TEXASSNAKES

LONE ★ STAR
FIELD GUIDE

TexasSnakes
ALAN TENNANT

THIRD EDITION

TAYLOR TRADE PUBLISHING
LANHAM | NEW YORK | BOULDER | TORONTO | OXFORD

Published by Taylor Trade Publishing
An imprint of The Rowman & Littlefield Publishing Group, Inc.
4501 Forbes Boulevard, Suite 200, Lanham, Maryland 20706

Distributed by NATIONAL BOOK NETWORK

Library of Congress Cataloging-in-Publication Data

Tennant, Alan, 1943–
    Lone Star field guide to Texas snakes / Alan Tennant.— 3rd ed.
        p. cm.
    Rev ed. of: A field guide to Texas snakes / Alan Tennant.
    ISBN 1-58979-209-2 (pbk. : alk. paper)
        1. Snakes—Texas—Identification. I. Title: Field guide to Texas snakes.
    II. Tennant, Alan, 1943– field guide to Texas snakes. III. Title.
    QL666.O6T464 2006
    597.96'09764—dc22   2005019889

∞™ The paper used in this publication meets the minimum requirements of American National Standard for Information Sciences—Permanence of Paper for Printed Library Materials, ANSI/NISO Z39.48-1992.

Manufactured in the United States of America.

CONTENTS

NOTE ON CONTENTS LISTING

The arrangement of snakes in the table of contents follows the now universal system of Latin and Greek genus, species, and subspecies nomenclature devised nearly two hundred and fifty years ago by Swedish botanist Carl von Linné, better known as Linnaeus. Beyond this convention, however, to facilitate field identification, snakes that look alike and/or share similar habitat are grouped together.

This grouping sometimes parallels these animals' genetic affinities. Yet, confusingly, snakes that look alike and behave similarly may not be closely related. (Their similarities are often due to the demands of a particular habitat, often referred to as parallel evolution.) On the other hand, snakes which look and behave differently may still be closely related.

In fact, the best way to determine kinship is through molecular comparisons of snakes' body proteins, combined with morphological data. This work has called into doubt many traditional ophidian classifications, but, following the most recent authoritative reference (Carl H. Ernst and Roger W. Barbor, 1989, *Snakes of Eastern North America*), the genetic relationships of North American snakes are currently thought to be as follows:

Family *Typhlopidae*
  Genus
  Ramphotyphlops

Family *Leptotyphlopidae*
  Genus
  Leptotyphlops

Family *Colubridae*
  Subfamily *Colubrinae*
    Genus
    Coluber
    Drymarchon
    Drymobius
    Masticophis
    Opheodrys
    Liochlorophis
    Salvadora
  Subfamily *Natricinae*
    Genus
    Nerodia
    Seminatrix
    Regina
    Storeria
    Thamnophis
    Tropidoclonion
    Virginia
    Clonophis
  Subfamily *Lampropeltinae*
    Genus
    Lampropeltis
    Cemophora

Rhinocheilus
Elaphe
Bogertophis
Pituophis
Arizona
Stilosoma
Subfamily *Xenodontinae*
  Genus
  Diadophis
  Carphophis
  Farancia
  Rhadinaea
  Tantilla
  Sonora
  Ficimia
  Gyalopion
  Heterodon
  Hypsiglena
  Leptodeira
  Coniophanes
  Trimorphodon

Family *Elapidae*
  Genus
  Micrurus

Family *Viperidae*
  Genus
  Agkistrodon
  Sistrurus
  Crotalus

PREFACE

In the end
We will preserve only what we love,
We will love only what we understand,
We will understand only what we have learned.

—Senegalese Conservationist Baba Dioum

Paleontologist Robert T. Bakker once observed that only with considerable difficulty had he been able to gain a perspective from which a thecodont—a stubby little Jurassic reptile—seemed as beautiful as a cheetah. The thecodont just had a different environment. An environment to which it adapted by squatting on the shores of ancient mud pans, gobbling down smaller creatures and living in the same tentative give-and-take with its neighbors that, extrapolated across the great panoply of living beings, reveals an infinitely complex system of delicately counterweighted life forces.

The system is so intricate that only a bit of its circuitry is yet available to our understanding, but its essence is clear. Cosmologically intermingled sets of opposing hungers and wills-to-live suspend each life form in a tenuous balance between dominance over its environment and extinction. In this unconscious genetic struggle each species' capacities contribute to the natural forces massed against its prey, its predators, and often, its neighbors. Collectively asserted, the efforts of those neighbor/competitors tend to oppose the species' own drive for biological success just enough for both sides to coexist, balanced, in communities ranging from those swarming through a drop of water to others carpeting the continents' great plains.

Although periodically reshuffled by the evolutionary changes typically brought about by environmental upheaval, over long spans of time these communities are comparatively stable. During these periods, this ongoing system of opposing interests maintains an only slightly-varying stasis, with dropout species quickly being replaced by variations of neighboring organisms, which venture evolutionary tendrils into every newly vacated environmental space.

As little more than blinking spectators to this most magnificent of mortal processes, we can only respect the contenders. Yet nothing could be further from our historical record: Wildlife of all kinds has always been something for mankind to overcome, to exploit, or to
x eliminate if it gets in the way.

Shedding the opacity of the cultural biases that have for thousands of years fueled this drive for dominance is the first step toward respecting our fellow beings. But it's not easy, because as Bakker recognized, the most difficult step in learning anything meaningful about the natural world is to begin to overcome the slanted human perspectives that determine so many of our biological empathies—especially where snakes are concerned.

In the prevailing cultural context, serpents are so scary and repugnant that, even to people who would hesitate to harm any other vertebrate, it has long seemed proper to kill a snake. Yet with the disappearance of so many formerly abundant animals, that viewpoint is changing. Gradually, we are starting to see how much we've lost in ridding ourselves of the bears and wolves, mountain lions, and rattlesnakes that threatened first our lives, then our livestock.

Too late, for the most part, awareness is dawning of the fundamental ignorance of seeing such creatures as villains, of filtering their appearances and actions through our provincial human perspectives of good and evil, beauty and ugliness—as though such narrow criteria could set standards for a system of harmonies that preceded our existence by billions of years and will certainly outlast us by an equivalent span. Culturally ingrained as it is, to choose certain striking beings—cheetahs, swallows, or redwood trees—to grace with our eccentric notion of beauty is to ignore how meager are our recently acquired cultural concepts when judged against a cosmic order whose structure binds the stately parade of stars and planets, shapes the flow of the tectonic currents that mold the continents, and has wrought the symmetry of serpents no less than that of tigers.

Moreover, assigning malfeasance to creatures we perceive as psychologically alien creates in us an illusion, an illusion that our species is different, a higher sort of creature.

It is this unconsciously arrogant notion that obscures from us our essence. We are but one minuscule thread in the planet's great organic tapestry—a thread, moreover, entirely dependent upon neighboring threads to maintain its place in the weave of life. In this intricate matrix, every single species of us is bound to our neighbors by myriad dovetailing pacts of mutual dependency—supremely complex pacts, pacts not of our choice nor over which we exercise control, but mutually dependent pacts, nevertheless, on which our joint survival ultimately depends.

This book is an attempt to bridge, in a single small area of knowledge, the large and growing gap between the data of the professional biological journals and the general, popular awareness of the natural world that largely determines our role in preserving or destroying it.

ACKNOWLEDGMENTS

In compiling this book, my debt to mapmaker, editor, consultant, and decades-long buddy Craig McIntyre, cannot be overstated. The same is true for Connie, Jeff, and Jonathan McIntyre.

In addition, contributing authors Joseph E. Forks and Gerard T. Salmon have devoted a major part of their lives to discovering the secret life of the gray-banded kingsnake, *Lampropeltis alterna*—the search for which, every spring and summer, brings hundreds of reptile enthusiasts to West Texas. What Forks and Salmon have learned about this intriguing member of Texas' herpetofauna is offered here for the first time: The intricate color patterns that vary markedly according to its geographically complex occurrence and descriptions of every known collecting site.

Beyond the contributions of this volume's contributing authors, I am indebted to Jim Stout for introducing me to field herpetology, to *Thamnophis* enthusiasts Bill and Donna Marvel, as well as to Damon Salceies and Troy Hibbitts for their careful observations of ophidian natural history, and to my very thorough researcher Melody Lytle. I am also most grateful to Kenny Wray for his enormous enthusiasm in helping in every way I asked; to Dr. Kathryn Vaughan, Dr. Jonathan Campbell, and Dr. Andrew Price for sharing their academic/governmental perspectives with me.

My sincere thanks, also, to those who graciously and laboriously read, corrected, and commented at length on several of the preliminary manuscripts: Dr. Neil B. Ford, University of Texas at Tyler; William W. Lamar; Dave Barker; Jim Stout; and A. J. Seippel.

Well before either book came into existence, however, only the generosity of many in the herpetological/medical/natural history community who contributed freely of their time and knowledge made these books possible. In addition to those previously cited they include Joseph M. Abell; Bob Binder; Johnny Binder; W. F. Blair; Bryan Blake; Dave Blody; Hugh Brown; Mark Brown; Jim Bull; Patrick Burchfield; Jim Constabile; Bill Degenhardt; Barbara Dillingham; Dr. James R. Dixon; Jim Dunlap; David Easterla; Rowe Elliott; Kevin Enge; Richard Etheridge; Mollie and David Francis; Dr. Frederick R. Gehlbach; Dr.

Thomas Glass; Jerry Glidewell; Charles Goodrich; Harry Greene; Ed Guidry; David M. Hardy; Terry Hibbitts; Toby Hibbitts; Richard Hix; Erik Holmback; Richard Hudson; J. P. Jones; John Jones; Tim Jones; Jack Joy; Alan Kardon; Robert E. Kuntz; Greg Lasley; the late wizard of herpetoculture, Jozsef Laszlo; John MacGregor; Ray Meckel; Dennie Miller; Paul E. Moler; William B. Montgomery; Susie and S. I. Morris; the late Eileen Morron; Rick Pratt; Hugh Quinn; Gus Renfro; Francis Rose; Dr. Craig Rudolph; Findlay E. Russell; Neils Saustrup; Barbara Scown; Dean Singleton; Larry and Marlene Smitherman; Jeannie Taylor; Luke Thompson; Earl Turner; Thomas Vermersch; Russ Walker; Brett Whitney; Michael A. Williamson; Sherri Williamson; Larry David Wilson; Tom Wood; Richard Worthington; and Jim Yantis.

Visually, this book is indebted both to the fine drawings of artists John Lockman and David Moellendorf; and to photographers Michael Allender, Dave Barker, Richard D. Bartlett, Michael J. Bowerman, T. L. Brown, Paul Freed, D. Craig McIntyre, George O. Miller, William B. Montgomery, Damon Salceies, and Robert Wayne Van Devender.

It is also important to acknowledge my debt to Roger Conant and Joseph T. Collins' *A Field Guide to the Reptiles and Amphibians of Eastern and Central North America* (Boston: Houghton Mifflin, 1991) as the source of several of the record lengths cited in this volume. Beyond the inspiration this volume provided, its co-author, Joe Collins, spent a good deal of time discussing with me speciation theory and ophidian evolution, for which I offer my thanks.

Finally, in the first book we worked on together, *A Field Guide to Snakes of Florida*, I wrote that my editor at Gulf Publishing, Tim Calk, was patient, fair, and supportive. Now he has become a friend.

Published material used in compiling the distribution areas of the maps includes G. G. Raun and F. R. Gehlbach, *Amphibians and Reptiles in Texas* (Dallas: Dallas Museum of Natural History, 1972); *Herpetological Review,* vols. 3–13; J. Glidewell, *Southwestern Naturalist* 19, no. 2 (1974): 213–23; D. Miller, "A Life History Study of the Gray-Banded Kingsnake, *Lampropeltis mexicana alterna,* in Texas" (master's thesis, Sul Ross State University, 1979); John E. Werler, *Poisonous Snakes of Texas and the First Aid Treatment of Their Bite* (Austin: Texas Parks and Wildlife, 1978); Roger Conant and Joseph T. Collins, *A Field Guide to Reptiles and Amphibians of Eastern and Central North America* (Boston: Houghton Mifflin, 1991); *Journal of Herpetology* 11, no. 2 (1977): 217–20; C. J. Cole and L. M. Hardy, *Bulletin of the American Museum of Natural History,* vol. 171 (New York, 1981); and J. S. Mecham, *Copeia,* 1956, 51–52.

Taylor Trade Publishing Director Rick Rinehart was a major force in bringing this third edition to print, an endeavor in which I was ably assisted by the editor, Adam Muhlig.

Alan Tennant
Marathon, Texas

We tried our best to make the third edition of this field guide an accurate, informative, and enjoyable reference to the diverse indigenous snakes of Texas. Friends and family accuse me of spending more time in Texas than in my home in the northeast, and those that have made my frequent trips and study of Texas' herpetofauna a much more enjoyable undertaking deserve mention. There are many, but most importantly: Dave and Tracy Barker, Jeff Barringer, Doug Beckwith, Dave Blody, Steve Boyd, Pat Cherryhomes, Dr. James Dixon, Dave Doherty, Doug Duerre, John Fraser, Joe Forks, Kathy Freeman, David Heckard, Troy Hibbitts, John Hollister, Jim McLean, Dennie Miller, Norm Nunley, Ray Queen, Jeff and Cathy Ross, Damon Salceies, Craig and Linda Trumbower, Russ Walker, and Dr. Kathryn Vaughan.

Gerard T. Salmon
Rhinebeck, New York

SNAKES AND THE LAW

Andrew Sansom
Former Executive Director
L. David Sinclair
Director, Wildlife Enforcement
Texas Parks and Wildlife Department
Austin, Texas

In Texas, snakes can be categorized into three distinct classes: (1) non-protected nongame, (2) protected or threatened nongame, and (3) endangered. These three classes are governed by statutes enacted by the Texas legislature and by regulations adopted by the Texas Parks and Wildlife Commission.

Statutes and regulations that affect the collection or hunting of non-protected, nongame snakes in Texas are currently minimal. Section 1.101, *Parks and Wildlife Code*, provides that "hunt" means capture, trap, take, or kill. Chapter 42, *Parks and Wildlife Code*, requires that a person hunting any animal (terrestrial vertebrate) in Texas must possess a hunting license.

There are no restrictions regarding means and methods for hunting snakes, provided a person is hunting on private property. Section 62.003, *Parks and Wildlife Code*, allows a person to hunt an animal from a motor vehicle within the boundaries of private property. No attempt may be made to hunt any wild animal from the vehicle on any part of a public road or public road right-of-way within the state.

If the collecting or hunting of snakes occurs on a public road, there are restrictions regarding the means and methods used. It is lawful for a person to drive a vehicle to any area along a public road, park the vehicle off the road, and walk the road right-of-way to collect or hunt snakes. While collecting or hunting snakes, using a vehicle on a public road in an abnormal, unlawful, or erratic manner—which includes driving slowly enough to create a safety hazard, stopping on the pavement or the roadbed, shining lights in ditches, or turning crossways in the roadway to spot snakes lying on the opposite ledges of the right-of-way—constitute probable cause to believe hunting from a vehicle on a public road is occurring in violation of section 62.003, *Parks and Wildlife Code.* (It may also be a violation of the *Texas Transportation Code.*) An officer may make a determination of whether a person is hunting from a vehicle by observing the driver's use or maneuvering of the vehicle on a public road during the collection or hunting process. A person who violates section 62.003, *Parks and Wildlife Code,* commits an offence that is punishable as a Class C *Parks and Wildlife Code* misdemeanor ($25–$500 fine). A second or subsequent violation of this statute within 5 years of the first offense is punishable as a Class B *Parks and Wildlife Code* misdemeanor ($200–$2,000 fine and/or a jail term not to exceed 180 days). In either case, each snake unlawfully hunted or collected constitutes a separate offense.

Snake collectors or hunters should know that it is against the law to (1) discharge a firearm on or across a public road as provided in Section 42.01, *Texas Penal Code,* punishable by a fine not to exceed $500; (2) hunt without a landowner's consent as provided in 61.022, *Parks and Wildlife Code,* punishable on first offense as a Class C *Parks and Wildlife Code* misdemeanor ($25–$500); a second or subsequent violation of this statute within 5 years of the first offense is punishable as a Class B *Parks and Wildlife Code* misdemeanor ($200–$2,000 fine and/or a jail term not to exceed 180 days)—both offenses result in an automatic loss of hunting license for a period of time from 1 to 5 years—and (3) trespass on the privately owned property adjacent to the roadway as provided in section 30.05, *Texas Penal Code,* punishable as a Class B misdemeanor with a fine not to exceed $2,000 and/or 180 days in a jail, unless the person possesses a deadly weapon. Then the offense is a Class A misdemeanor with a fine not to exceed $4,000 and one year in jail.

Snakes that are listed as protected or threatened nongame are regulated by the Texas Parks and Wildlife Department and no person may take, possess, transport, export, sell or offer for sale, or ship any species of snake listed as protected. It is not a violation to possess or transport live, mounted, or preserved specimens of species legally collected in another state, except that a copy of a valid out-of-state permit authorizing the possession of the specimens must accompany each specimen during transport within Texas and must be retained by the person or institution possessing the specimen. A person may possess, transport, export, sell, or offer for sale goods made from snakes listed as protected, provided the person possesses proof that the goods were obtained from lawfully taken snakes. A violation of the protected nongame statutes or regulations is a Class C *Parks and Wildlife Code* misdemeanor ($25–$500 fine).

The following species are protected or threatened nongame:

Big Bend Black-headed Snake	*Tantilla rubra cucullata*
Black-striped Snake	*Coniophanes imperialis*
Brazos Water Snake	*Nerodia harteri*
Concho Water Snake	*Nerodia paucimaculata*
Indigo Snake	*Drymarchon corais*
Louisiana Pine Snake	*Pituophis melanoleucus ruthveni*
Northern Cat-eyed Snake	*Leptodeira septentrionalis*
Scarlet Snake	*Cemophora coccinea*
Smooth Green Snake	*Liochlorophis vernalis*
Speckled Racer	*Drymobius margaritiferus*
Texas Lyre Snake	*Trimorphodon biscutatus*
Timber Rattlesnake	*Crotalus horridus*

Endangered species statutes are cited in Chapter 68, *Parks and Wildlife Code*. Snakes that are indigenous to Texas are endangered if included on the U.S. list of endangered native fish and wildlife or if they are on the fish and wildlife threatened with statewide extinction list as filed by the executive director of the Texas Parks and Wildlife Department. Currently there are no native species listed as endangered in Texas.

Section 68.015, *Parks and Wildlife Code,* is related to prohibited acts regarding endangered snakes for the purpose of propagating them for sale if the person has acquired a commercial propagation permit issued under the authority of Chapter 68, *Parks and Wildlife Code*. A permit may be issued if it is determined that the applicant has acquired initial breeding stock from a person permitted by the department or otherwise legally acquired. The applicant must not have violated the laws of the United States, Texas, or any state with respect to the acquisition of breeding stock. The original propagation permit may be issued for a period of 3 years at a cost of $550.

No person may possess, sell, distribute, or offer or advertise for sale any goods made from endangered snakes unless (1) the goods were made from snakes born and raised in captivity for commercial purposes under the provisions of Chapter 68, *Parks and Wildlife Code*, or (2) the goods were made from snakes taken in another state and the person presents documented evidence to the department to substantiate that fact. No person may sell, advertise, or offer for sale any species of snake not classified as endangered under the name of any endangered species.

Section 68.006, *Parks and Wildlife Code,* provides that a permit may be issued under the authority of Subchapter C, Chapter 43, *Parks and Wildlife Code,* to possess, take, or transport endangered snakes for zoological gardens, scientific research, or to take or transport endangered snakes from their natural habitat for propagation for commercial purposes and makes it a violation to conduct any of these activities without the permit. A person who violates any provision of Chapter 68, *Parks and Wildlife Code,* commits a Class C *Parks and Wildlife Code* misdemeanor ($25–$500 fine). A person who violates any provision of this chapter and who has been convicted on one previous occasion of a violation of this chapter commits a Class B *Parks and Wildlife Code* misdemeanor ($200–$2,000 fine and/or a jail term not to exceed 180 days). It is a Class A *Parks and Wildlife Code* misdemeanor ($500–$4,000 fine and/or a jail term not to exceed one year) if a person commits an offense of this chapter and has two or more previous convictions.

Public land under the control of the Texas Parks and Wildlife Department is also regulated for hunting. It is an offense to harm, harass, disturb, trap, confine, possess, or remove any wildlife from a unit of the state park system except by a permit issued by the director or as provided by Subchapter D, Chapter 62, *Parks and Wildlife Code.* Additionally, no person may take or attempt to take or possess wildlife from a wildlife management area, except in the manner and during the times permitted by the department under Subchapter E, Chapter 81. A violation of these statutes or rules is a Class C *Parks and Wildlife Code* misdemeanor ($25–$500 fine).

In addition to criminal fines that may be imposed, a person may be assessed a civil recovery fee for snakes unlawfully killed, caught, possessed, or injured in violation of the *Parks and Wildlife Code.* The recovery value for each nonprotected nongame snake is the commercial value of the species at the time it was illegally killed, caught, possessed, or injured. The recovery value for each individual protected or threatened snake equals $500, plus the commercial value at the time it was illegally killed, caught, possessed, or injured.

Examples of fees that may be assessed are as follows:

NONPROTECTED GAME SNAKES

Trans-Pecos Copperhead	*Agkistrodon contortrix pictigaster*	$63.00
Trans-Pecos Rat Snake	*Bogertophis Subocularis*	$63.00
Diamond-backed Rattlesnake	*Crotalus atrox*	$8.00

PROTECTED OR THREATENED NONGAME SNAKES:

Concho Water Snake	*Nerodia paucimaculata*	$515.00
Texas Indigo Snake	*Drymarchon corais*	$515.00
Texas Lyre Snake	*Trimorphodon biscutatus*	$503.00

A game warden or other peace officer commissioned by the department may search a game bag, receptacle, or vehicle if the warden or peace officer has a reasonable suspicion that it contains a wildlife resource that has been unlawfully taken. A wildlife resource includes animal, bird, reptile, amphibian, fish, or other aquatic life, the taking or possessing of which is regulated in any manner by the *Parks and Wildlife Code,* and a game warden or other peace officer commissioned by the department may inspect a wildlife resource that is discovered during a lawful search. In addition, to enforce the game and fish laws of Texas, a game warden may enter on any land or water where wild game or fish are known to range, and no action may be sustained against a game warden of the department to prevent his entering when acting in his official capacity.

Information provided in this section may change due to state or federal legislation or Texas Parks and Wildlife commission action. Any questions regarding these regulations may be directed to the Texas Parks and Wildlife Department Law Enforcement Division, but all indigenous snakes are protected in that a valid hunting license is required for collection from the wild. Further, a special group of nongame animals are listed with the Secretary of State as "threatened," and are therefore afforded greater protection than other species classified as "non-game." These species and subspecies include:

Black-hooded Snake, *Tantilla rubra cucullata*
Brazos Water Snake, *Nerodia harteri harteri*
Concho Water Snake, *Nerodia harteri paucimaculata*
Smooth Green Snake, *Liochlorophis vernalis*
Central American Speckled Racer, *Drymobius margaritiferus margaritiferus*
Texas Indigo Snake, *Drymarchon corais erebennus*
Louisiana Pine Snake, *Pituophis ruthveni*
Northern Scarlet Snake, *Cemophora coccinea copei*
Texas Scarlet Snake, *Cemophora coccinea lineri*
Black-striped Snake, *Coniophanes imperialis imperialis*
Northern Cat-eyed Snake, *Leptodeira septentrionalis septentrionalis*

A second group of snakes are affected by Texas Nongame Species List/Species Codes. These include:

Plains Garter Snake (*Thamnophis radix haydeni*) **trad**
Prairie Ring-necked Snake (*Diadophis punctatus arnyi*) **darn**
Western Diamond-backed Rattlesnake (*Crotalus atrox*) **crat**
Prairie Rattlesnake (*Crotalus viridis viridis*) **crvi**
Mottled Rock Rattlesnake (*Crotalus lepidus lepidus*) **crle**
Banded Rock Rattlesnake (*Crotalus lepidus klauberi*) **crkl**
Northern Black-tailed Rattlesnake (*Crotalus molossus molossus*) **crmo**
Western Massasauga (*Sistrurus catenatus tergeminus*) **site**
Desert Massasauga (*Sistrurus catenatus edwardsii*) **sied**
Pigmy Rattlesnake (*Sistrurus miliarius*) **simi**

If more than 25 specimens in the aggregate from the affected non-game species list are possessed (dead or alive), or if the animals are collected from the wild for commercial purposes, a permit must be obtained.

From: *April M. Chronister*
         512-389-4585
         Wildlife Permits Specialist
         Texas Parks and Wildlife Dept.
         4200 Smith School Road
         Austin, TX 78744

INTRODUCTION

This field guide describes every species and subspecies that is known to occur in Texas. The number assigned to each animal in the text is also used in the photographic captions.

The common and scientific names used here follow, for the most part, the nomenclature established by the Society for the Study of Amphibians and Reptiles in *Standard Common and Current Scientific Names for North American Amphibians and Reptiles,* third edition, by Joseph T. Collins et al. (Lawrence: University of Kansas Museum of Natural History).

The *species accounts* groups the snakes into sections that reflect (1) a snake's resemblance to other similarly patterned serpents; (2) its occupancy of similar habitat—aquatic snakes, for example; and (3) its taxonomic relationship to other members of the same section.

The *range maps* accompanying the text define the distribution of these animals. Even in well-studied areas the geographical range of many species and subspecies has not been determined with precision, however, and range demarcations are necessarily generalizations. Moreover, because the environmental conditions determining reptiles' presence in an area are in perpetual flux, range maps are best thought of as constantly altering cartographic kaleidoscopes, with the dark-shaded portion of each map representing only the temporary distribution of a particular species or subspecies.

The lightly shaded regions on some of the maps indicate zones of intergradation—areas where the ranges of two or more subspecies overlap. Genetic crosses found in these areas often exhibit characteristics of each of the neighboring subspecies, but because the boundaries of intergradation zones between adjacently ranging subspecies are even more variable than the boundaries between full species, specimens occurring in intergradation zones may (1) exhibit any combination of the characteristics of either of the subspecies involved or (2) closely resemble the nonintergrade form of either race.

Moreover, snakes are likely to occur only where proper environmental conditions exist. An animal may be quite common in some places, yet very rare in other areas well within its overall geographical distribution, because reptiles in general and snakes in particular are not found everywhere within their geographical ranges. This means that habitats that can support a significant population are likely to occur only in certain parts of their range. Elsewhere, less favorable conditions often mean that the species or subspecies may be or is entirely absent throughout much of its overall range.

Human intervention is changing Texas' natural ecosystems so rapidly that as habitat alteration causes extirpation of many animal and plant populations, other species and subspecies may expand their territory to occupy areas where they are currently unrecorded. It is far more likely that large numbers of species and subspecies will not be replaced.

Despite many snakes' rapid replacement rates, most varieties are now in decline. I have observed Texas herpetofauna for over 50 years, and it has become clear to me that the numbers of all reptiles, in particular those of terrestrial snakes, have dramatically diminished. This is due largely to two factors:

The vastly increased presence of man. Most important is the conversion of thousands of square miles of natural terrain to residential and commercial human usage—territory where few snakes are able to survive. Also significant is the enormously increased traffic on the state's expanding highway system. On these lethal networks of pavement, the constant passage of vehicles creates a 24-hour, year-round web of death to reptiles too unwary of cars to do much besides look up at the last moment.

Also deadly is the invasion of South American fire ants, which have devastated populations of both small fossorial and larger egg-laying snakes in the eastern half of the state.

Because none of these mortality factors show any signs of abating, we can expect the formerly rich herpetofauna of Texas to continue to decline. While no species or subspecies is likely to become extinct in the near future, many fewer reptiles of all kinds will be out there fulfilling the roles they would have played in a healthier ecosystem.

THE EVOLUTION
OF SNAKES

It seems natural to assume that snakes have always looked like the slender, tubular animals they are today, yet nothing could be further from the strange truths of evolutionary change. For tens of millions of years, snakes' immediate ancestors scrambled around on four legs—a circumstance reflected in the fact that a single taxonomic order, *Squamata*, contains only lizards and snakes. After an elaborate physical restructuring during the Mesozoic era, when some of those ancestral lizards radically pared down their four-legged bodies, the predecessors of today's snakes took on their current tubular shape.[1]

This radical evolutionary sacrifice meant giving up limbs, freer breathing, and superior circulation, as well as the sensory input of fine hearing and eyesight. Forgoing such genetically hard-won attributes could only have come about as a result of intense incentives for change—the most immediate of which was probably to avoid being eaten.

Small, warm-blooded dinosaurs are thought to have been among the primary predators of terrestrial lizards, running down some in the open and searching out others from vegetation and crevices, where lacertilians found it difficult to conceal their stiff bodies spiked with projecting legs. In response, at least one group of platynoids, probably the monitor-like aigialosaurs (though the long-necked aquatic dolichosaurs are also a possibility), may have gradually changed both their bodies and their behavior. Radically elongating their torsos eventually allowed these animals to forgo the dangers of life on the surface, for they are thought to have spent more and more time underground, where they were less likely to fall prey to saurian predators.

But learning to live permanently beneath the earth's surface would have been painfully procrustean. There's not much room below

---

[1]Similarly, a number of contemporary lizards, including the European slow-worm and the subterranean amphisbaenians, have also elected to do without legs and thus share the rope-like form of snakes. Unlike snakes, however, legless lizards retain bony pelvic and shoulder girdles, have many fewer vertebrae, and are consequently far less supple than true serpents.

ground, so this group of swiftly adapting, body-lengthening lizards had to become very small. Deep in their subterranean burrows, their senses were mostly limited to smell and taste. The neurological pathways connecting these sensory organs were already linked in the ancestral monitors, which had originated a sensitive forked tongue whose sticky surface gathered scent molecules from the air and soil, then carried those particles to a paired vomeronasal gland located in the roof of their mouths; those olfactorily active tongues then became a significant advantage for lizards embarking on a new life below the surface.

In a similar way, the great lateral flexibility of the monitor trunk lent itself to their fossorial descendants' need to squirm through tight subsurface milieus.[2] Wriggling worked better than walking in narrow subterranean tunnels, and in the course of the millions of years during which the post-monitors' bodies became ever smaller and slimmer, their limbs shrank into fetus-like stubs. This elaborate process—a triumph of adaptive evolution—entailed almost complete internal restructuring. To exclude the press of soil, these nascent snakes' eyes grew scale-cap goggles (transparent eyelids are still found on some contemporary burrowing monitors). Then, since vision was useless in the darkness below ground, those rigid eye caps hardened into an unbroken armor of facial scales covering eyes that ultimately atrophied into dots of vestigial ocular pigment. At roughly the same time, the dirt-gathering orifice of the ear permanently closed (presumably because it could be easily damaged from sudden pressure changes in the constricted airspace of subterranean passages) and with it went the lizard's delicate eardrum. At the same time, the auditory bones (which in other reptiles transmit airborne sounds from the eardrum to the aural nerves) fused to the lower jaw, leaving the evolving serpents deaf to all but a narrow range of earth-borne vibrations. The monitors' big carnivore teeth were sacrificed in favor of scaled-down dentition—adequate for the little subsurface-living lizards' minuscule new prey of annelids and insect larvae, and countersunk lower jaws developed to probe through soil without scooping up mouthfuls of terrain.[3]

Posteriorly, equally radical adjustments occurred. As their legs disappeared, these little animals' internal organs elongated and became staggered to fit within the increasingly tubular shape of their new bod-

---

[2]Within a single genus, South African snake-lizards show several intermediate stages of limb reduction: one has four fully developed legs, each with a five-toed foot; another has four rudimentary limbs with only two toes each; a third has vestigial hind legs bearing but one toe each and no external front limbs.

[3]Like most of their lizard forebears, all snakes are carnivores: no known serpent has ever opted for a herbivorous diet.

ies. But this was at the expense of impaired physiological efficiency. Among the more pronounced changes was the loss of the powerful lizard heart, for only a slender, less muscular heart—which suffers more backwash between chambers than the better-segmented hearts of lizards—could fit within these creatures' radically thinned bodies. Moreover, the corollary loss of a rigid lower thoracic shield left their fragile cardiovascular chambers vulnerable to external blows, and makes all contemporary serpents prone to serious injury in a fall. Respiratory efficiency also suffered, as many serpents, evolutionarily striving for the smallest possible diameter, adopted a single long lung. This prompted the development of subsidiary pulmonary capacity in other organs: the alveolar lining at the rear of most snakes' tracheas evolved some oxygen exchange capability, while the posterior end of the lung developed into a nonvascular air storage sac that enlarges the lung's capacity by some 20 percent.

The same sort of changes took place in the digestive tract. Unlike lizards, snakes' lengthy esophagus lost its separation from the stomach, which occupies much of the midbody, followed by a folded small and abbreviated large intestine.

For nascent snakes to so completely restructure their bodies was a risky evolutionary strategy—but over the long term it has proven to be a superior one. When the first Mesozoic monitors began their subterranean life, reptiles dominated the earth with more variety than all species of amphibians, birds, and early mammals combined. Then things changed; by the beginning of the Cenozoic, environmental cataclysms had eliminated the remaining small dinosaurs—on land no animal heavier than about 50 pounds survived—and cut the number of reptile species to less than a third of those that had flourished during the previous era.[4] The supple, miniaturized bodies that this group of chthonic lizard-snakes had evolved to evade their surface-living predators now allowed them to withdraw from the climatic vagaries that extirpated so many other terrestrial vertebrates and, figuratively speaking, slide relatively unharmed through the bottleneck of Cretaceous/Tertiary extinction.[5]

---

[4] The most likely hypothesis for this mass extinction now seems to be that a middle-size asteroid, probably the Alvarez Comet, struck the earth some 65 million years ago, detonating a dense cloud of dust that enveloped the planet for years, dimming the sun enough to eliminate most plant life and thus starving every terrestrial animal too large either to subsist on the remaining scraps of vegetation or get by on the limited prey offered by the few creatures that could.

[5] No more than 40 kinds of monitors are still found in restricted tropical ranges, while today snakes are by far the most widespread reptile, with over 2,500 species occupying a broad range of terrestrial, aquatic, and marine habitats.

Although most of the old predatory dinosaurs were gone, for the miniaturized, deaf and blind fossorial serpents, returning to life above ground presented immense problems.[6] One of the most pressing was the widely fluctuating surface temperature.[7]

Other reptiles—whose metabolic advantage lies in the fact that they consume only about 10 percent as much energy as a similar-sized bird or mammal—faced the same problem. But snakes were uniquely suited to cope with it. Avoiding falling air temperature or too-hot sun was mostly a matter of returning to the more temperate cosm beneath the surface, a realm their hard-won tubular shape and new flexibility let them access better than other reptiles. To make use of both worlds, however, snakes had to adopt new behavior—actively avoiding the surface's temperature extremes while making selective use of solar radiation to maintain the narrow range of temperature their increasingly sophisticated metabolisms required. This new strategy was thermoregulation, and for species active in daylight it took the form of basking. Heat-avoidance thermoregulation was simpler, entailing, for the most part, withdrawing into water or the cool realm below ground.

Although these emergent animals continued to rely heavily on the tactile and chemical sensations they had employed below the surface, there was now the need, once again, to see. So, with the genetic flexibility typical of snakes (which are resistant to the lethal gene combinations that cause most mutations of warm-blooded creatures to die), those formerly blind, burrowing Paleocene serpents reevolved the sense of sight.

As the opaque scales covering their vestigial eyes once more cleared into transparent lens caps, their retinal cells began to regenerate.[8] Physical reshaping has its limits, though, and genetically adaptable as snakes had proven themselves to be, they were unable to fully reevolve their ancestral lizard eyes.

Part of the problem was the lens cap they had developed underground to keep particles out of their eyes. It was there to stay. With-

---

[6]After the archeosaurian hunters vanished, snakes still faced a world filled with mammalian and avian predators whose big new brains required a stable internal climate, provided by a metabolic thermostat that meant they could forage well in a wide range of weather conditions.

[7]As legless creatures, terrestrial snakes are constantly in total contact with a substrate that heats and cools much more rapidly than the more temperate subterranean biological province. And no amount of physical reorganization could shield snakes, which like all reptiles lack a fully active temperature-regulating mechanism, from having to closely reflect the thermal level of their surroundings . . . and to die if that temperature varies more than 40°F in either direction.

[8]Unlike those of the diurnal ancestral monitors, however, their retinal cells took on an elongated, rod-like configuration better adapted to night vision.

out the pliant, focal length–altering optics that lizards share with birds and mammals, snakes can focus an image only by the relatively crude tactic of moving the entire, rigid lens farther from or closer to the retina—a retina unable to regenerate the high-resolution central focal zone enjoyed by even the earliest reptiles. As a result, snakes seem to have a sort of peripheral vision generalized across their entire field of view: sight that's quick to pick up movement but may lack sharp definition of detail.[9] Yet the old contractile iris of the lizards was able to re-form and even develop entirely new morphology. In advanced genera such as the vipers, a long, slit-like pupil allows the widest possible nocturnal aperture, while still narrowing enough for daylight vision.[10]

For primitive snakes emerging from restricted underground environments, locomotion presented equally complex problems. To expand into the newly available biological territory of the surface (much less grow large enough to exploit the caloric wealth of the warm-blooded prey now living there), serpents had to move with speed and agility. No sizable terrestrial creature had ever managed to do this without legs and feet, but snakes once more developed their own unique solution.

Without fore and hind limbs, serpents were no longer restricted to a short, mechanically effective distance between pelvis and shoulders, and over time snakes turned this freedom to their advantage. First, however, they had to evolve skeletal modifications far more elaborate than merely folding their limbs within their skins.[11] The most important was to develop a supple spinal column, which could be accomplished only by further miniaturizing the vertebrae, making room for many more spinal ball-and-socket joints. Some snake species ultimately produced a spine sufficiently flexible to tie itself into a knot—a suppleness that allowed snakes to move so well that they eventually developed two new methods of terrestrial locomotion.[12]

---

[9]Because snakes, as essentially limbless tetrapods, are unable to groom themselves, shield their eyes from twigs, or clean them with a paw, the protection of that eye-armoring lens cap may be worth the loss of visual acuity brought about by its rigidity.

[10]North of the Rio Grande, all venomous snakes except the coral snake, *Micrurus fulvious*, are pitvipers with vertically positioned, slit-like pupils. In other areas, species such as the arboreal, sight-hunting African twig snakes and the Asian whipsnakes developed horizontal pupilar slits.

[11]Some of the earliest snakes to evolve, during the late Oligocene, were the giant pythons and boas, which are characterized by both vestigial internal rear legs and tiny male-to-female claspers—the toe-tip remnants of long-vanished hind feet—that protrude from their flanks.

[12]The blind, burrowing *Typhlopidae* have 180 vertebrae, while the more advanced colubrids have as many as 435. (Mammals have 33.)

Both gaits called for sophisticated neuromuscular circuitry, although most of the time serpents use just one of the two. Called lateral undulation, the first means of locomotion is the mysterious, biblical "way of the serpent upon the rock" that allows snakes, without a visible means of propulsion, to slide effortlessly across uneven terrain. For centuries, this surreal-seeming slither mystified mankind, seeming magical because it is so different from the way mammals and birds scurry around. It is a gait far older than serpents, however, originating in the stride of ancestral monitors' side-to-side, head- and body-swinging walk. In this gait, the head and body bend to the right as the right foreleg moves back and the right hind leg simultaneously moves forward, a pattern reflected in serpents' sinuous, alternate flexing of the right- and left-side flank muscles, which draws S-shaped loops of the trunk forward and outward on either side of the snake's line of travel. Pressing rearward against protruding objects and surface irregularities, these loops then move gracefully rearward along the snake's body, imperceptibly levering the animal ahead. In agile genera like whipsnakes and old-world mambas, these alternating right- and left-side leveraging loops are slid rearward so rapidly that these swift serpents seem to fly along just above the surface. When traction is poor, the lateral loops of all snakes become proportionately larger as the serpent extends more of its belly length into the sideways search for something to press backward against. Extreme cases on loose sand call for "sidewinding." Here the only way to move in any direction is by extending the foremost body loop (which includes the neck) well to the side, then digging it in to scoop up a little ridge of sand to pull inward against. Anchored by this granular berm wedged up by its neck, a series of posterior body loops subsequently reach out to scoop up their own tiny ridges of sand to pull themselves toward. Finally, as muscular contractions sweep down the sidewinder's trunk, its body is drawn sideways across these notched depressions—which, after it has passed, remain as the sidewinder's distinctive, scalloped desert track. Worldwide, many other sand-dwelling serpent species use this form of locomotion, though all snakes employ an approximation of it when trying to negotiate slippery surfaces.

The other primary form of ophidian locomotion is rectilinear, or concertina, movement. It involves snakes' thin, flexible ribs, each pair linked to one of the midtrunk spinal vertebrae. The relatively loose architecture of serpents' bodies means that these ribs—which are controlled by more finely articulated muscles than those which initiate the larger movements of lateral undulation—are to some degree free to move fore and aft beneath the skin.

As they do, barely perceptible "rib walking"—one of the more fascinating attributes of ophidian morphology—takes place. It is the slowest but most energy-efficient serpentine gait, characteristic of heavy-bodied vipers such as rattlesnakes. Attached to the ends of each pair of ribs, a single, belly-wide ventral scale angles rearward like a shingle. When pressed down and back, its posterior edge digs against the surface to give snakes a belly hold for their trunk's lengthwise muscular ripples to push back against. Flowing back and forth along their bodies, the subtle contractions of dozens of muscle pairs let serpents swing successive pairs of ribs forward, then press them back in minuscule increments not unlike the movements caterpillars use to steadily hitch their multiple pairs of legs ahead. Used primarily for straight-line travel on the surface, below ground this gait allows serpents to inch their way through rodent tunnels too narrow for them to negotiate with lateral loops.[13] Among tree-climbing serpents, both gaits—straight-ahead concertina-creeping and backward-shoving lateral loops—may be used simultaneously. As one of its sideways coils levers the snake forward against twigs and stems, other body segments may find traction by lengthwise inching along a branch (some rat snakes and lyre snakes can dig in their belly scales firmly enough to creep straight up a rough-surfaced tree trunk or rock face). This calls for a very muscular midsection, and in such species the three major special muscles, *M. semispinalis-spinalis*, *M. longissimus dorsi*, and *M. iliocostalis*, are highly developed.[14] This sort of locomotive versatility also calls for great flexibility; tree-dwelling North American *Elaphe* have about 50 percent more vertebrae than most aquatic and terrestrial serpents.

Having learned to get around without the traditional vertebrate's stiff skeletal platform, by 35 million years before the present serpents had become mobile, surface-living creatures with rope-like suppleness possessed by no other land animal. This gave them the unique predatory advantage of striking. (Being able to reach out to snatch a food animal had long been an optimal hunting technique: frogs, toads, and a few lizards evolved projectable, jack-in-the-box tongues to snatch

---

[13]Rectilinear movement's minimal apparent motion can also enable snakes to approach wary food animals as long as they maintain a directly head-on perspective. From this angle (a telephone pole looks small when directly seen end-on) their quarry may perceive nothing but a flat disc apparently too small to be dangerous.

[14]A corollary characteristic developed by most tree-living serpents is bodies light and wiry enough to allow them to span branch-to-branch gaps at least half as great as their total length; a majority of terrestrial and aquatic serpents, in contrast, collapse across horizontal distances no more than a fifth their body length.

prey from a distance. But to catch anything larger than an insect, they still had to jump on it.)

Snakes had a better way, becoming the only contemporary reptile to develop a forebody so flexible and neuromuscularly sophisticated that it can instantly thrust the head and jaws well away from the inconspicuously coiled body to seize prey or—mouth agape—threaten an intruder. But even with this ability to seize large prey from a distance, snakes have never been able to dismember the prey. During the millions of years their subterranean prototypes fed only on soft invertebrates, the chewing teeth of serpents' lizard forebears were lost forever. But when their emergent descendants began to tackle chunkier prey, swallowing these sizable animals became a problem. The most primitive blind- and pipesnakes have inflexible jaws with limited gape, but later developing lineages came to need the big blocks of caloric energy available only by ingesting much larger prey, a strategy that let them spend most of their time hiding and digesting, thus minimizing their exposure to the dangerous world of predators.[15]

Yet fish and frog prey animals (as well as birds and small mammals) are frequently larger in diameter than the snakes that feed on them, so devouring these creatures called for radical feeding physiology. The solution was for snakes to expand. And without the limits of a limb-supporting thoracic cage or a rib-confining sternum, there was no structural reason that snakes could not eventually develop the capacity to flex their ribs so far outward that they were able to balloon themselves into shapes unattainable by any other vertebrate. Of course rib cages couldn't unfold this much without a very stretchy covering, but here too an endowment of singularly elastic skin remained from serpents' monitor ancestors.

The result was a singular biological success: the newly expandable serpents were eventually able to slip the largest possible bodies through narrow crevices in pursuit of lizards and rodents, then distend like a stretchy sock to draw themselves over plump prey. Safe from conventionally shaped carnivores in a space no larger than what had sheltered their prey, the snakes could remain to digest their meal.

In order to engulf big creatures, though, serpents had to find a way to fit them through their narrow skulls and jaws. But attenuated skulls, an essential part of their ancestors' tight-places survival strategy, made this almost impossible. The only way to get a small head over a large carcass is for the skull to temporarily come apart, and once again snakes' evolutionary answer lay in the biology of their monitor fore-

---

[15] Again, the seeds of this tactic lay with the ancestral varanids. Monitors are typically body distenders, swelling their bellies with big chunks of prey to keep it away from rivals.

bears. The cephalic expansion joints that had let ancient varanids partially dislocate their jaws to gulp down big chunks of meat evolved, among serpents, into more elaborate sutures. Connected by elastic, cartilaginous hinges, these joints were eventually able to separate far more widely than those of the monitors. Stretchy ligament bands allowed snakes' lower skulls to disjoint the lateral halves of their long lower mandibles, independently pivoting each side forward on its own linkage of loosely connected quadrate bones. Ultimately, aided by recurved teeth able to slip forward in ratchet-like steps over inward-bound prey, serpents' alternately advancing right and left jaw segments could draw a snake's head over a rat or rabbit several times thicker than the skull itself.

But ingesting large masses of flesh and bone impacted other aspects of snakes' metabolism. This included their breathing, for the buccal passage of a big carcass can take over an hour, during which every layer of soft tissue in a snake's throat is compressed to the utmost. That includes its airway, making a noncollapsible respiratory passage mandatory; the trachea of contemporary snakes is stiffened by closely spaced rows of cartilaginous rings that nevertheless retain sufficient articulation to preserve the neck's delicate flexibility.[16]

Pressing the swallowing mechanism to such biological lengths, however, meant that getting food into their stomachs was a slow process for snakes. This left them helpless for long periods and exposed them to injury inflicted by mammals capable of counterattack during the time it took to get them down. For this reason, being able to immobilize a biting, struggling victim before starting the lengthy process of swallowing it became a major biological incentive to small ophidian carnivores.

But immobilizing such prey meant either paralyzing it or killing it outright—new predatory ground for snakes, who had formerly swallowed most food animals alive. This meant more innovation. Among the earliest methods snakes evolved to subdue their victims was suffocation by constriction, a process developed from the same basic musculature that let arboreal species hang tightly onto tree branches. Each time a captive exhaled, a constricting snake's coils could be drawn tighter until, unable to expand its lungs, the victim died from a lack of oxygen. Yet for larger prey this process could require several minutes—during which the snake's coils were directly exposed to its prey's teeth and claws. In an evolutionary attempt to bypass this, by approximately the middle Miocene, 20 million years ago, other serpents had begun to develop a faster way of killing.

---

[16]Many tetrapods have cartilage-ringed tracheae, but because snakes typically swallow disproportionately large, solid food items, the difficulty of keeping their airway open is greater.

Forced into shallow wounds by the teeth, toxic saliva was proving effective among some species in minimizing the struggles of smaller prey, but more elaborate systems soon followed. Probably the first family to develop hollow hypodermic fangs from grooved, venom-introducing teeth was the *Elapidae*. Yet, despite having very powerful and intricate neurotoxic venom produced by separate venom glands, for the most part elapids still use the bite-and-squeeze venom delivery system. (Even the biggest cobras have small fangs because as rigid, upright pegs the teeth have to fit within the animal's mouth when it is closed.) Members of the viper family went further, evolving not only long, tubular anterior teeth, but articulated ones that fold back into bony slots in the roof of the mouth when the jaws are closed. When the viper is ready to strike these teeth can be instantly erected, swinging forward on hinged maxillary bones that rotate individually within sockets in the upper jaw. That means viper fangs can be quite long; those of the largest tropical bushmasters are capable of delivering venom over an inch below the surface.

Exposed by jaws that can gape open a full 180 degrees, forming a nearly flat oral wall, the angle of attack of viper fangs can even be adjusted in midstrike, giving the viper the choice of stabbing rather than biting large animals. (This option is solely a defensive one, though, since—except for the occasional misjudgment of juveniles new to hunting—no nonintrusive creature too big to be swallowed whole is ever attacked.)

Another advantage of viperid envenomation is speed. Delivered by a flashing strike and instantly forced into prey by big *compressor glandulae* muscles that surround the toxin storage glands, vipers' venom is injected so quickly that prey animals have no time to retaliate.[17] Nor do they usually have any inclination to do so. This is due to the immediate, intense pain these toxins cause as hydraulically pressurized dollops of venom are jetted through skin and muscle during the fraction of a second the snake's mouth is pressed against its prey.

This far quicker and safer way of injecting toxins was paralleled by the development of an equally sophisticated venom. Generated almost entirely from a pair of parotid glands—organs hyperdeveloped

---

[17]The pitviper strike has been measured at a speed of up to 11 feet per second—a bite that must be delivered so rapidly because small mammal prey reacts quickly enough to dodge anything slower. (Elapids, in contrast—which feed largely on less agile reptilian prey— make do with strikes only about half as fast. This lack of striking speed makes even deadly venomed cobras sure prey for quick, aggressive predators like the mongoose. But a mongoose confronted with a fast-striking rattlesnake aided by heat sensors would be envenomated before it managed its first feint.)

into complex lumens capable of generating 12 to 31 separate corrosive proteins—viper venom is a blend of tissue-disintegrating proteases, each directed toward a specific part of a prey animal's circulatory and/or nervous system.

Subsequently, the vipers' sensory skills were refined by a new ophidian subfamily, the *Crotalinae*, or pitvipers. These highly evolved reptiles' strike-guidance system centered on a pair of small depressions—the pits for which they are named—located on either side of the head between eye and nostril. The inner surface of these pits is lined with a thin membrane, sensitive to heat radiation and dotted with neural receptors. Collectively, these nerves signal the pitviper's brain along a neurological pathway so closely integrated with the optic tectum that impulses from both the eyes and the heat-sensing pits join to generate a single, thermally enhanced optical image.

This combination operates so well for that from the heat of a prey animal's small body a pitviper's overlapping, right–left stereoscopic infrared scan can effectively delineate its image even in total darkness; rattlesnakes deprived of vision with eye caps suffer almost no loss of predatory efficiency. Moreover, pitvipers' thermal pits are sensitive enough for them to distinguish newly slain prey from quiescent live animals—only living creatures are ever struck—while these organs are also used by both rattlesnakes and moccasins in seeking the warmer recesses of hillside caves for winter dormancy.[18]

But using its stereoscopic infrared scan to locate and accurately strike living prey involves only the initial phase of the pitviper's hunting strategy. Although a large amount of its toxins can kill in seconds any animal it is able to swallow, a pitviper's effectiveness as a small carnivore operating well beyond the conventional limits of its modest size depends largely on its venom *not* acting too quickly. To take full advantage of viperid toxin's digestive function, the venom's more lethal peptide enzymes must not shut down its victim's circulatory system until the venom's tissue-dissolving components have

---

[18] The distance at which these pits are effective has not been formally measured, but they are probably sensitive at a distance of at least 12 feet. Coasting down a Caldwell County incline on a bicycle, I drew an instantaneous angry whir and raised-forecoil defensive posture from a 4-foot-long *C. atrox* as I passed its hiding place in roadside Johnson grass—a reflexive response that was repeated on subsequent passes. My narrow-tired bike was nearly vibrationless on the smooth pavement and these encounters took place well after dark, with a slight breeze blowing my scent away from the rattler's visually shielded niche, so the snake almost certainly detected only the large block of my body heat suddenly passing through its thermal perceptual field. Another rattlesnake in my experience, an adult *C. molossus*, could perceive through the plate glass front of its cage the tiny glow of heat from a lighted cigarette held up a foot away, the back-and-forth movements of which it would accurately track with its snout.

had time to disperse throughout the creature's body. These digestive proteases so thoroughly disintegrate a prey animal's muscles and organs that what the viper swallows only a few minutes after the prey's death is a soft, predigested carcass that requires substantially less time to metabolize.

Ultimately, both the ancestral viper's long, erectile fangs and the later-evolved heat-sensing organs of the *Crotalinae* brought this group of snakes such predatory success that they came to enjoy the luxury of thick-girthed trunks much less athletic than those of non-venomous serpents that still had to pursue, capture, and wrestle food animals into submission.[19] Yet the corpulent bodies that pitvipers' sedentary, ambush-style predation permitted may have prevented these snakes from moving into every habitat they might otherwise have been able to occupy. One such potential home was the North American prairie.

In the Pliocene, Nearctic vipers may have spent most of their time near aquatic environments or within stands of cover, for numerous predators could have made the continent's vast grasslands a dangerous place for slow-moving, nonburrowing serpents. Yet the plains' rich supply of rodents and ground-nesting birds would have presented a major attraction to any serpent that could solve the problem of foraging across open country.

What these ancestral vipers may have needed was an antipredator device, a deficit that might have been solved when several genera of viperids amplified the fear-threat response of the many other serpents that twitch their tails in agitation, by developing on their caudal tips a loose-fitting column of hollow scales. Swollen like kernels of puffed rice, these scale segments, when shaken by the vipers' high-speed tail twitch, created the earliest-known aposematic buzz. Used first by *Sistrurus* and later by *Crotalus* genus rattlesnakes, that distinctive reverberating whir taught predators, as well as, perhaps, grazing mammals, to stay clear, for today the western plains are home to more than a dozen rattlesnake species, while no rattleless pitviper is common there.

Nevertheless, in the past hundred years the warning signal that allowed rattlesnakes to colonize the prairie has been their downfall,

---

[19]In addition, like other advanced ophidian genera, vipers are able to enhance their offspring's chances for survival in cool or extremely dry climates—environments that are dangerous to desiccation-prone reptilian eggs—by retaining the developing young within the more stable milieu of the female's body. Among such species the embryo is encased in a thin, water- and salt-permeable membrane that (in a metabolic antecedent to the placental nutrition of fetal mammals) may allow the unborn young to draw some sustenance from its mother's blood diffusing through the walls of the oviduct pressed against it.

for now the human attention it attracts usually means the death of the snake. In a similar way, after millennia of biological success, snakes are currently in worldwide decline as man's domination of the planet has driven species after species to the brink of extinction. The formerly profuse reptile fauna of the United States has been decimated by commercial and residential development, lumbering, chemical effluent, the invasion of South American fire ants, and commercial collecting for the pet trade, while the survival of over half of all pitvipers, including perhaps a third of North America's rattlesnake species, is threatened by mankind.

TEXAS SNAKE HABITATS*

Benjamin Tharp's *The Vegetation of Texas* (1939), W. Frank Blair's *The Biotic Provinces of Texas* (1950), and a synthesis of modern distributional data suggest that Texas has six primary natural regions:

1. The **Forest Region** of East Texas, principally composed of a pine/hardwood forest, fringed on the west by the oak-hickory forest called the Cross Timbers in North Central Texas.

2. The **Prairie Region,** of both North Central and Coastal Texas, defined by its original tall- or short-grass prairie, known as blackland prairie in Central Texas or, near the coast, salt-grass prairie.

3. The **Tamaulipan Region** of South Texas, comprising both tall-grass and short-grass prairie interspersed with clumps of woody plants that form thorn woodland, locally called chaparral or, more often, simply brush.

4. The **Edwards Plateau Region** of West Central Texas, containing both short-grass prairie and oak-juniper evergreen woodland, locally called cedar brakes.

5. The **High Plains Region** of the Texas Panhandle, covered for the most part with short-grass prairie but broken by mesas and canyons occupied by evergreen woodland.

6. The **Chihuahuan Desert Region** of Trans-Pecos Texas, which includes shrub desert in low basins, short-grass prairie on the rolling plains above, succulent desert and evergreen woodland on the lower and upper mountain slopes, respectively, and coniferous forest on a few high peaks.

Riparian or **Deciduous Woodland** follows creeks and rivers through all natural community types of the state.

Thirty-six percent of the 105 species and subspecies of snakes living in Texas are of eastern derivation. These animals range widely in eastern or southeastern North America but reach their western limits in Texas, where most are stopped by either the arid western plateaus

---

*Contributions by Frederick R. Gehlbach, Baylor University.

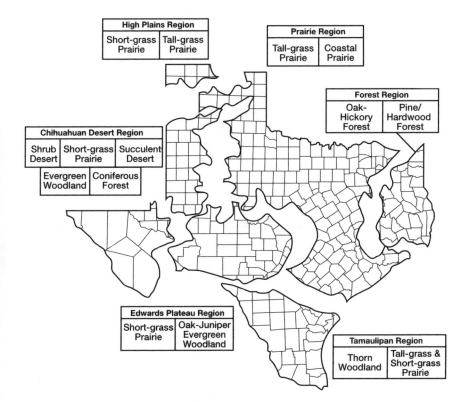

High Plains Region

| Short-grass Prairie | Tall-grass Prairie |

Prairie Region

| Tall-grass Prairie | Coastal Prairie |

Forest Region

| Oak-Hickory Forest | Pine/Hardwood Forest |

Chihuahuan Desert Region

| Shrub Desert | Short-grass Prairie | Succulent Desert |
| Evergreen Woodland | Coniferous Forest |

Edwards Plateau Region

| Short-grass Prairie | Oak-Juniper Evergreen Woodland |

Tamaulipan Region

| Thorn Woodland | Tall-grass & Short-grass Prairie |

or the short-grass prairie of the High Plains. The eastern hognose snake, the Texas rat snake, and the canebrake rattlesnake are examples.

The second important group of snakes (23% of the state's species) is basically western or southwestern, with eastern limits in Texas set by the central tall-grass prairie. The ground snake, the long-nosed snake, and the prairie rattlesnake are among this group. Additionally, there exists a small number (14%) of typically central North American or Great Plains species, such as the Texas blind snake, the Texas lined snake, and the western hog-nosed snake. A yet smaller group (9%) is of Chihuahuan regional derivation, and includes the Trans-Pecos rat snake, the western hook-nosed snake, and the rock rattlesnakes. A few (9%) transcontinental species also range across Texas, including ring-necked snakes, desert and speckled kingsnakes, and several garter snakes, while some essentially tropical snakes, such as the indigo, cat-eyed, and black-striped snakes, reach the northern limits of their range in the state's Tamaulipan Region. A single endemic, the Harter's water snake, is found entirely within Texas.

James Rogers (1976) analyzed these distributions and found that vertical landscape diversity and the number of coexisting small-mammal species were the chief positive influences on the number of local snake species. High altitude has a significant negative effect, however. The diverse ophidian population of the eastern and central portions of the state is, of course, the result of the strong eastern faunal element, but Texas' overall diversity is due to the addition of numerous western serpents plus the mix of important specialties from the Great Plains, Chihuahuan Desert, and Tamaulipan regions; no other state has as many snake species.

The following table is an approximation of the probable frequency, as best as is known, with which a snake species or subspecies makes use of or is able to inhabit a particular type of habitat. Various micro-habitats within these large geographic/geologic/vegetation areas are preferred by most snakes, and only a few species and subspecies such as racers, Texas rat snakes, bullsnakes, and western diamond-backed rattlesnakes occur throughout most of the terrain—*even in the Habitat Types where they are listed as* **C**, *or* **Common.**

Therefore, a species or subspecies designated as **C** in a given habitat means it is generally **Common** in that specific geographic area. That is, in a particular habitat type, this species or subspecies can be expected to occur—*somewhere*—on most sizable rural tracts of land containing both unaltered or minimally altered habitat and a variety of vegetation and terrain typical of the area, including lakes, ponds, or waterways. (The animal is unlikely to occur *everywhere* on such tracts of land for, even in areas where it may be listed as **Common,** most snake species and subspecies are found only in specific localities. Water snakes and ribbon snakes are found almost exclusively in and around bodies of water, for example, although most of their range is made up of dry land; many other species and subspecies are also usually restricted to such riparian corridors.)

Further, snake populations are notoriously unstable, with some species and subspecies being locally abundant in some locales, in some years, and nearly absent in the same areas at other times. Moreover, reptiles in general and snakes in particular are extremely seasonally oriented, weather-sensitive creatures. Many species and subspecies spend much, or all, of the year in hiding below the surface, and their movements abroad are subject to a huge range of seasonal and atmospheric conditions. Therefore, at any given time—even on tracts of land where a species or subspecies is abundant—one cannot necessarily expect to find the animal, for the subterranean lives of many snakes mean the snakes can be abundant in an area but only rarely be seen by humans. (Complicating this situation, snakes' population fluctuations can make them seem more abundant in an area—or, in years of prolonged drought, for example, much more rare—than that species or subspecies may prove to be over many years' observation.)

A **U,** or **Uncommon,** species would occur on only a few such tracts of land, even within the Habitat Types it normally occupies.

An **R** designation means a **Rare** species, or one that infrequently occurs even on large tracts of natural land within a particular habitat type.

A * symbol means that a species' or subspecies' occurrence in a given habitat type is not yet known. No habitat chart such as this has previously been published for Texas snakes, and as with all natural history studies, its data are still incomplete and subject to revision. We welcome information to this end.

Although Texas snakes are about equally divided between prey specialists/habitat generalists (eastern hognose, the crayfish snakes, Texas coral snake), habitat specialists/prey generalists (*Nerodia*-genus water snakes, western cottonmouth, the rock rattlesnakes), and prey-and-habitat generalists (western diamond-backed rattlesnake, bullsnake, Texas rat snake), the *prey*—invertebrate and vertebrate—of most native snakes tends to be habitat specialized, so that most species and subspecies occur more often in certain biotic communities than in others.

	Chihuahuan Desert Region				
	Shrub Desert	*Short-grass Prairie*	*Succulent Desert*	*Evergreen Woodland*	*Coniferous Forest*
1. Plains Blind Snake *Leptotyphlops dulcis dulcis*					
2. New Mexico Blind Snake *Leptotyphlops dulcis dissectus*	*	*	*	C	*
3. Trans-Pecos Blind Snake *Leptotyphlops humilis segregus*	C	*	C	*	*
4. Flat-headed Snake *Tantilla gracilis*					
5. Plains Black-headed Snake *Tantilla nigriceps*	*	U	U	*	*
6. Southwestern Black-headed Snake *Tantilla hobartsmithi*	C	C	C	*	*
7. Mexican Black-headed Snake *Tantilla atriceps*					
8. Black-hooded Snake *Tantilla rubra cucullata*	*	*	R	*	*
9. Texas Brown Snake *Storeria dekayi texana*					
10. Marsh Brown Snake *Storeria dekayi limnetes*					
11. Florida Red-bellied Snake *Storeria occipitomaculata obscura*					
12. Rough Earth Snake *Virginia striatula*					
13. Western Smooth Earth Snake *Virginia valeriae elegans*					
14. Mississippi Ring-necked Snake *Diadophis punctatus stictogenys*					
15. Prairie Ring-necked Snake *Diadophis punctatus arnyi*					
16. Regal Ring-necked Snake *Diadophis punctatus regalis*	U	U/R	U/R	U	U
17. Ground Snake *Sonora semiannulata*	C	C	C/U	U	*
18. Western Worm Snake *Carphophis amoenus vermis*					

	High Plains Region		Edwards Plateau Region		Tamaulipan Region		Prairie Region		Forest Region	
	Short-grass Prairie	Tall-grass Prairie	Short-grass Prairie	Oak-Juniper Evergreen Woodland	Thorn Woodland	Tall-grass and Short-grass Prairie	Tall-grass Prairie	Coastal Prairie	Oak-Hickory Forest	Pine/Hardwood Forest
		C	C	C	*	U	C	*		
	*	*								
	U	U	C	C	*	*	C	*	C/U	C
	C	C	C	*	*	R	U			
			C	*		*				
						R				
			U	C/U	C	*	C		C	C
								C		
									U	U
			*	C/U		U	C	U	C	C
			*	C			C/U	U	C/U	C/U
									U	U/R
	U	U	U	U			U	*		
	C	C	C	C	U	U	C/U			
									*	*

(table continued on next page)

21

	Shrub Desert	Short-grass Prairie	Succulent Desert	Evergreen Woodland	Coniferous Forest

	Shrub Desert	Short-grass Prairie	Succulent Desert	Evergreen Woodland	Coniferous Forest
19. Lined Snake *Tropidoclonion lineatum*					
20. Eastern Garter Snake *Thamnophis sirtalis sirtalis*					
21. Texas Garter Snake *Thamnophis sirtalis annecteans*					
22. Checkered Garter Snake *Thamnophis marcianus marcianus*	U	C/U	R	C	*
23. Western Plains Garter Snake *Thamnophis radix haydenii*					
24. Eastern Black-necked Garter Snake *Thamnophis cyrtopsis ocellatus*	U	U	U	C	*
25. Western Black-necked Garter Snake *Thamnophis cyrtopsis cyrtopsis*	U	U	U/R	C	C/U
26. Western Ribbon Snake *Thamnophis proximus proximus*					
27. Red-striped Ribbon Snake *Thamnophis proximus rubrilineatus*					
28. Gulf Coast Ribbon Snake *Thamnophis proximus orarius*					
29. Arid Land Ribbon Snake *Thamnophis proximus diabolicus*	U	U	R	U	*
30. Diamond-backed Water Snake *Nerodia rhombifer rhombifer*			C/U		
31. Yellow-bellied Water Snake *Nerodia erythrogaster flavigaster*					
32. Blotched Water Snake *Nerodia erythrogaster transversa*	U/R	U/R	U/R	U	
33. Broad-banded Water Snake *Nerodia fasciata confluens*					
34. Florida Water Snake *Nerodia fasciata pictiventris*					
35. Gulf Salt Marsh Snake *Nerodia clarkii clarkii*					

	High Plains Region		Edwards Plateau Region		Tamaulipan Region		Prairie Region		Forest Region	
	Short-grass Prairie	Tall-grass Prairie	Short-grass Prairie	Oak-Juniper Evergreen Woodland	Thorn Woodland	Tall-grass and Short-grass Prairie	Tall-grass Prairie	Coastal Prairie	Oak-Hickory Forest	Pine/Hardwood Forest
	*		C/U	U	*	U/R	C	C/U		
								R	R	R
				U	R	R	U/R	*		
	U	C	C/U	C/U	C	C	C	*		
	C	U								
			C/U	C						
	C/U									
							C		C	C
			C	C			C			
					C	C		C		
	C	C								
			C/U	C/U	C	C	C	C	C	C
									C	C
	C	C	C	C	C	C	C	C		
								C/U	C	C
						C Browns- ville Daly				
								C/U		

23

(table continued on next page)

	Chihuahuan Desert Region					
	Shrub Desert	Short-grass Prairie	Succulent Desert	Evergreen Woodland	Coniferous Forest	
36. Mississippi Green Water Snake *Nerodia cyclopion*						
37. Brazos Water Snake *Nerodia harteri harteri*						
38. Concho Water Snake *Nerodia harteri paucimaculata*						
39. Graham's Crayfish Snake *Regina grahamii*						
40. Gulf Crayfish Snake *Regina rigida sinicola*						
41. Western Mud Snake *Farancia abacura reinwardtii*						
42. Texas Patch-nosed Snake *Salvadora grahamiae lineata*						
43. Mountain Patch-nosed Snake *Salvadora grahamiae grahamiae*	*	C/U	C/U	C	*	
44. Big Bend Patch-nosed Snake *Salvadora deserticola*	C	U	C	*	*	
45. Rough Green Snake *Opheodrys aestivus*						
46. Smooth Green Snake *Liochlorophis vernalis*						
47. Eastern Coachwhip *Masticophis flagellum flagellum*						
48. Western Coachwhip *Masticophis flagellum testaceus*	C	C	C	C	C	
49. Central Texas Whipsnake *Masticophis taeniatus girardi*	U	U	C/U	C	*	
50. Desert Striped Whipsnake *Masticophis taeniatus taeniatus*	U		C/U	C	C/U	
51. Schott's Whipsnake *Masticophis schotti*						
52. Ruthven's whipsnake *Masticophis ruthveni*						
53. Southern Black Racer *Coluber constrictor priapus*						

	High Plains Region		Edwards Plateau Region		Tamaulipan Region		Prairie Region		Forest Region	
	Short-grass Prairie	Tall-grass Prairie	Short-grass Prairie	Oak-Juniper Evergreen Woodland	Thorn Woodland	Tall-grass and Short-grass Prairie	Tall-grass Prairie	Coastal Prairie	Oak-Hickory Forest	Pine/Hardwood Forest
								R	R	R
			C	C						
			C	C						
			U	*	R	R	U	C	U	U/R
								C	U	U
								U	C/U	C/U
			C	C	U	U	C	U		
			C	C	*	U	C	C	C	C
								R		
								U	C	C
	C	C	C	C	C	C	C			
			C/U	C						
					C	C	C			
					C	U				
									C	C

(*table continued on next page*)

	Chihuahuan Desert Region				
	Shrub Desert	Short-grass Prairie	Succulent Desert	Evergreen Woodland	Coniferous Forest
54. Buttermilk Racer *Coluber constrictor anthicus*					
55. Tan Racer *Coluber constrictor etheridgei*					
56. Eastern Yellow-bellied Racer *Coluber constrictor flaviventris*	R	R	R	R	
57. Mexican Racer *Coluber constrictor oaxaca*					
58. Central American Speckled Racer *Drymobius margaritiferus margaritiferus*					
59. Texas Indigo Snake *Drymarchon corais erebennus*	R		R		
60. Eastern Hog-nosed Snake *Heterodon platirhinos*					
61. Dusty Hog-nosed Snake *Heterodon nasicus gloydi*					
62. Plains Hog-nosed Snake *Heterodon nasicus nasicus*					
63. Mexican Hog-nosed Snake *Heterodon nasicus kennerlyi*	U	C/U	U		
64. Western Hook-nosed Snake *Gyalopion canum*	U	C/U	U	C/U	
65. Mexican Hook-nosed Snake *Ficimia streckeri*					
66. Louisiana Pine Snake *Pituophis ruthveni*					
67. Bullsnake *Pituophis catenifer sayi*					
68. Sonoran Gopher Snake *Pituophis catenifer affinis*	C/U	C	C/U	C	C
69. Texas Glossy Snake *Arizona elegans arenicola*					
70. Kansas Glossy Snake *Arizona elegans elegans*	C/U	C/U	C/U		
71. Painted Desert Glossy Snake *Arizona elegans philipi*	*		*		

26

High Plains Region		Edwards Plateau Region		Tamaulipan Region		Prairie Region		Forest Region	
Short-grass Prairie	Tall-grass Prairie	Short-grass Prairie	Oak-Juniper Evergreen Woodland	Thorn Woodland	Tall-grass and Short-grass Prairie	Tall-grass Prairie	Coastal Prairie	Oak-Hickory Forest	Pine/Hardwood Forest
								C	C
								C/U	C/U
C/U	C/U	C/U	C/U	U	U	C	C	C	C
				U	U				
				R					
				C/U	U				
U	U	U	U		U/R		C/U	C	C
		U	U			R	R	R	*
C	C								
				U	C/U				
		U							
				U	U				
								R	R
C	C	C	C/U	C	C	C	R		
				C	C	R		*	
*	*	R				*			

(*table continued on next page*) 27

	Shrub Desert	Short-grass Prairie	Succulent Desert	Evergreen Woodland	Coniferous Forest	
72. Texas Rat Snake *Elaphe obsoleta lindheimerii*						
73. Baird's Rat Snake *Elaphe bairdi*	U	U	C/U	C/U	C/U	
74. Great Plains Rat Snake *Elaphe guttata emoryi*	U	C/U	U	C/U	U	
75. Trans-Pecos Rat Snake *Bogertophis subocularis*	C/U	R	C/U	U	*	
76. Prairie Kingsnake *Lampropeltis calligaster calligaster*						
77. Speckled Kingsnake *Lampropeltis getula holbrooki*						
78. Desert Kingsnake *Lampropeltis getula splendida*	U	C/U	U	U/R		
79. Louisiana Milk Snake *Lampropeltis triangulum amaura*						
80. Mexican Milk Snake *Lampropeltis triangulum annulata*						
81. New Mexico Milk Snake *Lampropeltis triangulum celaenops*	U/R	R	U/R	R	R	
82. Central Plains Milk Snake *Lampropeltis triangulum gentilis*						
83. Gray-banded Kingsnake *Lampropeltis alterna*	R	R	U	U	R	
84. Northern Scarlet Snake *Cemophora coccinea copei*						
85. Texas Scarlet Snake *Cemophora coccinea lineri*						
86. Texas Long-nosed Snake *Rhinocheilus lecontei tessellatus*	C/U	C/U	C/U			
87. Texas Night Snake *Hypsiglena torquata jani*	C	C/U	C	U	*	
88. Black-striped Snake *Coniophanes imperialis imperialis*						

Chihuahuan Desert Region

High Plains Region		Edwards Plateau Region		Tamaulipan Region		Prairie Region		Forest Region	
Short-grass Prairie	Tall-grass Prairie	Short-grass Prairie	Oak-Juniper Evergreen Woodland	Thorn Woodland	Tall-grass and Short-grass Prairie	Tall-grass Prairie	Coastal Prairie	Oak-Hickory Forest	Pine/Hardwood Forest
		C	C	R	R	C	C	C	C
		U	C/U						
C/U	C/U	C	C	C	C	C	C	U	U/R
		*			R	C/U	C/U	C	U
U/R	U/R					C	C	C	C
		U	U	C/U	C/U	C/U			
						U	U	C/U	U
		R	R	C/U	C/U		C/U		
*	*								
	R								
		*	R						
								C/U	C/U
				R	*		R		
C/U	C/U	U	U	C	C				
U	*	U	U	C/U	C/U	*			
				U	U				

(table continued on next page)

| | Chihuahuan Desert Region | | | | |
	Shrub Desert	Short-grass Prairie	Succulent Desert	Evergreen Woodland	Coniferous Forest
89. Northern Cat-eyed Snake *Leptodeira septentrionalis septentrionalis*					
90. Texas Lyre Snake *Trimorphodon biscutatus vilkinsonii*	R		U/R	*	*
91. Texas Coral Snake *Micrurus fulvius tener*			R		
92. Southern Copperhead *Agkistrodon contortrix contortrix*					
93. Broad-banded Copperhead *Agkistrodon contortrix laticinctus*					
94. Trans-Pecos Copperhead *Agkistrodon contortrix pictigaster*	U		U	C/U	*
95. Western Cottonmouth *Agkistrodon piscivorus leucostoma*					
96. Western Pigmy Rattlesnake *Sistrurus miliarius streckeri*					
97. Western Massasauga *Sistrurus catenatus tergeminus*					
98. Desert Massasauga *Sistrurus catenatus edwardsii*		U			
99. Timber Rattlesnake *Crotalus horridus*					
100. Western Diamond-backed Rattlesnake *Crotalus atrox*	C	C	C	C	U
101. Northern Black-tailed Rattlesnake *Crotalus molossus molossus*	U	U/R	C	C	C
102. Prairie Rattlesnake *Crotalus viridis viridis*		U			
103. Mojave Rattlesnake *Crotalus scutulatus scutulatus*	U	U/R	C/U	U	*
104. Mottled Rock Rattlesnake *Crotalus lepidus lepidus*		R	C/U	C/U	C/U
105. Banded Rock Rattlesnake *Crotalus lepidus klauberi*			C/U	R	*

	High Plains Region		Edwards Plateau Region		Tamaulipan Region		Prairie Region		Forest Region	
	Short-grass Prairie	Tall-grass Prairie	Short-grass Prairie	Oak-Juniper Evergreen Woodland	Thorn Woodland	Tall-grass and Short-grass Prairie	Tall-grass Prairie	Coastal Prairie	Oak-Hickory Forest	Pine/Hardwood Forest
				R						
			C/U	C/U	C/U	C/U	U	C/U	C/U	C/U
							U	*	C	C
			C/U	C/U			C	C		
			U	U			U	C	C	C
								U/R	U/R	U/R
	C/U	C/U	R					U	R	
					*	U/R				
							U	U/R	C/U	U
	C	C	C	C	C	C	C	C		
				U						
	C	C								

SNAKE VENOM POISONING

With their bright, unblinking eyes that seem to reflect a preternatural serenity, their apparent ability to rejuvenate themselves by casting off their aged skins, and their uncanny agility—"the way of the serpent upon the rock"—snakes are distinctly different from other animals. For millennia, men have seen in them both intimations of transcendence (the serpent that tempted Eve was part of a long historical line of supernatural snakes) and the manifestation of supernatural power.

Throughout the world, early cultures placed great emphasis on both imagined aspects of serpents' nature. In the Toltec-Aztec-Maya civilizations of Middle America an early rattlesnake god—ultimately evolved into the feathered serpent Quetzalcoatl—became the deity whose potency sanctified the priesthood's control over the secular population. The same ability to kill with a pinprick inspired the Egyptian priesthood, from the time of earliest dynasties, to deify *Naja haje*, the Egyptian cobra, as the serpent-god Uraeus. Over the centuries Uraeus gradually rose among the celestial pantheon to a position second only to that of Ra, the sun king; later, *Naja haje* became the symbol of imperial authority, and the bejeweled face of a cobra glared from the brow of every royal headdress—whose flared neckpiece was itself designed to emulate the snake's spreading hood.

Not much was known about the snakes themselves; however, priests, postulating that mortal cobras derived their lethal virulence from Uraeus himself, sometimes cut open the limbs of bitten individuals to release the supernatural vapors assumed to have been implanted there.[1] Because no other explanation for the destructive

---

[1] In pre-Columbian North America, however, the affinity of snake venom for living protoplasm was widely recognized among native peoples, and stood as the rationale behind the most common American Indian antidote for snakebite, which was to slice through the fang marks and press the freshly opened body of a bird against the wound in the hope that some of the still-unbonded serum within might be drawn up into the unsaturated avian tissues. Although venom could not actually be drawn out in this way, the approach was rational enough for variations to be recommended by turn-of-the century medical officers looking for a better means of extraction than the dangerous and ineffective cut-and-suck regimen.

power of venomous snakebite existed, this belief persisted, largely unchallenged, until renegade physician Francesco Redi opposed the medical doctrines of seventeenth-century Florence (where it was believed that the virulent symptoms of envenomation were caused by the rage of the serpent, somehow passed, like the madness of a rabid dog, into its victim by means of its saliva). Redi maintained, instead, that the "direful effects" of snakebite were the result of a lethal poison held in the snake's "great glands," but apparently no one paid much attention.

Even with the much later advent of chemical analysis there was still little to support Redi's point of view. Late-nineteenth-century chemists were unanimous in finding that vipers' big buccal glands held no identifiable poison—at least not any substance, like the toxic alkaloids or burning acids, that they could recognize as a poison. Quite the opposite: snake venom seemed to be an apparently commonplace protein, so nearly indistinguishable from egg white in structure that in 1886 R. Norris Wolfenden, speaking for the Commission on Indian and Australian Snake Poisoning, reported: "It is quite impossible to draw any deductions as to the nature of the poison. It is merely a mixture of albuminous principles."

The first real clue to how this particular assemblage of reptilian body fluids could bring about the immediate physical deterioration of other animals came six years later, with French physician John de Lacerda's conceptualization of the tissue-disintegrating biological catalysts he termed *enzymes*. And indeed, much like the enzymes of stomach acid, harmless to the gut that contains them yet able to break down devoured flesh into its constituent amino acids, most components of North American pitviper venom have evolved to enzymatically disintegrate the internal tissues of the snake's prey. For contemporary victims of pitviper poisoning this is an important concept, since it emphasizes the progressive tissue-death aspect of venom poisoning over the commonly held belief that envenomation typically poses an immediately fatal threat.

W. C. Fields liked to tell people he always kept a bottle of whiskey handy in case he saw a snake—which he also kept handy. Few people still rely on Fields' remedy, but almost no one is aware that following

But, except for including thin sheets of latex to place between mouth and wound in some army snakebite kits, no improvement on the old method was developed until the 1920s, when Dudley Jackson (1929) slightly refined the old extraction approach by placing a series of heat-transfer suction cups over incisions both across the fang marks and around the perimeter of the expanding mound of edema that surrounds most serious pitviper envenomations. Although probably the best of the incision therapies, Jackson's approach was still unable to prevent the disabling tissue necrosis associated with severe crotalid envenomation and was entirely useless against the peptide-based venom of the coral snake.

most of the widely recommended first-aid procedures is nearly as dangerous. For example, cutting open a snakebite wound in the field is worse than doing nothing at all because attempts to suck or syringe out venom are inevitably futile and the incision, even if it is not large, can cause significant harm.

And there may be no need to do anything: the chances are good that the snake may not be venomous. The great majority of the several thousand snakebites that occur annually in the United States involve nonvenomous serpents and require nothing more than reassurance and a tetanus shot.[2] Then, because venomous snakes have control over whether or not they inject their toxins during a bite, envenomation doesn't always occur; punctures by pitvipers are entirely free of toxins about 15 percent of the time, and superficial envenomation is much more common than severe poisoning. Probably fewer than half of coral snake bites result in severe poisoning, and with either pitviper or elapids like the coral, unless heavy poisoning has been established it is irresponsible to destroy irreplaceable nerve and muscle tissue by following invasive first-aid procedures.

Many properties of snake venom, moreover, weigh heavily against a person's cutting into the fang marks left by a bite. One of these is the tendency of reptilian toxins to suppress the body's bactericidal and immune responses, particularly the action of its white blood cells, and without those leukocytes' prophylactic intervention an exceptionally receptive environment awaits the host of pathogens introduced by every deep field incision. In addition, rapid local dispersal of infective agents is ensured by the seepage of contaminated plasma and lymphatic fluid that, following envenomation, is suffused through tissues made more permeable by the fiber-dissolving effect of the venom's component hyaluronidase.

An even more pressing reason to avoid incision in the field is that the anticoagulant effect of pitviper venom on plasma fibrinogen so impairs the blood's ability to clot that opening an envenomated limb is likely to produce much more profuse bleeding than one would expect. It is always dangerous to risk bleeding in people whose level of fibrinogen is low, and following severe envenomation taking a chance on setting off heavy bleeding is particularly chancy because when people die of snakebite (which happens in less than 1 percent of poisonings inflicted by native species), loss of circulating blood volume is what kills them.

Therefore, maintaining sufficient circulating blood volume is crucial in the initial management of critical snakebite poisoning, and cutting open a limb which may bleed profusely is not the way to maintain

---

[2] Most envenomations occur in the southwestern states, and fewer than a dozen a year are fatal.

blood volume. Avoiding dehydration by having the victim drink as much as he is comfortable with is a good idea, however.[3]

Fortunately, in-the-bush surgery is usually out of the question anyway, because getting bitten by a venomous snake is such a terrifying experience that then being able to execute this classically prescribed procedure is impossible for most people. (It is also almost unbearable to be cut open after a pitviper bite because the digestive dissolution of blood within the subcutaneous tissue releases bradykinin from its disintegrating plasma and serotonin from its serum platelets, and both substances produce burning pain—which makes the skin so sensitive that the prospect of crude pocketknife incisions becomes nearly unthinkable.)

---

[3]After severe envenomation, some internal bleeding always takes place. Except in the most severe poisonings, however, or in the case of a small child, it ordinarily takes hours to lose a mortally significant quantity of blood internally because leakage through enzyme-perforated arterioles and venules normally only gradually allows the vascular fluids to pool in the interstitial spaces of an envenomated limb. (Eventually, though, a seemingly minimal amount of such swelling—Findlay E. Russell, dean of U.S. snake venom toxicology, estimated as little as a 2-centimeter increase in the circumference of a thigh—could account for the loss into the tissue spaces of nearly a third of the body's circulating blood volume, dropping vascular pressure enough to put a patient into shock.)

Ironically, the swelling of edema seldom threatens the limb itself. While huge serosanguinous blisters may bulge up around pitviper bites, the distension is usually soft and limited to the epidermal and outer cutaneous layers. As this fact has become widely known, the formerly common practice of surgically opening such swollen limbs—a technique long assumed to be necessary to relieve hydraulic pressure which might cause necrosis from restricted circulation—is now employed much less often, even in the most severe envenomations. (In treating some 200 venomous snakebites, Ken Mattox and his team at Houston's Ben Taub Hospital have used fasciotomy to relieve hydraulic tourniqueting less than a half-dozen times, while Russell, in treating more ophidian envenomations than anyone in North America, has never had to perform a fasciotomy due to excessive intracompartmental pressure.)

Finally, sophisticated surgical techniques for dealing with another, particularly pernicious type of deep pitviper envenomation have been developed by the late Dr. Thomas G. Glass, former professor of surgery at the University of Texas Medical School in San Antonio. Although most pitviper toxins reach only subcutaneous levels, occasionally a large rattlesnake accomplishes a much deeper penetration, sinking its fangs through skin, subcutaneous fatty layers, and the outer muscle fascia to deposit an infusion of venom within the muscle belly. While a rattler's toxins are much more destructive here, even a large amount of venom this far below the surface may produce few external symptoms because such areas are poorly supplied with nerve endings. (In subcutaneous tissues great pain, swelling, and discoloration accompany venom poisoning, but with deeper envenomations the toxins' proteolytic enzymes may be temporarily encapsulated within the underlying layers of muscle, and give few symptomatic indications of how severe the bite actually is. The trick, of course, is to be able to tell a real subfascial poisoning of this sort from the far more common, largely symptomless superficial snakebite in which little or no envenomation has occurred, and being able to do it in a hurry. If such a bite is accurately diagnosed, however, a considerable amount of the venom infusion can sometimes be removed by deep incision and debridement, although only in this unusual sort of poisoning is a major surgical campaign advised by medical authorities—and then only if it is executed by one of the handful of those experienced in the delicate excision of this sort of deep-lying lacunae.

Therefore, it is much better to avoid wrestling with the agony of such archaic procedures and to instead apply one's efforts to getting proper medical management. In the field, all one need remember is to immobilize an envenomated extremity, remove rings or shoes before swelling makes that difficult, then wrap the limb firmly but not tightly in a splinted elastic bandage. The important part is getting the victim to a good hospital.

All the old field-guide therapies—binding the limb with thin, circulation-cutting cords, packing it in ice, or cutting open the punctures—are dangerous procedures, treatments that invariably go awry because they are founded on a basic misunderstanding of the complex process that begins when a venomous snake bites a human being. The most common misconception is that a strike by a pitviper results in a lethal fluid oozing through the veins toward the heart. If this were the case one should probably do anything possible to arrest the venom's progress, but it isn't what happens at all.

Instead, from the moment it enters the body, venom is almost instantly incorporated into the surrounding tissues. Here, after only a few seconds, it is no more removable than ink dripped on a wet sponge. That is why cut-and-suck, or cut-and-pull with a syringe, or any other snakebite-kit extraction technique, is not a viable therapy for serious envenomation. More than 60 years ago, in experiments with cats and rabbits, F. M. Allen (1939) demonstrated that no benefit resulted even when, within five minutes, a large section of surrounding tissue was entirely removed from the site of an injection of either a western diamond-backed rattlesnake or eastern cottonmouth venom. During even this brief time between injection and tissue removal, Allen's laboratory animals had so thoroughly absorbed the venom's most lethal peptide components that every victim that had received a large enough dose to kill a surgically untreated control also died. This led Allen to conclude that large infusions of crotalid venom spread so quickly throughout a large mass of local tissue that even when an extensive excision immediately follows the bite, the seemingly normal tissue outside the excised area still contains enough venom to cause the animal's death.

These experiments illustrate the futility of trying to remove venom from a snakebite victim, but they also demonstrate that in most cases, after the venom's initial rapid bonding to local tissue, most of the components of pitviper toxin are no longer free to circulate. Thus, beyond the general vicinity of the bite they tend to disperse rather slowly throughout the rest of the body. This means that, to a considerable extent, temporarily localizing these toxins can be accomplished with the mild pressure of an elastic bandage.

Although at odds with most prevailing popular concepts of snakebite poisoning, this concept is consistent with the pattern of dispersal required by the predatory role that venom plays in a pitviper's life. For example, a majority of the 12 to 30 separate toxic peptides and enzymes these reptiles generate are not designed to kill large animals. Instead, their primary function is to predigest smaller vertebrate prey so that it is easier for a small-throated viper to swallow.

To accomplish this, the toxins do not have to move very far from the general region of a bite, so *crotalid* venom disperses only gradually throughout the body of a large victim such as a human being. But it methodically digests tissues as it goes. And, like all digestion, the process is complicated, since most of the venom's diverse proteases and kinases have a separate metabolic function, often a different target organ, and frequently a different way of getting there.[4] These toxins include hyaluronidase, collagenase, thrombin-like enzymes, L-amino oxidase (which gives venom its amber tint), phosphomonoesterase, phosphodiesterase, two kinds of kinases (both of which are similar to pancreatic secretions and, like pancreatic secretions, prepare soft tissue for more extensive breakdown by analogous solutions in the reptile's stomach), nucleotidase, at least one phospholipase, arginine ester hydrolase, and various proteolytic enzymes.[5]

Within the bodies of human beings bitten by pitvipers these enzymes gradually, and with great pain to the victim, disintegrate living tissues. Hyaluronidase, for example, breaks down connective fibers in the muscle matrix, allowing various proteases and trypsin-like enzymes to penetrate the limbs directly. Meanwhile, in concert with several endothelial cell-specific thrombin-like enzymes, other peptides simultaneously perforate the vascular capillary walls, allowing the seepage of plasma thinned by the simultaneous assault of another set of venom enzymes: phospholipase A combines with

---

[4]Many of these venom enzymes, moreover, operate most powerfully in complementary combinations.

[5]In poisoning by most pitvipers (although envenomations by western—Type A venom—populations of the Mojave rattlesnake, *Crotalus scutulatus*, may entail a large complement of neurotoxically active peptides) the venom's ultimate target is not the heart but the lungs. Among North American snakebite's few fatalities, pulmonary embolism is a common finding postmortem, but congestive pooling of blood in the lungs seldom has time to accumulate enough fluid to interfere with respiration before fatal shock from loss of circulating blood volume has occurred.

lipids in the blood to inhibit their coagulative function; toxic fibrinolytic and thrombin-like enzymes disintegrate the hematic fibrinogen also required for clotting; and a pair of related hemolysins, specifically keyed to the destruction of red blood cells, attacks the erythrocytes directly.[6]

Although nothing short of antivenin (which can be administered only in a hospital) is able to stop this process, besides wrapping the limb in an elastic bandage, mildly cooling the limb may offer a slight numbing of the pain. An ice pack on the forehead can also mitigate the intense nausea often associated with venom poisoning, and because toxin-induced intestinal spasms have sometimes been violent enough to provoke hemorrhage of the trachea, any reduction in their severity is of importance. (Severely chilling a bitten limb, however, is deadly to it. While the cell-disintegrating action of enzymes is to some degree slowed by extreme cold, it would take freezing a limb to achieve sufficient chilling to deactivate its infused venom enzymes.)[7]

By taking the conservative approach of simply wrapping the bitten limb or digit in an elastic bandage, splinting it to keep it immobile, then rewrapping the entire area, one allows essential oxygen

---

[6]The relative proportion of these elements in the venom mix varies considerably. Determined by the varying output cycles of each of more than a dozen secretory cells that release their separate toxins into a viper's paired storage bladders, or lumens, snake venom's composition varies from day to day. This makes it one of the most complex of biological substances and to some extent accounts for the disparity in potency observed between similarly sized snakes of the same species taken from the wild at the same time. (Since, at any given time, different venom ingredients are present in variable concentrations, their relative effect on each of a victim's organs may also be somewhat different.)

Outside the lumen, venom will even digest itself, for catalytic agents pumped into the serum from secondary secretory glands located downstream from the primary storage bladder metabolically break down venom's peptide components—which are themselves easily digested proteins.

[7]The worst of the cold-treatment therapies was ligature-cryotherapy. This regimen received popular attention during the 1950s as a way to avoid the obvious perils of incision and suction, but it instead combined two extremely destructive procedures: putting tourniquets around a limb or extremity, then radically chilling the constricted part by immersing it in ice, sometimes for hours. As might be expected, tissue deprived of the oxygen exchange and waste dispersal of normal blood flow while simultaneously being exposed to the cell membrane-cracking effect of lengthy chilling died so frequently that amputations following ligature-cryotherapy became almost routine.

Although this procedure is no longer followed in medical circles, a legacy of its erroneous concepts remains, and some literature still in print, as well as recent public-service television commercials, still refer to the option of packing envenomated limbs in ice.

dispersal, while the broad pressure of an elastic bandage—which moderately compresses the lymph vessels—slows the mostly muscular contraction-pumped flow of venom-saturated lymphatic fluid.[8] This singularly safe and effective field treatment dovetails with the medical consensus that now prevails concerning subsequent hospital management of severe reptile envenomation—an approach that relies heavily on the intravenous administration of antivenin, some-

---

[8]The most numerous components of pitviper toxin, its enzymatic venom fractions, are dispersed primarily through the lymph system. In contrast, the mostly neurotoxically targeted peptide components of *elapid* venoms, including those of all three North American coral snakes, disperse primarily through the bloodstream, where they are not subject to any mechanical constraint short of a total tourniquet. Only antivenin is effective in treating this sort of envenomation, and only in poisoning by such peptide-based venoms might employing a temporary arterial tourniquet be appropriate because, cinched down for more than a few minutes, such a tourniquet is likely to cause permanent injury to the limb, sometimes severe enough to require amputation. Applying a tourniquet is, in fact, such a dangerous procedure that binding a strap or cord around any envenomation, except perhaps that by a severe coral snake poisoning or of a toddler deeply envenomated by a big rattlesnake, is now decried by everyone involved in treating snakebites. The neurotoxically active polypeptides of coral snake venom are particularly dangerous. Because they evolved to quickly paralyze the other snakes on which many *elapids* feed, these polypeptides can effect the same paralysis in human victims of coral snakebite. Similar neurotoxically destructive proteins are also present, in smaller proportions, in nearly all snake venom, even that of genera such as the *viperids* (whose venom is principally comprised of hematoxic, or blood-targeted, components). But in the peptide-based venom of new world coral snakes these enzymes seem to be particularly targeted toward the neural membranes branching from the upper spinal cord, where they block acetylcholine receptor sites in the junctions between adjoining nuchal ganglia, impairing neuromuscular transmission and, by shutting down the autonomic triggering of respiration, can sometimes cause death by suffocation.

Other components of *elapid* venom are hemolytic, or blood- and circulatory-system directed. While generally less potent than the venom's neurotoxic elements, these cardiotoxically active components can be lethal in high doses. Neither Wyeth's equine-derived coral snake antivenin (Antivenin, *Micrurus fulvius*, Drug Circular, Wyeth, 1983) nor Savage Laboratories' new CroFab *crotalid*, or pitviper, antivenin is reported to neutralize these hemolytic elements, however. At a median dose of 6.5 vials, Wyeth reports, 35 percent of patients treated with its coral snake antivenin experienced side effects; in 50 percent of those cases, the side effects were severe, resulting in anaphylactic shock or serum sickness.

Another type of coral snake antivenin, with reportedly about the same dosage requirement, effectiveness, and problematic side effects, is manufactured by the Instituto Butantan in Sao Paulo, Brazil. Manufactured from antibodies generated by a mixture of the venom of two South American coral snake species, *M. corallinus* and *M. frontalis*, it may at some point be joined by a new, ovine-based *Micrurus* antivenin under development at St. Bartholomew's Hospital, Medical College, London, and the Liverpool School of Tropical Medicine, Liverpool, U.K. This antivenin is purported to neutralize both neurotoxic and cardiotoxic components of *Micrurus* venom—which, in preliminary trials, it reportedly did with a fourfold reduction in dosage. Because this antivenin is derived from sheep antibodies, the negative side effects of prior sensitization to equine-based serums used in previous inoculations are likely to be largely absent. (Antivenin from the same company—

times combined with antihistamines or epinephrine to stifle allergic reaction.

Although antivenin is still viewed with suspicion by both doctors and laymen—largely as a result of the poor reputation of earlier serums[9]—when administered by an experienced physician with immediate access to intensive care facilities, the newer antivenins (particularly the recently released CroFab™ serum)[10] seem to be fairly safe, although they must be administered with care. (Medical proponents of antivenin therapy maintain that not only are the life-threatening systemic failures that may follow heavy envenomation best offset by antivenin antibodies, but that these serums offer the only significant means of mitigating the often extensive local necrosis caused by pitviper toxins.)[11]

Nearly as biologically complex as the venom it is cultured to neutralize, antivenins have long been known to sometimes trigger allergic histamine shock, or anaphylaxis—a much more serious manifestation of the ordinary allergic response elicited by sensitizing agents from feathers to pollen. Therefore antivenin should never be used outside a hospital because, like any other immunization, antivenin therapy depends on establishing a protective titer of antibodies in the entire bloodstream. This normally requires far more antigen-bearing serum than conventional immunization—and once this sizable volume of for-

---

CroFab™ North American pitviper antivenin—is produced at the Protherics manufacturing facility in Blaenwaun, Wales, which also produces ViperaTab®, a European viper antivenin.)

[9] In particular, the old Institut Pasteur globulin often caused adverse responses because so much was asked of it by European doctors using it under primitive conditions in the bush to treat the devastatingly toxic bites of African and Indian cobras, mambas, and vipers.

[10] This new *crotalid* antivenin, CroFab™ (Crotalidae Polyvalent Immune Fab) was introduced in late January 2001. Its U.S. distributor is Savage Laboratories, a pharmaceutical division of Altana Inc., 60 Baylis Road, Melville, N.Y. 11747, (800) 231-0205. Altana Inc. is itself the U.S. subsidiary of Byk-Gulden, a multinational pharmaceutical company based in Konstanz, Germany.

According to literature released by Savage (http://www.savagelabs.com), "The majority of adverse reactions to CroFab™ reported in clinical studies were mild or moderate in severity—primarily rash, urticaria and pruritus. CroFab™ should not be administered to patients with a known history of hypersensitivity to papaya or papain unless the benefits outweigh the risks and appropriate management for anaphylactic reactions is readily available. . . . Adverse events involving the skin and appendages were reported in 14 of 42 patients. Three of the 25 patients who experienced adverse reactions experienced severe or serious adverse reaction. All adverse reactions resolved during the course of treatment."

[11] "The administration of an antivenin is important not just for saving lives, but for avoiding serious tissue and bleeding complications," according to Richard Clark, M.D., director of Medical Toxicology, University of California San Diego Medical Center, and medical director, San Diego Division, California Poison Control Systems.

eign protein has been infused into the blood, there is no getting it out.[12] Any allergic reaction that develops therefore must be mitigated with pharmaceutical intervention available only in a hospital—even intensive care—setting, because serum anaphylaxis could cause enough swelling to obstruct the respiratory passages, and even coronary attacks have occurred.[13]

Yet, administered by an experienced physician with immediate access to intensive-care facilities, antivenin can save lives. The most critical aspect of their use lies in the need for immediate intervention to offset any incipient allergic response, usually with antihistamines or epinephrine. This sort of reaction is relatively unlikely, though, since before antivenin can be administered each patient's sensitivity to its foreign proteins is determined by an allergic-reaction skin-test trial.[14]

If no allergic reaction occurs, antivenin can result in a marked decrease in the pain of ophidian venom poisoning. The reason lies in the way antivenin acts to prevent the proteolytic, fibrinolytic, and hemolytic action of snake venom. Introduced into the bloodstream, its antibody clusters are drawn to reptile venom's large, variably shaped toxic peptides and enzymes. (Venom enzymes are usually spherical; peptides may be tubular, coiled, or globular, but all of venom's toxic proteins are spiked externally with sharp-edged, key-like protuberances that work by penetrating the serum's target cells and disintegrating their structure.)

---

[12]This is why antivenin must never be injected directly into an envenomated extremity: you can't build up immunity in a finger alone.

[13]Anaphylaxis could perhaps always have been avoided if animals other than horses had been used to make antivenin but, until recently, only horses—the traditional source animals for all types of immunization vaccines—have been bled for the serum antibodies they produce in response to small, periodic injections of snake venom.

The problem is that horses have been used to produce so many antigen-bearing vaccines that people who have been inoculated against typhoid, tetanus, and diphtheria bacilli have often become sensitized to equine cellular matter. This does not create a problem when they receive the very small dose of foreign protein involved in subsequent conventional immunizations, but when the far larger volume of equine proteins required for treatment of severe venomous snakebite is suddenly dumped into their systems, they sometimes experience allergic anaphylaxis.

[14]Individuals vary so widely in their sensitivity to antivenin infusion that some people need nearly twice as long as others to build up the same blood level of antibodies, but if it can be tolerated, several vials of the vaccine may be given during the first hour. Infusion is then likely to be maintained at two or three vials per hour until an adequate plasma titer is established. According to literature released by Savage Laboratories, "'The availability of CroFab™ presents a safe treatment option for victims of venomous snakebite,' said Richard C. Dart, MD, PhD, Director, Rocky Mountain Poison and Drug Center, Denver Health Authority and Associate Professor of Medicine, Surgery and Pharmacy, University of Colorado Health Sciences Center."

To inhibit this process, antivenin antibodies physically encrust these protrusions so thickly that the toxins can no longer penetrate their target cells. Eventually, enough of their protective frosting is built up to attract the body's particle-devouring macrophagocytes—cleaner cells which, like giant amoebas, eventually engulf and digest most of the conglomerate specks of alien protein.

But they don't do it without potential problems. As the last of these deactivated antibody-antigen complexes precipitate out of the blood, up to two weeks after treatment, they may lodge in vascular vessel walls throughout the body, causing the skin rashes, hives, and temporary kidney impairment that collectively are known as serum sickness. Moreover, even after recovery from snake venom poisoning, a small cadre of the body's own antigens (spawned both by venom proteins and by the antivenin's foreign serum antibodies) may remain in the bloodstream, sensitizing the individual to any subsequently encountered foreign globulins—or, it is thought, to another snakebite.

Because neither the Wyeth *Micrurus* antivenin nor the newer Savage Laboratories CroFab™ pitviper antivenin is kept on hand by every hospital, an emergency source for the latter is the producer:

New *crotalid* (pitviper) antivenin:
CroFab™ (Crotalidae Polyvalent Immune Fab—Ovine)
Savage Laboratories Inc.
60 Baylis Road
Melville, N.Y., 11747
(800) 231-0205
(631) 454-9071

For North American coral snake antivenin: Wyeth Laboratories of Philadelphia, (610) 688-4400. Coral snake antivenin: (*Micrurus fulvius*, Drug Circular, Wyeth, 1983).

Another option is to contact the Antivenin Index, compiled by the Arizona Poison Center, which offers a comprehensive array of data on venomous snakebite and a list of all the antivenins currently stored in the United States, including those for foreign species. Their 24-hour emergency number is (602) 626-6016.

Finally, some authorities on envenomation by both native and exotic reptiles are as follows:

Arizona Poison Control System
Coagulation Research Laboratory
Department of Pediatrics
University of Arizona Health Sciences Center
Tucson, Arizona

Richard Clark, M.D.
Director of Medical Toxicology
University of California San Diego Medical Center
Director, San Diego Division
California Poison Control Systems
San Diego, California

Richard C. Dart, M.D., Ph.D.
Director, Rocky Mountain Poison and Drug Center and Associate
    Professor of Medicine, Surgery and Pharmacy
University of Colorado Health Sciences Center
Denver, Colorado

L. H. S. Van Mierop, M.D.
Department of Pediatrics (Cardiology)
University of Florida Medical School
Gainesville, Florida 32611

Damon C. Smith
Therapeutic Antibodies, Inc.
St. Bartholomew's Hospital Medical College
Charterhouse Square
London, EC1, U.K.

Venom Potency Table

The following comparative values for the relative venom toxicities of Texas' venomous snakes are based on the widely accepted standard known as the LD50. This stands for the Lethal Dosage, or amount of venom required to kill, within 24 hours, 50 percent of the laboratory mice injected with it. Used in slightly varying interpretations since the 1930s, it is the standard set (using the Spearman-Karber injection method and employing genetically uniform Swiss-Webster laboratory mice) by the World Health Organization in 1981.

As a comparative measure of venom potency, the numbers used here are a compilation of 13 major studies of venom potency conducted over the last 63 years on snakes from many different parts of the United States.[15]

Such collective averaging is valid only as an approximation of the general relative toxicity of the venoms of these species because of the great variability that exists in the makeup and potency of toxins taken from the same snake species. (Venom samples obtained from adult individuals of the same species, taken at the same time of year, are often found to be radically different in the relative proportions of their various hematoxic/neurotoxic venom components.) This variability is compounded by the slightly to highly variable differences between regional snake populations.

The venom potency numbers cited here therefore include the highest and lowest potency values (0 being the most toxic) recorded by any of these studies, as well as the mean.

---

[15]Compiled from Githens and Wolff (1939), Gingrich and Hohenadel (1956), Minton (1956), Russell and Emery (1959), Hall and Genarro (1961), Weinstein et al. (1962), Russell (1967), Cohen et al. (1971), Kocholaty (1971), Minton (1974), Glenn and Straight (1977), Glenn and Straight (1978), Russell (1980).

Species	High	Low	Mean
Western Diamond-backed Rattlesnake, *Crotalus atrox*	4.07	8.42	6.25
Western (Prairie) Rattlesnake, *Crotalus viridis*	2.0	2.37	2.19
Mojave Rattlesnake, *Crotalus scutulatus* (type A) Yuma, Arizona	0.13	0.54	0.34
Mojave Rattlesnake, *Crotalus scutulatus* (type B) unknown	2.29	3.8	3.05
Canebrake/Timber Rattlesnake, *Crotalus horridus*	2.69	3.80	3.25
Pigmy Rattlesnake, *Sistrurus miliarius*	6.0	10.29	8.15
Copperhead, *Agkistrodon contortrix*	7.8	16.71	12.26
Cottonmouth, *Agkistrodon piscivorus*	4.88	5.82	5.35
Coral Snake, *Micrurus fulvius*	0.53	0.73	0.63

SCALATION

Head Scales:
Nonvenomous Snake

Head Scales:
Pitviper

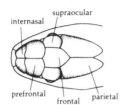

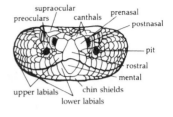

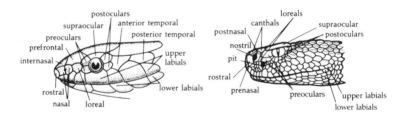

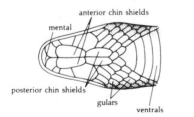

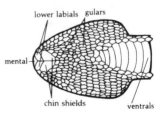

Undertail:
Nonvenomous Snake

*undertail:
nonvenomous
subcaudal scales

Note: The nonvenomous Texas longnose snake
has a single row of subcaudal scales.

Undertail:
Pitviper

*undertail: copperhead
and cottonmouth
subcaudal scales

Note: The venomous coral snake has a double
row of subcaudal scales.

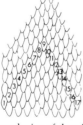

numbering of dorsal
scale rows

smooth scales

keeled scales

divided anal plate

single anal plate

IDENTIFICATION KEY

People who do a lot of looking at plants or animals develop a seemingly amazing ability to identify them from the merest glance. Typically, rather than instantly picking out the specimen's specific, subtle identifying characteristics, these people are recognizing the unique group of static and kinetic attributes that together make up what might be thought of as the creature's visual gestalt. This skill comes only after seeing a great many similar plants or animals, however, and until it is acquired, about the only way to distinguish difficult species is through the use of a taxonomic key.

This one is a tool to aid in the identification of most snakes found in the state. (It is, of course, possible to encounter the rare serpent not typical of its genus, such as an albino.) All numbered questions should be answered in sequence: a *Yes* answer to the first question leads to question 2. Where more than one question is asked, all answers must be *Yes* to take the *Yes* option. A magnifying glass may be helpful in picking out details of scalation, particularly when identifying small snakes.

If it is difficult to answer a question, assume the answer is *Yes,* and continue to the end. If the snake is not the one described in the text, return to the doubtful question and take the *No* option, continuing through the key until the correct genus can be established. Beyond genus level, the photographs, text, and distribution maps will establish a particular animal's species and subspecies.

1. Is the body covered with small dry scales? Does the animal lack legs, fins, movable eyelids, and external ear openings?

yes 2

no . . . . Not a snake.

2. Is there a pit (depression) on the side of the head, between the eye and the nostril?

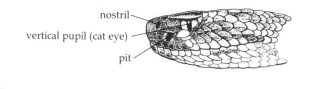

nostril

vertical pupil (cat eye)

pit

yes 3

no 10

3. Does the snake have a single row of scales under the tail? Does it have vertical pupils, like a cat's eyes?

single row   anal plate

yes 4

no . . . You have reached this point in error; return to question 2.

4. Are there rattles at the end of the tail?

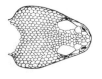

rattles

yes 5

no 9

5. Are there 8 or fewer large scales and many small granular scales on the top of the head?

yes 6

no 7

6. This is a rattlesnake of the genus *Crotalus* (99–105).

7. Are there 9 large scales on top of the head?

yes. 8

no . . . You have reached this point in error; return to question 4.

8. This is a rattlesnake of the genus *Sistrurus* (96–98).

9. This is a copperhead or cottonmouth of the genus *Agkistrodon* (92–95).

10. Is the snake red, yellow, and black, with the colors arranged in bands that completely encircle the body? Are the red and black bands noticeably wider than the yellow bands, with the red and yellow bands touching?

yes. 11

no 12

11. This is a Texas coral snake, genus *Micrurus* (91).

12. Does the snake resemble a worm: tiny, pinkish or flesh-colored, with a blunt tail and eyes that appear to be small, almost invisible dots? Are the scales on the belly not much wider than those on the back?

yes. 13

no 14

13. This is a blind snake of the genus *Leptotyphlops* (1–3).

14. Are all the dorsal (back) scales entirely smooth (not keeled or ridged)?

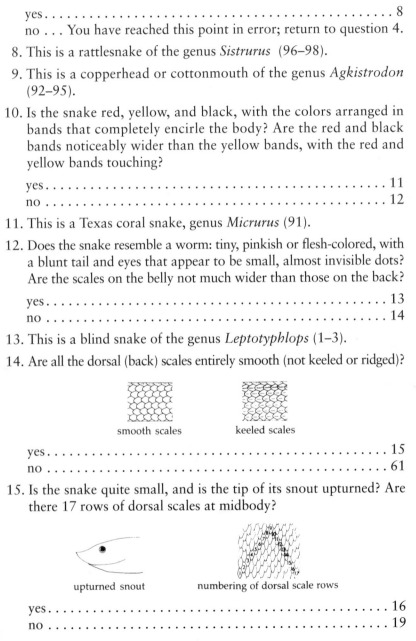

smooth scales   keeled scales

yes. 15

no 61

15. Is the snake quite small, and is the tip of its snout upturned? Are there 17 rows of dorsal scales at midbody?

upturned snout   numbering of dorsal scale rows

yes. 16

no 19

16. Is the top of the head patterned with 1 or 2 prominent blackish bands?

yes.. 17

no 18

17. This is a western hooknose snake, genus *Gyalopion* (64).

18. This is a Mexican hooknose snake, genus *Ficimia* (65).

19. Turn the animal over to locate the anal plate, which covers the vent and is located about two thirds of the way to the tail tip. Is the anal plate single (undivided)?

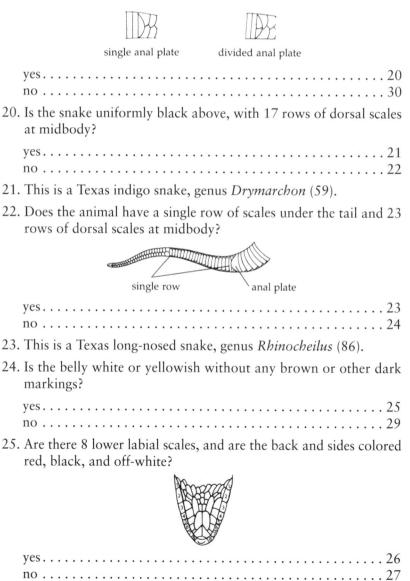

single anal plate   divided anal plate

yes.. 20

no 30

20. Is the snake uniformly black above, with 17 rows of dorsal scales at midbody?

yes.. 21

no 22

21. This is a Texas indigo snake, genus *Drymarchon* (59).

22. Does the animal have a single row of scales under the tail and 23 rows of dorsal scales at midbody?

single row   anal plate

yes.. 23

no 24

23. This is a Texas long-nosed snake, genus *Rhinocheilus* (86).

24. Is the belly white or yellowish without any brown or other dark markings?

yes.. 25

no 29

25. Are there 8 lower labial scales, and are the back and sides colored red, black, and off-white?

yes.. 26

no 27

26. This is a scarlet snake of the genus *Cemophora* (84, 85).

27. Is the dorsal color off-white blotched with brown? Is there a pale longitudinal line along the spine just behind the head? Are there 12 to 15 lower labial scales?

    yes. 28
    no . . . You have reached this point in error; return to question 2.

28. This is a glossy snake of the genus *Arizona* (69–71).

29. This is a kingsnake or milk snake of the genus *Lampropeltis* (77–83).

30. Are there 17 or fewer rows of dorsal scales at midbody?

    yes. 31
    no 50

31. Is the snake longitudinally striped, and does it have an enlarged, triangular-shaped rostral scale that curves back over the snout and has free edges?

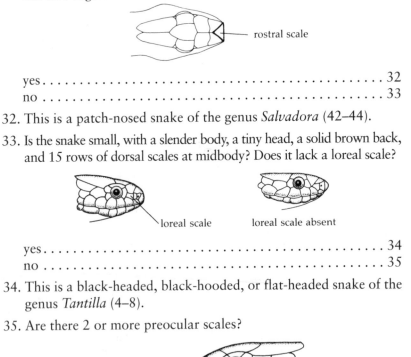

rostral scale

    yes. 32
    no 33

32. This is a patch-nosed snake of the genus *Salvadora* (42–44).

33. Is the snake small, with a slender body, a tiny head, a solid brown back, and 15 rows of dorsal scales at midbody? Does it lack a loreal scale?

loreal scale   loreal scale absent

    yes. 34
    no 35

34. This is a black-headed, black-hooded, or flat-headed snake of the genus *Tantilla* (4–8).

35. Are there 2 or more preocular scales?

preocular scales

    yes. 36
    no 45

36. Are the lower and upper preocular scales about the same size?

yes. 37
no 40

37. Is the nasal plate divided? Is the animal slate gray above, with a darker head and a black-speckled orangish belly?

divided nasal plate

yes. 38
no 39

38. This is a ring-necked snake of the genus *Diadophis* (14–16).

39. This is a western smooth green snake, genus *Opheodrys* (45).

40. Is the animal quite slender for its length, and are there 15 rows of dorsal (back) scales counted at midbody?

yes. 41
no 42

41. This is a whipsnake of the genus *Masticophis* (47–52).

42. Are there 17 rows of dorsal scales at midbody, and 13 rows just ahead of the anal plate?

yes. 43
no 44

43. This is a coachwhip of the genus *Masticophis* (47–48).

44. This is a racer of the genus *Coluber* (53–57).

45. Is the loreal scale in direct contact with the eye?

loreal scale

yes. 46
no 49

46. Is the back black, the lower sides pinkish? Are there fewer than 15 rows of dorsal scales at midbody?

yes. 47
no 48

47. This is a western worm snake, genus *Carphophis* (18).

48. This is a western smooth earth snake, genus *Virginia* (13).

49. This is a ground snake, genus *Sonora* (17).

50. Is the animal shiny black above and pink below, with a horny point on the tip of its tail?

yes 51
no 52

51. This is a western mud snake, genus *Farancia* (41).

52. Is the snake quite slender, and are its eyes proportionately very large, with vertical (cat-eyed) pupils?

yes 53
no 58

53. Are the back and sides light brown or buff narrowly banded with darker brown, and are 2 or more loreal scales present?

yes 54
no 55

54. This is a Texas lyre snake, genus *Trimorphodon* (90).

55. Are the back and sides yellowish, with wide, blackish-brown bands? Is the undertail orange or salmon?

yes 56
no 57

56. This is a northern cat-eyed snake, genus *Leptodeira* (89).

57. This is a night snake of the genus *Hypsiglena* (87).

58. Is the snake small and slender, its back and sides longitudinally striped with black and brown? Are there 19 rows of dorsal scales at midbody?

yes 59
no 60

59. This is a black-striped snake, genus *Coniophanes* (88).

60. This is a rat snake of the genus *Elaphe* (72–74).

61. Is the snake comparatively plump, with a snout whose tip is distinctly upturned? Are there 23 to 25 rows of dorsal (back) scales counted at midbody?

upturned snout   numbering of dorsal scale rows

yes 62
no 63

62. This is a hog-nosed snake of the genus *Heterodon* (60–63).

63. Is the anal plate single (undivided)?

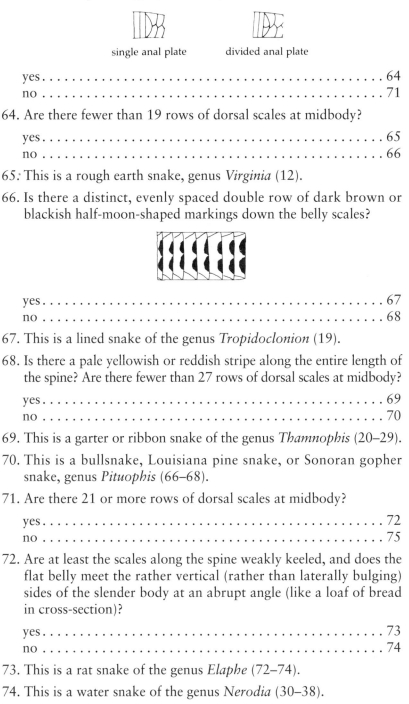

single anal plate   divided anal plate

yes. 64
no 71

64. Are there fewer than 19 rows of dorsal scales at midbody?

yes. 65
no 66

65. This is a rough earth snake, genus *Virginia* (12).

66. Is there a distinct, evenly spaced double row of dark brown or blackish half-moon-shaped markings down the belly scales?

yes. 67
no 68

67. This is a lined snake of the genus *Tropidoclonion* (19).

68. Is there a pale yellowish or reddish stripe along the entire length of the spine? Are there fewer than 27 rows of dorsal scales at midbody?

yes. 69
no 70

69. This is a garter or ribbon snake of the genus *Thamnophis* (20–29).

70. This is a bullsnake, Louisiana pine snake, or Sonoran gopher snake, genus *Pituophis* (66–68).

71. Are there 21 or more rows of dorsal scales at midbody?

yes. 72
no 75

72. Are at least the scales along the spine weakly keeled, and does the flat belly meet the rather vertical (rather than laterally bulging) sides of the slender body at an abrupt angle (like a loaf of bread in cross-section)?

yes. 73
no 74

73. This is a rat snake of the genus *Elaphe* (72–74).

74. This is a water snake of the genus *Nerodia* (30–38).

75. Are there 19 rows of dorsal scales at midbody?

yes. 76
no 77

76. This is a crayfish snake of the genus *Regina* (39–40).

77. Are there 17 rows of dark, weakly keeled dorsal scales, each bearing a dart-shaped yellow spot in its center?

yes. 78
no 79

78. This is a Central American speckled racer, genus *Drymobius* (58).

79. Are the back and sides bright green?

yes. 80
no 81

80. This is a rough green snake, genus *Opheodrys* (45).

81. Is there a prominent brown spot beneath the eye? Is the loreal scale absent?

loreal scale   loreal scale absent

yes. 82
no 83

82. This is a brown or red-bellied snake of the genus *Storeria* (9–11).

83. This is a rough earth snake, genus *Virginia* (12).

84. Is the animal mustard-brown above, with a thin, black H-shaped dorsal pattern?

yes. 85

85. This is a Trans-Pecos rat snake, genus *Bogertophis* (75).

BLIND SNAKES
Family *Typhlopidae*

Typhlopidae is a primarily tropical family consisting of three genera and more than 160 species. All are blind—as indicated by the Greek *atyphlos* (blind) and *ops* (eye)—with eyes buried beneath their almost translucent skin and covered by the same shiny round scales that occur everywhere on their bodies.

All blind snakes are primitive burrowing animals thought to resemble the earliest basal serpents from which all snakes are descended, for the first major ophidian division was between ancestral blind snakes and the progenitors of every other, more advanced ophidian lineage. Unlike those of other serpents, blind snakes' maxillary bones are not fused to the skull. Also, unlike more evolutionarily advanced serpents, the lower jaws of blind snakes bear no teeth, nor do blind snakes have the later-evolving capacity to widely gape open their jaws. None of the *Typhlopidae* are native to the United States, but one genus, *Ramphotyphlops*, occurs here in the form of a single, artificially introduced species, the Brahminy blind snake.

Brahminy Blind Snake
Genus *Ramphotyphlops*

Brahminy Blind Snake, *Ramphotyphlops braminus*

A BRAHMINY BLIND SNAKE
Ramphotyphlops braminus

The only member of the parthenogenetic, oviparous genus *Ramphotyphlops*, the Brahminy blind snake is the single serpent known to reproduce without males. Members of this all-female genus have a high number of chromosomes but, as might be expected of near-clonal animals, little variability in individual morphology. Like other blind snakes, they lack the large, laterally elongate ventral scales of more advanced ophidian families. Formerly thought to be fundamentally different from other serpents, blind snakes are now believed to be close to the base of ophidian evolution and crucial to understanding the evolution of all modern snakes from subterranean forebears.

Nonvenomous   The Brahminy blind snake is too small to bite humans.

Abundance   This primitive serpent, perhaps akin to the subterranean late Cretaceous snakes from which all modern serpents are probably descended, is native to Southeast Asia, but with the help of mankind now enjoys a near-global distribution. During the spring of 1997, the Brahminy blind snake—often referred to as the flowerpot snake because it tends to arrive in new geographic areas hidden in the soil of imported houseplants—was recorded for the first time in Brownsville by Richard Bartlett and Kenny Wray.

Size   *Ramphotyphlops braminus* is adult at about 5 inches in length. Though it may reach 6½ inches, this minuscule serpent is not much thicker than coat-hanger wire.

Habitat   In residential areas rich in well-watered soil the Brahminy blind snake may be abundant, occurring most often in the soft humus of flower beds.

Prey   Primarily the eggs, larvae, and pupae of ants and termites.

Reproduction   As the only parthogenetic serpent, *Ramphotyphlops braminus* is both egg-laying and live-bearing. Large groups of this all-female species—in which the ova begin cell division without spermatozoa—often live together in soil or rotting vegetation, where each one may produce up to eight genetically identical offspring. Between April and June these may be either born alive or deposited as eggs, which hatch in less than a week, with the 2-inch-long newborns being among the smallest of living serpents.

Coloring/scale form   Brahminy blind snakes resemble shiny black or dark brown earthworms (like worms, *R. braminus* is sometimes washed onto pavement by heavy rains). Its blunt head and tail seem nearly identical—there is no narrowing of the neck and the lower jaw is barely visible—while its vestigial eyes are no more than dots of black pigment. The Brahminy blind snake's nontapering posterior end is tipped, however, by a tiny spur. Unlike the transversely widened ventral scales of other serpents, the same sized and shaped scales occur in 14 rows that completely cover the blind snake's back, sides, and belly. Also unlike other snakes, there is no anal plate, for its vent is surrounded by the same minuscule scales.

Similar snakes   The **plains blind snake (1)** is a pale, fleshy color.

Behavior   The specialized spur on the Brahminy blind snake's tail tip is dug into the earth to obtain purchase for pressing its tiny body through soft soil. Then the tail tip is brought forward, planted, and used to once more lever the body ahead.

1 PLAINS BLIND SNAKE
Leptotyphlops dulcis dulcis

Nonvenomous   This miniature reptile is too small to bite humans.

Abundance   Locally common but unevenly dispersed across a broad section of the southern Great Plains. This 350-mile-wide band stretches from the Tamaulipan thorn woodland of the Rio Grande Valley north across Texas' Edwards and Stockton plateaus to the grasslands/cross timbers interface of northern Texas and southern Oklahoma. Before South American fire ants invaded the southern part of this range, where

L. d. dulcis was most abundant, plains blind snakes were often easy to find in areas of soft, loamy earth—especially in early spring before summer's drying and hardening of the soil's upper layers forced it deeper into the earth.

Size   Slender and only 2½ to 11 inches in length, *L. d. dulcis* looks like a large earthworm.

Habitat   This predominantly subterranean snake is sometimes found at the surface beneath leaf and plant litter or under decaying logs. Plains blind snakes also often inhabit the well-watered sod and rich garden humus of residential neighborhoods, where they are often turned up by those weeding or planting flower beds.

Prey   Blind snakes feed primarily on the eggs, larvae, and pupae of ants and termites. The adults of soft-bodied insects, usually commensals in ant and termite colonies, are reportedly taken as well. Harry Greene (1997) reports that "in feeding, *L. dulcis* first grasps a termite's abdomen, then breaks off its head by pressing it against the substrate, and finally swallows the soft hind parts. In contrast, that species arches its anterior over ant larvae and pupae, then forces its mouth down over the intact prey."

Reproduction   Egg-laying. During late June and early July, female blind snakes deposit 3 or 4 thin-shelled, half-inch-long eggs (sometimes in a nest cavity used by as many as a half dozen females) hollowed from decaying vegetation or loose, sandy soil. More than 40 eggs have been located in a single such site, with old broken shells indicating that these nests were used for a succession of breeding seasons.

Coloring/scale form   *Leptotyphlops dulcis dulcis* is much the same shape, size, and color as a large earthworm. Unlike blind snakes such as *Ramphotyphlops braminus*—which devotes some time to life on the surface—like other subterranean vertebrates the fossorial plains blind snake almost entirely lacks external pigmentation. This little snake seemingly has no facial features, for its vestigial eyes are no more than dots of nonfunctional pigment barely visible beneath translucent ocular scales. Each of these ocular scales extends to the mouth and is preceded by a single upper labial scale. Unlike those of other North American snakes, blind snakes' ventral scales are not transversely widened into long plates (14 rows of smooth scales encircle its whole trunk), and the tail is tipped with a tiny spur. See **Trans-Pecos Blind Snake.**

Similar snakes   The **New Mexico blind snake (2)** is distinguished by the 2 upper labial scales that occur just forward of the lower portion of each of its ocular scales. The **Brahminy blind snake (A)**, now found in the lower Rio Grande Valley, is a darker brown color.

Behavior   If people recognize them as reptiles at all, blind snakes are usually taken to be the newborns of larger snakes. Where soil conditions are ideal, several *L. d. dulcis* (which are often found in close proximity) are commonly mistaken for a nest of baby snakes. The specialized spur on the blind snake's tail tip is dug into its tunnel walls to obtain purchase in pressing through the soil; as might be expected of so vulnerable a creature, on open ground these animals never cease wriggling in search of cover in which to burrow. The slippery scales of all *Leptotyphlops*, as well as the viscous fluid this genus excretes when attacked, not only serve to protect it from the assaults of the ants and termites on which it feeds, but probably also make it difficult for larger predators to grasp. Frederick Gehlbach of Baylor University has documented blind snakes escaping from the talons of screech owls that have carried them back to feed their young—snakes which then survived on the insect larvae found in the owls' nest cavities and even laid eggs there. Though it is not a beneficial situation for the snakes, their predation on the owls' insect parasites allowed owlets in nests populated by blind snakes to suffer lower mortality and grow faster than owlets whose nest holes lacked resident *Leptotyphlops*.

2 NEW MEXICO BLIND SNAKE
Leptotyphlops dulcis dissectus

Like other *Leptotyphlops*, the New Mexico blind snake resembles a pale, shiny earthworm, particularly since adult specimens are no more than 6½ inches in length and not much thicker than coat-hanger wire. Blind snakes also resemble earthworms because they lack the belly-wide ventral scales of other snakes. Since there is no narrowing of either the neck or tail, blind snakes' blunt heads and tails seem nearly identical, for their vestigial eyes are almost invisible and their mouths and lower jaws are barely discernible. The blind snakes' posterior end is distinguished, however, by its minuscule tail-tip spur.

The New Mexico blind snake inhabits a curiously dissected range. One population (probably a relic group remaining from the area's wetter Pleistocene climate) inhabits the scattered grassland basins of Texas' Trans-Pecos, while another group occupies what little remains of the old prairie ecosystems of the Texas and Oklahoma panhandles. *Leptotyphlops dulcis dissectus* is differentiated from the **Trans-Pecos blind snake (3)**, which shares most of its Trans-Pecos range, by the 3 small scales—the Trans-Pecos has only 1—that separate the tops of its ocular plates. The **plains blind snake (1)**, a subspecies of the New Mexico race, is distinguished by the presence of 2 narrow upper labial scales—

Trans-Pecos blind snake
(L. h. segregus)

Plains and New Mexico
blind snakes
(L. dulcis)

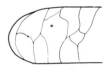

Plains blind snake
(L. d. dulcis)

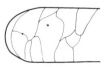

New Mexico blind snake
(L. d. dissectus)

dissectus means "cleft," in reference to their shared central suture—between the lower extension of the ocular plate and the nasal scale. The plains blind snake has but 1 such intervening scale. In other respects, these two races are identical, and intergrades between them are common. (Because these two races so closely resemble each other, no distinguishing characteristics are visible in a photograph; the New Mexico blind snake's two narrow upper labial scales are so small as to be visible only in an enlarged drawing.)

Behavior   Preyed on by a host of small carnivores, including desert scorpions, the New Mexico blind snake's ecology is probably identical to that of its subspecies, the plains blind snake. This may include a tendency for several females to deposit their egg clutches in the same nest cavity. Of necessity, in arid country where the substrate is loose enough for burrowing, *L. d. dissectus* descends quite deeply to avoid desiccation; individuals have been unearthed from several feet below the surface by road-grading machinery working the extremely dry, sandy terrain along the Rio Grande near Castolon.

3 TRANS-PECOS BLIND SNAKE
Leptotyphlops humilis segregus

Nonvenomous   This animal is much too small to bite humans.

Abundance   Widely but spottily dispersed over its arid range in Texas' northern Chihuahuan Desert, the Trans-Pecos blind snake is so inconspicuous that it is seldom noticed, although it can be fairly common in areas of moist soil.

Size   Slightly larger than the plains and New Mexico blind snakes, *L. h. segregus* reaches a maximum length of 13 inches.

Habitat   Trans-Pecos blind snakes—*segregus* refers to this animal's "distantly set-off" range, as assumed by L. M. Klauber, who described this subspecies in 1939—are recorded from a variety of terrestrial communities but are seldom if ever found in severe desert terrain. Their preferred habitat is the slightly more mesic, more richly soiled biotic communities of Trans-Pecos grasslands such as those in Presidio and southern Jeff Davis counties.

Prey   *Leptotyphlops humilis segregus* apparently feeds almost exclusively on the eggs and pupae of ants and termites, which it reportedly finds by following these insects' pheromone trails.

Reproduction   Egg-laying. See **Plains Blind Snake**.

Coloring/scale form   The shiny, flesh-colored back may have a brown tinge on 5 to 7 of its vertebral scale rows; the venter is pale pink. Along with 95 other species and subspecies of *Leptotyphlopidae* (many of them abundant in the American tropics), the Trans-Pecos blind snake has a cylindrical head and a tail of almost the same diameter as its midsection. Consequently both its ends look remarkably alike, although the head has tiny dots of vestigial ocular pigment while the tail is distinguished both by the tiny spur at its tip and by its

BLIND SNAKES

tendency to wriggle back and forth when the animal is disturbed, smearing musky cloacal fluid over the rest of its body. (Enhancing the protection afforded by the blind snakes' small, tightly overlapping scales, this musk functions as an olfactory armor by discouraging the bites and stings of ants, whose nests blind snakes must enter for food.)

Fourteen rows of small scales encircle the entire trunk, for no elongation of ventral scales into the big transverse plates of most serpents occurs. The anal plate is also absent, for the vent of *L. h. segregus* is surrounded by small scales.

Similar snakes Only other *Leptotyphlopidae* are similar. The **plains (1)** and the **New Mexico blind snakes (2)** are distinguished by the 3 small scales present in the center of the crown between the right and left ocular plates; a single midcrown scale separates the ocular scales of the Trans-Pecos blind snake. See **New Mexico Blind Snake.**

Behavior L. M. Klauber (1940) noted that this little serpent "progressed with less lateral undulation than other snakes. On smooth surfaces it employed the tail spine to aid in its motion. When placed in loose or sandy soil it burrowed immediately. It is never peaceful or quiet when above ground."

COLUBRID SNAKES
Family *Colubridae*

Colubridae is the vast and diverse family to which most North American snakes are assigned. This family is divided into four subfamilies: *Colubrinae*, *Natricinae*, *Lampropeltinae*, and *Xenodontinae*. (Most North American colubrids are nonvenomous, but a number of the species in the two subfamilies *Natricinae* and *Xenodontinae* are characterized by mildly toxic saliva and/or enlarged teeth at the rear of the upper jaw.)

Crowned, Flat, and Black-headed Snakes
Genus *Tantilla*

Flat-headed Snake, *Tantilla gracilis*
Plains Black-headed Snake, *Tantilla nigriceps*
Southwestern Black-headed Snake, *Tantilla hobartsmithi*
Mexican Black-headed Snake, *Tantilla atriceps*
Black-hooded Snake, *Tantilla rubra cucullata*

First described in 1853 in the famous *Catalog of North American Reptiles* by Smithsonian Institute Secretary Spencer Fullerton Baird and Frenchman Charles Frederich Girard, this oviparous genus is contained in the subfamily *Xenodontinae*. *Tantilla*—a name drawn from a gypsy dance, presumably because of the lively struggles of this genus' members to escape when handled— vary by species from common and well known to rare and poorly understood. In the eastern United States, these diminutive burrowers are called crowned snakes; in Texas they are known as flat-headed, black-headed, or black-hooded snakes.

Most are characterized by a black crown and sometimes a black nape, which may or may not be separated from the rest of the back by a light collar, as well as by 15 rows of smooth dorsolateral scales. The uniformly colored dorsum often approximates the hue of the substrate—typically sandy and well drained—on which a particular species is found.

These animals' fossorial lifestyle has perhaps generated the trunk-slimming evolutionary adaptation of a single ovary; the anal plate is divided and there is no loreal scale—the latter an important fact when trying to distinguish the flat-headed snake, a *Tantilla* species with muted head and nape colors, from the similarly gray-brown phases of the ground snake, *Sonora*.

Possessing both saliva toxic to their small, mostly invertebrate prey, as well as a pair of enlarged (but still tiny) teeth at the rear of each upper jaw with which to deliver this fluid, most *Tantilla* species are nevertheless much too small to harm humans.

4 FLAT-HEADED SNAKE
Tantilla gracilis

Nonvenomous   Although technically a rear-fanged opisthoglyph serpent with very mild salivary toxins that presumably help to immobilize its diminutive prey, the flat-headed snake is too small to harm humans.

Abundance   Formerly common. Historically among the most abundant of the little soil-colored serpents turned up in flower beds and gardens within a broad range stretching west from the Gulf Coast to the Pecos River, then north across the entire eastern two-thirds of the state. In the southern part of this range *Tantilla gracilis* has recently become less common, apparently due to the impact of invading South American fire ants that have taken over the hiding places and decimated the egg clutches of small terrestrial reptiles.

Size   Adult *T. gracilis* reaches a length of 10 inches; hatchlings measure only about 3 in.

Habitat   The flat-headed snake prefers loose, slightly damp soil in which to burrow; it consequently occurs most often in well-watered deciduous woods and grass/brushland communities.

Prey   The flat-headed snake's invertebrate prey seems to be at least partly partitioned among the several other small fossorial serpents that share its semisubterranean microhabitat. The stomach contents of most *Tantilla gracilis* examined in one study consisted of centipedes and earth-dwelling insect larvae such as cutworms and wireworms (ground snakes were found to eat mainly arachnids; ring-necked snakes, mostly earthworms).

Reproduction   Egg-laying. Reproduction among most *Tantilla* requires a long period of maturation, especially for a small reptile; females reach sexual maturity only in the spring of their third year. In one study, copulation was found to take place during the first half of May, with clutches of 1 to 4 oblong eggs being deposited in either shallow subsurface hollows or within decaying vegetation during the latter part of June. Depending on the temperature, these eggs hatched after about 60 days into neonates—which exactly resemble their parents—no more than 3 inches long.

Coloring/scale form Dorsolateral color is uniformly grayish tan except for the darker crown whose rear border is slightly concave. Flattened from top and bottom, the snout appears rounded from above; the venter is whitish to pale salmon. Although too small to note easily with the naked eye, there is a single postocular scale and no loreal (the second of the 6 upper labial scales touches, or almost touches, the prefrontal).

Similar snakes The **plains black-headed snake (5)** has 7 upper labial scales, a distinct black skullcap that stretches back to a point on the nape 3 to 5 scale rows behind its crown and a whitish-edged pink venter. **Earth snakes (12–13)** have a loreal scale and 17 rows of dorsal scales, with faint keels on the scales of at least the middorsal rows. (The rough earth snake also has 5 upper labial scales and more grayish coloration.) **Ground snakes (17)** living in the flat-head snake's range usually have a yellowish or reddish tan ground color as well as a partially crossbanded back and undertail; there is also both a loreal and paired postocular scales.

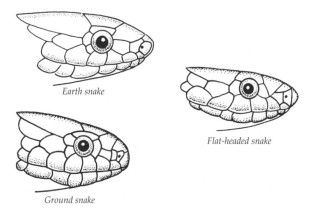

Earth snake

Flat-headed snake

Ground snake

Behavior Secretive and nocturnal, *T. gracilis* is active mainly between April and early November because temperature and soil moisture are the major factors determining its presence at the surface (the small bodies of *Tantilla*, being adapted to the more constant temperature below ground, have little resistance to the pronounced fluctuations of atmospheric temperature). Summer heat induces a period of aestivation, while low winter temperatures often force these animals to withdraw several feet into the ground, which they accomplish by insinuating themselves through tiny crevices in the earth. To facilitate this, the flat-headed snake's skull is no wider than its neck and is compressed from above and below into a penetrating wedge.

5 PLAINS BLACK-HEADED SNAKE
Tantilla nigriceps

Nonvenomous   The plains black-headed snake is too small and nonaggressive to harm humans.

Abundance   Moderately abundant in an extensive range that encompasses primarily the southern Great Plains, but stretches from the Tamaulipan thorn woodland along the Rio Grande northwest through the Chihuahuan Desert to the northern panhandle. In both the thorn brush of the Rio Grande plain and the short-grass prairie of the Texas and Oklahoma panhandles *T. nigriceps* is often common, although it is seldom noticed because its small size and cryptic microhabitat beneath vegetative ground cover enable it to escape human attention.

Size   Adults are 7 to 14¾ inches in length.

Habitat   This snake's primary environment is the thin subsurface layer where fallen vegetative litter meets the soil below; it is most often found at the surface in the slightly damp cavities beneath flat rocks and debris.

Prey   The plains black-headed snake's prey is primarily tenebrionid beetle larvae, centipedes, and small scorpions—the arthropods being envenomed by the toxic saliva forced into their bodies by this small hunter's enlarged upper rear teeth. Less vigorous prey such as snails, worms, spiders, and insect larvae, is also taken.

Reproduction   Egg-laying. See **Flat-headed Snake.**

Coloring/scale form   The dark skullcap—"nigriceps" is "black-headed" in Latin—is longer than that of other southwestern *Tantillas*, stretching back 3 to 5 vertebral scale rows to end in a point on the nape; there is a ruddy flush along the plains black-headed snake's midventral line. A single postocular and 7 upper labial scales (the second of which, due to the absence of a loreal, touches the prefrontal plate just ahead of the eye) are characteristic of this species. The anterior lower labial scales generally touch beneath the chin.

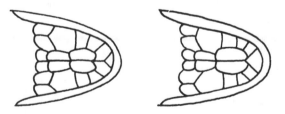

Underchin: plains black-headed snake   Underchin: southwestern black-headed snake

Similar snakes   The **flat-headed snake (4)** has 6 upper labial scales and a short brown skullcap whose slightly concave rear border extends rearward no more than 2 scale rows beyond its parietal plates. The straight posterior border of the dark skullcap of the **southwestern black-headed snake (6)** reaches no more than a single dorsal scale row onto its nape; its rostral scale is a bit more pointed, and its first pair of lower labial scutes do not touch under its chin. The **ground snake** (17) has both a loreal scale and a pair of postocular scales.

Behavior   See **Flat-headed Snake.**

6 SOUTHWESTERN BLACK-HEADED SNAKE
Tantilla hobartsmithi

Nonvenomous   See **Flat-headed Snake.**

Abundance   Probably moderately abundant. Named for venerable herpetologist Hobart M. Smith, this fossorial reptile occupies a primarily Chihuahuan Desert biotic community that reaches from Laredo to the northern Stockton Plateau, as well as westward across the Trans-Pecos. Here, *T. hobartsmithi* is seldom noted because its almost exclusively underground home enables it to escape human attention, although after heavy summer rain it is sometimes encountered as a roadkill.

Size   Maximum adult length is no more than 9½ inches.

Habitat   *Tantilla hobartsmithi* is a burrowing reptile usually found on the surface only after rainfall or where moisture has condensed under flat stones.

Prey   The stomachs of 37 southwestern black-headed snakes contained only butterfly, moth, and beetle larvae even though many other suitably sized invertebrates were to be found in the immediate vicinity.

Reproduction   Egg-laying. One female carrying a single egg was discovered on June 1 in Big Bend.

Coloring/scale form   The southwestern black-headed snake owes its current identity to studies by Charles Cole and Lawrence Hardy (1981) of the morphology of the tiny spines covering the hemipenes of these animals. Their work revised the classification of the **Mexican black-headed snake** into two different species. These authors believe *T. atriceps*, the Mexican black-headed snake, to be confined to a small range in south Texas, while the *Tantillas* once thought to make up this animal's western population—a population that lives northwest of Kinney, Edwards, and Sutton counties—are now believed to represent a separate species, *Tantilla hobartsmithi,* the southwestern black-headed snake. Within this species' large range, however, individual *T. hobartsmithi* display several types of head coloring. Each of these variants was once carefully charted since the different configurations were thought to define different species. Now, however, it is believed that local populations of *Tantilla hobartsmithi* include individuals with both short black cephalic caps and long ones—caps either bordered or not bordered with a pale nuchal collar—as well as specimens with either all-black or white-spotted snouts.

The shiny brown back and sides of the southwestern black-headed snake are perhaps slightly more reddish than those of other *Tantillas,* an orangish streak often lines the center of its forebelly, and its undertail is salmon colored. There are 7 upper labial scales, and the anterior lower labial scales usually do not meet beneath its chin.

Similar snakes   The cap of the **plains black-headed snake (5)** tapers to a point on the nape 3 to 5 scale rows behind the cephalic parietal scales, and the first pair of lower labial scales meets under its chin.

Behavior   Where *Tantilla hobartsmithi* lives below ground during most of the year is not known, for it has been found—foraging or perhaps seeking a mate, for most recorded specimens are male—only during moist periods in spring and summer.

7 MEXICAN BLACK-HEADED SNAKE
Tantilla atriceps

Nonvenomous   See **Flat-headed Snake.**

Abundance   In the *Bulletin of the American Museum of Natural History* (1981), Charles J. Cole and Lawrence M. Hardy revised the classification of the Mexican black-headed snake, *Tantilla atriceps*, into 2 separate species: (1) the *Tantilla* population found northwest of Kinney, Edwards, and Sutton counties, which is now defined as a different species, the **southwestern black-headed snake**, *T. hobartsmithi* and (2) a population of rare, predominantly subtropical snakes whose range lies primarily in the northern Mexican state of Tamaulipas and that retains the name Mexican black-headed snake, *Tantilla atriceps*. This species is known in Texas only from a pair of specimens collected over 100 years ago in Duval and Kleberg counties; whether it still occurs north of the Rio Grande is unknown. Nothing is recorded about its natural history in this country, and no photograph of a Texas specimen exists (the animal pictured here is from Nuevo Leon, Mexico).

Size   Maximum adult length is probably no more than 11 inches.

Habitat   In Mexico, *Tantilla atriceps* reportedly occupies both wooded and grassland/thorn brush communities.

Prey   The Mexican black-headed snake's food preferences are unknown, but like many other *Tantillas* it may prey on subterranean insects and their larvae.

Reproduction   Egg-laying. One to 3 eggs are deposited in early summer; reproduction is otherwise unknown.

Coloring/scale form   Specimens from Tamaulipas indicate that this snake displays its genus' typical brownish or grayish dorsolateral hue, slightly darker along the middorsal line. Its black crown reaches no farther rearward than the posterior border of its parietal scutes and does not touch the posterior corner of its mouth, which is bordered on each side by 7 upper labial scales. The Mexican black-headed snake's pale orange venter reddens beneath its tail.

Similar snakes   The **flat-headed snake (4)** has a brown skullcap with a slightly concave rear border, a lighter-hued undertail, and 6 upper labial scales.

Behavior   The *Tantilla* species and subspecies living in the southwestern United States are a northern branch of a family of predominantly tropical snakes that inhabit central and western South America.

68

8 BLACK-HOODED SNAKE
Tantilla rubra cucullata

Nonvenomous   The only *Tantilla* that grows large
enough to nip a human being, the black-hooded snake is
nevertheless harmless, despite its technical classification as
a rear-fanged opisthoglyph serpent. (All *Tantilla* have enlarged,
though still minuscule, grooved teeth in the rear of their upper jaws
and generate mild salivary toxins to help immobilize their small prey.)

Abundance   Threatened. Protected by the state of Texas. This rare fossorial
snake, endemic to the Trans-Pecos, was until recently known from only a few
specimens. It was thought to almost never emerge from its subterranean microenvironment except when surface conditions were optimal, for as many as 8 individuals have been found in a small area within a few days during humid weather
when soil moisture levels were high. Yet during the severe drought of 1998,
2 individuals were found near Jose Maria Spring in Val Verde County by Bill
Armstrong, manager of the Devil's River State Natural Area. One of these was
a hatchling discovered shortly after dawn on a dry, ash juniper/oak–covered slope
where one would never have expected to find such a tiny snake moving about in
the open, even with rain having fallen earlier in the week. Another neonate was
reported by Terry Maxwell and Kelly McCoy of Angelo State University.

Size   The black-hooded snake is a giant when compared to other *Tantilla*;
the few individuals on record have measured 8½ to 17¼ inches in length.

Habitat   Black-hooded snakes are known from 2 principal habitats: (1) elevations between 1,300 and 5,000 feet in the Chisos and Davis mountains; (2) both
broken and flat terrain in the low desert of Terrell and Val Verde counties.
(The easterly, desert-living population was for years known as the Devil's
River blackhead snake, *Tantilla rubra diabola*.)

Prey   According to Trans-Pecos *Tantilla* expert Troy Hibbitts, of the University of Texas at Arlington, the black-hooded snake's prey is primarily centipedes, particularly members of the genus *Scolependra*. Extremely abundant
in the black-hooded snake's range, these formidable chilopods reach 9 to 10
inches in length and, armed with the prominent fangs and toxic saliva for
which centipedes are noted, are powerful adversaries for black-hooded snakes
hardly larger than their prey. (The predatory power of these big centipedes
toward small snakes is not merely theoretical, for in 1975 David Easterla
observed a *Scolependra heros* devouring a Texas long-nosed snake of approximately the same length as the centipede.)

But a series of photographs shot by Hibbitts south of Alpine shows how
diminutive *Tantillas* regularly manage to overcome such aggressive prey. After
seizing a centipede at midbody, Hibbitts's *T. cucullata* hung on with determination, chewing on the chilopod's midsection despite the chilopod's
attempts to twist around and counterattack. (The black-hood's comparatively
heavy skull, armored with rimmed eye sockets, enables it to withstand the
centipede's fangs, but adult *T. r. cucullata* still tend to have scarred heads and
necks from encounters of this kind.)

Eventually, the black-hooded snake's mildly paralytic saliva—which is worked into the chilopod's body by its grooved rear teeth—overcame this particular centipede, which at last allowed the snake to swallow it. (In another instance, T. J. LaDuc reported a road-killed desert kingsnake in whose stomach was a freshly swallowed black-hooded *Tantilla*, which itself contained a *Scolependra* centipede.)

Reproduction   Egg-laying. A single captive-laid clutch, of 3 elongate eggs, has been recorded for *T. r. cucullata*. It was deposited June 13, while a female found dead in Big Bend National Park on July 16 contained a pair of eggs whose stage of development suggests that they would have been laid before the first of August. The neonate whose picture appears here—at an age never before seen or photographed—appears similar to most adults except that its pale nuchal collar is less clearly defined.

Coloring/scale form   The most distinctive marking of *T. r. cucullata* is its usually solid black head and anterior neck. There are several different nuchal-cephalic patterns, however. In one, except for some pale spots on the lower jaw, the head and neck are wrapped in a uniformly black hood; in another, the dark hood is interrupted across the nape by a light collar sometimes split by blackish pigment over the spine, with white spots occurring on the snout and upper labial scales. (*T. r. cucullata* from the Chisos Mountains often have light collars, while most of those from northern Brewster, Jeff Davis, and Presidio counties have solid dark hoods.)

Among the more easterly population, there is often a prominent white collar, a white-tipped snout, and a pronounced oval or irregularly shaped white spot just below and behind the eye. For 40 years this different coloring caused this population to be classified as the Devil's River blackhead snake, *Tantilla rubra diabola*, until it was found that color morphs typical of both populations sometimes occur together in the same area. Both the author and Damon Salceies have found disparate color phases in close proximity in Terrell County road cuts and in small canyons near Sanderson. The venter of all color patterns is off-white.

Similar snakes   Previously known as the Devil's River blackhead snake (*Tantilla rubra diabola*), the black-hooded snake may be renamed again. Dixon, Vaughn, and Wilson, of Texas A&M University, propose that the black-hooded snake be accorded full species status as *T. cucullata* (reserving *T. rubra* for a more southerly ranging group of exclusively Mexican snakes).

The dark crown of the **plains black-headed snake (5)** is pointed or convex along its rear edge, is not followed by a light collar, and does not extend onto the lower jaw. The **southwestern black-headed snake (6)** has an abbreviated dark skullcap that extends laterally only as far as the middle of its upper labial scales; its lower labials and chin are whitish. Although a narrow pale line is occasionally evident just behind the black cap, this area is not followed by a dark band. Both animals also have pinkish venters.

Behavior   Little is known of the subterranean habits of West Texas' pre-dominantly fossorial snakes, some of which were discovered only recently—Sherman Minton first described the black-hooded snake in 1956, while current authorities on these *Tantilla* species are Hibbitts, Kathryn Vaughn, and James Dixon of Texas A&M University, as well as Buzz Ross of the Fort Davis Rattlesnake Museum.

The sporadic above-ground forays of *T. r. cucullata* apparently occur mostly in June and July, almost always during humid conditions following recent precipitation: each of 6 individuals found on the roads, as well as 2 specimens collected in the field, turned up immediately after rainy periods.

Brown and Red-bellied Snakes

Genus *Storeria*

Texas Brown Snake, *Storeria dekayi texana*
Marsh Brown Snake, *Storeria dekayi limnetes*
Florida Red-bellied Snake, *Storeria occipitomaculata obscura*

The viviparous genus *Storeria*—whose name honors physician David H. Storer, author of the 1839 "Ichthyology and Herpetology of Massachusetts"—is contained in the colubrine subfamily *Natricinae*. It is thus closely related to the water and garter snakes, yet its two North American species, *S. occipitomaculata* and *S. dekayi*, are entirely terrestrial. Like their water and garter snake relatives, both these species are apt to void musk and smear feces on an aggressor, but unlike aquatic snakes they are secretive little animals that seldom, if ever, bite even when grasped.

Storeria have keeled dorsal and lateral scales and a divided anal plate. Brown snake species have 17 dorsolateral scale rows. Most red-bellied snakes, in contrast, have 15 such rows, but John MacGregor, of Nicholasville, Kentucky, has found what appears to be a first-generation *dekayi/occipitomaculata* hybrid, and it is possible that some of Louisiana's and East Texas' largely dark gray *Storeria* also carry genes from both species.

Brown and red-bellied snakes also usually lack the loreal scale, which is present in many other snake genera and located between the preoculars and the posterior nasal scale. (Like the handful of other serpents among whom mortality brings about an immediate change in pigmentation, red-bellied snakes tend to turn very dark after death.)

9 TEXAS BROWN SNAKE
Storeria dekayi texana

Nonvenomous   See **Marsh Brown Snake.**

Abundance   Common. Texas brown snakes are not limited in range to the state for which they are named. In a sometimes 300-mile-wide swath, their range extends from the Rio Grande straight up the Great Plains as far as north central Minnesota. In the southern part of this range, Texas brown snakes, as live-bearers, are apparently less susceptible than small egg-laying serpents to attacks by South American fire ants because their newborns seem to be sufficiently vigorous to slip away from these newly introduced insect predators.

Size   Most adults are 9 to 12 inches in length; the record is 18 in.

Habitat   Along the intricate north–south intersection of North America's eastern woodlands and Great Plains, this animal's macrohabitat includes both riparian bottomland and moist deciduous forest. Texas brown snakes also occur in grassland, including overgrown pastures, but they are not as common there as in places where leaf litter offers cover.

Prey   Brown snakes' primary prey is snails, which may be wedged into a crevice, then twisted out of their shells. Other food includes slugs, while earthworms are a secondary prey; arthropods, salamanders, minnows, and newly metamorphosed frogs are also taken.

Reproduction   Live-bearing. Breeding may take place both spring and fall, with spermatozoa from autumn pairings remaining in the female's oviducts until her spring ovulation. Most births occur between mid-June and the first week in August. One central Texas female found in late April devoured slugs and small earthworms until late May, by which time she had become too swollen with developing young to continue feeding (brown snakes exhibit the evolutionarily advanced trait of placental nourishment of their offspring during the latter stages of fetal development). On June 12 this female gave birth to 11 very active, 4-inch-long young. After their first shed at 9 to 11 days of age, these neonates were offered Q-tips swabbed with the scents of fish, tadpoles, and worms, but only the scent of slugs and snails elicited a feeding response. Other litters have contained 3 to 27 young, measuring from 3½ to 4½ inches in length.

Coloring/scale form   Dark-speckled reddish brown above, with a pale vertebral stripe, adult Texas brown snakes have white posterior labial scales. Below and behind the eye, the fifth through seventh upper labial scales are blotched with one or more big brown spots; another large brown marking occupies the side of the neck. The creamy venter has a few black dots along its sides. Neonates have dark-speckled gray-brown backs and sides, dark brown heads with little white on their cheeks, and a pale band across their napes. The dorsal scales lack apical pits and are arranged in 17 rows, and the anal plate is divided.

Similar snakes   A subspecies, the **marsh brown snake (10)**, has a small, dark horizontal bar across its light-hued temporal and postocular scales and generally unmarked pale labial scales.

Behavior Everywhere in the broad range of this species, brown snakes find favorable conditions in the soft soil of well-watered suburban yards, where they are often encountered by people engaged in gardening. Although generally secretive, during cool, damp weather these little animals may move about in the open even during daylight; in the hottest months brown snakes are nocturnal.

10 MARSH BROWN SNAKE
Storeria dekayi limnetes

Nonvenomous When threatened, this little reptile can present a formidable coil-and-strike demeanor, reaching forward, mouth closed, in tiny pseudostrikes. Despite the snake's small stature, the abruptness of its vigorous mock defense is sometimes enough to deter a not very determined predator.

Abundance *Storeria dekayi limnetes* is a locally common inhabitant of the northwestern Gulf coastal prairie. Here, in a 60- to 80-mile-wide strip of the seaside plain it replaces the Texas brown snake in both marshy grasslands and inland savannahs, where it typically hides in grassy hummocks.

Size Adult size is 9 to 13 inches; the record is 16 in.

Habitat Marsh brown snakes also shelter in the high-tide flotsam of the Texas coast's barrier islands—the type specimen from which this subspecies' description is drawn was collected under driftwood on Galveston Island—where *S. d. limnetes* is the predominant small "garden snake" found around houses.

Prey Away from the coast, the marsh brown snake feeds mostly on snails and slugs. On the saline barrier islands where snails are few and slugs cannot survive, *S. d. limnetes* preys on earthworms, arthropods, small salamanders, minnows, and newly metamorphosed frogs.

Reproduction Live-bearing. Most small serpents are so short-lived that they must reproduce rapidly, and although nothing is recorded of reproduction in this race, it is probably as prolific as other *S. dekayi*. See **Texas Brown Snake.**

Coloring/scale form All five U.S. brown snakes are also referred to as DeKay's snakes in reference to James Ellsworth DeKay, who early in the nineteenth century first recorded the northern race along the Atlantic seaboard. (The marsh brown snake's subspecies designation, *limnetes*, refers to the slim horizontal bar or line marking its temporal and postocular scales.) Its faintly

Texas brown snake

Marsh brown snake

dark-speckled back is brown, usually with a paler vertebral stripe; its sometimes partially speckled venter is off-white.

Similar snakes   A horizontally lined temporal scale and unmarked upper and
lower labial scales differentiate this race from its more inland subspecies, the
Texas brown snake (9).

Behavior   Like their relatives the garter and water snakes, brown snakes'
defensive behavior includes excreting musk from anal glands located in the
cloaca, then squirming about to smear both that musk and feces over the source
of their distress. Sometimes this species also flattens its body and rolls over,
mouth agape, as if injured. Although not popular as captive animals, brown
snakes thrive in terrariums—although as devoted burrowers they are almost
never seen—and live as long as 7 years.

11 FLORIDA RED-BELLIED SNAKE
Storeria occipitomaculata obscura

Nonvenomous   This shy little woodland animal does
not bite humans.

Abundance   Locally common throughout much of the
southeastern United States—a range that stretches from northern
Florida along the Gulf Coast into eastern Texas. At the western
boundary of its range in Texas this little serpent is rare, however, and
restricted in distribution.

Size   Most adults are 8 to 10 inches in length, with *S. o. obscura* reaching a
maximum of 16 in.

Habitat   The Florida red-bellied snake's favored habitat includes moist, heavily vegetated hardwood forest; this little reptile occupies, but is less often
found in, uplands and pine forest. Its microhabitat is most often leaf litter and
the underside of decaying logs.

Prey   Slugs are the Florida red-bellied snake's primary prey. Richard D.
Bartlett has fed newborns on bits of both common garden slugs and snails.
Earthworms are also taken, and as the soil dries during summer, *S. o. obscura*
follows its mollusk and annelid prey deeper into the earth along a soil-mois-
ture gradient.

Reproduction   Live-bearing. Litters of *S. o. obscura* number up to 23, with
the 2¾- to 4-inch-long young being born between early June and August.
Grayer than adults and usually lacking their dark dorsal spots, neonates are
marked with a pale band across the nape.

Coloring/scale form   The Florida red-bellied snake is characterized by
the three big pale spots behind its head, which often form a light-hued collar. Another prominent, black-bordered white spot occurs beneath the eye.
A double row of dark flecks usually runs along both sides of the speckled

back which, in the southern part of its range, is cinnamon or blue-gray in ground color. Yet *S. o. obscura* varies widely in color. Several individuals from East Texas were yellowish above with yellow venters and barely visible nuchal spots (the white spot marking the upper labial scales beneath the eye was present, but lacked a black lower border); another individual from the same area had a solid dark-brown back and blackish lower sides whose color extended onto the outer edges of its russet ventral scales. A third individual was brown-bellied, and also lacked the black border below its white subocular spot. Among all color phases the venter is usually red.

Similar snakes   Texas brown snakes (9) have a dark subocular spot, pale cheeks, bellies, and 17 midbody scale rows.

Behavior   Too small to defend itself in any conventional way, like most small snakes *S. obscura* may tuck its head beneath a body coil. Alternatively, like other *Storeria* it may employ a death-feigning display: rolling over mouth agape and flattening its body and head as though partially crushed. In a strange and enigmatic additional behavior pattern an occasional individual may draw back its teeth in a sort of miniature snarl. (John MacGregor reports from Kentucky that among the northern subspecies, *S. o. occipitomaculata*, this behavior is especially prevalent in gravid females.)

Earth Snakes
Genus *Virginia*

Rough Earth Snake, *Virginia striatula*
Western Earth Snake, *Virginia valeriae elegans*

In both species, *V. valeriae* and *V. striatula*, the anal plate is divided. Neither species of earth snake has prominent dorsal markings, but either may be finely peppered with tiny dark dots—appropriate coloration for these flat-snouted little snakes which spend most of their time burrowing into loose soil and are usually found at the surface beneath rocks and debris in moist woodland, forest edges, and clearings. *V. striatula* is contained in the colubrine subfamily *Natricinae*, most of whose members are water snakes. *Virginia*, however, is an entirely terrestrial genus characterized in part by dorsolateral scales that occur in either 15 or 17 rows.

Virginia valeriae have weakly keeled dorsolateral scales, at least posteriorly, while the dorsal—and particularly, the vertebral—scales of *V. striatula* are prominently keeled.

12 ROUGH EARTH SNAKE

Virginia striatula

Nonvenomous   This little snake is not big enough to bite humans.

Abundance   Formerly much more common, the rough earth snake is another species with separate eastern and western populations separated by the Mississippi River Valley. West of the Mississippi corridor, *Virginia striatula* is found in most of Louisiana and Arkansas, southern Missouri, and eastern Oklahoma, as well as in the eastern half of Texas—where its range stops abruptly at the edge of the state's arid western rangeland. This demarcation also halts the westward spread of fire ants, which cannot tolerate dry soil, although to the east these insects have taken over much of the rough earth snake's microhabitat beneath surface debris. In sheltered sites where, until recently, during damp spring weather dozens of rough earth snakes could be found, nothing now exists but myriad fire ant swarms.

Size   *Virginia striatula* may reach 12½ inches in length, but even at this size it is no thicker in diameter than a pencil.

Habitat   Macrohabitat is primarily open woodland, either pine or deciduous. Here, rough earth snakes are largely fossorial, generally appear at the surface only when the soil is moist from recent rain. Microhabitat is the sheltered, semisubterranean layer found beneath fallen leaves, pine needles, and the rusting metal siding that litters abandoned farms.

Prey   The stomachs of 45 *V. striatula* contained only earthworms.

Reproduction   Live-bearing. According to J. K. Stewart, "*Virginia striatula* represents a stage in . . . evolution in which placental nourishment supplements yolk nutrition [with a consequent] enhancement of newborn quality." Sixteen litters ranged in number from 3 to 8 offspring, with the young measuring 3 to 4½ inches in length.

Coloring/scale form   Rough earth snakes are unmarked grayish brown above (newborns have a pale collar) with slightly darker pigmentation around the eyes and on the upper labial scales; the belly is creamy white. There are 17 midbody rows of dorsal scales—several of the vertebral rows are keeled, hence the "rough" of its common name, while the "striatula," or "striped," of its Latin designation refers to the faint line running down the center of these scales. A horizontally elongate loreal scale touches the front of the eye, and there are 2 small postocular scales, typically 5 upper labials, and usually a divided anal plate.

Similar snakes   Flat-headed snakes (4) have tan backs, dark-crowned heads with no loreal scale, a single postocular, and smooth dorsal scales.

Behavior   The rough earth snake's lightly shielded head is less effective in rooting through hardened soil than the hooked or armored rostral scutes of larger burrowing serpents, but its pointed snout allows it to penetrate the moist loam where its annelid prey is most plentiful. (Since *V. striatula* tends to be a rather shallow burrower, even a few warm midwinter days bring these little reptiles to the surface.)

13 WESTERN EARTH SNAKE

Virginia valeriae elegans

Nonvenomous   Western earth snakes do not bite humans.

Abundance   Generally locally common in Texas, especially in the oak–juniper savannah of the central Edwards Plateau.

Size   Adult western earth snakes measure 7 to 13 inches in length.

Habitat   Microhabitat is most often the damp soil beneath tree litter, the underside of logs, and the often humid layer of topsoil and detritus found beneath human-generated debris.

Prey   Western earth snakes feed mainly on earthworms, but snails, insects, and other small invertebrates also sometimes constitute prey.

Reproduction   Live-bearing. One 11-inch-long North Texas female gave birth on August 20 to 7, 4-inch-long charcoal-gray neonates.

Coloring/scale form   The uniformly reddish-tan dorsum is unmarked except for a pale, dimly defined vertebral stripe, and the dark hairline seams (that resemble keels) found in the centers of some of the scales adjacent to the faintly keeled vertebral scales located on the posterior portion of the back. Otherwise, the 17 midbody rows of dorsal scales are smooth. The venter is unmarked white, sometimes with a yellowish wash, the forward edge of the eye is touched by a horizontally lengthened loreal scale, and a pair of small postoculars borders the rear of the eye. There are usually 6 upper labial scales, and the anal plate is divided.

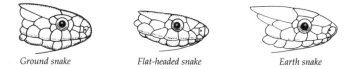

| Ground snake | Flat-headed snake | Earth snake |

Similar snakes   The **rough earth snake (12)** is grayer, without a russet cast; it has 5 supralabial scales and several rows of keeled vertebral scales. The **flat-headed snake (4)** has a slimmer body with a flattened, dark-capped head, a salmon-pink venter, no loreal scale, a single postocular, and 15 rows of smooth dorsal scales. The **ground snake (17)** has 15 or fewer rows of smooth dorsal scales, a small preocular separating its eye from its loreal scale, and a faintly braided appearance due to its lighter-hued scale borders.

Behavior   Although primarily fossorial, western earth snakes often appear at the surface when the soil is moist on warm spring nights. (Among sumac-covered limestone ledges in eastern Kansas, Abilene Zoo director Jack Joy found *V. valeriae* only on two or three April days, when these animals suddenly appeared under nearly every large stone. In the same spot, during the summer he turned up numerous worm and ring-necked snakes but never another western earth snake.) In hot weather the lack of moisture in surface soil brings about subterranean aestivation, although *V. valeriae* may emerge as late as December in central Texas, when these animals are sometimes present beneath boards and sun-warmed sheets of fallen metal siding.

Ring-necked Snakes

Genus *Diadophis*

Mississippi Ring-necked Snake, *Diadophis punctatus stictogenys*
Prairie Ring-necked Snake, *Diadophis punctatus arnyi*
Regal Ring-necked Snake, *Diadophis punctatus regalis*

The genus *Diadophis*, known scientifically since Carolus Linneaus's classification of the natural world in 1766, is part of the colubrine subfamily *Xenodontinae*. It is characterized by smooth dorsolateral scales, a loreal scale, and a divided anal plate. It is restricted to the United States, Canada, and northern Mexico, where a single species, *D. punctatus*, occurs in a number of races, all of which intergrade with geographically adjacent groups. All, except for the Florida Keys ring-neck and the regal ring-neck of the Southwest, among which the pale nuchal collar may be muted or lacking, can be identified by their yellowish cream to brilliant orange to orange-red nuchal collars.

Harmless to humans and traditionally classed as nonvenomous, ring-necked snakes actually have a mildly toxic saliva to aid in overcoming their small prey. When startled, members of these species elevate their posterior bodies to display their often bright undertail coloring. This an aposematic display that may signal danger to avian carnivores by suggesting the coral snake's bright hues. Or it may indicate unpalatability, for small mammalian hunters sometimes regurgitate ring-necked snakes or even release them after a single bite, wiping their mouths against the ground as if trying to rid themselves of an unpleasant taste. Ophidian predators such as coral and kingsnakes generally eat ring-necked snakes without distress, but John Mac-Gregor reports some fatalities among captive *Lampropeltis* that had just eaten a ring-neck.

14 MISSISSIPPI RING-NECKED SNAKE

Diadophis punctatus stictogenys

Nonvenomous   Ring-necked snakes are members of the uneven-toothed subfamily *Xenodontinae*, a group characterized by slightly longer (but in the case of ring-necks, still minuscule) posterior teeth. The salivary glands of this subfamily secrete enzymes that slowly immobilize small prey, but ring-necks almost never bite when handled and pose no danger to humans.

Abundance   Historically abundant in moist East Texas woodland but becoming less so because many of its sheltered microhabitats are now infested with

South American fire ants. These fierce little insects are especially destructive to oviparous snakes like the ring-necks, whose eggs are vulnerable to the ants' depredations.

Size   Adult Mississippi ring-necked snakes are 10 to 12 inches in length.

Habitat   Throughout its range *D. p. stictogenys* is primarily a forest-living animal, though it is also often found along the wooded borders of damp meadows and in overgrown fields near water. As with most semifossorial snakes, the principal factor determining its presence is the availability of cover: either the natural shelter of fallen logs and plant detritus or human-generated debris such as discarded sheets of metal siding.

Prey   Ring-necked snakes are scent hunters which search woodland ground cover for smaller snakes as well as for salamanders, skinks, small frogs, earthworms, slugs, and insect larvae. The Mississippi ring-neck is a midlevel hunter in this ophiophagous predatory pyramid, however, for in the wild it has been found in the stomachs of larger serpent-eaters such as the coral snake, and captive kingsnakes feed readily on ring-necks.

Reproduction   Egg-laying. Two to 8 elongate, ¾-inch-long eggs are laid during summer in moist soil or within a rotting log; the 3- to 4-inch-long young can emerge in as little as 5 weeks. In contrast to the activity pattern of many serpents, among which the males move about most widely, female *D. punctatus*, which are also larger than males, travel farthest beyond their home territories on journeys to their sometimes communally used nesting sites.

Coloring/scale form   The Mississippi ring-neck's slate-gray dorsum, separated from its black head by a bright yellow nuchal collar, is unmistakable. Its venter, cream beneath the snout, shades to yellow at midbody and darkens to orange under the tail. Among eastern-living individuals the belly and underchin—referred to by the Greek "stiktos" for "spotted"—are patterned with a double row of tiny black spots; in the Texas population most individuals have black ventral crescents. There are usually 15 forebody rows of dorsal scales.

Similar snakes   The Mississippi ring-neck is a race poorly differentiated from both its easterly subspecies, the southern ring-neck, and its western subspecies, the prairie ring-neck. In fact, the Mississippi ring-neck may be only an intergraded form between these two races. The **prairie ring-necked snake (15)** more often has 17 forebody rows of dorsal scales and a reddish undertail.

Behavior   Like other brightly undertailed *Diadophis*, the Mississippi ring-neck employs a defensive combination of color and posture that includes hiding its head beneath a body coil, twisting its caudal section over to expose its orange-red underside, and voiding musk and feces.

SMALL BURROWING SNAKES

15 PRAIRIE RING-NECKED SNAKE
Diadophis punctatus arnyi

Nonvenomous   See **Mississippi Ring-necked Snake**.

Abundance   Variable. In the southern part of a huge range
that stretches from central Texas north across Oklahoma and most
of Kansas and Missouri *D. p. arnyi* is uncommon in many places.
Yet in other parts of the Great Plains the prairie ring-necked snake can outnumber all other serpents. Herpetologist H. S. Fitch once captured 279 individuals beneath two dozen pieces of sheet metal on a single hilltop field in
eastern Kansas.

Ring-necked snakes follow one another to such communal shelters using
the scents left by their musky dermal pheromones; when 40 individuals were
released in an enclosure containing 12 evenly spaced plates, the four plates
under which the first 5 snakes took shelter subsequently attracted the whole
group, leaving the other identical hiding places unoccupied.

Size   Adults are 10 to 14 inches long; the record is 16½ in.

Habitat   Despite its name, the prairie ring-neck often occurs beneath a
canopy of tree branches; in the western part of its range it also occupies open
grassland and mountain slopes, however.

Prey   See **Mississippi Ring-necked Snake**.

Reproduction   Egg-laying. See **Mississippi Ring-necked Snake**.

Coloring/scale form   Separating this subspecies' black head from its dark
gray back is a golden neck ring which, in only 17 of the 220 individuals examined by Troy Hibbitts, of the University of Texas at Arlington, was interrupted
over the spine by dark pigment. The gray lips, chin, and throat are speckled
with black, while both the yellow venter and the orange-red undertail are randomly marked with little black half-moons. The dorsal scales occur in 15 or
17 forebody rows (about half the population has 15 rows, the other half, 17).

Similar snakes   The **Mississippi ring-necked snake (14)** usually has 15 anterior rows of dorsal scales and a row of small, dark, paired half-moons lining
the center of its belly. According to Hibbitts, throughout the Trans-Pecos the
prairie ring-neck intergrades with its western subspecies, the **regal ring-necked
snake (16)**, a slightly larger, lighter gray race that often lacks a pale neck ring
and has 17 dorsal scale rows on its forebody and an orange venter whose
color (unlike the prairie race) extends 1 or 2 scale rows up onto its lower sides.
In the Guadalupe Mountains some ring-necks are prairie type, some are intermediate between it and the regal ring-neck, and some are pure examples of
the western regal subspecies.

Behavior   Prairie ring-necked snakes, whose name honors Samuel Arny, a
nineteenth-century Kansas collector who recorded this race's type specimen,
are very localized reptiles. Marked specimens may be recaptured as much as
a year after their release so close to the same spot that this animal's usual
range is thought to be no more than 400 feet in diameter. Travel beyond this
distance probably represents only a seasonal movement between winter bru-

mation and summer egg-laying sites. If adequate refuge from low winter temperatures is not available within its small summer territory, *D. p. arnyi* may venture several hundred yards in search of higher, rocky ground with deep crevices to provide the subsurface drainage necessary for successful dormancy because flooded dens cause considerable mortality among snakes which, due to cold weather, are unable to relocate to drier quarters.

16 REGAL RING-NECKED SNAKE
Diadophis punctatus regalis

Nonvenomous   When threatened, even large regal ring-necked snakes usually do no more than evert their brightly colored undertails.

Abundance   Common. Widely distributed (mostly as an intergrade with the prairie ring-necked snake) across the Trans-Pecos and Stockton Plateau regions, *D. p. regalis* is seldom seen because it keeps to the cover of shrub or cactus roots and rock crevices.

Size   *Diadophis punctatus regalis* is named for its comparatively statuesque—if not quite regal—proportions. Troy Hibbitts, who has studied these animals intensively in their natural habitat, has recorded nine specimens from the Trans-Pecos measuring more than 19½ inches in length, while in Santa Fe County, New Mexico, herpetologist William B. Love photographed the 32½-inch record length regal ring-neck whose picture is included here.

Habitat   In northwestern Texas the regal ring-necked snake (which occurs here primarily as an intergrade with its more easterly prairie subspecies) occupies both grassland and mesquite/brush habitats. In the Trans-Pecos this animal inhabits environments ranging from the evergreen-covered slopes of the Davis and Guadalupe mountains to the limestone-floored desert of Terrell and Val Verde counties. Microhabitats include the spaces beneath large rocks and fallen yucca logs, as well as the interior and shriveled roots of dead agaves, often those situated near sporadically flowing streambeds.

Prey   Like other ring-necked snakes, *D. p. regalis* feeds primarily on reptiles, principally smaller snakes. These are grasped and chewed vigorously until immobilized by the salivary toxins that flow into the punctures made by the ring-neck's enlarged upper rear teeth.

Reproduction   Egg-laying. Two to 5 proportionately large, elongate eggs are laid in early summer.

Coloring/scale form   Regal ring-necked snakes vary widely in dorsal coloring. Some are unmarked light gray above, while others exhibit a full or partial pale nuchal band. Hibbitts has found that pale-collared *D. p. regalis* are most likely to be found in the contact zone with the golden neck-ringed prairie subspecies, although individuals with light-hued nuchal bands occur throughout areas where solid-hued individuals predominate. The yellowish lower labial scales are marked with tiny black spots which extend rearward within the band of yellowish orange ventral pigment that extends 1 or 2 scale rows

SMALL BURROWING SNAKES

81

upward from the venter onto the lower sides. Randomly placed black half-moons spot the yellow to dark gray forebelly; posteriorly, the venter is less heavily spotted as it darkens to red under the tail. There are usually 17 rows of dorsal scales on the forebody.

Similar snakes   An intergrade with the regal race throughout West Texas, the **prairie ring-necked snake (15)** is slightly smaller and darker, with a prominent yellow neck band and a black crown. Its yellowish orange ventral coloring does not extend as far up its sides (only $\frac{1}{2}$ scale row) as that of the regal ring-neck.

Behavior   See **Prairie Ring-necked Snake.**

Ground Snakes
Genus *Sonora*

Ground Snake, *Sonora semiannulata*

As part of the colubrine subfamily *Xenodontinae*, the genus *Sonora* (whose type specimen, described in *The Catalog of North American Reptiles* in 1853, came from Sonora, Mexico) is characterized by a blunt, rounded head only moderately wider than its neck, smooth dorsal scales that occur in either 13 or 15 rows, 6 or 7 upper labial scales, and a divided anal plate. In color and pattern combinations, few snakes in North America rival the variability of *Sonora*. Individual *S. semiannulata* may be uniformly russet, buff, greenish buff or gray (often with a slightly darker crown), or sharply banded with contrasting shades of its dorsal hues or at least two tones of gray or pink. There may be a prominent terra-cotta-colored vertebral stripe, sometimes broken by broad black saddles, while each light-hued dorsolateral scale may have a dark central spot. This highly variable coloration makes it difficult to distinguish ground snakes from other small snake species, but this genus' most important identifying characteristic is the loreal scale (usually distinct but sometimes partially fused to another scute) that separates the second upper labial scale from the prefrontal.

A secretive, oviparous group of small serpents, *Sonora* is usually associated with well-drained plains, prairies, semideserts, and desert edge habitats; here, *S. semiannulata* may be numerous where flat surface rocks are abundant. Using their weakly toxic saliva, ground snakes feed on arthropods and, occasionally, tiny geckos and their eggs, but they pose no danger to humans.

17 GROUND SNAKE
Sonora semiannulata

Nonvenomous   *Sonora semiannulata* does not bite humans.

Abundance   Widely distributed and locally common throughout a broad range that stretches from southern Kansas and Missouri to southwestern Texas.

Size   Most adults measure less than 12 inches; the record is 16⅜ in.

Habitat   Ground snakes inhabit a wide range of terrestrial milieus: mountain slopes to low-lying desert, juniper brakes to High Plains grassland. *Sonora semiannulata* seems to be most abundant, however, in the oak–juniper savannah of north central Texas and in the succulent and shrub desert of the Trans-Pecos; it is present but less numerous on most of the Great Plains and in the thorn woodland of the Rio Grande Valley. Ground snakes are also often found in suburban areas, especially in disturbed sites such as dumps or empty lots piled with debris.

Prey   *Sonora semiannulata* preys principally on invertebrates, mainly spiders, as well as on centipedes and scorpions.

Reproduction   Egg-laying. Despite its small size and inoffensive nature, *S. semiannulata* is known for combat rivalry among breeding males. Most female ground snakes deposit their clutches of 4 or 5 eggs during early to midsummer.

Coloring/scale form   A variety of dorsolateral color and pattern characterizes *S. semiannulata*. In fact, several different combinations may be found among the small population inhabiting a single rocky bluff.

Yet geographic variations also exist. Individuals from central Texas are most often uniformly yellowish tan above, with a small dark band across the nape. In the northwestern part of the state a majority of ground snakes exhibit up to 35 dark vertebral crossbars; these bars may completely encircle the tail and are the source of this reptile's Latin name, for *semiannulata* means "partially ringed." Individuals from the Trans-Pecos area are often a beige/salmon above, sometimes accentuated with an orange-red vertebral stripe broken by dark crossbars, but silvery individuals also occur here. Along Big Bend's famous River Road both red and gray solid-colored individuals are found alongside distinctly banded varieties. Ground snakes' lower sides are typically a lighter pinkish or yellowish tan, with tiny blocks forming a dashed lateral line.

All *Sonora* have light-hued venters, often boldly cross-barred beneath the tail but usually without markings forward of the vent. Dorsolaterally, ground snakes' two-toned, dark-centered scales give this species a woven or textured appearance.

Similar snakes   Flat-headed snakes (4) have smaller, ventrodorsally flattened, dark-crowned heads, unmarked backs, salmon-colored midbellies, and no loreal scale. Earth snakes (12, 13) have 17 rows of dorsal scales that lack the ground snake's two-toned-scale pigmentation; unlike the ground snake, the earth snake's loreal scale touches its eye.

SMALL BURROWING SNAKES

83

Behavior   Like most small serpents, *S. semiannulata* is unable to tolerate the daily surface temperature variations of its Great Plains and desert habitat. The author has seen these animals, taken from subterranean sites, die after only a few minutes, even in deep shade, when the air temperature was above 100°F. (This means that within most of this species' range, during late spring and summer ground snakes can function above the surface only at night.) Some *S. semiannulata* exhibit a head-hiding, tail-waving defensive posture called a flash display because the animal typically suddenly everts, or flashes, its bold undertail patterning. This behavior may have evolved in imitation of the defensive display of the similarly tail-waving, venomous coral snake.

Worm Snakes
Genus *Carphophis*

Western Worm Snake, *Carphophis amoenus vermis*

The oviparous genus *Carphophis* is classified in the colubrine subfamily *Natricinae*. Here, according to researchers, this genus may contain either 1 full species with 3 subspecies or 2 full species (the latter view is perhaps more widely accepted, with the eastern species, *Carphophis amoenus*, being divided into 2 subspecies).

Worm snakes are small burrowing serpents with smooth, shiny scales which—except when their colors are muted by approaching ecdysis—display a beautiful opalescent sheen. The head is small and pointed and the eyes are tiny. The dorsal scales are arranged in only 13 rows, the tail terminates in a tiny spine, and the anal plate is divided.

18 WESTERN WORM SNAKE
Carphophis amoenus vermis

Nonvenomous   The western worm snake is harmless to humans.

Abundance   The westernmost race of an essentially eastern forest serpent, *C. a. vermis* occupies only the far northeastern corner of the state. One of the few recorded Texas specimens was found at the southwestern limit of its range, near Clarksville. However, in every part of its range its small size and secretive behavior may make *C. a. vermis* very difficult to find, despite the fact that it is often abundant enough to occur in small colonies.

Size   Adults are 7½ to 11 inches long.

Habitat   In its relatively dry (for a worm snake) western milieu *C. a. vermis* is restricted to damp areas similar to its species' primary eastern habitat of mesic woodland, well-vegetated stream banks, brushy meadows, and overgrown farmland. Usually discovered in spring beneath stones, rotting logs, vegetative debris, or leaf mold, the western worm snake seeks moisture during the drier months by withdrawing to depths of as much as 6 feet.

Prey   Western worm snakes feed primarily on earthworms, slugs, grubs, and soft-bodied invertebrates.

Reproduction   Egg-laying. In late summer, about 7 weeks after they are deposited in an earthen cavity, the 1 to 8 thin-shelled eggs (which measure 1¼ by ⅝ inch) hatch into 3- to 4-inch-long young.

Coloring/scale form   Named "beautiful worm" in Latin, this creature's distinctive dorsolateral coloring results from the striking longitudinal demarcation which separates its salmon-hued venter and lower sides from its almost iridescent, purplish black back. Like that of other burrowing snakes, the western worm snake's head is no wider than its neck, while its sharply pointed terminal caudal scute is similar to the pointed tail tip of the unrelated *Leptotyphlopidae*, which also use their tail tips as anchoring pins to press through the soil.

Similar snakes   In Texas, *C. a. vermis* is the only small burrowing snake with a horizontal black-and-salmon color demarcation along its sides.

Behavior   When the organic foodstuff of decomposing leaves draws earthworms to the surface in spring, *Carphophis* is active in the upper layers of the soil; when both air and ground temperature reach 58 to 78°F and the soil is damp, these animals may even forage abroad during the day. Later in the year, as midday heat dries the surface, annelids retreat deeper into the earth and worm snakes go down with them.

When restrained, *C. a. vermis* tries to thrust itself forward, suddenly pressing either its pointed snout or its sharp tail tip between the holder's fingers. This produces a startling sensation so much like the prick of a tooth that one's reflexive response is to drop the snake. Less often, the western worm snake may expel a yellowish musk from its anal glands, spreading the unpleasant-smelling mucus about in its efforts to escape.

LINED, GARTER, AND RIBBON SNAKES

Lined Snake
Genus *Tropidoclonion*

Lined Snake, *Tropidoclonion lineatum*

Like others in its colubrine subfamily *Natricinae*, the mostly grassland- and prairie-living genus *Tropidoclonion* (first scientifically described by dinosaur fossil hunter Edward Drinker Cope in 1860) is closely related to both the water snakes and to the garter and ribbon snake genus, *Thamnophis*. Its only U.S. species, the lined snake, is often mistaken for a small garter snake.

Tropidoclonion lineatum is most easily distinguished from its garter snake relatives by its belly markings: a double row of black half-moons extends from neck to tail tip. Its keeled dorsal scales occur in 19 rows at midbody and in 17 rows just anterior to the vent. There are 5 or 6 upper labial scales, and the anal plate is undivided.

19 LINED SNAKE
Tropidoclonion lineatum

Nonvenomous   Lined snakes do not bite humans, but if threatened, a large individual may flatten its neck and attempt to bluff an assailant with mock strikes.

Abundance   Common. Throughout Texas' central and north central plains, as well as in the remnant prairie of the northern panhandle, *T. lineatum* is a familiar grassland snake that is also often seen in areas of altered and softened soil near rural houses.

Size   Adults are between 8 and 12 inches, but J. P. Jones, former reptile director of the Fort Worth Zoo, recorded one gravid Tarrant County female of 21½ inches.

Habitat   Despite its kinship to aquatic snakes, *Tropidoclonion lineatum* is an entirely terrestrial, semifossorial inhabitant of open, grassy environments; in wooded areas it lives mostly in open meadows. Its primary natural aboveground microhabitat is the narrow space beneath rocks lying on the surface.

Prey   is primarily earthworms, but *T. lineatum* is one of the few vertebrates to feed on the toxic little crustaceans known as sow bugs, which frequently line snakes' damp retreats.

Reproduction   Live-bearing. In Oklahoma, 23 broods of 4- to 5-inch-long newborns were deposited between August 9 and 31.

Coloring/scale form   The lined snake's slender, gray-to-olive ground-colored, usually dark-speckled dorsum bears a pale vertebral stripe. Midway down its side, a pale lateral stripe, often ill-defined, is bordered both above and below by dark checks that resemble another pair of stripes. The throat and belly are creamy (the midventral region may have a yellowish cast) with a double row of black, rearward-arched ventral half-moons; the pointed head, no wider than the neck, is adapted for burrowing.

Similar snakes   Lined snakes were formerly differentiated into the separate subspecies, the central lined snake, *T. l. annectens*, and the New Mexico lined snake, *T. l. mertensi*. These are now rejoined with the race formerly called the Texas lined snake, *T. l. texanum*, to form a single species, the **lined snake (19)**, *Tropidoclonion lineatum*. Lined snakes' relatives, the **garter snakes (20-25)**, have heads twice the width of their necks when seen from above and 8 upper labial scales vertically edged with black along their sutures; none has a double row of ventral half-moons.

Behavior   Lined snakes are seldom seen in the open; they typically remain coiled beneath cover during the day, emerging only at night during damp weather. A favored prey of milk and kingsnakes, *T. lineatum* is detected by these predators from the scent of its musky odor. In suburban areas, lined snakes often hide in the sunken concrete cylinders that house residential water meters, and meter readers may see more *T. lineatum* than any herpetologist.

Garter and Ribbon Snakes
Genus *Thamnophis*

Eastern Garter Snake, *Thamnophis sirtalis sirtalis*

Red-sided Garter Snake, *Thamnophis sirtalis parietalis*

Texas Garter Snake, *Thamnophis sirtalis annectens*

Western Plains Garter Snake, *Thamnophis radix haydenii*

Checkered Garter Snake, *Thamnophis marcianus marcianus*

Eastern Black-necked Garter Snake, *Thamnophis cyrtopsis ocellatus*

Western Black-necked Garter Snake, *Thamnophis cyrtopsis cyrtopsis*

Western Ribbon Snake, *Thamnophis proximus proximus*

Red-striped Ribbon Snake, *Thamnophis proximus rubrilineatus*

Gulf Coast Ribbon Snake, *Thamnophis proximus orarius*

Arid Land Ribbon Snake, *Thamnophis proximus diabolicus*

The genus *Thamnophis* is contained in the colubrine subfamily *Natricinae*. Greek for "bush serpent," the term *Thamnophis* was coined by L. J. F. Fitzinger in 1843, and these animals are indeed at home in brushy environs, especially along lake and stream shores. Both garter and ribbon snakes are genetically closely allied with the water snakes, for *Thamnophis* is probably ancestral to *Nerodia*, the water snake genus.

Almost all garter and ribbon snakes share a pale vertebral line and light-hued side stripes, but determining particular species can be difficult, especially where melanistic populations occur (in some places up to 20 percent of *Thamnophis* are black). In fact, a number of *Thamnophis* species are distinguishable only by the position of the scale row on which their pale lateral line occurs, the overall number of dorsal scale rows, the labial scale count, and whether the labial scales are barred or unmarked. (The keeled scales of garter and ribbon snakes occur in 17 to 21 rows, though this number varies not only by species but individually.) Usually there is an undivided anal plate.

Most small garter snakes are reluctant to bite, but if grasped some of the larger ones can nip vigorously (though garter snakes are nonvenomous, bites have caused mildly adverse reactions). All *Thamnophis* are likely to smear musk and feces about in defense—making themselves as unpalatable as possible to a predator. Another tactic is to flatten and laterally expand their bodies, which not only makes them appear larger but displays the often bright red skin between their scales.

20 EASTERN GARTER SNAKE
Thamnophis sirtalis sirtalis

Nonvenomous   Most wild-caught individuals only emit musk, flatten their necks and feign strikes, sometimes bumping one's hands with their snouts, but the few that choose to bite may hang on tenaciously. Very rarely, slight toxic reactions have been noted as a result of bites by this subspecies. Although *T. s. sirtalis* is not dangerous, it should be handled with care.

Abundance   Common. In areas of suitable habitat—particularly along heavily vegetated waterways crossing prairie, meadow, and marshland—eastern garter snakes can be abundant anywhere in their broad range.

Size   Average adult length is 20 to 28 inches, although the largest recorded eastern garter snake measured 49 in.

Habitat   Primarily open or semi-open lowland, especially stream banks and suburban ditches containing water.

Prey   *Thamnophis sirtalis sirtalis* will prey on almost any smaller creature, but a majority of its diet consists of aquatic or semiaquatic life: small fish, frogs, and salamanders. Terrestrial food animals such as toads and earthworms are sought by scent and seized with the aid of sight, but aquatic prey is often taken without using either of these senses. For example, as an eastern garter snake moves along the margins of a shallow pond, in response to movements in the water it may thrust its foreparts below the murky surface, wagging its open mouth from side to side as it gropes for fish or tadpoles.

Reproduction   Live-bearing. Most litters are born during June and July in Texas, and number from 6 to nearly 60. This great range in litter size generally reflects the size of the mother, with large females giving birth to many more young.

Coloring/scale form   Garter snakes are named for men's old striped sock garters ("sirtalis" also means "striped" in Latin), and although *T. s. sirtalis* is somewhat variable in both color and pattern (individuals found along the Gulf Coast sometimes have red markings amid the dark pigment separating their straw-colored vertebral and lateral stripes), a distinct light brown to yellowish green vertebral stripe is always evident. A similarly colored lateral stripe occupies the second and third scale rows above the pale venter at least among the most commonly pigmented color phase. *T. s. sirtalis* has 19 midbody rows of dorsal scales and the anal plate is undivided.

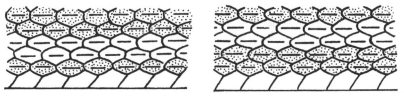

Lateral stripe marking: garter snake   *Lateral stripe marking: ribbon snake*

Similar Snakes   **Western** and **Gulf Coast ribbon snakes (26, 28)** are slimmer, with proportionately longer tails, a rearward-curved white spot in front of the eye, and a pale side stripe on the third and fourth scale rows above the belly.

Behavior   On land, *T. s. sirtalis* is a deliberate, scent-trail forager. Harry Greene reports this species' ability to distinguish recent worm castings from older feces in order to concentrate hunting near the fresher droppings. Individual eastern garter snake ranges are about 2 acres, with the average activity area found in one 3-year study being about 600 by 150 feet; the greatest distance traveled by any of the project's subject snakes was less than ⅙ mile. Few small serpents reach old age in the wild, but as one of the most-studied snakes in the laboratory, captive eastern garter snakes have lived for as long as 14 years.

21 TEXAS GARTER SNAKE
Thamnophis sirtalis annectens

Nonvenomous   When first picked up, Texas garter snakes generally choose to emit musk and bump aggressively with the snout rather than bite, but a large one can nip with determination.

Abundance   Uncommon, but still fairly numerous in scattered locales. According to ecologist Frederick R. Gehlbach of Baylor University, populations of *T. s. annectens* were historically highest in the original tall-grass prairies of Texas and Oklahoma. Over 95 percent of this marvelous ecosystem of successionally maturing grasses, which typically reached 7 feet in height by midsummer, has now been cleared for agriculture. Before tractors smoothed its pocked surface into cotton and sorghum fields, that prairie's vegetation concealed millions of pothole ponds, however, each a miniature wetland harboring its own springtime complement of breeding anurans, and the Texas garter snakes that fed on them.

Size   Adult Texas garter snakes average 18 to 30 inches in length.

Habitat   In addition to its primary tall-grass prairie habitat, open woodland and riparian bottomland are also inhabited, for the author has also found Texas garter snakes in shady juniper canyons along the eastern edge of the Edwards Plateau.

Prey   Like other most other U.S. garter snakes, this race will take almost any moving animal small enough to swallow. Earthworms, minnows, tadpoles, frogs, and small toads are its main prey, however.

Reproduction   Live-bearing. See **Eastern Garter Snake**.

Coloring/scale form   With its dark back split by a broad orange stripe that occupies both the vertebral scale row and more than half of each adjacent scale row, *T. s. annectens* is a visually striking reptile. (When threatened, by spreading its ribs the Texas garter snake can splay its lateral scales to reveal the bright red skin hidden along its sides.) On the forward third of its trunk, its yellowish lateral stripe occupies most of the second, all of the third, and about half of the fourth scale row above the whitish or light green venter. There are 19 midbody rows of dorsal scales and the anal plate is undivided.

Similar snakes   Within its range, only *T. s. annectens* has pale side stripes that involve the fourth lateral scale row above the belly (in the **eastern, checkered,** and **black-necked garter snakes (20, 22, 25)**, these stripes do not touch the fourth scale row).

Behavior   During the hot summer months, Texas garter snakes are active morning and evening, and their lack of wariness makes *T. s. annectens* an interesting animal to watch. At a limestone pool among Edwards Plateau cedar brakes, one 20-inch-long individual had no hesitation in attacking anurans much too large for it to swallow and hung on to a leopard frog for 20 minutes, never managing to engulf more than a single hind leg.

22 CHECKERED GARTER SNAKE

Thamnophis marcianus marcianus

Nonvenomous   Large checkered garter snakes may nip if handled roughly.

Abundance   *Thamnophis marcianus marcianus* is often abundant in the southern part of its U.S. range, and during late spring and early summer checkered garter snakes were by far the most numerous terrestrial serpents observed in rural South Texas. By the late 1990s, however, only a handful of these animals could be seen in a night's drive over roads which, ten years earlier, had produced sightings of as many as 80 *T. m. marcianus* in an evening. Habitat had not changed in this area, so the checkered garter's decline there may be due to increased vehicular traffic.

Size   Adult *T. m. marcianus* average 15 to 28 inches in length; the record specimen measured 42½ in.

Habitat   In North Texas and the Trans-Pecos, the checkered garter snake prefers grassy areas near water; in the Tamaulipan thorn brush of the Rio Grande plain these animals are more widely dispersed; in both areas their periods of greatest activity are closely tied to rainfall, for precipitation brings out the annelid and anuran prey of *T. m. marcianus,* while the humid air following rainfall allows this olfactorily oriented predator to follow the prey's scent.

Prey   Captive checkered garter snakes feed readily on worms, tadpoles, frogs, and small mice. A variety of other small vertebrate, insect, and annelid prey is taken in the wild, while *T. m. marcianus* is also among the handful of serpents that sometimes feed on carrion. See **Eastern Black-necked Garter Snake.**

Reproduction   Live-bearing. Most checkered garter snakes give birth between late May and September. The October 6 deposition of 38 newborns, averaging just over 7¾ inches in length, by a 28-inch-long south Texas female is the latest date on record. (Before birth, developing checkered garter snakes are partially nourished through their mother's placenta.) Immediately after their birth the young, which exactly resemble their parents except with more vivid coloring, tend to be relatively sluggish in the wild, and throughout the Rio Grande brush country it is not unusual to find healthy neonates lying quietly in the middle of mesquite-shaded cow paths.

Coloring/scale form   The checkered garter snake's white or very light yellow vertebral stripe is flanked, on each side of its gray-green ground-colored back and sides, with a double row of black squares. (Checkered garter snakes living on the Edwards Plateau have a tendency toward melanism. Two black *T. m. marcianus* from this area were displayed at the San Antonio Zoo, and other melanistic individuals have come from Kerr and Medina counties.)

The checkered garter snake's most distinctive marking, however, is the prominent pale yellow crescent behind its jaw, posteriorly bordered by a large

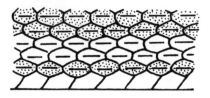

Lateral stripe marking: checkered garter snake

black nuchal spot. Laterally, a light-hued stripe occupies only the third row of scales above the belly on the foreparts, but widens to include the second scale row over the rest of the body; the otherwise unmarked whitish yellow ventral scales sometimes have blackish edges. The dorsal scales are arranged in 21 rows at midbody and the anal plate is undivided.

Similar snakes   Texas (21) and both **black-necked garter snakes (24, 25)** lack a prominent yellow crescent behind the jaw and have only 19 midbody rows of dorsal scales. The **western plains garter snake (23)** has a less prominent yellow nuchal crescent, while its anterior lateral stripe occupies the third and fourth scale rows above its venter.

Behavior   Named *T. m. marcianus* for Captain Randolph B. Marcy, who in 1852 delivered to the Smithsonian Institute the original type specimen obtained during an expedition along the Red River, the checkered garter snake ranges from Kansas to Belize. It is also an ancient species. The fossilized remains of a snake thought to be *T. marcianus* were recovered in Hardeman County, Texas, strata dating from the Wisconsin Glacial Period of 50,000 to 100,000 years ago.

Marcy's garter snakes follow the typical ophidian pattern of foraging at dawn and dusk in spring and fall, then becoming both nocturnal and less active during the hottest months; with cooler autumn weather checkered garters become active once more. In the manner of ring-necked, ground, and other subcaudally red or banded snakes, occasional individuals exhibit a defensive posture (first photographed by Donna Marvel beside a Rio Grande irrigation ditch) in which the tightly curled yellowish underside of the posterior third of the trunk is suddenly everted.

23 WESTERN PLAINS GARTER SNAKE
Thamnophis radix haydenii

Nonvenomous   This animal will not bite unless handled, when it may snap abruptly in its own defense, especially when its tail is touched. (If its foreparts are touched, the plains garter usually responds only by ducking its head beneath a body coil.)

Abundance   Common. Named for frontier geologist Ferdinand V. Hayden, *T. r. haydenii* is a common snake where good habitat prevails in the northern panhandle.

Size   Adults average 20 to 28 inches in length; the record is 40 in.

Habitat   This subspecies' popular name suggests a grassland range, but within most of its huge central and northern Great Plains range its microenvironment is more likely to involve the borders of streams, washes, and gullies that cross the prairie, where it is sometimes locally abundant.

Prey   Amphibians and other small vertebrates as well as insects (especially grasshoppers and, among the young, earthworms) are the principal prey of *T. r. haydenii*.

Reproduction   Live-bearing. Litters average 29 of the approximately 7-inch-long offspring. Like other *Thamnophis,* male western plains garter snakes follow the pheromone trails that sexually receptive females leave on vegetation in order to find their mates.

Coloring/scale form   Dorsally, the western plains garter snake resembles a checkered garter snake. Its white or very light yellow vertebral stripe is flanked with a closely spaced double row of black squares. Below these checkers, a prominent pale yellow lateral stripe occupies the third and fourth scale rows above the belly—a position higher on the sides than that of any other garter snake and one unique to *Thamnophis radix.* Below it another row of square black spots appears. With 21 rows of dorsal scales, *T. r. haydenii* also has more numerous dorsal scales than any other garter snake but the checkered. Its off-white to pale greenish ventral scales often bear a line of dark distal spots, and its anal plate is undivided.

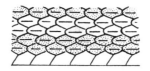

Lateral stripe marking: western plains garter snake

Similar snakes   This is sometimes a difficult animal to distinguish from the **checkered garter snake (22),** whose range overlaps that of the western plains garter in the Texas and Oklahoma panhandles. The checkered garter's light yellow, posteriorly black-bordered neck crescent is more prominently defined, however, and its light-hued side stripe does not reach the fourth scale row above its belly line. **Ribbon snakes (26-29)** are more slender, with proportionately longer tails, unspotted backs, unmarked whitish lips and bellies, a prominent, recurved white spot just ahead of the eye, and 19 rows of dorsal scales.

Behavior   Seasonally active from March to November, western plains garter snakes retire below ground during the hottest weeks of summer, for they are quite sensitive to high temperatures, becoming overheated at more than 90°F. *Thamnophis radix* is relatively hardy in cool weather, however, for on sunny autumn days too chilly for most reptiles to be abroad, large numbers of western plains garter snakes sometimes crawl onto asphalt roads where they remain, absorbing warmth from the blacktop, until many are slain by traffic.

24 EASTERN BLACK-NECKED GARTER SNAKE

Thamnophis cyrtopsis ocellatus

Nonvenomous   *Thamnophis cyrtopsis ocellatus* generally defends itself only by discharging feces and musk, but
a large individual may nip if molested.

Abundance   Common. Endemic to Texas, the eastern black-necked
garter snake's range is confined to this state's central hill country. Here, due
to its vivid colors and diurnal foraging, it is often noticed in the suburban
neighborhoods spreading westward from San Antonio, New Braunfels, San
Marcos, and Austin. In these new residential developments, houses are often
built during the winter over the brumation crevices of *T. c. ocellatus*, and
when these beautiful little serpents emerge in spring they find themselves on
the new residents' doorsteps—sometimes causing consternation because in
popular mythology a bright orange and black snake, however small and
innocuous, means danger.

Size   Adults average 16 to 20 inches in length; the record is 43 in.

Habitat   The eastern black-necked garter snake's primary habitat is moist,
wooded ravines and streamside bottomland; heavily foliaged residential neighborhoods approximate this environment and support sizable populations of
T. c. ocellatus.

Prey   In an extensive study of predation in this and two other *Thamnophis*
species in Travis County, M. J. Fourquette (1954) found that the eastern
black-necked garter takes mainly tadpole prey during spring and early summer, then adult frogs the rest of the year. Along the Balcones Fault west of
Austin, Fourquette found that the snake's anuran prey was primarily the
locally abundant cliff frog, although slimy salamanders, red-spotted toads,
and ground skinks were also noted. In this area, the eastern black-necked
garter snake competes for food mainly with the red-striped ribbon snake,
which also favors amphibian prey. The garter snake takes primarily amphibians it finds on land, however, while the predominantly aquatic ribbon snake
seeks frogs and salamanders in water.

Reproduction   Live-bearing. The average brood is 9 young, each 8 to 10½
inches in length.

Coloring/scale form   First described by C. B. R. Kennicott in 1860, the eastern black-necked garter snake takes its name from the Greek *cyrto*, "curved,"
and *aopsis*, "appearance"—a reference to the hemispherical black blotch
located just behind its jaw. Flanking this snake's orange vertebral stripe, a
row of large black dorsolateral blotches, separated by tiny light and dark bars,
encroaches downward into the forward portion of its broad yellow side stripe
(which occupies the second and third scale rows above its venter), giving this
stripe a wavy appearance. Posteriorly, these blotches diverge into a double
row of staggered black spots. The dorsal scales are arranged in 19 rows at
midbody and the anal plate is undivided.

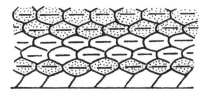

Lateral stripe marking: eastern and western black-necked garter snakes

Similar snakes   No other *Thamnophis* occurring within the range of *T. c. ocellatus* has a single row of very large black blotches on either side of its neck. The **western black-necked garter snake (25)**, with which the eastern race intergrades throughout the western Edwards Plateau and eastern Trans-Pecos, has black checkerboard dorsolateral patterning on the rear of its body. The **checkered garter snake (22)** has three staggered rows of small black dorsolateral squares, while the pale side stripe of the **Texas garter snake (21)**, unlike that of *T.c. ocellatus*, occupies part of the fourth scale row above its belly.

Behavior   Both eastern and western black-necked garter snakes are diurnally active during even the hottest summer months, but almost always remain near some sort of aquatic habitat. Vision is used for capturing elusive nearby prey, but sight is less important than scent in finding the general locale of appropriate food animals such as earthworms, anurans, and fish. Despite its gaudy appearance, the eastern black-necked garter's bright vertebral stripe nevertheless functions as a sophisticated sort of camouflage. As *T. c. ocellatus* slides away from danger, its black dorsal spots and orange vertebral pigment flash intermittently through intervening leafy undergrowth, focusing a predator's visual attention on what seems to be a flickering but stationary ribbon of orange.

25 WESTERN BLACK-NECKED GARTER SNAKE

Thamnophis cyrtopsis cyrtopsis

Nonvenomous   Western black-necked garter snakes nip humans only when molested or handled roughly.

Abundance   Common. In scattered well-watered habitats sparsely distributed across the northern Chihuahuan Desert, this reptile may be abundant. In Brewster County, Sherman Minton (1959) found, "In late July, almost every pool in the little canyon below Boot Spring was occupied by 2 to 6 of these snakes. They were sunning on rocks or swimming in pursuit of *Hyla arenicolor* [canyon treefrog] tadpoles, which were found in the stomachs of all those collected."

Size   Adults average 16 to 28 inches; the largest western black-necked garter on record measured 41¾ in.

Habitat Due to the presence of water there, *T. c. cyrtopsis* is more often a mountain canyon dweller than a resident of low-lying desert, but near desert springs it may be common.

Prey See **Eastern Black-necked Garter Snake.**

Reproduction Live-bearing. Broods of 3 to 25 young have been recorded.

Coloring/scale form On the forebody, a broad, pale orange vertebral stripe divides a single row of large black dorsolateral squares; posteriorly, this row of black markings splits into a doubled, checkerboard-like row. The crown is bluish gray, strikingly set off from the big black neck patch that is the source both of this subspecies' common name and (from "cyrto," or "curved") its scientific name. The western black-necked garter snake's whitish side stripe occupies the second and third scale rows above its venter; its chin is also white, with dark-edged labial scales. Its venter is white as well, sometimes with a greenish or yellowish brown cast. There are 19 rows of dorsal scales at midbody, and its anal plate is undivided.

Similar snakes The subspecies **eastern black-necked garter snake (24)** (with which the western race intergrades throughout the western Edwards Plateau and eastern Trans-Pecos) has a single row of much larger, rounded or V-shaped dark nuchal blotches, the lower tips of which reach downward into its wide yellow lateral stripe, giving this stripe a wavy look. The **checkered garter snake (22)** is not usually found in the upland locales where the western black-necked garter most often occurs, but is distinguished by the prominent yellow crescent located just behind its jaw, by the anterior restriction of its pale side stripe to the third row of scales above its belly, and by its 21 midbody rows of dorsal scales. **Ribbon snakes (26-29)** are more slender, with proportionately longer tails, unmarked white upper labial scales, and a white, half-moon-shaped spot just forward of the eye. Ribbon snakes also lack the garter snakes' black-blotched back.

Behavior *Thamnophis cyrtopsis cyrtopsis* is frequently encountered basking on creek-side rocks from which, if disturbed, it flees by swimming across the surface to the opposite bank. Here it typically seeks shelter under overhanging rocks or vegetation. If cornered, this little animal may flatten its body against the ground and writhe as menacingly as possible. Such a strategy is of no use against large ophidian predators, however, for a freshly devoured 22-inch-long western black-necked garter was disgorged by a Sonoran gopher snake captured south of Fort Stockton by the author.

26 WESTERN RIBBON SNAKE
Thamnophis proximus proximus

Nonvenomous   See **Red-striped Ribbon Snake.**

Abundance   Western ribbon snakes are generally common in areas of suitable habitat throughout both the southern Great Plains and its complex interface with the eastern woodlands. *T. p. proximus* inhabits a long sweep of this terrain stretching from northeastern Texas to northern Kansas and Missouri. Other subspecies range as far south as Costa Rica.

Size   Adults are 20 to 34 inches long, with such slender bodies that 3 female western ribbon snakes between 27 and 34 inches in length—as with all *Thamnophis*, females are larger than males—averaged less than 6 ounces in weight.

Habitat   Where the eastern Texas forest thins into the open country of the central plains, agriculture now prevails, but it is not as hostile to ribbon snakes as to larger snake species. The drainage ditches bordering crop fields offer an approximation of ribbon snakes' natural creek-side microenvironment, and *T. p. proximus* may occur near any such strip of fresh water with vegetative cover along its banks. It is also often found in arid brush country but seldom far from a source of water.

Prey   Western ribbon snakes' prey varies with the seasons; 92 percent of the stomach contents of one central Texas sample trapped during late spring consisted of tadpoles. At other times frogs and toads (whose digitaloid skin toxins garter snakes are metabolically equipped to digest), lizards, and small fish may be this snake's principal prey. Besides being prey to mammalian and avian carnivores, ribbon snakes are themselves devoured by big, fast-moving snakes like racers and coachwhips.

Reproduction   Live-bearing. One female *T. p. proximus* captured near Stanford, Oklahoma, gave birth to 21 young on August 8, while three litters from Northeast Texas were deposited July 10 and 18, and August 20. Of these three, the two smaller females each gave birth to 18 young, the larger one to 23. All the neonates were about the same size: between 9½ and 10 inches in length, slimmer than a pencil at midbody, and about ¹/₁₀ ounce in weight.

As with most snake species, mortality among first- and second-year juveniles is high. Donald Clark (1974) reports heavy winter die-offs among juvenile western ribbon snakes, presumably because their smaller ratio of bulk-to-surface area renders them more vulnerable to desiccation during their critical November-through-February brumation period. Among Clark's East Texas population, sufficient rainfall before and during denning appeared to be the primary factor determining survival of juvenile *T. p. proximus*, for dry autumn weather limited the abundance of small frogs and resulted in low fat levels among the young about to enter winter dormancy. Little precipitation later in the year, combined with very cold winter weather, then resulted in an estimated mortality of 74 percent of this vulnerable age-group during brumation.

Coloring/scale form The western ribbon snake's unmarked dark gray-brown dorsum is split by a broad orange vertebral stripe. Like that of all ribbon snakes, its yellowish lateral stripe occupies the third and fourth scale rows above its yellowish green venter. Its white upper labial scales are unmarked, although the lips, lateral stripe, and belly of individuals living north and east of Dallas often have a bluish cast. Two tiny white dashes punctuate the rear of its blackish crown, while a rearward-curved white spot occurs just in front of each eye. The dorsal scales are arranged in 19 rows at midbody and the anal plate is undivided.

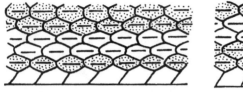 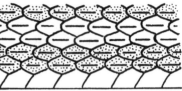

Lateral stripe marking: garter snake
(All garter snakes have the same side-striped spacing.)

Lateral stripe marking: ribbon snake

Similar snakes Of the several races with which *T. p. proximus* intergrades, the **Gulf Coast ribbon snake (28)** typically has a brownish to olive-green back and sides and an olive-tan to dull gold vertebral stripe. The **red-striped ribbon snake (27)** is characterized by a dark gray back, a wine-red vertebral stripe, and gray-green lower sides, while the **arid land ribbon snake (29)** usually has a gray-brown back (individuals from the Canadian and Cimarron River drainages sometimes have a darker ground color), with both a distinctively thin, black ventrolateral seam and a broad orange vertebral stripe that lightens to gold on the nape.

Behavior During late August and September newborn ribbon snakes can sometimes be found sheltering in tall creek-side grass or under planks; in the taller growth along lake and stream shorelines these juveniles are sometimes somewhat arboreal; near the Red River nine small western ribbon snakes were observed basking on the branches of a brush-filled gully.

27 RED-STRIPED RIBBON SNAKE
Thamnophis proximus rubrilineatus

Nonvenomous Like most *Thamnophis*, ribbon snakes, if seized roughly, can nip and hang on tenaciously despite their small heads.

Abundance Common. Endemic to Texas, the red-striped ribbon snake is found primarily in the oak–juniper savannah of the state's central Edwards Plateau; intergrade individuals combining characteristics of one or the other of the three ribbon snake races whose range surrounds that of *T. p. rubrilineatus* occur in a wide perimeter around the red-striped race's central range.

Size   Most adults are 24 to 36 inches long. Typically, the red-striped ribbon snake is quite slender, but three-way intergrades between it and the Gulf Coast and arid land ribbon snakes (the latter the longest *Thamnophis proximus*) can grow much larger. Such animals inhabit South Texas' Tamaulipan thorn woodland and may attain more than twice this species' usual girth, becoming so thick-bodied that they resemble the similarly colored Texas garter snake.

Habitat   Like other ribbon snakes, *T. p. rubrilineatus* is almost always found near water, where it is easily observed because of its diurnal activity pattern. When not actively foraging, it basks on rocks, logs, and the raised cypress knees that occur along watercourses. Basking individuals typically remain motionless until closely approached or even touched, at which point they streak away across the water's surface to hide beneath overhanging rocks or vegetation on the opposite bank. During late August and September newborn red-striped ribbon snakes can often be found sheltering under flat, creek-side limestones.

Prey   Ribbon snakes' prey is seasonally variable but is almost always obtained from aquatic environments. In spring, tadpoles constitute much of the diet; at other times, small fish, salamanders, and adult frogs and toads—whose digitaloid skin toxins ribbon snakes are metabolically equipped to digest—are principal food animals. On land, ribbon snakes use scent tracking to locate fossorial food animals such as earthworms, as well as to ferret lizards and small anurans from beneath grass and litter.

Reproduction   Live-bearing. Breeding takes place from April through June. Litters of up to 20 are deposited between July and September.

Coloring/scale form   The narrow vertebral stripe splitting the dark gray back of this subspecies can vary from deep wine red (*rubrilineatus* means "red-striped") near the tail to bright orange at the nape, although entirely orange-striped specimens turn up throughout the range. As on other ribbon snakes, there is usually a white dot on the rear of each parietal scale as well as a larger white spot immediately in front of each eye. There are 19 rows of dorsal scales, and the anal plate is undivided.

Similar snakes   The 4 geographical races of *Thamnophis proximus* interbreed to produce clinal variations intermediate between the red-striped ribbon, the **Gulf Coast ribbon snake (28)** (which typically has a brown to olive-green back and sides and an olive-tan to dull gold vertebral stripe), the **arid land ribbon snake (29)** (whose orange vertebral stripe bisects an olive-brown to gray back and tan lower sides), and the **western ribbon snake (26)** (whose dark gray-brown back is split by a broad orange vertebral stripe).

Behavior   Ribbon snakes' conspicuous vertebral stripe is believed to help them evade predators. Seen through thick vegetation, as the snake moves away from a viewer this bright line between its unmarked dark sides appears to remain stationary as the snake slides deeper into the bushes. Even knowing full well that such a partially hidden snake is moving away, it is still a surprise to see its tail tip suddenly slip from view; predators may get the same surprise because so many carnivores manage to catch only the ribbon snake's tail tip—which is easily twisted off—that nearly 20 percent of the *Thamnophis proximus* in one Kansas study lacked complete tails.

28 GULF COAST RIBBON SNAKE

Thamnophis proximus orarius

Nonvenomous   See **Red-striped Ribbon Snake.**

Abundance   Common. Although to the north and west
of its primary range *T. p. orarius* intergrades with the three
ribbon snake races whose territories border its own, its principal
distribution is along and up to 100 miles inland from the Gulf Coast.

Size   See **Red-striped Ribbon Snake.**

Habitat   *Thamnophis proximus orarius* inhabits marshes, moist prairie, and
the low dikes and roadbeds that prevail in its coastal haunts, rising a few
inches above surrounding wetlands. One favored microhabitat is the levees
that impound rice field irrigation lakes. These reptiles are also found in grassy
dunes no more than 30 yards from the Gulf's breaking surf, but wooded
inland terrain is occupied as well.

Prey   Ribbon snakes typically forage along aquatic shorelines, taking insects,
crustaceans, and small vertebrates. Nearly as tied to water as the *Nerodia* to
which they are related, ribbon snakes rely on diving into water for protection.
Without this refuge they seem to be quite vulnerable, for the author has seen
small Gulf Coast ribbon snakes heavily preyed on by cattle egrets in the drying bed of the Nueces River.

Reproduction   Live-bearing. Breeding begins early in the year. Gravid *T. p.
orarius* have been discovered as early as April, and by July, 88 percent of
females examined in one study were found to be pregnant. Recorded broods
for *Thamnophis proximus* have ranged from 5 to 27.

Coloring/scale form   First defined as a subspecies in 1963 by Douglas Ross-
man, this race is notable for its mint-green upper labial scales, chartreuse venter, and a less contrasting dorsal pattern than inland-living ribbon snakes. *T.
p. orarius* has a brownish green back whose pale vertebral line is almost the
same color as its olive-tan side stripes. (*T. p. orarius* from South Texas often
have cream-colored vertebral stripes, however, while those from East Texas
and Louisiana may have a golden spinal stripe and backs and sides nearly as
dark as those of the western ribbon snake.) There is usually a white spot on
the rear of each parietal scale, a vertical white spot immediately in front of
each large eye, 19 rows of dorsal scales, and an undivided anal plate.

Similar snakes   The 4 races of *Thamnophis proximus* interbreed freely, producing intermediate forms which vary clinally as the range of each subspecies
merges with that of adjoining races. In their pure forms, however, the **western ribbon snake (26)** has a darker back and a broad orange vertebral stripe,
the **red-striped ribbon snake (27)** has a slightly narrower vertebral stripe
(which can shade from wine-red near the tail to bright orange at the nape)
that splits a dark gray back, and the **arid land ribbon snake (29)** has a gray-
brown back with both a thin black ventrolateral seam and a broad orange
vertebral stripe that lightens to gold on its nape.

Behavior   In studying a woodland population of Gulf Coast ribbon snakes on the Sarpy Wildlife Refuge, a cypress gum swamp northwest of New Orleans, Donald Tinkle (1957) established that in this subtropical climate ribbon snakes are active almost year-round—although their most extensive foraging occurred immediately after warm summer rains when frogs and toads were abroad. Tinkle found that his marked snakes occupied home territories several acres in extent although, because they foraged throughout the study area, he encountered them most frequently on earthen ridges extending into a wetland. Here, in cool spring weather they basked in the sunny upper layers of blackberry vines; in summer they sought the shade of the wooded parts of the ridges.

29 ARID LAND RIBBON SNAKE
Thamnophis proximus diabolicus

Nonvenomous   Ribbon snakes nip only if they are molested.

Abundance   Common. The arid land ribbon snake's ability to penetrate westward along river courses and to subsist around even small bodies of water allows this westernmost race of *T. proximus* to occupy large areas of West Texas, often as an intergrade with the western ribbon snake. One particularly abundant population is resident along the shores of Amistad Reservoir while other *T. p. diabolicus* occupy the banks of the Big Bend portion of the Rio Grande as well as pats of the Devil's and Pecos rivers' riparian corridors.

Away from these watercourses, however, this animal's broad distribution is due in large measure to mankind. Since the late nineteenth century, ranchers have been pumping water from panhandle aquifers into stock tanks—artificial ponds that provide frogs and toads an aquatic reproductive niche and provide them with flies drawn to the manure-covered banks. As a result, these anurans' ribbon snake predators, which were previously restricted to the heads of narrow creeks on the dry prairie, have colonized the myriad man-made waterholes now scattered across the High Plains.

Size   The longest of Texas' ribbon snakes, *T. p. diabolicus* has been recorded to just over 4 feet in length. See **Red-striped Ribbon Snake**.

Habitat   See **Red-striped Ribbon Snake**.

Prey   Any small vertebrate (even many suitably sized invertebrates, although annelids are not usually eaten) moving within a ribbon snake's sight may constitute prey, but pond-dwelling frogs and toads are a major component in the diet of many *T. p. diabolicus* because, like their relatives the garter snakes, ribbon snakes are able to feed on toads due to the enlarged adrenal glands that allow them to partially neutralize toads' toxic epidermal secretions. These secretions contain the digitaloid poisons which cause dogs that have bitten a toad to gag and froth at the mouth, and can slow or even stop the heartbeat of small predators not metabolically equipped to counter their neurologically suppressive effect.

Reproduction   Live-bearing. See **Gulf Coast Ribbon Snake.**

Coloring/scale form   Because the type specimen was taken near the Devil's River, this snake owes its subspecies name to the Greek *diabolikos*. Its back is usually gray-brown—though individuals from the Canadian and Cimarron river drainages sometimes display a darker ground color—with a broad orange vertebral stripe that lightens to gold on the nape. There is also a distinctive thin black ventrolateral seam. As on other ribbon snakes, a white spot usually appears on the rear of each parietal scale, and there is a prominent white spot immediately in front of each eye. There are 19 rows of dorsal scales, and the anal plate is undivided.

Similar snakes   Throughout the Texas and Oklahoma panhandles *T p. diabolicus* intergrades with the **western ribbon snake (26)**, which generally has a darker back and a slightly narrower vertebral stripe. Likewise, on the Stockton and western Edwards plateaus the arid land ribbon snake intergrades with the **red-striped ribbon snake (27)**, the latter having a ruddier vertebral stripe than the arid land race. As far northwest as Laredo on the Rio Grande plain, the arid land ribbon snake's range overlaps that of the olive-backed, vertebrally greenish tan striped **Gulf Coast ribbon snake (28)**, although in this area the genetic influence of the red-striped ribbon snake is also sometimes evident. See **Red-striped Ribbon Snake.**

Behavior   The arid land ribbon snake's behavior, although partially adapted to the drier conditions of its range, is fundamentally similar to that of other subspecies of *Thamnophis proximus*.

Aquatic Snakes

Genus *Nerodia*

Diamond-backed Water Snake, *Nerodia rhombifer rhombifer*
Yellow-bellied Water Snake, *Nerodia erythrogaster flavigaster*
Blotched Water Snake, *Nerodia erythrogaster transversa*
Broad-banded Water Snake, *Nerodia fasciata confluens*
Florida Water Snake, *Nerodia fasciata pictiventris*
Gulf Salt Marsh Snake, *Nerodia clarkii clarkii*
Mississippi Green Water Snake, *Nerodia cyclopion*
Brazos Water Snake, *Nerodia harteri harteri*
Concho Water Snake, *Nerodia harteri paucimaculata*

A part of the colubrine subfamily *Natricinae*, the aquatic genus *Nerodia* is named for the Greek sea nymph, Nereis. Adult female *Nerodia* are usually larger than males and are so fertile that when pregnant large individuals may reach comparatively immense girths. Perhaps because they live in predator-filled surroundings, all of the 52 *Nerodia* species are adept at self-defense. If restrained, they almost always try to bite as well as smear a combination of musk and feces on their assailant. Moreover, as with many snakes possessing a Duvernoy's gland, the saliva of *Nerodia* contains complex proteins which, along with the host of microorganisms present in their mouths, can produce inflammatory reactions around the site of their bite.

All American water snakes are live-bearing, with some giving birth to very large litters (a Florida green water snake just under 5 feet long contained 128 well-developed young). In lifestyle, water snakes vary from semiaquatic to almost exclusively aquatic. Most are dark, heavy-bodied serpents that fishermen, boaters, and hikers invariably confuse with the venomous cottonmouth. This often brings about the death of the water snake, but long before human intervention, the resemblance of large *Nerodia* to the cottonmouth may have conferred some protective benefits.

Warm spring and rainy summer nights are the peak activity period for water snakes, and on such nights vehicles can take a terrible toll on *Nerodia* since the snakes often linger on roads where frogs and toads congregate. In cooler weather, water snakes may bask all day if it is sunny. This exposes them to predators, and at this time *Nerodia* tend to be especially wary, dropping into the water and diving at the first sign of disturbance. They may surface quickly, sculling slowly in place or swimming parallel to the shore to assess the danger, but if frightened again they often submerge and remain hidden for long periods.

Water snakes have heavily keeled scales whose rough surface tends to collect a thin film of mud, obscuring these animals' sometimes distinct dorsolateral patterning: the intricacy of these markings is usually fully evident only when aquatic snakes are wet or have recently shed their skins. In nearly all instances, *Nerodia* have a divided anal plate, although occasionally an undivided anal plate occurs among members of the several races of *N. erythrogaster*.

30 DIAMOND-BACKED WATER SNAKE
Nerodia rhombifer rhombifer

Nonvenomous   If cornered, large diamond-backed water snakes can be vigorous biters, with an extraordinary ability to excrete and spew musk.

Abundance   Variably abundant across a variety of environments that stretch from the desert banks of the Pecos River in western Texas to wooded swamps in the eastern part of the state, on the southern Gulf coastal plain and Rio Grande Valley N .r. *rhombifer* is the most common aquatic serpent.

Size   Most adults are 20 to 34 inches, with females typically attaining greater length, and considerably more girth, than males. The record is just over 60 in.

Habitat   Within its range, *N. r. rhombifer* may be found around almost any rural body of water, including small, temporary ponds (man-made objects left along the banks are a frequent source of shelter). During rainy periods, however, diamond-backed water snakes often forage in moist grassland a considerable distance from water.

The same sort of overland travel occurs in southwestern Texas, where *N. r. rhombifer* inhabits more arid terrain than almost any other aquatic snake. Because waterways in this area are prone to seasonal drying, diamond-backed water snakes are often forced to make long journeys to permanent water holes, and at this time the young are particularly vulnerable to predation by carnivorous wading birds such as herons and egrets. Yet no sooner have autumn rains refilled rivers and ponds than adult *N. r. rhombifer* (usually traveling at night) reappear in their home territories among outlying stock tanks. (These temporary pools almost always harbor a great many tadpoles and frogs, prey which is able to prosper here only because these ponds' periodic evaporation kills predatory fish that would eat anuran tadpoles.)

Prey   The diamond-backed water snake's prey species vary considerably with locale, but in most situations this snake feeds primarily on frogs and rough fish (few game fish, which are too fast for water snakes to capture, are taken). One predatory technique involves swimming parallel to the shore, then seizing the frogs that, flushed from their bankside resting places, often leap directly into the swimming snake's path. As with other water snakes, carrion may also be an important part of the diet, for, drawn by both scent and vibrations in the water, *N .r. rhombifer* is commonly seen nosing around the dead and dying fish held by fishermen's stringers or, after dark, coming ashore in search of fish heads and offal at fishing camps.

Reproduction   Live-bearing. Unusual among serpents is the sexual dimorphism of diamond-backed water snakes, among which males are characterized by underchin tubercles that could offer sensory clues during courtship. Because of its large size, *N .r. rhombifer* is able to produce large numbers of offspring. Twenty-two litters, all deposited between the first of August and mid-October, averaged just over 37 young; these neonates ranged from 8$\frac{1}{4}$ to 10$\frac{1}{4}$ inches in length.

Coloring/scale form   Blackish brown lines form a diamond- or chain-link fence–shaped network (the *rhombus*—"rectangular"—of its Latin name), which crosses the olive to grayish brown back; these lines also intersect dark vertical bars along its sides. The yellowish venter is randomly marked with small black crescents, there are 25 to 31 midbody rows of dorsal scales, and the anal plate is divided.

Similar snakes   The diamond-backed water snake's heavy body and indistinct dark coloring (especially when its pattern is obscured by a film of dried mud) often cause it to be mistaken for the **western cottonmouth (95)**. This aquatic pitviper is distinguished, however, by its slit-purpled eye and the sunken, heat-sensing pit located between its eye and nostril.

Unlike the rounded heads of water snakes, the cottonmouth's angular skull is characterized by flat, undercut cheeks which abruptly intersect its crown. *Nerodia* water snakes typically swim and dive vigorously, moreover, while a swimming cottonmouth's entire body is buoyantly suspended on the surface. (The aggregations of aquatic snakes often seen in shrinking water holes during late summer are almost always nonvenomous *Nerodia* rather than the "nest of cottonmouths" they are commonly taken for.)

Behavior   One predatory strategy involves sensitive lateral areas spaced along this animal's trunk. When these spots are touched, *N .r. rhombifer* snaps sideways in an automatic strike response that maximizes its chances of seizing prey. Another such strategy is moving constantly from one water source to another as each pond's prey is exhausted; stocking a batch of hatchery-bred sunfish (some of which are sure to be in poor condition and consequently easy to catch) will often draw a visit from several scent-hunting diamond-backed water snakes already present in the general vicinity.

31 YELLOW-BELLIED WATER SNAKE

Nerodia erythrogaster flavigaster

Nonvenomous   Often after a preliminary defensive display in which it may discharge feces and foul-smelling musk excreted by glands within its cloaca, the yellow-bellied water snake will bite in self-protection. This behavior is usually accompanied by a flattening of the neck and head and short, sham strikes—but if pressed, large *Nerodia* can be nasty biters, causing long scratches as they quickly jerk their heads back from their assailant.

Abundance   Common. With a range that joins the territories of this race's adjacently ranging subspecies, the red-bellied race to the east and the blotched water snake to the west, *N. e. flavigaster* is common throughout the eastern quarter of the state.

Size   Most adults are 30 to 48 inches in length; the record is just over 59 in. Because large *N. erythrogaster* are heavy-bodied, an individual this massive would be almost certain to be misidentified as a cottonmouth. (Actually, the majority of "moccasins" found around rural and suburban ponds within this animal's range are really large yellow-bellied water snakes.)

Habitat   *Nerodia erythrogaster flavigaster* is found in most rural wetland environments, more often in wooded than in open areas; it seems, however, to be most numerous in swamps, the luetic water of oxbow river segments, bayous, and the marshy verges of floodplain lakes and ponds.

Prey   Young yellow-bellied water snakes eat minnows, tadpoles, and aquatic insects; adults feed primarily on frogs and other amphibians, for as they mature, *N. erythrogaster* gradually alter their early preference for the smell of fish to that of frogs and other amphibians. One instance of this preference was noted by Bill Marvel:

"At 2 p.m. on March 16 I was standing beside a roadside ditch when a 36-inch yellow-bellied water snake backed out of the water with a 10-inch lesser siren grasped about mid-body. The snake crawled up the embankment, where it began "walking" its jaws along the siren's body toward the head. The siren attempted to escape by burrowing among the grass roots and by twisting movements that forced the snake to turn on its back. Although the snake crawled across my boots during this struggle it did not seem to notice my presence. After it had swallowed the siren it raised its head, flicked its tongue, then crawled back into the ditch and swam away under water. The whole operation took about 45 minutes."

It is characteristic of water snakes, particularly *N. erythrogaster*, to drag large fish or other prey animals out of the water, gaining traction against the ground as leverage in overcoming the struggles of their prey. See **Blotched Water Snake.**

Reproduction   Live-bearing. See **Blotched Water Snake.**

Coloring/scale form   *Flavor*, which is Latin for "yellow," combined with *gaster*, Greek for "belly," aptly describes this yellow-bellied western race of *N. erythrogaster*. (*Erythrism* means "red," the belly color of the eastern subspecies.)

Slightly paler on its lower sides, the dark, unpatented dorsum of the yellow-bellied water snake varies from gray-green to almost black. (The dorsolateral markings of juvenile *N. e. flavigaster* differ greatly from the coloring of adults; their faintly pinkish ground color is conspicuously patterned over the forebody with dark dorsal bands which break up posteriorly into dark saddles alternating with vertical lateral bars.) The lips are yellow, with dark labial sutures; there are 23 midbody rows of dorsal scales, and the anal plate is usually divided.

Similar snakes   The albumin proteins of water snakes indicate that the snakes are close relatives of the **garter** (20–25) and **ribbon snakes** (26–29). (*Nerodia* are thought to be a Pliocene evolutionary departure toward aquatic life on the part of some members of the older, more terrestrially adapted garter snake genus *Thamnophis*.)

Behavior   See **Blotched Water Snake.**

32 BLOTCHED WATER SNAKE
Nerodia erythrogaster transversa

Nonvenomous   When restrained, like other reptiles attempting to discourage a predator by making themselves unappetizing, *N. e. transversa* often forcibly expels the contents of its cloaca, accompanied by musk discharged from glands located within the cloacal cavity.

Abundance   Common. Across the central half of Texas *N. e. transversa* is the predominant water snake, while even as far west as the arid Trans-Pecos, individuals have been found in the Devil's River near Juno and along the Pecos River's almost dry course throughout northwestern Val Verde County.

Size   Most adults are 2 to 3 feet in length; the record is 58 in.

Habitat   Major riparian corridors in the west; any watercourse, pond, lake, or their intervening grassy or wooded lowlands in the central and northern parts of the state. The chocolate-blotched newborns of this race are more typically found in shallower, more dappled microenvironments—both small streams and the inlets of larger bodies of water—than are the more uniformly colored adults.

At the mouth of such inlets, the young sometimes lie for hours, anchored against the bottom. With their snouts pressed into the incoming flow, they may be anticipating small prey washed downstream, monitoring the onrushing stream of scent flowing past.

Prey   Most reptiles partition habitat; snakes usually partition prey species. Like other diverse ophidian populations, Texas' several sympatric water snake species to some degree partition their food resources, with *Nerodia erythrogaster* taking mostly fish and frogs.

How they capture large examples of this prey is remarkable. The author once watched a blotched water snake drag a catfish too large and vigorous to be swallowed (or even gripped by its jaws for long in the water) out onto the bank of a stock pond. Here, the snake actively searched for an embedded stick or rock around which to anchor a body coil, thus preventing the flopping fish from dragging them both back into the pond until, many minutes later, the snake finally succumbed from being out of water.

Reproduction   Live-bearing. Breeding takes place on land, in spring. Like their relatives the garter snakes, water snakes are characterized by large numbers of offspring. *Nerodia erythrogaster transversa* fits this pattern, for after a 3½-month gestation period, litters containing from 5 to 27 young, ranging from 7½ to 10½ inches in length, are born in late summer.

AQUATIC SNAKES

Coloring/scale form   Blotched water snakes are gray-brown above, often with a hint of olive. Over the spine, short, dark-edged pale bars are evident, while dimly defined dark vertical bars mark the sides. (The most westerly *N. e. transversa* live in shallow, rocky streambed channels like those frequented by eastern juveniles. Here, strongly contrasting dorsolateral patterning is a more cryptic adaptive choice, and to benefit from this camouflage adults retain the distinct dorsal patterning of juveniles.)

Among both geographic groups the belly is yellow, with the edges of larger animals' ventral plates lightly tinged with brown. There are 23 to 27 midbody rows of dorsal scales and the anal plate is divided.

Similar snakes   Intergrades between the blotched and **yellow-bellied water snake (31)** occur in East and Central Texas, but the typical yellowbelly is unmarked above, with light yellow posterior edging on its ventral scales (the young, however, are indistinguishable from juveniles of other races of *Nerodia erythrogaster*). Because blotched water snakes are stout-bodied, short-tailed serpents which darken with age, they superficially resemble the **western cottonmouth (95)**. But the cottonmouth has a vertically slit pupil, unlike the circular pupil of all water snakes. As a pitviper, the cottonmouth also has a dark heat-sensing pit between its eye and nostril and an angular head whose flat, undercut cheeks abruptly intersect its crown.

Behavior   For the most part *Nerodia* water snakes have not made radical physical accommodation to aquatic life. Instead, they have adapted behaviorally to take advantage of the benefits of living in the water. Most important is their technique for gaining heat in cooler aquatic milieus by basking. Sometimes seen draped along tree limbs overhanging water (like most aquatic serpents *N. e. transversa* is a good climber), blotched water snakes are also encountered crossing roads in the evening, especially following rainstorms that bring out breeding frogs.

During temperate weather blotched water snakes are crepuscular or diurnal foragers, but during the hottest months they are active mainly at night. Like other *Nerodia*, these reptiles are far more mobile than is commonly supposed. Individuals marked by the author have shown that at least some blotched water snakes are fairly wide ranging, periodically visiting several different stock ponds at least a half mile apart.

33 BROAD-BANDED WATER SNAKE
Nerodia fasciata confluens

Nonvenomous   If cornered, *N. f. confluens* may discharge odorous musk from its cloaca, flatten its forebody, and strike repeatedly in self-defense. Yet, like other large, dark-bodied water snakes that resemble the cottonmouth, it is harmless to humans unless harassed.

A   **Brahminy Blind Snake,**
Ramphotyphlops braminus

I   **Plains Blind Snake,**
Leptotyphlops dulcis dulcis

2   **New Mexico Blind Snake,**
Leptotyphlops dulcis dissectus

3 **Trans-Pecos Blind Snake,**
Leptotyphlops humilis segregus

4a **Flat-headed Snake,**
Tantilla gracilis

4b **Flat-headed Snake,**
Tantilla gracilis

5 **Plains Black-headed Snake,**
Tantilla nigriceps

8a **Black-hooded Snake,**
Tantilla rubra cucullata (western population)

8b **Black-hooded Snake,**
Tantilla rubra cucullata (eastern population)

9 **Texas Brown Snake,**
Storeria dekayi texana

10   Marsh Brown Snake,
Storeria dekayi limnetes

11a   Florida Red-bellied Snake,
Storeria occipitomaculata obscura

11b   Florida Red-bellied Snake,
Storeria occipitomaculata obscura

12   Rough Earth Snake,
Virginia striatula

13   Western Earth Snake,
Virginia valeriae elegans

14   Mississippi Ring-necked Snake,
Diadophis punctatus stictogenys

15a   Prairie Ring-necked Snake,
Diadophis punctatus arnyi

15b   Prairie Ring-necked Snake,
Diadophis punctatus arnyi

M. J. Bowerman

16a   Regal Ring-necked Snake,
Diadophis punctatus regalis

W. B. Love

16b   Regal Ring-necked Snake,
Diadophis punctatus regalis

M. J. Bowerman

17a   Ground Snake,
Sonora semiannulata

17b   Ground Snake,
Sonora semiannulata

17c   Ground Snake,
Sonora semiannulata

18   Western Worm Snake,
Carphophis amoenus vermis

19   **Lined Snake,**
Tropidoclonion lineatum

20   **Eastern Garter Snake,**
Thamnophis sirtalis sirtalis

21   Texas Garter Snake,
Thamnophis sirtalis annectens

22   Checkered Garter Snake,
Thamnophis marcianus marcianus

23   Western Plains Garter Snake,
Thamnophis radix haydenii

24a   Eastern Black-necked Garter Snake,
Thamnophis cyrtopsis ocellatus

24b   Eastern Black-necked Garter Snake,
Thamnophis cyrtopsis ocellatus (sub-adult)

25a   Western Black-necked Garter Snake,
Thamnophis cyrtopsis cyrtopsis

D. Duerre

25b Western Black-necked Garter Snake,
Thamnophis cyrtopsis cyrtopsis (sub-adult)

D. Marvel

26 Western Ribbon Snake,
Thamnophis proximus proximus

27   Red-striped Ribbon Snake,
Thamnophis proximus rubrilineatus

28   Gulf Coast Ribbon Snake,
Thamnophis proximus orarius

29   Arid Land Ribbon Snake,
Thamnophis proximus diabolicus

30a   Diamond-backed Water Snake,
Nerodia rhombifer rhombifer

30b Diamond-backed Water Snake,
Nerodia rhombifer rhombifer (juvenile)

31 Yellow-bellied Water Snake,
Nerodia erythrogaster flavigaster

32a Blotched Water Snake,
Nerodia erythrogaster transversa

32b   Blotched Water Snake,
Nerodia erythrogaster transversa

32c   Blotched Water Snake,
Nerodia erythrogaster transversa (juvenile)

33   Broad-banded Water Snake,
Nerodia fasciata confluens

34a   Florida Water Snake,
Nerodia fasciata pictiventris

34b   Florida Water Snake,
Nerodia fasciata pictiventris

35   Gulf Salt Marsh Snake,
Nerodia clarkii clarkii

36 Mississippi Green Water Snake,
Nerodia cyclopion

37 Brazos Water Snake,
Nerodia harteri harteri

38 Concho Water Snake,
Nerodia harteri paucimaculata

39 Graham's Crayfish Snake,
Regina grahamii

40 Gulf Crayfish Snake,
Regina rigida sinicola

41a   Western Mud Snake,
Farancia abacura reinwardtii

41b   Western Mud Snake,
Farancia abacura reinwardtii (ventral display)

42   Texas Patch-nosed Snake,
Salvadora grahamiae lineata

43   Mountain Patch-nosed Snake,
Salvadora grahamiae grahamiae

44 **Big Bend Patch-nosed Snake,**
Salvadora deserticola

45 **Rough Green Snake,**
Opheodrys aestivus

46 **Smooth Green Snake,**
Liochlorophis vernalis

47a   Eastern Coachwhip,
Masticophis flagellum flagellum

47b   Eastern Coachwhip,
Masticophis flagellum flagellum (juvenile)

48a   Western Coachwhip,
Masticophis flagellum testaceus

48b   Western Coachwhip,
Masticophis flagellum testaceus (juvenile)

48c   Western Coachwhip,
Masticophis flagellum testaceus
(red color phase found in
West Texas' Trans-Pecos)

49   Central Texas Whipsnake,
Masticophis taeniatus girardi

50   Desert Striped Whipsnake,
Masticophis taeniatus taeniatus

51a   Schott's Whipsnake,
Masticophis schotti

51b   Schott's Whipsnake,
Masticophis schotti (hatchling)

52 **Ruthven's Whipsnake,**
Masticophis ruthveni

53a **Southern Black Racer,**
Coluber constrictor priapus

53b   Southern Black Racer,
Coluber constrictor priapus (juvenile)

54   Buttermilk Racer,
Coluber constrictor anthicus

55 **Tan Racer,**
Coluber constrictor etheridgei

56 **Eastern Yellow-bellied Racer,**
Coluber constrictor flaviventris

57a Mexican Racer,
Coluber constrictor oaxaca

57b Mexican Racer,
Coluber constrictor oaxaca

57c Mexican Racer,
Coluber constrictor oaxaca (hatchling)

58   Central American Speckled Racer,
Drymobius margaritiferus margaritiferus

59a   Texas Indigo Snake,
Drymarchon corais erebennus

59b   Texas Indigo Snake,
Drymarchon corais erebennus (juvenile)

60a   Eastern Hog-nosed Snake,
Heterodon platirhinos

60b   Eastern Hog-nosed Snake,
Heterodon platirhinos (defensive tail-coiling and
neck-spreading)

60c   Eastern Hog-nosed Snake,
Heterodon platirhinos (black color phase)

Kevin Enge

60d   Eastern Hog-nosed Snake,
Heterodon platirhinos (defensive head/
neck-spreading)

M. J. Bowerman

61   Dusty Hog-nosed Snake,
Heterodon nasicus gloydi (hatchling)

M. J. Bowerman

62   Plains Hog-nosed Snake,
Heterodon nasicus nasicus

63 Mexican Hog-nosed Snake,
Heterodon nasicus kennerlyi

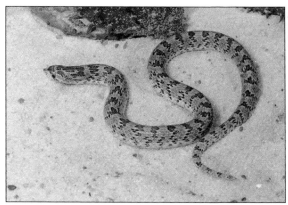

64 Western Hook-nosed Snake,
Gyalopion canum

65 Mexican Hook-nosed Snake,
Ficimia streckeri

M. J. Bowerman

66a Louisiana Pine Snake,
Pituophis ruthveni

W. B. Love

66b Louisiana Pine Snake,
Pituophis ruthveni (juvenile)

L. Jarrell

67a Bullsnake,
Pituophis catenifer sayi (pale, Southwestern
Plains form)

67b **Bullsnake,**
Pituophis catenifer sayi (russet, Central
Plains form)

68 **Sonoran Gopher Snake,**
Pituophis catenifer affinis

69 **Texas Glossy Snake,**
Arizona elegans arenicola

70   **Kansas Glossy Snake,**
Arizona elegans elegans

71   **Painted Desert Glossy Snake,**
Arizona elegans philipi

72a Texas Rat Snake,
Elaphe obsoleta lindheimerii

72b Texas Rat Snake,
Elaphe obsoleta lindheimerii (juvenile)

M. J. Bowerman

73a Baird's Rat Snake,
Elaphe bairdi

M. J. Bowerman

73b Baird's Rat Snake,
Elaphe bairdi (juvenile)

74a   Great Plains Rat Snake,
Elaphe guttata emoryi (East and North Texas
dark phase, large-blotched form)

74b   Great Plains Rat Snake,
Elaphe guttata emoryi (South and West Texas
paler, smaller-blotched form)

75a   Trans-Pecos Rat Snake,
Bogertophis subocularis

75b Trans-Pecos Rat Snake,
Bogertophis subocularis

75c Trans-Pecos Rat Snake,
Bogertophis subocularis (pale or "blonde"
color phase)

75d Trans-Pecos Rat Snake,
Bogertophis subocularis (hatchling)

76   Prairie Kingsnake,
Lampropeltis calligaster calligaster

77   Speckled Kingsnake,
Lampropeltis getula holbrooki

78a   Desert Kingsnake,
Lampropeltis getula splendida

78b **Desert Kingsnake,**
Lampropeltis getula splendida (juvenile)

79 **Louisiana Milk Snake,**
Lampropeltis triangulum amaura

80 **Mexican Milk Snake,**
Lampropeltis triangulum annulata

81a   New Mexico Milk Snake,
Lampropeltis triangulum celaenops

81b   New Mexico Milk Snake,
Lampropeltis triangulum celaenops

81c   New Mexico Milk Snake,
Lampropeltis triangulum celaenops

82a   Central Plains Milk Snake,
Lampropeltis triangulum gentilis

82b   Central Plains Milk Snake,
Lampropeltis triangulum gentilis (juvenile)

83a **Gray-banded Kingsnake,**
Lampropeltis alterna (light-hued, Blair color phase with
orange saddles; central Val Verde County)

83b **Gray-banded Kingsnake,**
Lampropeltis alterna (light-hued, alterna phase without orange saddles;
central Val Verde County)

M.J. Bowerman

83c   Gray-banded Kingsnake,
Lampropeltis alterna (dark-hued Blair color phase;
southern Val Verde County)

M.J. Bowerman

83d   Gray-banded Kingsnake,
Lampropeltis alterna (darker-hued Blair color phase;
central Val Verde County)

83e **Gray-banded Kingsnake,**
Lampropeltis alterna (hatchling; light-hued
alterna color phase; central Val Verde County)

83f **Gray-banded Kingsnake,**
Lampropeltis alterna (light-hued alterna
color phase; western Brewster County)

83g **Gray-banded Kingsnake,**
Lampropeltis alterna (medium-
hued alterna color phase; Jeff Davis
County)

83h **Gray-banded Kingsnake,**
Lampropeltis alterna (dark-hued
color phase, intermediate between
Blair and alterna; southern
Brewster County)

83i **Gray-banded Kingsnake,**
Lampropeltis alterna (light-hued Blair color
phase; western Terrell County)

84a **Northern Scarlet Snake,**
Cemophora coccinea copei

84b   Northern Scarlet Snake,
Cemophora coccinea copei

84c   Northern Scarlet Snake,
Cemophora coccinea copei

85   Texas Scarlet Snake,
Cemophora coccinea lineri

86 Texas Long-nosed Snake,
Rhinocheilus lecontei tessellatus

87a Texas Night Snake,
Hypsiglena torquata jani

87b Texas Night Snake,
Hypsiglena torquata jani (far West Texas
pale phase)

88a   Black-striped Snake,
Coniophanes imperialis imperialis

88b   Black-striped Snake,
Coniophanes imperialis imperialis

89   Northern Cat-eyed Snake,
Leptodeira septentrionalis septentrionalis

90a   Texas Lyre Snake,
Trimorphodon biscutatus vilkinsonii

90b   Texas Lyre Snake,
Trimorphodon biscutatus vilkinsonii

90c   Texas Lyre Snake,
Trimorphodon biscutatus vilkinsonii (hatchling)

91   Texas Coral Snake,
Micrurus fulvius tener

92   Southern Copperhead,
Agkistrodon contortrix contortrix

93a   Broad-banded Copperhead,
Agkistrodon contortrix laticinctus

93b Broad-banded/Southern Copperhead
Intergrade, *Agkistrodon contortrix laticinctus*

94a Trans-Pecos/Broad-banded Copperhead
Intergrade, *Agkistrodon contortrix pictigaster*

94b Trans-Pecos Copperhead,
Agkistrodon contortrix pictigaster

95a **Western Cottonmouth,**
Agkistrodon piscivorus leucostoma

95b **Western Cottonmouth,**
Agkistrodon piscivorus leucostoma (juvenile)

96 **Western Pigmy Rattlesnake,**
Sistrurus miliarius streckeri

97 **Western Massasauga,**
Sistrurus catenatus tergeminus

98 **Desert Massasauga,**
Sistrurus catenatus edwardsii

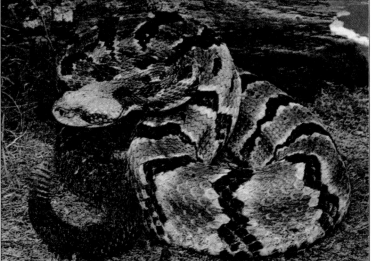

99a **Canebrake Rattlesnake,**
Crotalus horridus atricaudatus (large male, East Texas type)

99b **Canebrake Rattlesnake,**
Crotalus horridus atricaudatus (newborn)

99c **Canebrake Rattlesnake,**
Crotalus horridus atricaudatus

M. J. Bowerman

100a Western Diamond-backed Rattlesnake,
Crotalus atrox

J. H. Evans

100b Western Diamond-backed Rattlesnake,
Crotalus atrox (newborn)

101a Northern Black-tailed Rattlesnake,
Crotalus molossus molossus

101b Northern Black-tailed Rattlesnake,
Crotalus molossus molossus

102a Prairie Rattlesnake,
Crotalus viridis viridis

102b Prairie Rattlesnake,
Crotalus viridis viridis

103a Mojave Rattlesnake,
Crotalus scutulatus scutulatus

103b Mojave Rattlesnake,
Crotalus scutulatus scutulatus

104a Mottled Rock Rattlesnake,
Crotalus lepidus lepidus

104b Mottled Rock Rattlesnake,
Crotalus lepidus lepidus

104c Mottled Rock Rattlesnake,
Crotalus lepidus lepidus

104d Mottled Rock Rattlesnake,
Crotalus lepidus lepidus

105 Banded Rock Rattlesnake,
Crotalus lepidus klauberi

Abundance   Uncommon in much of its extensive East Texas range. *N. f. confluens* is most abundant along the upper Gulf Coast. In the marshes of Chambers and Jefferson counties it is the predominant water snake.

Size   Adult length averages 20 to 30 inches; the record is 45 in.

Habitat   Broad-banded water snakes occur around wooded inland lakes, ponds, and slow-moving bayous. They seem to be most common, though, in coastal wetlands (sometimes among the brackish sloughs behind barrier dunes not far from breaking Gulf surf), as well as in seasonally flooded prairies.

Prey   *Nerodia fasciata* preys primarily on fish, frogs, toads, salamanders, and crayfish taken on both diurnal and nocturnal forays; one predatory technique involves slowly nosing across the bottom of shallow ponds.

Reproduction   Live-bearing. Mating has been reported to occur in April, followed, after 70 to 80 days of gestation, by litters of up to 50 young. Only the largest *Nerodia fasciata* deliver this many offspring, however, and most broods are closer in number to the 15 young—all between 8½ and 9 inches in length and about ⅕ ounce in weight—deposited July 20 by a 32½-inch-long female captured in Smith County.

Coloring/scale form   Ground color is dark yellow to golden brown, usually with less than 20 very wide, dark-edged gray-brown to black dorsolateral crossbands, making this the most handsome of all *Nerodia*. Juveniles are more boldly patterned, while very old individuals may be almost entirely dark brown. A prominent blackish eye stripe, characteristic of all banded water snakes, extends from the eye across the gray-brown cheeks through the last supralabial scale. The dappled yellow venter is marked either with squarish brown blotches or, occasionally, crossbars. There are 21 to 25 midbody rows of dorsal scales and the anal plate is divided.

Similar snakes   No other aquatic snake in this animal's Texas range shares the contrasting colors of its bold dorsolateral patterning.

Behavior   On sunny days, broad-banded water snakes spend hours basking on partially submerged logs or on shoreline tree limbs (like most water snakes, *N. fasciata* is a good climber), but in wintry weather these animals retire to bankside dens or burrow beneath vegetative debris.

Also like other water snakes, *N. fasciata* is a vigorous traveler across dry land. During anurans' breeding season, drawn by the congregations of frogs and toads that gather to deposit their eggs in ditches, temporarily puddle-filled depressions, and flooded prairies, it may venture a mile or more from any permanent body of water.

34 FLORIDA WATER SNAKE
Nerodia fasciata pictiventris

Nonvenomous   Florida water snakes will bite only if molested. Because this animal has a stout body that becomes darker and more heavily proportioned with age (and since individuals often flatten their heads and strike repeatedly in self-defense), large *N. fasciata* are frequently mistaken for the venomous cottonmouth.

Abundance   Far from its normal Florida range, a population of *N. f. pictiventris* has become established in southeastern Cameron County at the mouth of the Rio Grande. Texas' colony of Florida water snakes owes its existence to the live animal business operated in Brownsville by W. A. "Snake" King, which between 1907 and 1956 imported and sold thousands of wild creatures to zoos, circuses, and snake charmers.

To provide food for King's large cobras, hundreds of water snakes were imported from the Southeast and held in ramshackle cages, many of which were torn open by a violent hurricane in September 1933. In addition, rather than maintaining these expendable "food snakes" during slack seasons, King's firm annually released large numbers of southeastern water snakes in the local resacas and parks—from which, it was hoped, they might later be recaptured. That not all King's *N. f. pictiventris* were recovered is evident from the appearance there of newborn Florida water snakes a half century after their predecessors' introduction.

Size   Most adults measure between 22 and 40 inches. The record length is much larger, however, at 62½ inches.

Habitat   Aquatic habitat is generally the margins of lakes, ponds, rivers, and streams. Here, a favored microenvironment is the shelter provided by floating vegetation such as lily pads, hyacinths, and other aquatic plants.

Prey   *Nerodia fasciata* takes a variety of aquatic life, including crayfish, salamanders, frogs, and fish.

Reproduction   Live-bearing. Following a late-winter breeding season, Texas females give birth by June, when young Florida water snakes appear in bankside vegetation. Litters usually number 20 to 30 young measuring 5 to 9 inches long, but as many as 57 offspring can be deposited by the largest females.

Coloring/scale form   The Florida water snake's grayish cheeks are paler than its dark crown and are marked, behind the eye, with a chocolate-colored stripe that extends posteriorly through the last supralabial scale. Otherwise, this animal's dorsal coloring is variable. Its ground color ranges from tan to dark brown, with reddish brown to black crossbands and dark intervening lateral blotches; older individuals may be so heavily pigmented as to appear almost black.

If its back is both variable and nondescript, the Florida water snake's belly is its signature. Named for its painted stomach (*pictum* in Latin), *N. f. pictiventris* is distinguished by the bold—red to dark brown to black—wavy markings that border its yellowish ventral scales. The young have a light beige ground color, with contrasting dark dorsolateral crossbands. There are 23 to 27 rows of dorsal scales at midbody, and the anal plate is generally divided.

Similar snakes   Unlike any water snake, the **cottonmouth (95)** has a triangular slab-sided head, a dark pit midway between its nostril and its vertically slit pupil, and a single row of scales beneath its tail, where water snakes have a double row.

Behavior   See **Broad-banded Water Snake.**

35 GULF SALT MARSH SNAKE
Nerodia clarkii clarkii

Nonvenomous   *Nerodia clarkii clarkii* is named after a student of Smithsonian Secretary S. F. Baird, Lieutenant John Henry Clark, who collected the type specimen; it bites only if harassed.

Abundance   Formerly numerous on the Gulf Coast, *N. c. clarkii* is now less common due to the commercial development and pollution of so much of Texas' tidal wetlands.

Size   Adults are 15 to 30 inches long; the record is 36 in.

Habitat   Salt marsh snakes live in brackish and saltwater estuaries and saltgrass meadows (*N. c. clarkii* is seldom found in freshwater). Favored microhabitats include the shelter of littoral debris, crayfish and fiddler crab burrows, and matted vegetation in the salt grass-lined margins of tidal mud flats.

Prey   *Nerodia clarkii* preys primarily on fish, especially shallows-living species such as killifish and small mullet (which are often taken when they become trapped by the falling tide), as well as crayfish and shrimp.

Reproduction   Live-bearing. Little else is known, but the 9- to 10½-inch-long young which, except for slightly bolder dorsolateral striping, resemble the adults, weigh only ¼ to ⅓ ounce at birth.

Coloring/scale form   On each of the Gulf salt marsh snake's upper sides, a pair of dark brown dorsolateral stripes stands out against the snake's pale grayish ground color. Its venter is reddish brown, with a central row of cream-colored oval blotches often flanked by a lateral row of pale spots. The dorsal scales occur in either 21 or 23 rows at midbody, there is a double row of subcaudal scales, and the anal plate is divided.

Similar snakes   Salt marsh snakes were once classified as a subspecies of the freshwater-living banded water snake, *Nerodia fasciata*. Because salt marsh snakes have morphological differences and rarely enter freshwater, however, they are currently classified as a separate species, but where their ranges overlap, intergraded animals that may exhibit both the pale cheeks and lateral blotches of the **broad-banded water snake (33)** and the longitudinal gray dorsolateral stripes of the salt marsh snakes. **Crayfish snakes (39-40)** have dark, unstriped backs and 19 or fewer rows of dorsal scales.

AQUATIC SNAKES

Behavior   The fluid conservation difficulties faced by marine reptiles such as sea turtles, sea snakes, and, to a lesser extent, brackish water-living species like the salt marsh snakes, are as severe as those confronting desert dwellers. Not only is fresh water absent from most of this animal's natural habitats, but seawater—which is saltier than the snake's body fluids and is ingested along with every prey animal—exerts an osmotic draw on the animal's tissues' electrolyte balance.

Scaly reptilian skin is a good barrier against external dehydration, but because intestinal membranes are salt permeable, if seawater is ingested it pulls the less salty fluid of blood and body tissues into the stomach. Among North American snakes only *N. clarkii* has established itself in an entirely saline niche, a metabolic feat salt marsh snakes manage by drinking rainwater when it is available, sometimes leaving their salty environs to seek fresh water, and at other times swallowing nothing but prey animals whose body fluids are as dilute as their own.

36 MISSISSIPPI GREEN WATER SNAKE

Nerodia cyclopion

Nonvenomous   The Mississippi green water snake is often confused with the venomous cottonmouth—especially since, as a dark-hued, thick-bodied aquatic serpent *N. cyclopion* may flatten its head and body and strike if molested. When handled, many individuals discharge an odorous musk from the cloaca and may also disgorge recently taken prey.

Abundance   From the Louisiana border to Corpus Christi Bay on the Gulf Coast, the Mississippi green water snake is present only as an uncommon species, for its main range is eastward throughout Louisiana and north up the Mississippi River Valley as far as southern Illinois.

Size   Most adults measure between 30 and 45 inches; the record is 50 in.

Habitat   For the most part, the Mississippi green water snake inhabits inundated lowland forest and tree-lined sloughs and is scarce in open estuarine milieus.

Prey   Robert H. Mount reports that in Alabama "fish appear to be by far the most important food. Amphibians are eaten infrequently."

Green water snake

Other water snakes

Reproduction   Live-bearing. Breeding occurs from April to June, with litters being deposited between late June and early September. These average 15 to 25 offspring, although the largest females may give birth to many more young. Unlike the adults, the 6- to 8-inch-long newborns are distinctly spotted and crossbarred.

Coloring/scale form   The dorsum is olive green, marked with both dark and pale speckling among younger animals; it is more darkly pebbled among older adults. The definitive characteristic of *Nerodia cyclopion*, however, is the row of small subocular scales that separates the lower edge of its eye from its supralabial scales.

The venter of the Mississippi green water snake is also distinctive. Its pale yellowish forebelly darkens posteriorly to gray, where it becomes heavily infused with yellow half-moons. This animal's dorsal scales occur in 27 to 29 rows at midbody and its anal plate is divided.

Similar snakes   In Texas, **all other water snakes** lack subocular scales.

Behavior   Mississippi green water snakes are occasionally seen during the day basking at the water's edge, but this species is largely a nocturnal forager most often observed—both in the water and on shore—by spotlighting after dark.

37 BRAZOS WATER SNAKE
Nerodia harteri harteri

Nonvenomous   Brazos water snakes will nip only if seized or molested.

Abundance   Threatened. **Federally protected, and protected by the state of Texas**. *Nerodia harteri* is the only species of snake unique to Texas, and while it is restricted in range, it is not close to extinction.

Size   Most adults measure 16 to 32 inches; the record is just over 35 in.

Habitat   *Nerodia harteri* typically hides under stones in shallow water or shelters beneath flat, bankside rocks. Until the late 1980s this species had almost never been reported from any environment other than stony-bottomed shallows located along the upper Brazos River and its tributaries. This habitat has always been limited, and with long stretches of the river now planned for deepwater reservoir impoundments, both *Nerodia harteri harteri* and its subspecies, the Concho water snake, *Nerodia harteri paucimaculata*, were thought to be in danger of extinction.

The ecological attention this situation received ultimately resulted in an intensive investigation by James Dixon, Jim Mueller, and others of Texas A&M University. When Dixon's 5-year-long study of both races of *N. harteri* appeared in 1992, it held that, although only a few thousand individuals of both races had been thought to exist, their numbers were probably far greater. Both Brazos and Concho water snakes—although perhaps originally almost exclusively riffle dwellers—had apparently adapted to life in the newly constructed lakes that replaced much of their original shallow streambed habitat, and the Brazos race is now found along rocky shorelines in both Lake Granbury and Possum Kingdom Lake.

Prey   The opportunity to seize small fish as they become momentarily vulnerable in rocky riffles has historically been the primary factor determining the Brazos water snake's microhabitat. How it manages, over long periods, to forage and evade predation and human intrusion in environments far removed from these shallow rapids remains to be seen.

Reproduction   Live-bearing. The September and early October parturition of 4 females captured while gravid resulted in the birth of litters numbering 7 to 22 young that measured 7¼ to 9 inches in length.

Coloring scale/form   The type specimen of *N. h. harteri*—captured in 1940 by veteran Palo Pinto County reptile fancier Phillip "Snakey" Harter—is defined by its medium brown vertebral stripe, flanked by a double row of brown spots (each row has 58 to 65 spots, more than any other indigenous water snake). The ground color is tan, the throat is pale yellow, and the venter carrot-colored, with the ends of each ventral scale spotted or darkened. The posterior chin shields are separated by 2 rows of small scales, the dorsal scales occur in 21 to 25 (usually 23) midbody rows, and the anal plate is divided.

Similar snakes   The subspecies **Concho water snake (38)** has slightly less prominent ventral markings and a single row of small scales between its posterior underchin shields.

Behavior   *Nerodia harteri* is a frequently diurnal forager whose exposed streambed habitat requires it to hide under submerged rocks from predators—where it can remain without breathing for more than an hour—and to move fast when necessary. If discovered in these hiding places, Harter's water snakes typically streak diagonally downstream toward the opposite bank.

38 CONCHO WATER SNAKE
Nerodia harteri paucimaculata

Nonvenomous   See **Brazos Water Snake.**

Abundance   Endangered. Federally protected and protected by the state of Texas. The only snake species unique to Texas, *Nerodia harteri* has always been restricted in range, with the Concho water snake inhabiting even narrower geographic boundaries than its subspecies, the Brazos water snake.

Recently, these boundaries have been narrowed still further. Since 1968, nearly half the Concho water snake's original streambed-shallows home has been inundated by the construction of Spence Reservoir in Coke County. This left just 69 miles of the Concho water snake's Concho and upper Colorado River habitat, where some 41 riffle sites in Tom Green, Concho, Coleman, and McCulloch counties were thought to contain almost the entire world population of an estimated 330 to 600 Concho water snakes. The impending construction of Stacy Dam was scheduled to flood much of this remaining habitat and severely cut downstream flow during dry weather, with the result that

Concho water snakes were expected to be confined to less than 22 miles of sparsely riffled and sometimes dried-up streambed—a remnant environment also vulnerable to development because these shallows are the only spots to build low-water road crossings. Yet a 1992 study by James Dixon of Texas A&M University indicates that both the Brazos and Concho water snake races may have successfully adapted to the newly constructed lakes that have replaced much of their streambed habitat, for Concho water snakes are now found along rocky portions of the banks of Lakes Spence, Ivy, and other impoundments, and are reportedly under consideration for declassification as a threatened animal.

Size　Adult length ranges from 16 to 32 in.

Habitat　Some 135 miles southwest of the Brazos River headwaters where *N. h. harteri* is found, the same sort of fast-flowing upper Colorado and Concho river riffles are home to Texas' even more range-restricted, endemic race of the Harter's water snake, *N. h. paucimaculata* (still waters in this area are inhabited by the quite different blotched water snake, *N. e. transversa*).

Prey　See **Brazos Water Snake.**

Reproduction　Live-bearing. See **Brazos Water Snake.**

Coloring scale/form　Not described until 20 years after its Brazos subspecies, the Concho water snake has a paler dorsum and less conspicuous ventral spots—hence its designation *paucimaculata*, or "sparsely spotted." A single row of small scales separates its posterior underchin shields, its dorsal scales occur in 21 to 25 (usually 23) rows, and its anal plate is divided.

Similar snakes　The subspecies **Brazos water snake (37)** has a double row of small scales between its underchin shields. The **blotched water snake (32)** has vertebral crossbars and dark lateral blocks.

Behavior　See **Brazos Water Snake.**

Crayfish Snakes
Genus *Regina*

Graham's Crayfish Snake, *Regina grahamii*
Gulf Crayfish Snake, *Regina rigida sinicola*

Part of the colubrine subfamily *Natricinae*, the genus *Regina* contains four species; all have 19 midbody rows of dorsal scales and a divided anal plate, while *R. rigida* and *R. grahamii* have keeled scales. The Gulf crayfish snake is a comparatively stout, shiny serpent; the Graham's crayfish snake is rather slender and dull-scaled.

Both these *Regina* species are found in aquatic milieus but often leave the water to bask and to hide beneath shoreline litter and rocks, and both have developed a strong predatory adaptation to feeding on crayfish. The Graham's crayfish snake is a specialist predator on soft-shelled (freshly molted) crayfish, while the Gulf crayfish snake is less discriminating, taking both hard- and soft-shelled crayfish. (Studies have recently disclosed that a component in the saliva of crayfish snakes renders their prey immobile and thus easily swallowed.)

39 GRAHAM'S CRAYFISH SNAKE
Regina grahamii

Nonvenomous   This slender, unaggressive snake seldom if ever bites human beings, even if it is handled.

Abundance   Uncommon within a Texas range that stretches from arid mesquite brushland along the Nueces River to the forested wetlands of Louisiana.

Size   Small and slender, most adult Graham's crayfish snakes measure only 18 to 30 inches in length; their maximum length is 47 inches.

Habitat   *Regina grahamii* inhabits sloughs, rice field irrigation ditches, and, where crayfish are abundant, muddy bottomland pastures. The aquifer-fed headwaters of rivers emerging from Texas' Balcones Fault constitute another habitat—Graham's crayfish snakes are common in the headwaters of the San Antonio River—while in the westernmost part of its range, *R. grahamii* occupies riparian valleys running through agricultural fields, dry prairie, and even thorn desert.

Prey   The first to report on this animal's diet was John K. Strecker (1926), who wrote that *Regina grahamii* "feeds largely on crayfish and a small species of fresh-water prawn." Recent studies have found that the stomachs of Graham's crayfish snakes contain only freshly molted crayfish, the scent of which elicits instinctual feeding behavior among neonates.

Reproduction   Live-bearing. Lawrence Curtis and R. J. Hall (1949) first observed courtship, which occurs early in May, at night, in the water. At this time, a group of pheromone-drawn male Graham's crayfish snakes may entwine themselves around a single female, forming a compact mass within which only one copulation evidently occurs. More often, however, breeding pairs are solitary, floating wrapped together, their tails hanging downward.

Deposited in August and September, recorded litters have ranged from 6 to 39 (26 broods averaged just over 17 young, 7 to 9½ inches in length). Strecker also reported finding 4 or 5 newborns sheltering together under flat rocks at the water's edge. Males may breed as early as their second spring, but females do not do so until their third year.

Coloring scale/form   Among *Regina grahamii* the back and upper sides are dark grayish brown, except for a pale vertebral line. A wide, yellowish tan lateral stripe—edged by a serrated black seam—occupies the first three scale rows above this animal's cream to yellowish belly, where a midventral row of brown dots is better defined toward its tail; the belly's distal margin is delineated by a line of angular black spots. The 19 midbody rows of dorsal scales are keeled, and the anal plate is divided.

Similar snakes   The **Gulf crayfish snake** (40) has a shiny, chocolate-colored back and a venter marked with a double row of dark brown crescents. The **Gulf salt marsh snake** (35) has a gray-striped back and sides, at least 21 rows of dorsal scales, and a dark venter whose midline bears a row of cream-colored ovals.

Behavior   Named for soldier, engineer, and naturalist James Duncan Graham, a member of the 1852–1853 Mexican Border Survey that first described much of Texas' herpetofauna, *Regina grahamii* forages at night during the summer months but engages in more crepuscular activity in spring and fall. Because of its reclusive temperament, the Graham's crayfish snake is able to subsist in urban park ponds where its presence is often something of a surprise. On rainy spring nights Graham's crayfish snakes are sometimes found crawling across suburban lawns in Waco, Texas—the only time *R. grahamii* is ever seen in this area.

40 GULF CRAYFISH SNAKE
Regina rigida sinicola

Nonvenomous   Like all crayfish snakes, this shy little reptile seldom bites human beings even if it is handled.

Abundance   Probably uncommon. Certainly *Regina rigida sinicola* is not often or easily found throughout most of its two broad ranges. The more westerly of these includes eastern Texas.

Size   Adults average 20 inches in length; the maximum size recorded for *R. r. sinicola* is 31½ in.

Habitat   The Gulf crayfish snake seems to be found most often in cypress sloughs and waterways through bottomland forest. Yet, in places where crayfish are common, it also occurs—in open country—in irrigation ditches, wet marl prairies, and muddy pastures.

Prey   Like other crayfish snakes, *Regina rigida sinicola* preys almost entirely on crayfish; the young, however, are reported to also feed on dragonfly nymphs as well as freshly molted crustaceans—the scent of which triggers a pronounced feeding response even among predatorily naive newborns.

Reproduction   Live-bearing. Eleven newborns measured between 7 and 8½ inches in length.

Coloring/scale form   The Gulf crayfish snake's back is shiny chocolate brown, sometimes with dimly darker-striped sides above a yellowish tan lateral stripe (split by a thin black seam) that occupies the first and second scale rows above its belly line. Among *R. r. sinicola* the dorsal scales are keeled and there are two prefrontal scales per side. Both its labial scales and the unpatterned sides of its throat are yellowish, and its pale yellow venter (which among females has 55 or more subcaudal scales, 63 or more among males) is

AQUATIC SNAKES

marked with a double row of rearward-arced dark crescents that form a single line beneath its chin and tail.

Similar snakes   The yellowish lateral band of the **Graham's crayfish snake (39)** reaches up its sides three scale rows above the belly line, where it is separated from the grayish brown back by a faintly serrated dark horizontal line. The Graham's crayfish snake's belly also bears, throughout its length, only a single row of small midventral spots.

Behavior   Crayfish snakes are predominantly nocturnal, although Paul E. Moler of the Florida Game and Fresh Water Fish Commission has observed diurnal foraging in this species. *R. r. sinicola* forages mainly between March and early November but even during this time it is almost never observed except during drainage ditch excavation or at night after heavy rain. Its predators can include giant salamanders. One 40-inch-long two-toed amphiuma trapped by Florida Game and Fresh Water Fish Commission biologist Kevin Enge disgorged a large crayfish snake.

Mud and Rainbow Snakes
Genus *Farancia*

Western Mud Snake, *Farancia abacura reinwardtii*

The genus *Farancia* is contained in the rear-fanged, mildly venomed colubrine subfamily *Xenodontinae*. The two species in this genus—*F. abacura* and *F. erytrogramma*—are very specialized reptiles with moderately thick girths and heavy necks, rather small heads, and tails that terminate in a spine-like tip. Their shiny black ground-colored backs and upper sides contrast sharply with their bright red or carmine bellies (the mud snakes are carmine-banded only along their lower sides while the rainbow snakes are dorsolaterally striped and speckled with red and pink flecks). The predominantly smooth scales of both species are arranged in 19 midbody rows, and the anal plate of both species is usually divided.

These specialized bodies are the mud snakes' adaptation to swampy or entirely aquatic environments where, when adult, both species are narrowly focused predators that feed mostly on large salamanders, although some captives accept frogs.

Female mud snakes can attain more than 5 feet in length (males are noticeably smaller), and when gravid, to shelter their eggs they dig burrows in the soil or beneath vegetative debris. These cavities are often comparatively sizable, for female mud snakes typically coil atop their large clutches during the eggs' entire incubation period.

41 WESTERN MUD SNAKE
Farancia abacura reinwardtii

Nonvenomous   This big, surprisingly docile serpent seems entirely unwilling to bite, even when first handled in the field.

Abundance   Common but seldom seen, in suitable habitat the western mud snake occurs sporadically throughout its broad range. This animal was formerly abundant in most marshes just inland from the Texas and Louisiana coasts, but the last 20 years' industrialization of this area has reduced the western mud snake's numbers dramatically. Along Highway 87 in Chambers and Jefferson counties, however, *F. a. reinwardtii* is still numerous in roadside bar ditches and luetic grassland a few hundred yards behind the Gulf beaches.

Elsewhere in its range this animal is seen less often. Scattered populations occur throughout inland East Texas (including one in Panola County at the north end of Toledo Bend Reservoir). Here, despite mud snakes' secretive, aquatic/burrowing habits they can be among the most numerous serpents seen crossing low-lying roads on rainy spring nights.

Size   Adult western mud snakes may reach over 6 feet in length—most measure between 30 and 48 inches—although at hatching they average a comparatively tiny 6¾ in.

Habitat   *Farancia abacura reinwardtii* may be found in and around most freshwater environments in eastern Texas, but it seems to especially favor turbid bodies of water with swampy margins and profuse aquatic vegetation. Marshes of all kinds are usually good mud snake habitat, while these reptiles also sometimes occupy salt grass prairie; one microhabitat is the underside of logs and debris on hummocks in flooded bottomland forest.

Prey   A prey-specific predator, *F. a. reinwardtii* has a heavily muscled neck, jaws, and trunk adapted to overpowering the giant salamanders—sirens and amphiuma—that are its principal prey. (Its horny tail tip may have evolved to help the mud snake overcome these vigorous, difficult-to-hold animals by giving it a point of purchase on the amphibians' slippery sides.) Captives also rarely accept other salamanders, frogs, eels, or fish as food.

Reproduction   Egg-laying. Western mud snakes lay their eggs during July and August, and do so prolifically: one clutch numbered 60, another 104. The eggs are parchmentlike in texture and adherent, forming a glued-together mass. They are typically deposited in a moist subsurface cavity, usually excavated in sandy soil, inside which the female may remain coiled about her clutch throughout its 8- to 12-week incubation period, presumably so that her respiration might help maintain the chamber's humidity.

At least five mud snake nests, one in northern Florida and four in Louisiana, have been located within the nests of American alligators. The big piles of composting vegetation that alligators amass to warm their eggs with the heat of decay also benefit the eggs of *Farancia abacura*—whose incubation period

AQUATIC SNAKES

is similar to that of alligator eggs. Young mud snakes also benefit from this commensal nesting because female alligators defend their nests from raccoons and other carnivores, while the elevation of their nest mounds minimizes the chance of damage by flooding.

Coloring/scale form   Western mud snakes may live on wet soil, but they are anything but muddy in color. Their backs and upper sides are glossy blue-black, marked along the belly line with 52 or fewer round-topped, reddish pink blotches; among juveniles, these carmine ventral blotches extend up the sides as far as the lower back. The belly has a bright red and black checkerboard pattern that, beneath the tail, becomes a series of similar-hued crossbands, while the dorsal scales are smooth except for the vertebral rows above the vent, where they may be keeled. There is no preocular scale, the terminal caudal scale is enlarged and hardened into a point, and the anal plate is usually divided.

Similar snakes   No other indigenous serpent bears the mud snake's bold and distinctive color pattern. The **western cottonmouth (95)** is brownish or black-ish gray above, lacks reddish scallops along its lower sides, and has an angular, slab-sided head characterized by sunken facial pits and vertical pupils.

Behavior   Western mud snakes are aquatic, nocturnal animals, often bur-rowers but never climbers. The horny tail tip (which captured *F. a. reinwardtii* typically press against the captor's hands), besides helping grip slippery prey may have evolved to offer these creatures a point of purchase for traction in viscous mud.

Patch-nosed Snakes
Genus *Salvadora*

Texas Patch-nosed Snake, *Salvadora grahamiae lineata*
Mountain Patch-nosed Snake, *Salvadora grahamiae grahamiae*
Big Bend Patch-nosed Snake, *Salvadora deserticola*

The genus *Salvadora* is a part of the colubrine subfamily *Colubridae*. It con-tains two species of moderate-size-, primarily terrestrial oviparous snakes characterized by an enlarged, free-edged, wraparound rostral scale, 17 mid-body rows of smooth dorsolateral scales (occasionally weakly keeled along the posterior back), and a divided anal plate. Both species are sandy brown to buff in dorsolateral ground color, with varying combinations of dark and light vertebral and lateral striping (the middorsal area is the most richly hued, and is separated from the lighter sides by prominent dark stripes). The ven-ter is whitish but may be clouded with darker pigment.

Salvadora are swift-moving relatives of the racers (*Coluber constrictor*), and like them are active throughout the day even in the hottest weather, rely-
ing on their acute vision both for hunting and for quickly noting potential

danger. Lizards, which patch-nosed snakes sometimes pursue up into shrubs, are these reptiles' primary prey, but amphibians, smaller snakes, and nestling rodents are also taken opportunistically.

42 TEXAS PATCH-NOSED SNAKE
Salvadora grahamiae lineata

Nonvenomous   See **Mountain Patch-nosed Snake.**

Abundance   Common. In central and southern Texas *S. g. lineata* can occur in almost every well-vegetated, rural terrestrial habitat. It is probably most abundant, however, in the interspersed open woods and farmland of the state's central cross-timbers.

Size   Most adults are between 20 and 34 inches long; the author has seen many dozens of these animals, but never one approaching the record size of nearly 4 feet.

Habitat   The Texas patch-nosed snake's most likely microhabitat is the shelter it finds beneath flat rocks and fallen sheet metal/building materials left in overgrown pastureland and along woodland/meadow boundaries. *Salvadora grahamiae lineata* occupies a similar habitat in the oak–juniper savannahs of Texas' Edwards Plateau, while it is present, but less abundant, in the thorn brush ecosystem of the Rio Grande Valley.

Prey   As captives, most Texas patch-nosed snakes prefer lizard prey. Yet, from the stomach contents of wild individuals, mice, frogs, smaller snakes, and reptile eggs—the latter presumably rooted from buried nest cavities with the aid of the enlarged rostral scale at the tip of the snake's snout—are also reported.

Reproduction   Egg-laying. Reproduction was first recorded by Roger Conant in 1940: a Palo Pinto County female laid 10 adhesive-shelled yellowish white eggs 1⅛ inches in length and ⅝ inch in diameter on April 1—a time when many other serpents in central Texas have just begun courtship. Two other clutches of 5 and 7 eggs were deposited during the first week in May by a pair of Travis County females; these hatched 88 days later into young slightly paler than the adults, with whitish sides. The neonates were very active, vibrating their tails and striking excitedly about.

Coloring/scale form   As an adult, *S. g. lineata* has a blackish brown back split by a prominent, golden yellow stripe along the spine which occupies the vertebral scale row plus half of each adjacent row. The Texas patch-nosed snake's sides are buff to olive-brown, bordered below by a thin brown line: the *lineata* of its Latin name. On the snake's foreparts, this line seams the third row of scales above its belly; on its posterior trunk, the line occupies the second lateral row of scales above the belly. Aberrant color morphs also occur, however: east of Harlingen, Craig McIntyre photographed an amelanistic Texas patch-nosed snake that had a light brown back instead of black, yet its pale longitudinal stripes resembled those of other patch-nosed snakes. An enlarged, slightly elevated rostral scale tips this animal's snout like a patch, giving it its common name. (The Latin species name, *grahamiae*, refers to James Duncan Graham, a naturalist member of the 1852–1853 Mexican Border Survey that first systematically cataloged much of the southwest's herpetofauna.) The 17 midbody rows of dorsal scales are smooth, there are 7 or sometimes 8 upper labial scales, and the anal plate is divided.

Similar snakes   In northeastern Terrell County the Texas patch-nose begins to intergrade with its western subspecies, the **mountain patch-nosed snake** (**43**). This race has pastel gray to pinkish sides, a yellow to faintly peach-hued vertebral stripe 3 scale rows in width, and usually 8 upper labial scales. **Garter** and **ribbon snakes** (**20-29**) have darker backs and sides, lack a flat, rostral-scaled snout and have at least 19 midbody rows of keeled dorsal scales and an undivided anal plate.

Behavior   Despite its enlarged rostral *S. g. lineata* is not a fossorial animal: rather than diving into a hole when flushed from hiding, this fast-moving serpent typically streaks away into brush or tall grass. Partly because its diurnal orientation means it is abroad during the warmest part of the diel cycle, the Texas patch-nosed snake seems to be active in unusually cool weather: these animals forage in central Texas as late as mid-December and, after brief brumation, as early as mid-February.

43 MOUNTAIN PATCH-NOSED SNAKE
Salvadora grahamiae grahamiae

Nonvenomous   The upper rear teeth of *Salvadora grahamiae* are slightly enlarged, a characteristic of many colubrids whose saliva is somewhat toxic to their small prey, but this beautiful little animal poses no danger to humans. In the field, when first handled, mountain patch-nosed snakes may flail about and even give a single panicky nip. If treated gently, however, they calm down quickly and are unlikely to bite again.

Abundance   Common. Widely distributed throughout its Trans-Pecos range, in suitable habitat *S. g. grahamiae* occurs from low-lying desert floor to montane elevations over 7,000 feet.

Size   Slightly smaller than the closely related Texas patch-nose, adult *S. g. grahamiae* usually measure 18 to 30 inches in length. The record is 37½ in.

Habitat   Named for James Duncan Graham, astronomer and biological field collector on the 1852–1853 Mexican Border Survey, *S. g. grahamiae* occupies a variety of stony and/or brushy northern Chihuahuan Desert habitats. In the stony desert west of the Devil's River, it is sometimes discovered in the heart-root cavities of decaying agaves and sotol, or beneath yucca logs. Near the top of Guadalupe Peak the author has also found it in alligator juniper–dwarf oak woodland.

Prey   This snake's primary prey is lizards, especially whip-tails, but smaller serpents, reptile eggs, and mice are also eaten; its lightly armored snout is used to press into the subsurface nooks where these creatures sometimes shelter, as well as to dig for buried lizard eggs.

Reproduction   Egg-laying. See **Texas Patch-nosed Snake.**

Coloring/scale form   The mountain patch-nosed snake's delicate form and subtle coloring make it one of the most attractive reptiles in North America. Its broad (usually 3 full scale rows in width), yellow to faintly peach-hued vertebral stripe is flanked by contrasting brownish black stripes that set off its silvery tan to pinkish beige sides. An enlarged rostral scale overlaps its adjacent nasal scales and folds back over the snout, giving the patch-nose its distinctive squared-off profile as well as its common name. There are usually 8 upper labial scales, and the posterior chin shields beneath its jaw either touch or are separated by a single small scale.

Similar snakes   The more easterly ranging subspecies **Texas patch-nosed snake (42)** has a narrower, more richly hued vertebral line. This is bordered by a pair of wider, blackish brown dorsolateral stripes. Its buff-colored sides are split by a thin dark seam along the third scale row above its belly. A separate species, the **Big Bend patch-nosed snake (44),** is distinguished by a line of dark hash marks along the fourth lateral scale row above its peach-colored venter, by its 9 upper labial scales, and by the 2 or 3 small scales that separate its posterior underchin shields.

Behavior   Quick and elusive in brush or near cover, the mountain patch-nose must still rely on ambush to obtain most of its extremely fast-moving prey. This may entail a deliberate process of advancing, in a series of short glides, each time its lizard quarry becomes preoccupied with its own foraging. Once in striking range, the author saw a medium-sized *S. g. grahamiae* seize a crevice spiny lizard larger than its own diameter, then hang on doggedly as its victim dragged it back and forth. After half an hour the patch-nose had worked its way along the tiring lacertilian's body to its snout where, by stretching its delicate head and jaws over the larger skull of the lizard, the patch-nose somehow squeezed its bulky prey into its throat.

44 BIG BEND PATCH-NOSED SNAKE

Salvadora deserticola

Nonvenomous   Slender, delicate *Salvadora deserticola* generally does not bite even when first handled in the field.

Abundance   This predominantly Mexican-ranging reptile is somewhat uncommon within its restricted range northeast of the Rio Grande from El Paso to Big Bend.

Size   A majority of adults are 20 to 45 inches in length.

Habitat   The Big Bend patch-nose inhabits low-lying shrub desert, tobosa/grama grassland, and catclaw/creosote/blackbrush flats, as well as a variety of broken upland terrain. One individual was found by the author in a cholla/sotol/alligator juniper savannah at over 5,000 feet elevation.

Prey   Lizards, snakes, reptile eggs, and small rodents are reported as the primary prey of *S. deserticola*—all but the latter thought to be often rooted from sand-filled depressions with the aid of its enlarged rostral scale.

Reproduction   Egg-laying. Little is known, but reproduction may be similar to that of the single *Salvadora* species, the mountain patch-nosed snake, which shares the Big Bend patch-nosed snake's range.

Coloring/scale form   This attractive serpent has yellowish gray sides separated from its wide, peach-colored dorsal stripe by a flanking pair of dark brown dorsolateral stripes. Its sandy beige sides are marked with a line of dark-hued hash marks along the fourth scale row above its pinkish orange venter. The Big Bend patch-nosed snake's enlarged rostral scale (which overlaps the adjacent nasal scales) covers the tip of the snout in a distinctive flat patch from which its common name is derived. Its lips and throat are unmarked white—there are 9 upper labial scales, and either 2 or 3 small scales separate its posterior underchin shields.

Underchin: Texas and mountain patch-nosed snakes   *Underchin: Big Bend patch-nosed snake*

Similar snakes   The **mountain patch-nosed snake (43)** has 8 upper labial scales and posterior underchin shields that either touch or are separated by a single scale.

Behavior   Like many diurnal, desert-living serpents, the Big Bend patch-nose is inclined to midday basking in cool weather: Sherman Minton (1959) found it abroad as early as March 6 in Brewster County. Later in the year, during the heat of July, August, and September, *S. deserticola* adopts a predominantly crepuscular activity pattern but (unlike many arid terrain snakes which retire into subsurface aestivation during summer) it remains abroad. At this time it often forages in the more moist environments of riparian canyons, however, or even frequents irrigated areas because diurnal hunters like patch-nosed snakes transpire more water than nocturnal/fossorial serpents.

Its daylight hunting also makes *S. deserticola* susceptible to avian predation. Minton found the remains of a Big Bend patch-nose in the nest of a red-tailed hawk, and a roadrunner has been photographed offering one of these slender colubrids to its fledglings.

Green Snakes
Genus *Liochlorophis** and *Opheodrys*

*The smooth green snake has recently been placed by systematists in the genus *Liochlorophis*.

Smooth Green Snake, *Liochlorophis vernalis*

Rough Green Snake, *Opheodrys aestivus*

Both *Liochlorophis* ("smooth green snake" in Greek) and *opheodrys* (also Greek, for "forest-living snake") are members of the colubrine subfamily *Colubrinae*. While distantly related, the members of these two oviparous genera are rather different in morphology—the scales of the rough green snake are keeled and arranged in 17 midbody dorsolateral rows; those of the smooth green snake are smooth and set in 15 rows—as well as in both habitat and lifestyle. (The anal plate of both is divided, however.)

As predators, *Liochlorophis* and *Opheodrys* share the acute vision of insect hunters, have similar slender bodies, and display almost the same uniquely bright green dorsolateral and whitish or yellow-green ventral coloring. Yet the rough green snake is an agile arborealist that feeds on caterpillars, crickets, and spiders while the smooth green snake ascends branches far less readily than the rough green snake and is almost always found on the ground, where it hunts insects and spiders and shelters beneath surface debris such as matted vegetation, flat rocks, and discarded boards and newspapers.

45 ROUGH GREEN SNAKE
Opheodrys aestivus

Nonvenomous   The rough green snake (which is also known in the South as "vine snake," a tropical family to which it is not related) is unlikely to bite humans.

Abundance   Abundant. With the exception of the higher elevations of the Appalachians, *Opheodrys aestivus* is widespread throughout the southeastern two-thirds of the United States, where, in moist, heavily forested woodlands its numbers may be so high that the collective biomass of *Opheodrys aestivus* rivals that of any other vertebrate. Unique to Texas is the rough green snake population living in the xeric oak woodland of Val Verde and northeastern Terrell counties.

Size   Adults average 22 to 32 inches; the record is 45⅝ in.

Habitat   Thickly foliaged trees and shrubs are preferred environment because their closely spaced stems allow *O. aestivus* to move about easily, well off the ground. Within this milieu the thickest vegetation occurs along the sunlit edges of woods bordering the open space of ponds, meadows, and dirt roads, and this small reptile's abundance here makes it so easy to capture that thousands (almost all of which immediately died) were taken every year for the pet trade.

Prey   Plucked from leaves and stems, insects make up most of the rough green snake's prey. In one Arkansas study, 85 percent of its diet consisted of caterpillars, spiders, grasshoppers, crickets, and odonates. Of these, caterpillars, as the preferred food, are positively selected for since they constituted more than twice as large a percentage of the total as their prevalence in the sample area would suggest. See **Smooth Green Snake.**

Reproduction   Egg-laying. Spring and summer rainfall influences reproduction among rough green snakes because the greater abundance of insect prey available in wet years increases females' body fat and thus their egg-laying capacity. Four to six eggs is the norm in most years, but during a wet summer a clutch of 15 *O. aestivus* eggs was taken from a central Texas stone wall by Tim Cole, a fact that indicates commensal egg deposition by more than one female. On July 2 these eggs hatched into 8-inch-long young, all of which immediately began feeding on small crickets.

Rainfall enhances the survival of such clutches—most of which are laid in plant litter between April and July—since the small size of the rough green snake's eggs makes them particularly prone to desiccation. The slender, grayish hatchlings can reach adult size in a year but do not breed until their second spring.

Coloring/scale form   Often called "grass snake," emerald-bodied *O. aestivus* is color-adapted, instead, to the verdant hue of tree leaves. (After death, these little snakes soon turn a dull blue.) The lips, chin, and belly are yellow, and the nostril lies across the juncture of adjacent nasal scales. The keeled dorsal scales are arranged in 17 rows at midbody.

Similar snakes   The **smooth green snake (46)** shares only a small amount of territory with the more southerly ranging rough green; it has 15 rows of smooth dorsal scales. The **eastern yellow-bellied racer (56)** is a much more robust, gray-green serpent with smooth scales; each of its nostrils is centered in a single nasal plate.

Behavior   Entirely diurnal, slow-moving, unwary *O. aestivus* depends entirely on its bright, leaf-green color for camouflage, and when approached it may sway with the wind to match the movement of surrounding foliage. Occasionally, a rough green snake may also indulge in a brief, mouth-gaping defensive display, but these little animals are very reluctant to bite.

During warm weather this diurnal forager sleeps at night in a loop draped along a branch, its head resting either on the branch or on a body coil. Here, its luminous venter reflects the beam of a flashlight so clearly that in places where rough green snakes are numerous they are easily found by scanning vegetation along forest roads. Despite the Latin name *aestivus*, or "summer," rough green snakes are abroad well into cool autumn weather as long as foliage remains on the trees. Later in the year, *O. aestivus* spends the leafless months below ground where, in hardened clay several inches beneath the surface, Robert Webb reported finding one brumating Oklahoma individual.

46 SMOOTH GREEN SNAKE
Liochlorophis vernalis

Nonvenomous   This small snake is harmless to humans.

Abundance   Common in much of its range, yet **threatened** in some areas and **protected by the state of Texas.** This little snake remains common in places, but in most of its range it has completely disappeared from areas where it was formerly abundant. The reason is not known, but its abrupt decline may be due partly to the increasingly mechanized cultivation of the crop fields which have replaced its original meadowland habitat. More likely, this little snake's dwindling numbers parallel the decline of many other insect-eating animals whose prey is now saturated with pesticides. (Largely because of this, like a drying puddle shrinking into disparate droplets, the smooth green snake's formerly broad range has fragmented into numerous small, disjunctive pockets scattered throughout eastern and central North America.)

One of these isolated populations may still occupy Texas's upper coastal plain, where *L. vernalis* is known from fewer than 10 specimens, all collected in Austin, Chambers, Harris, and Matagorda county grasslands. (Arnold Gorman of the Florida State Museum, an expert on this species, has suggested that rather than constituting a natural population these individuals may have been escaped captives, although that would seem to be less likely than their being a relict group still living in a pocket of what was once a much broader range.)

Size   Most adults are 12 to 15 inches long; the record is 26 in.

Habitat   In the northern and western portions of its territory *L. vernalis* is a resident of grassy meadows—especially those on the periphery of open woodland. It is less often found in damp forest, shrubby clearings, and overgrown orchards, where smooth green snakes are likely to hide beneath boards, newspapers, and other human-generated debris, especially when preparing to shed. Although able to climb, this species is less likely to do so than the predominantly arboreal rough green snake.

Prey   Almost exclusively sight hunters, smooth green snakes are active only during daylight, foraging through dense grass and occasionally climbing into low bushes where John MacGregor has seen as many as 10 Kentucky individuals basking in close proximity. Like the similarly sight-hunting rough green snake, the smooth green snake has a slightly concave channel lining each side of its snout just ahead of its eye. This enhances its forward vision and even gives each eye a small zone of overlapping stereoscopic vision that presumably provides a window of depth perception which helps *L .vernalis* more accurately gauge the distance to its quick-moving insect prey. Nevertheless, unlike the more agile tree- and shrub-living rough green snake, the smooth green species typically forages more deliberately along the ground, searching for grass-living insects such as crickets, grasshoppers, caterpillars, and other larvae.

GREEN SNAKES

Reproduction   Egg-laying. During the summer months up to 12 (usually 3 to 6 per individual mother) eggs are deposited in decaying wood or vegetation. In Missouri, G. T. Hillie found 3 newly hatched young buried beneath a decomposing wooden fence post. There are reports from the northern part of the smooth green snake's range of an exceptionally short incubation of as little as 4 days, a period which would be due not to exceptionally rapid development of the eggs, but to the female's retaining her clutch for most of its normal gestation. Many of the 5- to 6-inch-long hatchlings have an olive to light brown dorsal hue that only later becomes brilliant green.

Coloring/scale form   *Liochlorophis vernalis* is the new scientific name of the smooth green snake which, until recently, was known as *Opheodrys vernalis*. Both green snakes were formerly placed within the genus *Opheodrys*, but the smooth scalation of *L. vernalis*, along with its distinct body configuration and different ventral scale count, has prompted Hobart M. Smith and the late Jonathan C. Oldham to offer a new genus designation for this animal.

Smooth green snakes are bright green above with lighter hues, typically yellow or white, ventrally. The lips and chin are also whitish. Texas specimens and several Upper Midwest populations retain their gray to olive-brown juvenile coloration into adulthood, while deceased individuals turn blue shortly after death. This snake's smooth dorsolateral scales are arranged in 15 midbody rows, its nostril lies across the juncture of adjacent nasal scales, and its ventral scales range widely in number, varying between 116 and 154.

Similar snakes   The **rough green snake (45)** is proportionately slimmer and more wiry, and has 17 rows of keeled dorsal scales and 144 to 171 ventral scales. The **eastern yellow-bellied racer (56)** is a much larger, gray-green serpent that at the length of the adult smooth green snake still exhibits a contrasting, dorsally brown-blotched juvenile pattern. Each of the racer's nostrils is centered in a single nasal plate.

Behavior   This unobtrusive little serpent relies on camouflage to avoid detection. If startled, it most often ceases all movement but at times may gape when threatened, displaying the dark interior of its mouth. Aggregations of smooth green snakes sometimes assemble for winter brumation (in Michigan, 148 individuals were found hibernating together), but during warm weather these animals are solitary.

WHIPSNAKES, RACERS, AND INDIGO SNAKES

Whipsnakes
Genus *Masticophis*

Eastern Coachwhip, *Masticophis flagellum flagellum*
Western Coachwhip, *Masticophis flagellum testaceus*
Central Texas Whipsnake, *Masticophis taeniatus girardi*
Desert Striped Whipsnake, *Masticophis taeniatus taeniatus*
Schott's Whipsnake, *Masticophis schotti*
Ruthven's Whipsnake, *Masticophis ruthveni*

Masticophis is part of the colubrine subfamily *Colubrinae*, within which it is genetically allied with the racer genus *Coluber* (only whipsnakes and racers, for example, lay eggs with granular-surfaced shells that exhibit a star-shaped indentation on one end). Like wiry-bodied—*mastix* is Greek for "whip"—big-eyed diurnal snakes the world over, whipsnakes actively pursue their prey. The narrow yet blunt-snouted head is nevertheless larger in diameter than the slim neck; there are 15 to 17 midbody rows of smooth dorsolateral scales, and a divided anal plate.

Whipsnakes are alert serpents that sometimes hunt by periscoping their heads above tall grass to make use of their acute vision—upon which *Masticophis* seem to rely almost as much they do on the chemical cues most snakes use when seeking prey. Watching their surroundings so closely also lets whipsnakes keep track of avian activity. This helps them avoid hawks, one of their major predators, and may enable them to spot arboreal bird nests beyond the scent-locating range of terrestrial snakes. Other prey includes lizards and smaller snakes, including their own kind, as well as mammals— all of which are seized and immobilized by the strong jaws but not constricted.

47 EASTERN COACHWHIP
Masticophis flagellum flagellum

Nonvenomous   If cornered, this long, wiry serpent vibrates its tail and doesn't hesitate to strike and bite— often 2 or 3 times in succession. Instead of hanging on to an aggressor, however, *M. flagellum* typically pulls away quickly, leaving shallow scratches.

Abundance   Common. The eastern coachwhip is one of the most numerous large terrestrial serpents in its broad range.

Size   The record individual measured 102 inches in length, although a coachwhip this size would be very unusual, for the majority of adult *M. f. flagellum* are between 50 and 72 in.

Habitat   Coachwhips occur in virtually every rural environment: forest, marsh, pastureland, borders of cultivated fields, the banks of both inland and estuarine watercourses, and sandy coastal strands. Probably because of the abundant rodent, lizard, and smaller snake prey often found there, eastern coachwhips seem to be particularly abundant around abandoned farms.

Prey   Coachwhip prey can include almost any smaller vertebrate. Spiny and tree lizards probably comprise much of the eastern subspecies' diet, but the droppings of wild individuals have contained the remains of other snakes, mammals, birds, frogs, and even small turtles. Insects are probably the primary prey of juveniles.

Serpentine greyhounds adapted for sight hunting, coachwhips have evolved their specialized bodies only after giving up other adaptations. J. A. Ruben's research suggests that *M. flagellum*, like other whipsnakes, has gained speed and agility but foregone some constrictive ability by evolutionarily lengthening the segmental spacing of its three major epaxial muscle groups, although whipsnakes employ a quasiconstriction by pressing a prey animal against the ground with a body coil. Despite its adaptations for sight hunting, the coachwhip's final feeding response is often determined by vomerolfaction: only if a prey animal smells right do coachwhips bite down. For example, *M. flagellum* hatchlings with no prior exposure to their natural prey snap instinctively at cotton swabs rolled over the skin of lizard and snake species abundant within their range.

Reproduction   Egg-laying. Little is recorded about courtship and nesting among free-ranging *M. f. flagellum*, but the 10- to 15-inch-long hatchlings, which emerge in July and August, have dimly defined brown anterior dorsal crossbars on their tan backs and whitish, anteriorly spotted venters. This patterning is so different from the dark-backed adults that young coachwhips are frequently assumed to belong to another species.

Coloring/scale form   Adult *M. f. flagellum* exhibit unique, two-toned coloring. The unmarked dark forebody gradually fades to progressively lighter shades of brown and tan on the posterior two-thirds of the trunk, and even the occasional entirely black individual usually has a russet-tinted tail.

Ventral color matches that of the dorsum, while the dark-bordered caudal scales create a crosshatched, braided whiplike pattern from which this animal's common name is derived.

Coachwhips' heads are also distinctive. Elongate yet wider than the wiry neck, with big eyes that are shielded above by a projecting parietal scale plate and bordered along their forward edges by a pair of small preocular scales. The dorsal scales are arranged in 17 rows at midbody, but occur in only 13 rows just ahead of the vent.

Similar snakes   Where the ranges of the eastern and **western coachwhips (48)** overlap, intergrades are common. To the west of this zone, the western race is distinguished by its much lighter-hued, beige to brownish dorsolateral color, often barred with wide light and dark crossbands. Its venter resembles that of the juvenile eastern coachwhip: creamy, with a double row of dark dots beneath the neck. Adult **southern black racers (53)** lack the eastern coachwhip's dark anterior, lighter posterior color demarcation, as well as its crosshatched tail; racers also have 15 rows of dorsal scales just ahead of the vent.

Behavior   Like other whipsnakes, *M. f. flagellum* is exceptionally alert, perhaps even curious. To get a better look at an intruder, an adult surprised in the field may, like a slim-necked cobra, raise its head and forebody well off the ground. The author has noticed himself being observed in this way by coachwhips which had fled a short way, then paused to look back over tall grass—their direct gaze a startling contrast to the absence of long-distance vision in most snakes.

Because *M. flagellum* can traverse open ground more swiftly than any other North American serpent—and, when pursued, streak up into low trees—coachwhips are able to evade predators well enough to forage in comparatively unsheltered environments. Nevertheless, their diurnal movement across open terrain leaves *M. flagellum* vulnerable to predation by raptors, and both red-tailed and red-shouldered hawks are commonly observed with a still-writhing coachwhip in their talons.

The nervous energy that fuels this vigorous, dangerous, open terrain–hunting lifestyle generates in coachwhips a constant need to both feed and constantly move about, and as a result they tend to be frustrated cage pacers which should not be held in confinement—though they are such tough, resilient captives that one individual lived for nearly 17 years in the laboratory.

48 WESTERN COACHWHIP

Masticophis flagellum testaceus

Nonvenomous   Western coachwhips are agile biters; cornered by a human being, a large individual may strike past its assailant's hands at his face or body. See **Eastern Coachwhip.**

Abundance   Among the most common large, nonvenomous serpents in terrestrial rural environments throughout the western three-fourths of Texas, *M. f. testaceus* is particularly abundant in late summer or early autumn, when its dimly brown-banded, big-eyed hatchlings appear on every dirt road.

Size   Most adults are between 4 and 5½ feet in length, although the record is 6 feet 8 in. The young are 12 to 14 inches long at hatching.

Habitat   *Masticophis flagellum testaceus* occupies almost every terrestrial, nonurban habitat in northern, southern, central, and western Texas. In the open terrain of the western part of this range the author has watched these snakes forage over hundreds of yards in just a few minutes.

Prey   Any western coachwhip, at various seasons and different stages in its life, could have potentially fed on grasshoppers and other invertebrates, lizards, other snakes, and any bird or mammal small enough to be overcome. See **Eastern Coachwhip**.

Reproduction   Egg-laying. The 10- to 15-inch-long hatchlings, which emerge in July and August, are slender, pale earth-colored little serpents notable for their speed, their proportionately large, orange-irised eyes, and their pronounced supraocular scales, as well as the crosshatch-patterned tails they share with adults of their race. See **Eastern Coachwhip**.

Coloring/scale form   Although its head and neck are often slightly darker than its trunk, the western coachwhip's coloring tends to follow the prevailing ground color of the terrain that it occupies. Geographically, *M. f. testaceus* populations become paler hued as one moves westward into rockier, less-vegetated territory. Many individuals living in the east central part of the Texas range have broad light and dark gray-brown dorsolateral crossbands, while on the limestone of the Edwards Plateau unmarked silvery tan coachwhips predominate. West of the Pecos River, this color morph is replaced by brick red (the subspecies name means "dark pink" in Latin) to vermilion-hued western coachwhips. One might think that such bright coloring would make these animals virtual bull's-eyes to every predator, but mammalian carnivores are color-blind, and to even color-visioned humans and raptors these coachwhips' silvery red dorsums somehow almost disappear into even the attenuated vegetation of their desert homes. In Jeff Davis, Brewster, and Presidio counties, on the dark red rhyolite formations of the Davis Mountains, dark pink *M. f. testaceus* are the prevailing color phase (in all areas the young are tan, with thin, dimly defined brown vertebral bars).

In this region, some truly spectacular "red racers" are even marked with wide bands of pink and dark red or charcoal, though silvery tan individuals also inhabit this area. Aside from the brilliant coloring of the Trans-Pecos population, however, the western coachwhips' most distinctive characteristic is the light and dark crosshatch patterning of its tail. Since each dorsal caudal scale is two-toned (the forward portion is paler than its trailing edge) the tails of *M. f. testaceus* have the look of a braided rope or, to an earlier generation's eyes, a woven rawhide buggy whip. Yet even those distinctive caudal scales are quite smooth; they are arranged in 17 rows at midbody (in 13 rows just anterior to the vent), while a unique pair of lorilabial scales—the lower one very small—borders the anterior edge of the eye. The venter is anteriorly marked by a double row of black spots.

Similar snakes   The **eastern coachwhip** (47) has uniformly blackish foreparts and a lighter-colored, dark to light brown midbody and tail. Other **whipsnakes (49–52)** are even wirier serpents than the coachwhip, with narrow white lateral stripes, reddish undertails, and 15 midbody rows of dorsal scales.

Behavior   This extremely temperature-tolerant reptile is often seen sliding across broiling pavement or rocky, barren ground in midsummer temperatures above 100°F. No other serpent besides other whipsnakes, whose lean configuration is similarly resistant to heat and desiccation, is abroad during such conditions, but this ability to be active when lizards, a primary prey group, are most active, is a considerable predatory advantage. Because their temperature tolerance also applies to cold, even in the relatively high elevation Trans-Pecos western coachwhips are regularly seen abroad during mild midwinter weather.

Summer or winter, this animal's mobile, mostly diurnal predatory style renders it vulnerable to predation by carnivorous birds. Hawks are commonly seen perched on power line poles holding captured coachwhips, while juvenile *M. f. testaceus* are preyed on by roadrunners. But daytime is not the only time coachwhips forage. On several occasions the author has found western coachwhips feeding at night on seasonal invasions of big lubber grasshoppers. Night or day, vehicles also cause many coachwhip deaths, for despite their alertness and good vision, whipsnakes are typically unwary of even heavily traveled highways.

49 CENTRAL TEXAS WHIPSNAKE

Masticophis taeniatus girardi

Nonvenomous   See **Desert Striped Whipsnake.**

Abundance   Common. Despite its geographically descriptive name, the central Texas whipsnake is probably seen more often in the Trans-Pecos portion of its range. It is likely to be equally abundant in the central hill country, but because of the thickly vegetated juniper brakes it inhabits there, it is relatively unfamiliar even to rural residents of the area.

Size   Despite its considerable length—adult size is 28 to 72 inches—*M. t. girardi* is so slender that even the largest individuals have heads no bigger than a man's thumb; one healthy 3½-foot-long individual captured by the author weighed but 5½ ounces.

Habitat   In central Texas, oak–juniper woodland is this animal's favored habitat. In the Trans-Pecos, *M. t. girardi* is found in a wider range of environments. Dry watercourses, low-desert canyons, rocky slopes up to nearly 8,000 feet in elevation, and evergreen mountain forest are all commonly inhabited.

Prey   Food animals include lizards, snakes, and small rodents. Newly caught central Texas whipsnakes are typically voracious, immediately taking several

133

mice in succession. After settling into confinement their metabolisms slow, however, and established captives eat no more than a mouse every week or two.

Reproduction   Egg-laying. See **Desert Striped Whipsnake.**

Coloring/scale form   *Masticophis taeniatus girardi* is named in honor of Charles Frederich Girard, French-born collaborator with Spencer Fullerton Baird in first describing some 24 southwestern ophidian species and subspecies. Its dorsal coloring varies to the extent that individuals from central Texas are grayish black above, with whitish scales on the nape and a row of tiny white flecks on both the lowest dorsal scale row above the belly and on the outer tips of the gray- and white-mottled ventral plates (posterior to the vent, these shade to pink). Chihuahuan Desert–living *M. t. girardi* may fit this description, or they may have brownish dorsolateral crossbands or be uniformly mahogany above, often with charcoal anterior bellies. All color morphs have a white lateral stripe—made up of long white patches separated by dark intervening scales—that runs along the third and fourth scale rows above the belly. There are 15 midbody rows of smooth dorsal scales.

Similar snakes   Throughout the northern Trans-Pecos, intergrades occur with the subspecies **desert striped whipsnake (50)**, which is distinguished by its brown to rusty dorsolateral color and its pair of mostly unbroken white lateral stripes. The uppermost of these stripes is longitudinally split by a blackish streak; the lower white stripe touches the outer edge of its venter. Along the southern edge of the Edwards Plateau, the **Schott's whipsnake (51)** is distinguished by its bluish to olive dorsolateral color, its pair of unbroken white lateral stripes, and the orange flecks often found on its neck and anterior sides.

Behavior   Although few serpents in the wild live much beyond the prime of life, even among animals as high-strung as whipsnakes a few survive to old age. In Big Bend, D. Craig McIntyre came upon a 6-foot-long central Texas whipsnake that showed signs of age ordinarily seen only in captive serpents at the end of long lives in confinement. Drinking deeply from a stock tank, this individual was quite lethargic despite the warm weather and made no attempt to escape when approached.

50 DESERT STRIPED WHIPSNAKE
Masticophis taeniatus taeniatus

Nonvenomous   A nervous, excitable animal, *M. taeniatus* flees rapidly from danger, but if cornered or seized may defend itself with several rapid nips.

Abundance   Desert striped whipsnakes intergrade with the central Texas whipsnake throughout the Trans-Pecos; whether *M. t. taeniatus* exists as a pure subspecies anywhere within this area is in doubt.

Size   See **Central Texas Whipsnake.**

Habitat *Masticophis taeniatus taeniatus* inhabits both gravel-floored succulent desert and evergreen montane woodland up to nearly 8,000 feet in elevation. Because the rocky faces of highway road cuts constitute prime habitat for their lizard prey, desert striped whipsnakes are sometimes seen in these manmade canyons. Here, trapped between the cuts' vertical faces they often fall victim to traffic, for during hot weather it is not unusual to see road-killed *M. t. taeniatus* in such spots, although especially for fast-moving, diurnal, open-ground hunters like whipsnakes both accidental death and predator mortality peak during these periods of maximum activity.

Prey The desert striped whipsnake feeds primarily on lizards and snakes—small western diamondback rattlers have been reported as prey—as well as rodents, nestling birds, and insects. Whipsnakes are not good constrictors, however, and typically simply pin prey animals to the ground while disabling them by biting their heads. See **Eastern Coachwhip**.

Reproduction Egg-laying. Harry Greene reports that related striped whipsnakes may travel hundreds of yards in the course of evaluating a number of rodent burrows as potential clutch-deposition sites. Like other whipsnakes, *M. t. taeniatus* lays clutches of 3 to 12 relatively large, granular-surfaced eggs. The 12- to 15-inch-long hatchlings—no thicker than a pencil and colored like their parents except that their pale nuchal marking is more pronounced—are not uncommon in late summer or early autumn.

Coloring/scale form The desert striped whipsnake is descriptively named. Below its rusty brown dorsal ground color 3 prominent pale lateral stripes (*taeniatus* is "striped" in Latin) line its sides. The uppermost of these stripes is off-white in color, 2 scale rows in width, and longitudinally split by a blackish seam. This pale stripe's lower border is defined by a dark lateral stripe, and below this a second white stripe touches the outer edge of the belly. Ventral coloring is charcoal to mottled gray or white on the forebody, shading to coral beneath the tail. The dorsal scales are arranged in 15 rows at midbody.

Similar snakes As do other whipsnakes, the desert striped whipsnake intergrades with any race of *M. taeniatus* whose range abuts its own; throughout the northern Trans-Pecos this merging involves the **Central Texas Whipsnake** **(49)**, which in typical form is distinguished by a black back, distinct white neck patch, and a series of elongate white dashes—sometimes compared to highway traffic lane dividers—that runs along its anterior sides.

Behavior Whipsnakes are among the most radically shaped of serpents. Their gracile configuration allows them speed and agility, but their wiry bodies are primarily an adaptation to resist heat and desiccation. This is vital for such diurnal, desert-living lizard hunters because it allows *M. taeniatus* to forage during the midday activity peak of its lacertilian prey. (Another advantage of the whipsnake's narrow body is that it allows this wire-like reptile to almost disappear by freezing partially upright, transforming its thin profile into what appears to be an inconspicuous plant stem.) At the same time, this animal's large eyes enable it to orient itself visually with respect to major topographical features that would be beyond the distance-sight capabilities of most reptiles.

51 SCHOTT'S WHIPSNAKE
Masticophis schotti

Nonvenomous   See **Ruthven's Whipsnake.**

Abundance   Named in honor of Arthur C. V. Schott, a surveyor with the 1852–1853 Mexican Boundary Survey. *Masticophis schotti* is seasonally active in Duval, Brooks, Jim Wells, Webb, Kleberg, and Kenedy counties, but it is not numerous.

Size   Most adult Schott's whipsnakes are 40 to 56 inches long—the record is 66 inches—but even the largest adults are not much thicker than a fountain pen and weigh only a few ounces.

Habitat   *Masticophis schotti* inhabits the coastal plain south of the Balcones Fault. Here, between the oak and juniper brakes of the hill country to the north (home of the central Texas whipsnake) and the Tamaulipan thorn brush to the south (where the Ruthven's whipsnake predominates), the prevailing biome is mesquite/live oak/prickly pear savannah, and the resident whipsnake species is the Schott's.

Prey   Lizards are this species' principal prey, but rodents are also taken—recent captives typically eat mice immediately—as well as other snakes; cannibalism of its own kind by *M. schotti* is reported. The young probably feed largely on insects and lizards.

Reproduction   Egg-laying. Three Texas clutches reported by Howard Gloyd, laid in May and June, consisted of 3, 10, and 12 eggs. None hatched, but reproductive success was achieved during 1996 when a gravid Webb County female cared for by Kenny Wray laid 9 nearly 2-inch-long, rough-surfaced eggs on May 1. Four were infertile, but 72 days later the remaining egg hatched into a 12¾-inch-long offspring whose brick-red cephalic wash and salmon-hued venter were quite different from the coloring of adult *M. schotti* (its photograph, the first ever taken of a hatchling, is included here).

Coloring/scale form   Formerly known as *Masticophis taeniatus schotti*, the Schott's whipsnake has been redefined by James Dixon and others of Texas A&M University as the separate species, *Masticophis schotti*. Its bluish to greenish gray back and sides contrast sharply with its pair of white lateral stripes and the reddish orange scales scattered along its off-white lower neck. Its venter is cream-colored beneath the chin, stippled with bluish gray at midbody, and deep yellow to salmon below its tail. Its smooth dorsal scales are arranged in 15 rows at midbody.

Similar snakes   Along the southern Edwards Plateau, the adjacently ranging **Central Texas Whipsnake (49)** is gray-black, with a prominent white nuchal patch and a series of white dashes—sometimes likened to highway lane dividers—along its anterior sides; it lacks the Schott's pair of unbroken white dorsolateral lines. To the south, **Ruthven's whipsnake (52)** is greener, lacks distinct white lateral stripes, and has both gray or dark orange spots on its white or pale yellow throat and possesses a bright red undertail.

Behavior Fast-moving small animals, especially lizards, instantly attract this diurnal hunter's attention. Such prey is seldom hotly pursued, however, but instead is stalked, using a stop-and-go technique in which the whipsnake pauses while its quarry looks up. Then, when the lizard's attention is diverted by its own foraging, the whipsnake quickly advances a few inches, then a few more. Once grasped by the jaws, prey too large to be immediately engulfed is held down with a loop of the trunk and disabled by repeated bites to its head.

52 RUTHVEN'S WHIPSNAKE
Masticophis ruthveni

Nonvenomous *Masticophis ruthveni* is nervous and quick to flee danger, but if cornered it does not hesitate to nip in its own defense, after which it may quickly retract its head and neck, raking its teeth across its adversary's skin and leaving shallow scratches.

Abundance Formerly abundant. Ruthven's whipsnake is now seldom seen outside the scattered patches of uncut mesquite savannah and thorn woodland still found in the Rio Grande valley, where it is sometimes seen as a roadkill near the Cameron County Airport. *Masticophis ruthveni* is also still common on the Laguna Atascosa National Wildlife Refuge.

Size Most adults are 40 to 56 inches long; the record is 66⅛ in.

Habitat This semitropical whipsnake is native to Tamaulipan thorn woodland. Until midcentury this massive thorn thicket, named for Mexico's northeasternmost state, spread a tangle of catclaw acacia, paloverde, tamarisk, cenizo, and ocotillo from the Rio Grande almost halfway to San Antonio. This was once among the United States' richest biotic communities in species diversity, but its lush vegetation grew on fertile, level land, and the agricultural boom of the 1950s leveled most of its native vegetation, decimating the tropical birds, mammals, and reptiles that historically ranged only as far north as this thorn-jungled tip of southern Texas.

Prey See **Schott's Whipsnake**.

Reproduction Egg-laying. See **Schott's Whipsnake**.

Coloring/scale form The central dorsum of adult Ruthven's whipsnakes is an unmarked bluish to olive green; the lighter-hued, blue-green lower sides are faintly marked behind the jaw with rusty orange spots. (The leading edge of some of the anterior vertebral scales is cream-colored, a hue that shades to olive or reddish gray toward the tail.) The pale yellow forebelly changes to blue-gray, lightly mottled with salmon on the middle third of the trunk, then brightens to pink around the vent, finally becoming deep red beneath the tail.

Juveniles have a faintly russet crown and nape and a black-edged pale side stripe on adjacent portions of the third and fourth scale rows above the belly; they generally lack the light anterior vertebral scale margins of adults, as well as most of their dark ventral stippling. The dorsal scales occur in 15 rows at midbody.

Similar snakes   Formerly classified as *Masticophis taeniatus ruthveni*, a sub-species of more northerly whipsnakes, Ruthven's whipsnake has now been defined as the separate species *Masticophis ruthveni* by James Dixon of Texas A&M University. The **Schott's whipsnake (52)** has much more conspicuous white lateral stripes, a paler forebelly, and a deep yellow posterior venter shading to salmon beneath the tail.

Behavior   In his 1928 monograph, A. I. Ortenberger (who named this snake in honor of his teacher, Alexander Grant Ruthven, president of the University of Michigan) concluded that little was known of the snake's ecology. Even brief field observation reveals, however, that like other whipsnakes *M. ruthveni* is a seemingly curious animal: with abrupt darting movements it investigates any unusual activity within its territory, while Craig and Connie McIntyre observed one Laguna Atascosa individual alertly poised in ambush—well above the ground in the thorny branches of a mesquite. Since most of its U.S. habitat has been lost to agricultural and residential development during the past 30 years, however, further information regarding its natural history will probably come from northern coastal Mexico. See **Schott's whipsnake.**

Racers
Genus *Coluber*

Southern Black Racer, *Coluber constrictor priapus*

Buttermilk Racer, *Coluber constrictor anthicus*

Tan Racer, *Coluber constrictor etheridgei*

Eastern Yellow-bellied Racer, *Coluber constrictor flaviventris*

Mexican Racer, *Coluber constrictor oaxaca*

Along with whipsnakes of the genus *Masticophis*, racers are part of the colubrine subfamily *Colubrinae*. An oviparous genus first scientifically described by Carolus Linneaus in 1758, members of the *Coluber* group produce leathery eggs with roughly surfaced shells and a distinctively crimped, starburst pattern on their ends. Racers' scales are smooth, arranged in 17 rows at mid-body (usually 15 rows just anterior to the vent), and their anal plate is divided. These serpents are notable for their alert demeanor, readiness to bite if molested, and considerable speed. They also climb well and spend a great deal of time in shrubs and low trees, but unlike other arboreal ophidian predators such as the rat snakes, racers do not constrict their prey, despite the scientific species name *constrictor*. Instead, these snakes simply grasp a food animal in their jaws and swallow the struggling creature alive.

At least 12 subspecies of *C. constrictor* are found from the Atlantic to the Pacific (10 of which occur east of the Rocky Mountains), while *Coluber* is absent from large parts of the southwestern and north central United States, as well as from the area along the continental divide. Adults of most of these subspecies are uniformly black, gray, or bluish or brownish green above, but the dark ground color of two subspecies, the buttermilk, *C. c. anthicus*, and tan, *C. c. etheridgei*, racers is variably patterned with light-hued spots and blotches. (Hatchlings and juveniles of all subspecies are strongly patterned with dark dorsal blotches or crossbars on a tan to light brown or grayish ground color.)

53 SOUTHERN BLACK RACER
Coluber constrictor priapus

Nonvenomous   Racers are comparatively high-strung snakes that will bite in self-defense.

See **Northern Black Racer**.

Abundance   Elsewhere in its range, *Coluber constrictor priapus* is among the most successful and abundant large terrestrial snakes, but it occurs in Texas only in the far northeastern corner of the state.

Size   Most adults are 20 to 56 inches in length; the record is 72 in.

Habitat   Like other *Coluber*, the southern black racer is a habitat generalist that thrives in a variety of rural and even suburban areas. Its preferred environment, however, seems to be deciduous forest–meadowland interface—a vegetative transition zone characterized by the thick, low-level shrubbery that racers favor.

Prey   This wide-spectrum predator takes whatever smaller creatures—including animals from insects and their larvae to vertebrates such as frogs, toads, lizards, snakes, birds and their eggs, and rodents—are most available within its range. In captivity, racers' high metabolism requires them to eat every few days. See **Eastern Yellow-bellied Racer**.

Reproduction   Egg-laying. Seven to 18 granular-textured oval eggs, about 1 by 1⅝ inches and bearing characteristic starlike markings on their ends, are laid in a humid subsurface cavity (a few of these nests are communally used year after year). The 9- to 11-inch-long hatchlings emerge in July and August and, because they are otherwise defenseless, may feign death when handled.

Coloring/scale form   The southern black racer's dorsum is a satiny charcoal gray to jet black, with some white generally visible on its chin and throat; the remainder of its belly ranges from yellowish gray to as dark a charcoal as its back. This subspecies' slender body and elongate head follow the same configuration as those of other racers, but its eye is notable for its dark, orange-red iris. Very different in coloring from the adults, young southern black racers are conspicuously patterned with chestnut-brown vertebral saddles, grayish lateral spots, and pale, often posteriorly pinkish bellies. They do not turn uniformly dark above until they reach about 22 inches in length.

Similar snakes   The equally dark but larger and longer-tailed **eastern coachwhip (47)** has a lighter-hued posterior body marked by dark-edged crosshatching; it also bears a uniformly dark chin and throat and 13 rows of dorsal scales just anterior to its vent.

Behavior   One study found that during spring and summer several *C. c. priapus* maintained small, well-defined home territories around the rocky outcroppings of grassy, oak-studded hillsides in Grayson County. Other southern black racers have been observed more than 10 feet high in trees, where they sought refuge after having eluded a pursuer on the ground; *C. c. priapus* tends to be far less wary, however, when hidden in thick branches where it is inclined to freeze, sometimes until actually touched. In contrast, when preparing to shed their skins, these animals most often seek the higher humidity of an animal burrow or shady shelter beneath either natural or man-made debris.

As reflected in the name "racer," *C. constrictor* is capable of a maximum burst speed of about 12 miles per hour, or 18 feet per second. Though exhaustion is reached in less than 30 seconds, well short of the maximum endurance of birds and mammals, this is great stamina for a terrestrial reptile and can only be achieved because of racers' sophisticated physiology. For example, Plummer and Congdon found that among this race's northern subspecies, within 30 seconds of seizing a mouse a racer's heart rate can shoot up to 3 times its resting level. At the same time, its arterial blood pressure increases nearly fourfold, providing a rush of circulating oxygen that lets *C. constrictor* respond nearly as rapidly from a resting state as a bird or mammal. As field experience has repeatedly confirmed, a reptile need not be a warm-blooded dinosaur to make use of a quick-reacting neuromuscular system, or to sustain that system with considerable cardiovascular stamina.

54 BUTTERMILK RACER
Coluber constrictor anthicus

Nonvenomous   Like other racers, *C. c. anthicus* will nip in self-defense. Even in distress these animals often bluff by striking openmouthed, however, and though all *Coluber constrictor* can be quick tempered, their jaws lack the strength to inflict more than scratches.

Abundance   Common in local areas (during one week in mid-May, 9 buttermilk racers were found on the grounds of a Lake Houston golf course). The buttermilk racer's unusually shaped home range encompasses a broad arc that more or less encircles eastern Texas' heavily wooded Big Thicket, which is home to this subspecies' adjacently ranging race, the tan racer, *C. constrictor etheridgei*.

Size   Most adults are 30 to 60 inches long; the record is 70 in.

Habitat   The buttermilk racer favors brushy, forest-edge habitats that include the borders of overgrown fields, meadows, and partially open areas where it

54 is able to shelter in briar patches and undergrowth. This habitat preference has benefited *C. c. anthicus* because most of East Texas' old growth forest has been cut for timber, leaving a patchwork of such woodland-interface habitats at the edges of new residential subdivisions and golf courses.

Prey   In the single study of this subspecies' diet, mice were found in the stomachs of 25 adults, lizards were found in 8, frogs in 7, rats in 5, and 3 had eaten birds.

Reproduction   Egg-laying. During the breeding season in April and May, male racers become quite aggressive, with several sometimes courting a single female. Deposited during June, July, and early August, the granular-surfaced eggs, notable for the distinctive starburst pattern on their ends and measuring up to $1\frac{5}{8}$ inches in length, are deposited in a variety of sites. These include the tunnels of small burrowing mammals, beneath rotting boards or sheets of iron siding, and in loose soil along the margins of plowed fields. Of three *C. c. anthicus* clutches laid at the Houston Zoo, 2 clutches were made up of 18 eggs, the third of 27. All the eggs hatched about 46 days later into 10- to 11-inch-long young whose off-white ground color was blotched with brown vertebral saddles and small lateral spots.

Coloring/scale form   Named for the supposed similarity of its dappled dorsum to the light-hued droplets of fat sprinkled throughout old-time homemade buttermilk, *C. c. anthicus* is notable among racers for its unique dorsolateral patterning. The ground color of its foreparts is dark bluish or greenish gray, a hue that becomes lighter and browner toward the rear of its body, though in Angelina, Polk, Tyler, and northern Jasper and Newton counties many buttermilk racers are less distinctly marked due to intergradation with the uniformly gray-brown subspecies, *C. c. etheridgei,* and may be patterned only with a white-spotted dark patch on the nape.

Covering the dark ground color of phenotypically pure buttermilk racers, however, is a sometimes spectacular spattering of off-white scales, densely packed on some individuals, scattered and few in number on others. The lips, chin, and lower sides of the neck are pale yellow, while the belly is gray, often with a few little yellow spots.

Similar snakes   The subspecies **tan racer (55)** is almost entirely light gray or brown above, although sometimes it is marked with a few white dorsolateral scales. Another subspecies, the **eastern yellow-bellied racer (56),** is olive to bluish green above, with a bright yellow venter. (Young buttermilk racers' dark vertebral saddles, big, yellow-irised eyes, and 17 anterior rows of dorsal scales set them off from adults of the similar-sized burrowing serpents found in the same leaf-litter microenvironment.)

Behavior   Even in areas of suboptimal habitat, buttermilk racers probably occupy ranges of no more than 25 acres; few have been known to travel as far as three-quarters of a mile. See **Southern Black Racer.**

55 TAN RACER
Coluber constrictor etheridgei

Nonvenomous   See **Eastern Yellow-bellied Racer.**

Abundance   *Coluber constrictor etheridgei* is not uncommon within its very limited range.

Size   This subspecies has been recorded to nearly 6 feet in length. Most adults are 3 to 5 feet long, however, while hatchlings measure 8 to 12 inches.

Habitat   An inhabitant of the longleaf pine/oak/sweetgum forest of Texas' Big Thicket, the tan racer also occupies dense second-growth woodland. Yet, as this old climax forest has given way to fields, subdivisions, and golf courses, much of the tan racer's former territory has been usurped by the more open-clearing-living buttermilk racer. First scientifically described by Larry David Wilson in 1970, this animal's subspecies name honors Richard Etheridge, a San Diego State University zoology professor who, as a high school student in 1946, collected the type specimen.

Prey   See **Eastern Yellow-bellied Racer.**

Reproduction   Egg-laying. The only data for this subspecies is that on May 28, a female from east of Woodville, Texas, deposited 20 eggs—a high number for a racer, although this species' propensity for communal nesting contributes to large clutches laid together by several females—each a little more than an inch in length.

Coloring/scale form   The individual pictured here is grayish, but the tan racer's dorsolateral coloring is also often light brown (at first glance this animal resembles a western coachwhip with a scattering of pale dorsal scales). Sometimes there is a white-spotted patch of dark bluish or greenish gray on its nape, while its venter is unmarked light gray, with a few yellowish spots.

Similar snakes   East Texas' more widespread **buttermilk racer (54)** has a darker, generally gray-blue or gray-green back patterned with much more profuse off-white dorsolateral scales. (Intergrades between the two races are common. These animals usually exhibit the dark forebody of the buttermilk subspecies, but with fewer white dorsal scales, and with the brownish tail of the tan racer.) Hatchling racers are impossible to distinguish by subspecies, but can be told from other small terrestrial serpents by their dark vertebral saddles, their proportionately large heads and big yellowish eyes, and by their singular combination of a divided anal plate and 17 rows of smooth dorsal scales at midbody, 15 just ahead of the vent.

Behavior   As with other racers, *C. c. etheridgei* is most easily found in early spring while it is still lethargic, hiding beneath woodland ground cover or human detritus. Later in the year, in the dense forest they inhabit these racers are almost impossible to either find or capture when they are warm and agile, an activity period that peaks between May and July. Using the measure of individuals seen crossing pine woods logging roads, these animals then seem to retire during the hottest and driest part of late summer, emerging for another foraging peak in October. Foraging is generally divided into morning and afternoon periods, especially when the temperature at those times is between 70 and 85°F.

56 EASTERN YELLOW-BELLIED RACER

Coluber constrictor flaviventris

Nonvenomous   If cornered, *C. c. flaviventris* may vibrate its tail, and if restrained is likely to snap with agility. Compared to even a small mammal, however, racers are unable to exert much pressure with their jaws, and pricks or scratches are all that result from a bite.

Abundance   The most widely distributed member of its genus, the eastern yellow-bellied racer occupies an enormous range that extends from the Texas Gulf Coast and arid Trans-Pecos north past the Oklahoma border as far as southern Alberta.

Size   Although reported to reach nearly 6 feet in length, adult *C. c .flaviventris* generally measure between 30 and 54 in.

Habitat   Although in much of its range the eastern yellow-bellied racer keeps to wooded cover and traverses overgrown fields mainly on hunting forays, in the west, entire populations live in open grassland. Here, *C. c. flaviventris* is often found in more vegetated areas such as brush-filled gullies or wooded riparian corridors, where it typically shelters under flat rocks, bushes, or clumps of bunchgrass. Derelict buildings with fallen boards and siding constitute another favored microhabitat.

Despite its name, the eastern yellow-bellied racer also inhabits arid western deserts. One individual, found near Marathon by the author, may be part of a relict population that has survived in a small mesic refuge remaining from the wetter Trans-Pecos of Pleistocene times. Yet a second specimen was then discovered nearby in the entirely waterless, rocky desert north of Sanderson.

Such animals have been linked with either the subspecies Mexican racer, *C. c. oaxaca*, or the far western subspecies, *C. c. mormon*, but both these Trans-Pecos individuals were phenotypically perfect eastern yellow-bellied racers, and their presence in the northern Chihuahuan Desert simply broadens our perspective of the variety of environments in which this extraordinarily adaptable subspecies can survive.

Prey   Despite the name *constrictor*, racers are not constrictors. Small prey such as insects are simply snapped up, but when feeding on larger vertebrates—birds, frogs, lizards, other snakes, and rodents are recorded—rather than suffocating their prey, racers simply overpower small creatures, pinning them against the ground with a body coil and disabling them by bites to the head.

Like other racers, *C. c. flaviventris* will eat any creature it can capture (the author once found a 2-foot-long eastern yellow-bellied racer in a coop housing half-grown chickens far too big for it to swallow), including large insects. Cicadas are important prey for many woodland snakes, and during the periodic emergence of tens of thousands of these plump insects, eastern yellow-bellied racers feed on them almost exclusively.

Reproduction   Egg-laying. With the approach of their early summer partu-rition, female racers move to denser vegetation that they frequent at other times in order to hide their eggs beneath litter or bury them under a layer of sandy soil. See **Buttermilk Racer.**

Coloring/scale form   Adult eastern yellow-bellied racers are a lovely, unmarked blue-gray-green above, with a bright yellow venter. The pale ground-colored young are sharply blotched with brown, but during their sec-ond year, after reaching 16 to 18 inches in length, in an ontogenetic pattern change they start to lose their juvenile coloring, beginning on the tail. There are usually 7 upper labial scales.

Similar snakes   In the northeastern portion of its Texas distribution, the east-ern yellow-bellied racer's range abuts that of the **southern black racer (53)**, an animal whose back is satiny charcoal gray to jet black, with some white generally visible on the chin and throat. In East Texas, the subspecies **butter-milk racer (54)** has a darker, gray-blue or gray-green back and sides pat-terned with profuse off-white scales. In southwestern Texas, the eastern yellow-bellied racer's territory overlaps that of the **Mexican racer (57)**, a more southerly and westerly subspecies with a slightly darker back and lighter sides, a greenish yellow venter, and 8 upper labial scales. (Intergrades between any two of these racer subspecies are common.)

Behavior   Racers' comparatively advanced physiology is the primary factor that gives rise to a subtle quality one notices when handling these snakes. Unlike a majority of serpents, racers have an almost mammalian presence: they clearly take note of what is going on around them. A newly captured individual may seem to have settled down in one's hands but, in a way not seen among most other serpents, it typically continues to pay attention to its circumstances and, if a chance for escape arises, it is instantly ready to take advantage of the opportunity. See **Southern Black Racer.**

57 MEXICAN RACER
Coluber constrictor oaxaca

Nonvenomous   *Coluber constrictor oaxaca*, like other racers, is adept at self-defense. If cornered it will strike energetically and bite repeatedly, although it is incapable of inflicting anything more than pricks and scratches.

Abundance   Uncommon even in undisturbed parts of its South Texas range, the Mexican racer is most prevalent in the brush country of the lower Rio Grande Valley. Many intergrade individuals have been found far to the west, however, in a disjunct range that includes Val Verde, Terrell, Jeff Davis, and Brewster counties.

Size   Slightly smaller than other racers, most adult *C. c. oaxaca* measure 18 to 36 inches in length, and any individual over 40 inches long would be very large. Hatchlings are from 8 to 11 inches in length.

Habitat   In the United States, phenotypically pure examples of the Mexican racer are restricted to Texas' subtropical southern Gulf Coast, where *C. c. oaxaca* inhabits the grassy sand dunes, called lomas, which abut the saline Laguna Madre. Inland, the Mexican racer is a resident of shrubby fields and open woodlands and riverbanks, as well as suburban vacant lots and city parks. The Tamaulipan thorn woodland is also a principal habitat, where this subspecies shelters in clumps of prickly pear or beneath boards and debris around unworked farms and stock tanks.

Prey   Like other racers, *C. c. oaxaca* is an opportunistic feeder. Because of their prevalence in its environment, lizards and frogs seem to be the principal prey of adults, but small rodents, nestling birds, and insects are also taken. Juveniles reportedly feed on locusts, crickets, cicadas, and nontoxic caterpillars, as well as on very small lizards and frogs when these are available. In addition, an unusual and previously unrecorded prey species for *Coluber constrictor oaxaca* is reported by herpetologist Gus Renfro, who has found that individuals captured in the coastal dunes often defecate the shell fragments of fiddler crabs.

Reproduction   Egg-laying. Little is known about the reproduction of the Mexican racer. Clutches probably vary from the 3 eggs produced by one small captive female to more than a dozen. Sometimes, though, deriving reproductive data for an uncommon animal like *C. c. oaxaca* can be an exercise in forensics. For example, one freshly traffic-killed, 3-foot-long female discovered on June 25 by D. Craig McIntyre had milky skin and eye coverings. When she was found to be near the end of pregnancy, it became clear that her epidermal condition meant that at the time of her death she was entering her pre-egg-laying shed.

From this, a tentative copulation date sometime in mid-May could be deduced, using the gestation period of the Mexican racer's numerous subspecies. In addition, counting ahead the usual 15 days from the beginning of her pre-laying shed to egg deposition would give an expected laying date of around July 10, and since captive *Coluber constrictor*'s incubation times are 50 to 65 days, this particular Mexican racer's hatchlings would in all likelihood have emerged sometime in early to mid-September. (An attempt was made to salvage and incubate her 13 fully formed and shelled eggs, but since they were still in the oviduct—where serpents' eggs are supplied with oxygen by their mother's respiration—by the time the eggs were removed all the embryos had suffocated.)

Coloring/scale form   Adult *C. c. oaxaca* have a mostly unmarked olive-gray back, generally only slightly darker along the spine although some individuals have a more distinct dusky vertebral stripe. Their sides are gray-green, greenish brown, or greenish yellow, with some specimens showing dark blue or black skin between their scales—colors that may also appear on the forward margins of the scales themselves. The upper and lower labial scales, the chin, and the venter are pale yellow to off-white, often with a pronounced greenish tinge; a few individuals have pinkish throats. There are usually 8 upper labial scales.

Unlike the young of other racers, which generally have rounded brown vertebral saddles, juvenile *C. c. oaxaca*—which are tan to buff in ground color—are marked, across the forward part of their backs, with jagged-edged dark bands that fade or disappear posteriorly. Brown flecks are scattered over their sides, while both the crown and the posterior back are grayish brown.

Similar snakes The **eastern yellow-bellied racer (56)**, which to the north intergrades with the Mexican racer, is a slightly more robust race with 7 upper labial scales.

Behavior Mexican racers spend considerable time in shrubs and bushes, where their coloring serves as ideal camouflage. They are always alert to nearby movement, and will often raise their heads above body level, apparently to better assess their circumstances. If approached, they may freeze, dart quickly away for several yards, and suddenly stop again—their abrupt transition to a complete lack of movement almost magically blending them, like slender green stems, into the surrounding foliage.

Speckled Racers
Genus *Drymobius*

Central American Speckled Racer, *Drymobius margaritiferus margaritiferus*

This tropical group of alert, fast-moving oviparous serpents—whose genus, *Drymobius*, is part of the colubrine subfamily *Colubrinae*—is represented in the United States by a single species restricted to the lower Rio Grande River Valley. Its 17 rows of dorsal scales have apical pits and are weakly keeled along its spine, and its anal plate is divided.

Drymobius margaritiferus margaritiferus is also a uniquely colored snake. It has a flat black ground color, yet the spot of bright yellow in the center of each of its scales, coupled with a dab of blue on the scale's anterior edge, somehow gives a fast-moving individual (for these colors are most visible when the snake flexes its trunk) a bluish green cast that almost glows.

58 CENTRAL AMERICAN SPECKLED RACER
Drymobius margaritiferus margaritiferus

Nonvenomous Its rarity and restricted habitat—as well as its speed and shyness—ensure that in Texas the Central American speckled racer seldom encounters human beings. If cornered, however, it is so agile that avoiding a nip is difficult.

Abundance Threatened. Protected by the state of Texas. The only member of its mostly tropical genus to inhabit the United States, *D. m. margaritiferus* reaches the northern limit of its range at the southernmost tip of the Rio Grande Valley in Texas' Cameron and eastern Hidalgo counties.

Size Most adults are 30 to 40 inches in length; the record is 50 in.

Habitat From southern Texas to the Yucatan Peninsula, *D. m. margaritiferus* occupies dense thickets or palm groves where the layered floor of decaying fronds remains undisturbed. Its other preference is the proximity of freshwater, where its amphibian prey is likely to be plentiful. Because little of the region's native woodland is left north of the Rio Grande, the Central American speckled racer's continued existence here is in doubt, but among the few places it can sometimes still be found is the Audubon Society's 60-acre Palm Grove Sanctuary, the stands of Texas palms that remain in Cameron County's riparian woodland near Brownsville, and the brushy creekbeds remaining in Hidalgo County. See **Ruthven's Whipsnake**.

Prey Central American speckled racers are terrestrial, diurnal predators which most often feed on anurans; on a jungled Mexican riverbank, the author found a large *Drymobius* by following the shrill cries of a frog held in its jaws.

Reproduction Egg-laying. Between April and August Central American speckled racers typically deposit clutches of 2 to 8 nonadhesive, smooth-shelled eggs approximately 1⅝ inches in length by ⅝ inch in diameter. For the size of the parent, these are rather small, and after an incubation of some 8 weeks, they produce hatchlings no more than 6 to 7 inches in length.

Coloring/scale form The vividly patterned dorsum of *Drymobius margaritiferus* is evocative of oriental lacquer work. Each dark dorsal scale bears a yellow-white, dart-shaped spot, a bluish margin near its anterior base, and a black perimeter. Hans Schlegle, who named this snake in 1837, described this patina of glossy dots by combining the Latin *margarita*, or "pearl," with *ferre*, which means "to carry." (*Drymobius* is Greek and means "of the forest.")

The lower sides are yellowish green, the neck is washed with turquoise, and a black stripe runs from the eye across the posterior lemon-yellow labial scales—the sutures of which are edged with black. This is a vivid combination, but compared with adults, the young are even more intensely colored. Although their backs are often overlaid with dark vertebral blotches or crossbands, their pale yellow spots are both brighter and larger in proportion to the size of their scales than those of older individuals. Both adults and juveniles have greenish yellow bellies, with ventral scales whose trailing edges are bordered, beneath the tail, with black.

Similar snakes No other snake within its U.S. range resembles the Central American speckled racer.

Behavior In southern Mexico, Guatemala, and Belize, *Drymobius margaritiferus* is abundant in thickly vegetated riparian milieus, where it constantly searches damp places for prey. In these countries speckled racers are also seen in both open savannah and woodland, as well as in overgrown fields and even village backyards.

Indigo Snakes

Genus *Drymarchon*

Texas Indigo Snake, *Drymarchon corais erebennus*

Indigo snakes are large, racer-like, oviparous serpents whose genus, *Drymarchon*, first described by L. J. F. Fitzinger in 1843, is part of the colubrine subfamily *Colubrinae*. The classification of *Drymarchon corais*, the single species in this genus, is in some doubt, however, because some researchers believe the Florida and Texas indigo snakes are really two separate species rather than geographic races of the single species, *Drymarchon corais*. All *Drymarchon* are heavy-bodied reptiles that are good at defending themselves, partly because of their size. *D. corais* is among the largest of all colubrines (*archos* is Greek for "ruler"), and occasional individuals exceed 8 feet in length. In an impressive defensive display, provoked indigos may vibrate their tails noisily, hiss, compress their necks vertically, and bite vigorously with strong jaws that can produce deep lacerations.

Individual indigo snakes range over wider territories than any other North American serpent—behavior that brings them into conflict with people and their vehicles; faced with human population expansion, both races are in serious decline. The smooth, almost mirror-finished scales of both subspecies are arranged in 17 midbody rows, and the anal plates are undivided.

59 TEXAS INDIGO SNAKE

Drymarchon corais erebennus

Nonvenomous   Every adult *D. c. erebennus* is a dramatic animal when encountered in the field: strikingly beautiful and impressive in its obvious lack of fear. Moreover, most individuals allow themselves to be handled without aggression; this is astonishing behavior in a reptile of the indigo's size and power. Yet, when very warm and active, *D. c. erebennus* can bite hard, shaking its head vigorously enough to inflict deep cuts.

Abundance   Threatened. Federally protected, and protected by the state of Texas. Despite receiving complete legal protection, the Texas indigo snake is slowly declining. The heavy collecting for the pet trade that formerly impacted the eastern indigo population has not occurred to a major extent with the Texas race, and this animal's current decline is almost entirely due to a loss of habitat.

The widespread conversion of its native terrain into agriculture has recently restricted *D. c. erebennus* to uncleared portions of South Texas' vanishing mesquite savannah and Tamaulipan thorn woodland. (Another population, too small to figure in this animal's overall numbers, occupies desert terrain as far west as the eastern Trans-Pecos. Here, Damon Salceies recorded a large adult in Sanderson Canyon, while D. Craig McIntyre reported a vehicle-killed 2-foot-long adolescent in the same region, confirming breeding success by this Pecos River–area group.)

Nevertheless, fragmentation of its home range by human incursion remains the central problem in preserving the Texas indigo. For every adult, hundreds of acres of hunting territory are necessary to support enough food animals to support its high metabolism, while males cover even more terrain in search of receptive females. This means that only in parts of the South Texas brush country and the less-rich eastern Trans-Pecos is there enough open space to allow even a small, viably breeding population of these active animals.

Size   Along with its similarly sized eastern subspecies, *D. c. erebennus* is the largest nonvenomous snake in North America; individuals of the Texas race over $8\frac{1}{2}$ feet in length are recorded.

Habitat   Among the New World's most widely distributed species, *Drymarchon corais* occurs in environments ranging from grassy prairie to coastal sandhills to limestone-floored desert. In Texas, it is most plentiful in the thorn brush woodland and mesquite savannah of the southern coastal plain. Here, tree-filled riparian corridors constitute its favored habitat, while its microhabitat includes mammal burrows, which are both essential defensive retreats from the brush country's host of large mammalian predators, and because in order to shed its skin the indigo requires the relatively moist environment that in arid terrain it can find only in underground tunnels.

Prey   In foraging, the Texas indigo moves rapidly through burrows and across the bare ground between patches of thorn thicket in a singularly unwary manner; on these forays one can sometimes actually hear it sniffing for prey at the entrance of burrows in its search for any vertebrate big enough to attract its attention and small enough to be swallowed.

Not a true constrictor, *Drymarchon corais* typically seizes its prey and, if the prey is large, the snake thrashes it back and forth against the ground while biting its head. This tactic is effective in subduing even large pitvipers, to whose venom adult indigos seem to be immune. (A rattlesnake seized at midbody will strike its assailant many times before being overpowered and swallowed and rural South Texans have long valued indigos for predation on local pitvipers.)

The Texas indigo snake's preferred prey, however, is rodents—new captives immediately take rats—as well as frogs and nonvenomous snakes. A great many of these prey animals are taken, moreover, because *D. c. erebennus* has such an active metabolism that warm and active adults may feed several times a week if prey is abundant.

Reproduction   Egg-laying. Breeding occurs in late fall, after which female indigo snakes retain sperm until early spring fertilization. (Sometimes sperm are retained much longer. One female *Drymarchon* deposited fertile eggs after 4 years of isolation.) After 70 to over 100 days of incubation, the 4 to 11 pebbly surfaced, 3-inch-long, $1\frac{1}{2}$-inch-wide eggs hatch into dorsally blotched young that are 18 to 26 inches long. Sexual maturity is not reached until 3 years of age—the longest adolescence of any native serpent.

Coloring/scale form   The adult Texas indigo snake's dorsum is covered with very large, smooth, glossy scales (both this animal's species and subspecies names are drawn from the Greek for "black") that seem freshly waxed. Dark facial striping is evident on most individuals' slightly brownish foreparts, while the venter is a cloudy, orange-mottled blue-gray. There are 17 midbody rows (14 on the posterior trunk) of dorsal scales, with partial keels occurring on some of the vertebral scale rows of adult males.

Similar snakes   No other terrestrial serpent in southwest Texas has an entirely black back and sides.

Behavior   The Texas indigo snake is seasonally territorial. In spring and summer males roam for miles, but in winter both sexes remain near their residence dens, which they periodically leave during warm spells. On their home terrain these animals seem to be familiar with every stick and bush, for if pursued they may make false runs in two or three different directions before doubling back toward their real den.

Indigo snakes' dramatic appearance has created a demand for the pet trade, but besides being illegal to capture, *Drymarchon* are so given to voiding musk and feces that handling even veteran captives is usually an ordeal because unlike arboreal snakes such as boas, which are comfortable draped over one's arms, the terrestrial indigo is ill at ease off the ground and typically makes such an effort to be free of human contact that it is clear it should have been left in the wild.

Brown-Blotched
Terrestrial Snakes

Hog-nosed Snakes
Genus *Heterodon*

Eastern Hog-nosed Snake, *Heterodon platirhinos*
Dusty Hog-nosed Snake, *Heterodon nasicus gloydi*
Plains Hog-nosed Snake, *Heterodon nasicus nasicus*
Mexican Hog-nosed Snake, *Heterodon nasicus kennerlyi*

This unusual group of oviparous, thick-necked serpents has so many bizarre habits, physical structures, and patterns of musculature that the genus *Heterodon* has been considered for classification as a separate family, set apart from other colubrids. Currently, though, this genus remains classified in the colubrine subfamily *Xenodontinae*. All *Heterodon*, a term which means "different-toothed," are characterized by an upturned snout, enlarged teeth in the rear of the upper jaw, and saliva that contains mild toxins.

Hog-nosed snakes are stout for their length, have a moderately to prominently upturned, dorsally keeled rostral scale, 23 to 25 rows of strongly keeled dorsolateral scales, and a divided anal plate. Three species occur in the United States, with only *Heterodon nasicus*, the western hog-nose, being divided into different races. Hog-nosed snakes tend to be active by day, but during the hottest weather the western hog-nose, which generally inhabits open, less shady environments, switches to crepuscular or nocturnal foraging. The more easterly *H. platirhinos* is a specialist feeder on toads, while the western hog-nose races also feed on lizards and small rodents.

The most distinctive behavioral attribute of *Heterodon*, however, is this genus' characteristic defensive strategy. In this strategy, which is utilized most often by the eastern hog-nose, a threatened individual may huff and puff, flatten its head like a viper, and bluff-strike. Or it may spread its ribs, writhe its body, and if severely distressed, open its mouth to loll out its tongue and flop over onto its back as if dead. At this point, nothing will make a hog-nose show any sign of life except turning it right side up, when it typically rolls itself back over into its upside-down imitation of a corpse.

60 EASTERN HOG-NOSED SNAKE
Heterodon platirhinos

Very mildly venomous but harmless *Heterodon platirhinos* has a pair of small, lance-shaped rear teeth, but these are located too far back in its mouth to be used in defense. Despite its threatening, viperlike gestures in self-defense—behavior that has given rise to the common name "spreading adder"—the eastern hog-nose is harmless to humans.

Abundance   Common. *Heterodon platirhinos* may be locally abundant, within its enormous and complexly bordered range, in almost any area that favors its anuran prey (in most cases this means heavy ground cover and moist, sandy soil in which both toads and hog-nosed snakes can burrow). For example, although *H. platirhinos* is fundamentally a woodland animal, this snake's territory extends upstream along the riparian corridors of streams such as the Nueces, Colorado, Red, and Canadian, which flow down across Texas' central grasslands, giving the western boundary of *H. platirhinos*' range an intricate, multifingered configuration.

Size   Adults are usually 20 to 33 inches in length; the record is $45\frac{1}{2}$ in.

Habitat   *Heterodon platirhinos* inhabits a variety of usually sandy-substrate terrestrial environments, especially mixed hardwood forest/grassland boundaries. For some reason, these animals often turn up in disturbed areas, where the author has repeatedly found them associated with flood-cut riverbanks.

Prey   This scent-hunting predator of amphibians locates the bulk of its prey beneath leaf litter and even layers of soil, then roots them out with the upturned, plowsharelike rostral scale for which it is named. In Greek, *platirhinos* means roughly "spade-nosed." Most of the prey is toads, which are abundant and unwary largely because few other predators can tolerate their toxic skin secretions. *Heterodon platirhinos* has become such a predatory specialist on toads, however, that it has evolved a refined set of adaptations that allow it to feed almost exclusively on the plentiful anurans.

These adaptations include enlarged posterior teeth hinged to the maxillary bone at the rear of its upper jaw. (After its flexible lower jaw has partially engulfed a toad and maneuvered it as far back into the mouth as possible, the hog-nose swings these long upper teeth forward to puncture the amphibian's swollen torso, for toads are themselves behaviorally adapted to balloon their bodies with air to make themselves as difficult as possible to swallow.) Through these puncture wounds the hog-nose then introduces its stringy, opalescent saliva, whose neurotoxins soon leave its prey too limp to continue its struggle.

Another separate set of adaptations deals with metabolizing the toad's bufotoxin, a group of heart-suppressing digitaloid compounds excreted by the toad's epidermal glands. To offset the compound's effect and maintain its proper heart rate, *H. platirhinos* has developed huge adrenal glands, $\frac{1}{4}$ by 2 inches long in large adults, with a weight 10 times heavier, in proportion to their bodies, than the adrenals of other snakes.

Frogs are also a principal food of *H. platirhinos*, and lizards may occasionally be taken; in captivity hatchling hog-noses will accept crickets. This reptile also readily scavenges carrion (the author has seen an eastern hog-nosed snake trying to pull a road-killed leopard frog off the pavement), but since this species is disinclined to take the domestic mice that most captive snakes are fed, *H. platirhinos* was seldom maintained in confinement until it was discovered that many could be enticed to feed on mice by rubbing the rodents against a toad to acquire its scent.

Reproduction   Egg-laying. Mating occurs March through May, though not in every year and sometimes not even in alternate years. Deposition of the 4 to 61 (average 22) eggs occurs in mid- to late summer. At 1¼ by ¾ inches, the eggs are more rounded than those of most serpents. Hatchlings measure 6½ to 9½ inches in length and, in an unusual developmental pattern, typically experience their first shed while still in the process of emerging from the egg.

Coloring/scale form   *Heterodon platirhinos* varies enormously in dorsolateral coloring. Individuals can have a khaki green, yellowish, or reddish brown ground color, elaborately patterned with almost any combination of darker spots and splotches. Some eastern hog-nosed snakes are entirely black, but most individuals have a yellowish ground color blotched with darker brown. (As *H. platirhinos* ages, many individuals undergo an ontogenetic color change in which their bold juvenile patterning darkens so much that older specimens are almost entirely dusky.) Whatever its age or coloring, the eastern hog-nose almost always exhibits a big dark-hued blotch just behind its jaw, which extends posteriorly along the sides of its neck. Likewise, among all color morphs the underside of the tail is much lighter than the (occasionally orange-blotched) gray belly.

Because of this reptile's variability in color and pattern, however, it may be best to identify *H. platirhinos* by its configuration of a stocky trunk, a short head scarcely distinct from its wide neck, and an upturned, pointed snout backed by a raised keel and flanked by sharp-edged labial ridges. Behind this turned-up rostral scute, the prefrontal scales touch, while a prominent bulge over the little dark eyes is emphasized by a brown band that masks the forecrown.

Similar snakes   The more westerly ranging **dusty, plains,** and **Mexican hog-nosed snakes (61–63)** have a sandy ground color more or less uniformly patterned with brown dorsolateral spots; their bellies and undertails are heavily pigmented with black. **Copperheads' (92–94)** dorsolateral bands completely cross their backs and sides; their slender viperid neck is much narrower than their flat-crowned head, and a dark pit is visible between the nostril and the large, pale, vertically slit-pupiled eye.

Behavior   The strongly keeled dorsolateral scales of *H. platirhinos* give it tank-treadlike traction to root through the earth, using its muscular trunk and wedged snout like a small plow to force loosened soil to the sides. In the open, this animal's deliberate pace makes it an easy target for predators, and in defense it has developed elaborate death-feigning behavior. This usually initially entails spreading its long nuchal ribs to bow out its neck into an approximation of a pitviper's flattened head, hissing, and making feinting pseudostrikes in imitation of a venomous serpent's aggressive behavior.

However, the hog-nose strikes with its mouth closed. In fact, unless one has recently handled a toad, even prodding this snake's snout with a finger won't prompt it to bite, but if its antagonist persists, the eastern hog-nose may conceal its head under its tightly spiraled tail and, presumably to make itself unappealing as a meal, it may then writhe convulsively, regurgitate, defecate, discharge musk from its cloaca, and turn belly up, its tongue hanging loosely from its slackened jaw. If placed right side up, some eastern hog-noses will even flop back over into their death pose, righting themselves only after they no longer find themselves being watched—a situation they are evidently able to monitor even from their belly-up mortality-imitation posture.

61 DUSTY HOG-NOSED SNAKE
Heterodon nasicus gloydi

Very mildly venomous but harmless to humans
Heterodon means "different-" or "multiple-toothed," in reference to this genus' combination of conventional anterior teeth and hinged upper rear fangs. Although mildly toxic to its small mammal, lizard, and amphibian prey, the seromucous parotid gland secretions in the saliva of *H. nasicus* pose no danger to humans because the tips of the animal's long rear teeth lie so far back in the throat that they cannot be used for a biting defense.

Abundance   Uncommon. *Heterodon nasicus gloydi* occurs in widely separated populations scattered throughout three distantly disjunct ranges. The largest of these separate ranges is a stretch of open prairie grassland that extends from the Pecos River northward through Oklahoma. A second range, quite different in habitat, encompasses the scattered woodland and bottomland pasture and crop fields along the Brazos River and its tributaries from the Gulf Coast inland almost as far as Texas' Edwards Plateau. A third entirely separate range, but one with a biotic community similar to that of the Brazos valley, is the mixed pasture and woodland of northeastern Texas.

Size   Most adult dusty hog-nosed snakes are 17 to 25 inches long; the record is nearly 3 feet.

Habitat   *Heterodon nasicus gloydi* occupies a geographically diverse assortment of mostly sandy-soiled habitats: short-grass prairie, grassy areas in rocky

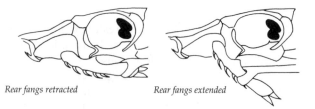

Rear fangs retracted   *Rear fangs extended*

semidesert, and pasture/pine/hardwood forest interface. On the upper coastal islands the dusty hog-nose lives both on salt-grass prairie and dunes and in residential areas.

Prey   A generalized feeder, mainly on small mammals, *H. n. gloydi* is also reported to prey on amphibians, lizards, and smaller snakes—all subdued by its parotid salival secretions—as well as on reptile eggs and the young of ground-nesting birds. Carrion is also occasionally eaten.

Reproduction   Egg-laying. Despite the long foraging season of this race's southern range, breeding may occur primarily in alternate years. Deposited between early June and August, the 4 to 23 eggs hatch after 52 to 64 days into young 6 to 7½ inches in length; sexual maturity is reached at 18 to 24 months.

Coloring/scale form   In 1952 R. A. Edgren divided the western hog-nosed snakes—all of which have buff ground-colored backs blotched with big brown dorsal spots and smaller brown lateral patches—into the 3 subspecies recognized today. The dusty hog-nose race, *Heterodon nasicus gloydi*, is named for Howard K. Gloyd, author of *The Rattlesnakes, Genera Sistrurus and Crotalus*. It has fewer than 32 medium-sized brown dorsal blotches between snout and vent in males, and fewer than 37 in females. (Males can be identified by their thicker-based tails.) This race's predominantly black belly has scattered yellowish white blotches, 9 or more small azygous scales separate the prefrontal plates of its forecrown, and there are 23 midbody rows of dorsal scales.

Similar snakes   The subspecies **plains hog-nosed snake (62)** (with which the dusty hog-nose intergrades in the northern part of its range) has more than 35 slightly smaller dorsal blotches in males, more than 40 in females and, like the dusty hog-nose, has 9 or more small azygous scales separating the prefrontal plates of its forecrown. Another subspecies, the **Mexican hog-nosed snake (63)**, is dorsally patterned much like the dusty hog-nose but is darker-hued above, with an orange-bordered black belly and no more than 6 azygous scales between its prefrontal plates. The **eastern hog-nosed snake (60)** never has a pale tan ground color broken only by small brown vertebral and lateral splotches; its undertail is always much lighter in hue than its unmarked, dark gray venter.

Behavior   See **Plains Hog-nosed Snake**.

62 PLAINS HOG-NOSED SNAKE

Heterodon nasicus nasicus

Very mildly venomous   *Heterodon nasicus nasicus* does not ordinarily bite humans. Its defensive behavior includes imitation strikes made with the mouth firmly shut. However, if it does happen to clamp onto a human finger (the only place it can gain a biting surface) either subspecies of western hog-nose may hang on with determination. One such bite, which occurred during the spring of 2002 to Joe Monahan, involved a slight anticoagulant effect that took place after the snake had chewed on his finger for several minutes. This was followed by mild swelling and numbness that after several hours reached almost to his elbow. No permanent damage occurred, however.

Abundance   Uncommon. Nevertheless, *H. n. nasicus* is widely dispersed across a huge swath of short- and mixed-grass prairie covering a 200-mile-wide north–south section of the Great Plains reaching from southern Saskatchewan and Alberta to the Texas panhandle, then south throughout the central Trans-Pecos where this animal intergrades with the Mexican hog-nose.

Size   Adults are some 15 to 25 inches long; the largest specimen on record, a male from Hale County, Texas, measured 35¼ in.

Habitat   The plains hog-nosed snake's macrohabitat is short- and mixed-grass Great Plains prairie. Yet within this sweep of mostly smoothly rolling grassland, *H. n. nasicus* is most often found in broken terrain where canyons or large draws provide at least seasonal water, gravelly or sandy soil allows burrowing, and leaf litter or ground cover offers shelter to both this hog-nose and its prey.

Prey   See **Dusty Hog-nosed Snake.**

Reproduction   Egg-laying. Reproduction is similar to that of the dusty hog-nose, but the shorter foraging season of this race's more northerly range makes it difficult for females to build the fat reserves necessary for annual pregnancy. Since many female *H. n. nasicus* examined in midsummer are not gravid, much of the population may breed only in alternate years, a fact that makes contact between males and the only periodically fecund females unusually important. But since hog-nosed snakes winter in scattered, solitary denning niches, males have less access to females than do communally wintering serpents, and during the first weeks after springtime emergence they must wander widely in search of mates. (Another brief period of potential copulation occurs in the fall, with spermatozoa from these pairings remaining viable in the female's cloaca throughout the winter.)

Coloring/scale form   The plains hog-nosed snake's sandy ground-colored dorsum is marked with more than 35 brown vertebral blotches between snout and vent in males, more than 40 blotches in females. (Males can be identified by their thicker-based tails.)

   This animal's sides are patterned with both large brown spots and similarly colored dots and speckles. There is the prominent brown band, or mask—typical of *Heterodon*—through the eyes and across the forehead, while the plains hog-nose's characteristic big brown nuchal blotch reaches from the rear of the crown back across the sides of its neck. (A few individuals—which may or may not be intergrades with the somewhat differently marked Mexican hog-nose—characterized by almost unmarked dorsums have been found in Val Verde County.)

   Sections of the plains hog-nosed snake's mostly coal black belly are edged with white, yellow, or pale orange, 9 or more small azygous scales separate the prefrontal plates of the forecrown, and there are 23 midbody rows of dorsal scales.

Similar snakes   Across the southwestern boundary of its range, the plains hog-nose intergrades with its southerly subspecies, the **dusty hog-nosed snake (61)**. In pure form, this race has fewer than 32 medium-sized brown dorsal blotches between snout and vent in males, and fewer than 37 in females; as on the plains hog-nose, there are 9 or more small azygous scales separating the prefrontal plates of its forecrown. Another subspecies, the **Mexican hog-nosed snake (63)**, with which the plains hog-nose intergrades throughout the Trans-Pecos, is marked like the dusty race, but has a more prominent rostral than either the plains or the dusty subspecies, as well as a distinctly orange-bordered black belly; fewer than 6 azygous scales are found between its prefrontal plates. (Jim Costabile reports that in northern Brewster and Jeff Davis counties all three subspecies appear to interbreed, with individuals typical of each race turning up only a few miles apart.)

Behavior   Field studies of *H. n. nasicus* in central Kansas show it to be most active morning and evening, sheltering at night and during cold weather by burrowing into sandy soil; on the surface it is often found submerged in leaf litter.

63 MEXICAN HOG-NOSED SNAKE
Heterodon nasicus kennerlyi

Mildly venomous but harmless. See Dusty Hog-nosed Snake.

Abundance   Uncommon in pure form. *Heterodon nasicus kennerlyi* was formerly thought to occupy two widely separated parts of Texas: a primary range on the southern Gulf Coast and lower Rio Grande plain and a secondary habitat encompassing the Trans-Pecos. Now, however, it appears that in the central part of the Trans-Pecos the Mexican hog-nose is replaced by its northern subspecies, the plains hog-nosed snake, *Heterodon nasicus nasicus*. Intergrades between these two races occur throughout the remainder of the region, with the Mexican form predominating in southwestern Presidio County. (To further complicate the genetic picture, the hog-nosed snakes living north of Alpine and Marathon and south of Interstate 10 appear to constitute a three-way intergrade population between the Mexican hog-nose, the more northerly plains race, and the more easterly living dusty hog-nose.)

   In contrast, in the mesquite savannah and Tamaulipan thorn brush of South Texas the pure form of *Heterodon nasicus kennerlyi* is widespread but—because of its semifossorial lifestyle—is seldom seen. Here, most records are of individuals found during damp weather in May and June, then again in September; at these times, over the course of a few days several individuals may turn up in places where no others have been seen for months.

Size   See **Plains Hog-nosed Snake.**

Habitat   In South Texas, Mexican hog-nosed snakes occur most often in grassland, including both inland pastures punctuated with mesquite and prickly pear and the more arid milieu of grass-covered coastal sand dunes. Another, less frequented habitat is the region's thorn woodland, where *H. n. kennerlyi* is frequently found near arroyos or watercourses where its anuran and small rodent prey is likely to be found.

Intergrades between the Mexican and plains hog-nosed snakes are most often found, in the Trans-Pecos, on the short-grass prairie of Presidio and northern Brewster and Jeff Davis counties, although *H. n. kennerlyi* has occasionally been found in rocky, desert-like terrain near the Rio Grande.

Prey   See **Dusty Hog-nosed Snake.**

Reproduction   See **Dusty Hog-nosed Snake.**

Coloring/scale form   Coloring is somewhat similar to that of other western hog-nosed snake subspecies but is darker dorsally, with larger, chocolate-brown vertebral and lateral blotches. Prominent orange pigmentation occupies a good bit of the sides of the otherwise glossy black venter. In its phenotypically pure form, no more than 6 azygous scales separate the prefrontal plates of this race's forecrown, while its rostral scute is considerably larger and more heavily ridged.

Nevertheless, much of Texas' Trans-Pecos appears to be an intergrade zone for this animal, for while many individuals exhibit the dark dorsal color and pattern of the Mexican race, this is combined with the smaller rostral of the plains hog-nose, the latter's only sparingly orange-marked venter, and the up to 10 small azygous scales that separate the prefrontal plates of the plains hog-nose's forecrown.

Similar snakes   A subspecies, the **dusty hog-nosed snake (61)** has fewer than 32 medium-sized brown dorsal blotches between snout and vent in males, and fewer than 37 in females. (Males can be identified by their thicker-based tails.) In pure form, this race has 9 or more small azygous scales separating the prefrontal plates of its forecrown and a less prominent rostral scale. Another subspecies, the **plains hog-nosed snake (62)**, has more than 35 slightly smaller dorsal blotches in males, more than 40 in females, 9 or more small azygous scales separating its prefrontal plates, and a similarly reduced rostral scale. The **Mexican hook-nosed snake (65)** is a smaller serpent with 17 rows of dorsal scales and a shallow depression rather than a raised keel behind its tiny upturned snout. Exhibiting almost the same dorsal coloring, size, and body shape as the Mexican hog-nose is the **desert massasauga (98)**; at night, in the beam of a flashlight, only by looking for the viper's rattle is it possible to tell at a glance which animal is at hand. (This is an interesting case of parallel habitat selection, for this little pitviper shares both of the Mexican hog-nosed snake's widely separated ranges.)

Behavior   Named for Caleb Kennerly, who collected the type specimen while medical officer of the 1855–1860 Pacific Railroad Surveys, *H. n. kennerlyi* is fossorial for much of the year. Thus it is always a treat to come across a Mexican hog-nose on one of its sporadic forays, which occur generally just before dark. Because this slow-moving little reptile is vulnerable on the surface to a host of predators—hawks and owls, bobcats, coyotes and foxes, raccoons, and bands of snake-eating javelinas—it is possible that the Mexican hog-nose is so adapted to the relative safety of fossorial life that it need not employ the defensive death feigning of other hog-nosed snakes. Several individuals found by the author could not be induced to engage in this behavior even when first handled in the field.

Western Hook-nosed Snake
Genus *Gyalopion*

Western Hook-nosed Snake, *Gyalopion canum*

First described in 1861 by pioneer paleontologist Edward Drinker Cope, the genus *Gyalopion* is a member of the colubrine subfamily *Xenodontinae*. In the United States this subfamily contains 2 genera (*Ficimia* is the other) of the diminutive, minimally rear-fanged burrowing spider eaters known as hook-nosed snakes. Although these genera differ, their external characteristics are similar, with both resembling diminutive hog-nosed snakes.

Both genera are oviparous, burrowing snakes, widely distributed in northern Mexico, that emerge from burrows only after nightfall. Both feed primarily on spiders, both have 17 rows of smooth dorsal scales and a divided anal plate, and both use similar defense mechanisms: writhing and popping the cloacal lining in and out, producing a snapping sound.

Yet there are significant differences. In the United States *Gyalopion* is the more westerly of the two genera of hook-nosed snakes, occurring only in west central Texas and the Trans-Pecos (the Mexican hook-nose is restricted to the Rio Grande valley). Its single species, *G. canum*, has a smaller rostral scale backed by the conventional pair of prefrontal scales, and its crown is strongly patterned with wide, black-edged brown bands.

64 WESTERN HOOK-NOSED SNAKE
Gyalopion canum

Nonvenomous   This little snake never bites humans.

Abundance   Fairly common. For nearly a century *Gyalopion canum* was thought to be extremely rare; now, due to increased reporting of observations, this species is known to occur widely over both Texas' Stockton Plateau and its Trans-Pecos region.

Size   Most western hook-nosed snakes are between 6½ and 11 inches in length; the record is a 17¼-inch-long Andrews County specimen found by Damon Salceies.

Habitat   *Gyalopion canum* is primarily an inhabitant of short-grass prairie above 2,500 feet in elevation. After the summer rains have started it is often found in high meadows of the Davis Mountains. Western hook-nosed snakes also occur, although less frequently, at lower elevations on Texas' north central plains and in the oak–juniper savannah of the western Edwards Plateau.

Its microhabitat on the surface is the shelter found beneath flat rocks and any sort of vegetative or man-made debris. This shelter's slightly enhanced humidity and damp earth substrate draw predatory spiders, centipedes, and scorpions in search of the smaller insects that find such conditions attractive. It is here that the western hook-nosed snake, in turn, discovers much of its arachnid and arthropod prey.

Prey   *Gyalopion canum* feeds on spiders, centipedes, and scorpions.

Reproduction   Egg-laying. All that is known about this species' reproduction is that in early July a captive female laid a single, proportionately large 1⅛-inch-long egg.

Coloring/scale form   The buff dorsolateral ground color of the western hook-nosed snake is both dark speckled and crossed with black-edged brown or reddish brown, zigzag-edged vertebral bars. These taper to points just above its off-white venter. This little snake's bulbous forehead emphasizes the small depression, or in Greek, *gyalopion*, below. This prominent brow is crossed with a black-bordered brown band that partially masks the eyes and extends posteriorly past the rear of its jaw. Above this band, rusty to dark brown bands and splotches, a pattern that varies from individual to individual, usually include a longitudinal brown patch on the rear of the skull and nape.

Yet the most distinctive characteristic of this stub-tailed little reptile is the tiny upturned hook formed by the enlarged rostral scale which tips its snout. This hyperdeveloped scale splits the internasal scales which lie just behind it and reaches back as far as the juncture of the prefrontal scales. The otherwise smooth dorsal scales are dotted with inconspicuous apical pits.

Similar snakes   The **Mexican hook-nosed snake (65)** is more olive-gray, has a darker, largely unpatterned crown and narrower, solid brown dorsolateral crossbands. There are usually no internasal scales because this species' enlarged rostral scale occupies their space and extends rearward between its prefrontals all the way to its frontal scale. The sympatrically ranging **dusty, intergraded plains,** and **Mexican hog-nosed snakes (61–63)** are more robust reptiles with 23 rows of keeled dorsal scales and a proportionately larger upturned rostral scale with a raised keel along its anterior edge.

Behavior   Found at the surface mainly under rocks, this slow-gaited burrower emerges only after dark or, following summer rains, at dusk. Besides hiding, its primary protective strategy is to perhaps discomfit some predators by engaging in a series of sudden gyrations and producing distinct popping sounds by extending and retracting the lining of its cloaca through its vent.

Mexican Hook-nosed Snake

Genus *Ficimia*

Mexican Hook-nosed Snake, *Ficimia streckeri*

The genus *Ficimia* is a member of the colubrine subfamily *Xenodontinae,* which in the United States contains two genera (*Gyalopion* is the other) of the diminutive, minimally rear-fanged burrowing spider eaters known as hook-nosed snakes. Although these genera differ, their external characteristics are similar, with both resembling diminutive hog-nosed snakes. Both are oviparous, use similar defense mechanisms (writhing and popping the cloacal lining in and out, producing a snapping sound), and both have 17 rows of smooth dorsal scales and a divided anal plate. The crown of the Mexican hook-nose is largely devoid of a dark pattern; however, its enlarged rostral scale reaches all the way back to its frontal scale, and it is found only in the lower Rio Grande Valley (the western hook-nosed snake lives in west central Texas and the Trans-Pecos).

65 MEXICAN HOOK-NOSED SNAKE

Ficimia streckeri

Nonvenomous   *Ficimia streckeri* does not bite human beings.

Abundance   Common. Within its limited South Texas range, during May and June this primarily Mexican species is often seen at night on the back roads of Webb, Brooks, Jim Hogg, Duval, Zapata, and Starr counties.

Size   Almost all Mexican hook-nosed snakes are between 5½ and 9 inches in length, but the record is a comparatively huge 19 in.

Habitat   Widely distributed throughout the Tamaulipan thorn brush biome of the Rio Grande plain, like most herpetofauna in this often dry country, *F. streckeri* is attracted to moisture and is most likely to be found in the vicinity of stock ponds and irrigation canals.

Prey   A feeding specialist like many snakes, *F. streckeri* exhibits a marked preference for spiders; centipedes and other small invertebrates may also be taken. In an example of parallel evolution, this little snake has developed a hooked, upturned rostral scale which, along with its slightly bulbous forehead, closely resembles the cephalic configuration of the only distantly related western hook-nosed snake. (The upturned rostral of the much larger hog-nosed snakes is used both for digging for shelter and to root out hidden prey, but it is not clear whether the Mexican hook-nosed snake's similar-looking rostral is also directed toward uncovering hidden food animals—spiders are seldom fossorial—or whether its miniature snout plow is used primarily for burrowing to evade predators.)

Reproduction   Egg-laying. No other reproductive behavior is recorded for *F. streckeri*.

Coloring/scale form   The Mexican hook-nosed snake's ground color is olive- to grayish brown, patterned with 50 or more thin, dark, narrowly spaced vertebral crossbars which extend from its nape—where there is a single wider crossband—to its tail tip. Except for a large brown spot below its eye, its lips, throat, and lower sides are pale buff; its belly is off-white. There are usually no internasal scales because this species' enlarged, upturned rostral scale, which has a surprisingly sharp point, occupies this area, separates the two prefrontal scales, and reaches all the way back to its frontal scale. (The Mexican hook-nosed snake's forehead exhibits the bulging brow characteristic of serpents which have evolved a hyperdeveloped rostral.) The otherwise smooth dorsal scales are pocked with tiny apical pits.

Similar snakes   The **western hook-nosed snake (63)** has a smaller rostral scale that does not extend rearward as far as its frontal scale, leaving room for a conventional pair of internasal scales. Its crown is marked with a back-edged brown partial mask, and its similarly black-edged dorsal crossbands are wider than those of *F. streckeri*. The **Mexican hog-nosed snake (63)** has 23 rows of keeled dorsal scales and a proportionately larger rostral backed by a perpendicular reinforcing ridge.

Behavior   *Ficimia streckeri*—whose name honors herpetologist John K. Strecker, former head librarian of Baylor University and the founding force behind its Strecker Museum—is also a slow-moving creature whose principal means of self-defense is its exceptional burrowing ability. When picked up, it vigorously noses downward through one's fingers; when set free it will disappear into soft earth within moments. The Mexican hook-nose's other defensive tactics include slowly weaving its miniature elevated head and forebody in a surprisingly adept approximation of the defensive posture of a pitviper, while a direly threatened individual may suddenly flip itself back and forth, making a sharp little popping sound by extending and retracting its cloacal lining through its vent.

Pine, Gopher, and Bull Snakes
Genus *Pituophis*

Louisiana Pine Snake, *Pituophis ruthveni*
Bullsnake, *Pituophis catenifer sayi*
Sonoran Gopher Snake, *Pituophis catenifer affinis*

Defined by John Edward Holbrook in 1842, the genus *Pituophis* means pine snake—*pitu* and *ophis* in Greek—a name that describes the pinewoods-living eastern species first seen by Europeans. A part of the colubrine subfamily *Colubrinae*, the members of this genus are large, oviparous snakes with heavily keeled dorsal scales and the ability to constrict powerfully. The rostral—the scale on the tip of the snout—is characteristically prominent among *Pituophis*, strongly convex, usually higher than it is wide, and extends upward between the internasal scales. All *Pituophis* covered here have four prefrontal scales; their dorsal scales are arranged in 29 or more rows at midbody, and the anal plate is undivided. (Despite having a somewhat different morphology, the genus *Pituophis* is closely related to rat snakes and kingsnakes, and captives of all three groups have interbred, producing viable, fertile young.)

Within this genus, pine snakes have proportionately narrower heads, while the heads of bull and gopher snakes are somewhat wider (it was long thought that there were but two species of *Pituophis*, the pine snakes, *P. melanoleucus*, and the bull- and gopher snakes, *P. catenifer* in the United States; the theory that the Louisiana pine snake, *Pituophis ruthveni*, is a separate species is now accepted by many authorities).

Because adult pine, bull-, and gopher snakes are heavy-bodied and comparatively slow moving, when threatened they tend to rely on an assertive defense rather than flight. This most often entails a sort of mostly bluffing belligerence in which these species vibrate their tails like a pitviper, swell their necks, and—helped by their unique glottal structure—hiss very loudly.

Although all *Pituophis* can climb, their lifestyle is primarily terrestrial (pine snakes are not arboreal but take their name from the pine woods they inhabit). This genus's burrowing skill is essential to its pursuit of rodents such as pocket gophers, on which some species are prey specialists, within their underground tunnels. Burrowing is also crucial to pine, bull-, and gopher snakes' excavation of the deep subsurface chambers in which they deposit their relatively few, but comparatively large eggs (greater numbers of eggs are sometimes found in the same chamber since communal nesting is well documented among *Pituophis*). Hatchlings are correspondingly sizable, with some exceeding 20 inches as they emerge from their shells, and in late summer can be extremely numerous.

66 LOUISIANA PINE SNAKE
Pituophis ruthveni

Nonvenomous This rare serpent is seldom seen by man, but like other *Pituophis* it may defend itself by hissing and rattling its tail. (Air expelled past a flap of tissue on the glottis produces the loud, wheezy hiss, while the distinct whirring sound, which is often mistaken for the caudal buzz of a rattlesnake, comes from vibrating the tail tip in dead leaves.) If closely approached, all large *Pituophis* may rear the anterior third of the body into an elevated S shape and strike, but their small heads and short teeth make them a much less fierce adversary than this mostly bluffing defensive behavior would suggest.

Abundance Endangered. **Protected by the state of Texas.** Despite its precariously depleted population, in historical times the Louisiana pine snake's range was moderately large, and included most of west and central Louisiana as well as Texas' Big Thicket lowlands north of Harris County. Yet *Pituophis* *ruthveni* was never a commonly seen animal, since its secretive subterranean life lets it avoid contact with humans.

With the advent of large-scale timbering in this area's longleaf pine forest, however, as well as with the control of wildfires—which historically kept open the forest's interior savannahs where rodent prey was plentiful—*Pituophis ruthveni* lost most of its habitat. Louisiana pine snakes apparently suffered a radical decline in population, and until recently this species was known primarily from historical records and some 17 individuals preserved in museum collections. It was thought that only small populations of *Pituophis ruthveni* remained, scattered throughout disjunct pockets of old-growth timber like the solitary stand in Wood County, Texas, where Neil Ford of the University of Texas at Tyler studied an isolated group of Louisiana pine snakes.

During the past three years, however, a federally funded study undertaken by Craig Rudolph of the Southern Forest Experimental Station has located more than a dozen additional specimens in East Texas and Louisiana National Forests and has begun to unravel the population dynamics of this still very rare reptile.

Size   Most adult Louisiana pine snakes are between 3 and 5 feet in length; the record is just under 6 ft.

Habitat   Louisiana pine snakes don't live in trees. They are terrestrial/burrowing residents of Louisiana and East Texas longleaf pine/hardwood forest. But as lumber industry–affiliated forest management has led to monoculture crops of slash pines for pulping into newspaper, this environment has become less suitable for the Louisiana pine snake's primary prey, the Baird's pocket gopher.

Prey   Pocket gophers are such important prey to pine snakes that their population density is usually the most important factor determining the presence of *Pituophis ruthveni* in a climax forest. Pocket gophers have formidable defenses against predators; however, in order to feed on these rodents, the Louisiana pine snake has developed a pair of singular hunting techniques.

Unlike generalized ophidian predators such as rat snakes, which are more tentative subsurface hunters, the Louisiana pine snake typically dives straight down gopher burrows. It has to move fast because gophers are rapid diggers and can quickly throw up a plug of dirt, blocking the burrow behind them. A creeping rat snake encounters a dead-end tunnel, but the pine snake, with its burrower's conical skull and muscular neck, is better adapted to overcome this defense. *P. ruthveni* observed in Rudolph's glass-walled subterranean chamber in Nacadoches promptly twisted their heads sideways and scooped this rapidly erected obstacle out of their path. When the pine snakes' quarry was overtaken, since there was no room to constrict the gopher in the narrow confines of its tunnel, Rudolph reports *P. ruthveni* forcing past the gopher, pinning it against the side of its burrow, and suffocating it with the pressure of a body coil.

Other recorded food animals include rodents and young cottontails as well as ground-nesting birds and their eggs, while the stomachs of three road-killed individuals examined in Louisiana contained only amphibian remains. *Pituophis ruthveni* drift-fence trapped in Texas have contained no prey except for two that had fed on turtle eggs. (These animals were probably empty because they would have been unlikely to come to the surface except when moving from one feeding area to another, or during males' annual search for a female's pheromone scent.)

Reproduction   Egg-laying. Nothing is recorded for this species in the wild, but among captives, compared to other *Pituophis* this cryptic burrower, which faces few predators, deposits fewer but larger eggs, devoting more resources to each well-nourished offspring. See **Bullsnake.**

Coloring/scale form   Fewer than 40 irregularly shaped chocolate dorsal saddles mark the posterior dorsal three-quarters of most *P. ruthveni*, but a pair maintained at the Lufkin Zoo varied markedly in coloring. The male, taken from the western edge of the range in the Angelina National Forest, had a light brown ground color, dark dorsal blotches and a black crossbarred tail, a grayish tan crown, and a dark mask through its eyes and across its forehead. The female, no larger than the male although perhaps older, was captured in Newton County on the Louisiana border and was an almost uniformly brown serpent. Her brownish dorsal mottling, which extended to both crown and tail, obscured almost all of her vertebral saddles and caudal bands.

Among a majority of Louisiana pine snakes the venter is creamy, with brown or black spots along its sides; the vertebral rows of the 28 or 29 midbody rows of dorsal scales are more heavily keeled than the lateral rows, and the slightly bulbous rostral scale is higher than it is wide.

Similar snakes   Called pine snakes in the East, bull snakes in the Midwest, and gopher snakes in the West, members of the genus *Pituophis* share similar configuration and ecology. Yet their relationships are cloudy. The Louisiana pine snake's woodland habitat is certainly both geographically separate and ecologically distinct from the easternmost range of the bullsnake, *P. catenifer*, as is its smaller, lighter-skulled head and less heavily scaled snout, and these animals indeed seem to be different species.

An even larger geographic gap exists between the Louisiana pine snake's range and that of the three eastern races of *P. melanoleucus*, however. This, according to Steven Reichling (1995), along with the Louisiana pine snake's dissimilar dorsolateral coloring and lifestyle, indicates sufficient difference in their respective evolutionary trajectories to warrant classification of the Louisiana pine snake as the separate species *P. ruthveni*.

Behavior   Rudolf and his colleagues have also documented the Louisiana pine snake's reliance on underground shelter to escape forest fires. Nine of his research group's transmitter-equipped *P. ruthveni*, all of them living in prescribed burn areas, avoided injury by retreating at the last minute into pocket gopher burrows. Three individuals that were observed as ground fires approached did not flee or respond in any way until flames were within a few feet, then rapidly sought burrow entrances, even when that meant moving a short way toward the advancing fire.

BROWN-BLOTCHED TERRESTRIAL SNAKES

67 BULLSNAKE
Pituophis catenifer sayi

Nonvenomous Named for Thomas Say—who collected the type specimen as chief zoologist on Major Steven H. Long's 1820s Rocky Mountain explorations—*Pituophis catenifer sayi* varies widely in temperament. Both because of the differences between individual snakes and variables such as temperature and hunger, some wild adults allow themselves to be picked up without distress while others rear their heads and forebodies into an elevated S-shaped curve, hiss, and attempt to bite. None will strike unless molested, however. See **Louisiana Pine Snake**.

Abundance Very common. Along with the western diamond-backed rattlesnake, bull- and gopher snakes are the most abundant large serpents in West Texas, particularly in late summer when the year's neonates first appear.

Size Most adult bullsnakes are from 4 to 6 feet in length, but *P. c. sayi* can grow much larger. The largest specimen ever taken is the 8-foot, 6½-inch-long Wichita County, Texas, giant captured by Dr. Robert Kuntz of San Antonio's Southwest Research Center.

Habitat One of the most widely distributed snakes of the central United States, *P. c. sayi* occupies every sort of either wooded or open-country terrain from the Gulf Coast across the Great Plains to the foothills of the Rocky Mountains.

Prey *Pituophis catenifer sayi* feeds primarily on burrowing rodents, especially pocket gophers and ground squirrels. Although less fossorial than the eastern pine snakes, which live in much softer soils, the bullsnake's muscular neck, heavy skull, and enlarged rostral scale enable it to root through even gravelly strata in pursuit of this prey.

Gophers are not helpless in such situations, however, and may push up a plug of soil to seal their tunnels behind them—sometimes successfully, for the author has seen a large bullsnake turn away from a burrow just backfilled by a frantically digging gopher. (This bullsnake's reluctance to dig may have been because, as a well-fed resident of the gopher colony, it may not have felt the need to press every predatory opportunity.) Within the confines of these burrows, bullsnakes find it easy to overcome fleeing gophers, however, by pinning them against the walls of their tunnels with a lateral body loop.

In such situations, even a single *P. c. sayi* exerts a major predatory impact, for these are voracious reptiles, and around crop fields where mice, cotton rats, or gophers proliferate, an undisturbed population of bullsnakes can lower rodent numbers enough to eliminate the need for poisoning. Other prey, such as young rabbits, ground-nesting birds, and nestling prairie dogs, is also usually warm-blooded, while juveniles are reported to take lizards as well as insects.

Reproduction Egg-laying. Courtship involves males' springtime olfactory tracking along a female's pheromonal scent trace. Up to 24 eggs (the record number deposited by a robust, 6½-pound female maintained by *Pituophis* enthusiast Jim Costabile) are deposited in loose soil during June and July. These leathery, adhesive-shelled eggs, which measure from 2 to more than

3½ inches long, adhere to form a single large cluster. In late summer and early autumn the young appear in great numbers, and, at up to 20 inches in length they are, along with neonate indigo snakes, diamond-backed rattlesnakes, and the slightly larger offspring of the Louisiana pine snake, the biggest newborn North American serpents. Yet, because of heavy predation by both mammalian predators and soaring raptors, bull and gopher snakes must be extremely prolific to maintain their large populations.

Coloring/scale form Of native snakes, only *Pituophis catenifer* has a khaki-hued, brown-freckled crown much paler than its brown-blotched back. Patterned with more than 40 brown vertebral blocks, the bullsnake's back is very differently marked from its tail, where dark brown crossbands stand out against a mustardlike ground color. A slightly elevated transverse ridge—from which the bullsnake's common name is derived—crosses its forehead like the boss of a bull's horn; along it a dark band angles back through the eye and across the pale cheeks. This reptile's cephalic scalation is also unique: 4 small prefrontal scales back its enlarged rostral scale. Arranged in 29 to 37 rows (usually 33 at midbody), the dorsal scales have apical pits and are most strongly keeled along the spine, while the laterally speckled venter is off-white.

Similar snakes The **Sonoran gopher snake (68)** is a slightly paler, sometimes more reddish subspecies whose rostral scale is a bit broader than that of the bullsnake (the bullsnake's rostral scale is narrower than it is wide). The Sonoran race intergrades with the bullsnake across the Trans-Pecos, where Terry Hibbitts, of the University of Texas at Arlington, found that both sorts of rostral scales occur with about equal frequency. The **Louisiana pine snake (66)** is darker and usually less distinctly patterned, with fewer than 40 nonrectangular vertebral blotches. Adult **Texas rat snakes (72)** have dark brown heads, 27 rows of dorsal scales, 2 prefrontal scales, and a divided anal plate. **Texas** and **Kansas glossy snakes (69–70)** have a pale longitudinal line along their napes, a white venter, and 2 prefrontal scales.

Behavior See **Sonoran Gopher Snake.**

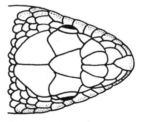

Prefrontal scales: bull, pine, and gopher snakes

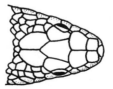

Prefrontal scales: glossy snakes

68 SONORAN GOPHER SNAKE
Pituophis catenifer affinis

Nonvenomous   Some adults among this western race of *Pituophis catenifer* are docile and can be picked up without protest. Others assume a perfect replica of the pre-strike posture—raised forebody loop and lowered, flattened head, its posterior splayed wide to approximate a viper's triangular skull—characteristic of a large rattlesnake. See **Louisiana Pine Snake.**

Abundance   Common throughout the western United States, *P. c. affinis* appears in Trans-Pecos Texas primarily as an intergrade with the more easterly ranging bullsnake.

Size   Most adults are between 3½ and 5 feet in length, although one very long, slender individual, found in the Davis Mountains by python breeder Dave Barker, measured just over 8 feet in length.

Habitat   The western Texas habitat of this subspecies includes short-grass prairie, shrub, and succulent desert, as well as barren and evergreen-wooded mountain slopes up to at least 7,000 feet, an elevation where *P. c. affinis* has been found by the author.

Prey   This big snake's prey consists primarily of small burrowing mammals, especially deer mice, pocket gophers, and ground squirrels. In gopher and ground squirrel colonies, an adult *P. c. affinis* simply takes up residence in the burrows. Young rabbits and the eggs and nestlings of ground-living birds are also taken, and while other snakes are seldom mentioned as prey, the author observed this subspecies immediately devour an adult western black-necked garter snake with which it was momentarily placed in a collecting bag. Captive-born juvenile gopher snakes also take lizards and large insects.

Reproduction   Egg-laying. C. M. Bogert and V. D. Roth (1966) report dominance rivalry among male Sonoran gopher snakes. In these contests, the combatant most successful in the pair's preliminary head-rearing skirmishes attempts to maintain its superiority by holding its forebody above that of its adversary for as much as an hour, from time to time dropping its anterior trunk onto the snake below. Incubation takes from just under two months to 75 days, mostly depending—as is the case with all squamate eggs—on the prevailing temperature. See **Bullsnake.**

Coloring/scale form   Throughout eastern Trans-Pecos Texas, the Sonoran gopher snake intergrades with the **bullsnake.** In this area the gopher snake is lighter and sometimes slightly more reddish in color; farther west some individuals have a pinkish tan cast, slightly more numerous rusty brown vertebral rectangles, and a comparatively somewhat broader rostral scale. The Sonoran gopher snake's throat is always white, however, shading to pale yellow at midbody; posteriorly, scattered dark spots tip the outer edges of its ventral scales. As on other *Pituophis*, four prefrontal scales border the rear of its enlarged rostral, and its 29 or more midbody rows of dorsal scales are heavily keeled, especially along the spine.

Similar snakes Of 15 Guadalupe Mountains *Pituophis catenifer,* 8 had comparatively taller, slightly narrower, bullsnake-type rostral scales; 5 were intermediate between the bullsnake and gopher snake; and 2 had the comparatively lower, broader rostral scale typical of the Sonoran gopher snake. See **Bullsnake (67).**

Behavior Diurnal as well as nocturnal, gopher snakes may be abroad at any hour; this fact accounts for considerable daytime predation by red-tailed and other hawks. In the Trans-Pecos, where ground cover is sparse enough to observe a large snake's movements from a distance, the author has followed individual *P. c. sayi* for nearly a quarter mile as they foraged across the desert. Most of the time these animals crept along slowly but deliberately. Foregoing lateral undulation in favor of energy-efficient concertina, or rectilinear, locomotion (inching the ventral scutes ahead in successive waves of belly muscle contraction), they investigated every burrow and crevice by poking in their heads for up to 30 seconds, in what was probably a careful olfactory scrutiny, before proceeding.

Because Sonoran gopher snakes cross roads with the same slow gait, they are vulnerable to being run over by traffic. Generally terrestrial, like its more easterly race, the bullsnake, *P. c. sayi* may scale trees both in search of nestling birds and as a last resort when pursued. Although predominantly diurnal in spring and fall, during hot weather gopher snakes are often active throughout the night.

Glossy Snakes
Genus *Arizona*

Texas Glossy Snake, *Arizona elegans arenicola*
Kansas Glossy Snake, *Arizona elegans elegans*
Painted Desert Glossy Snake, *Arizona elegans philipi*

Arizona—a genus whose name means "dry land" due to this burrowing serpent's preference for arid, sandy soils—is part of the colubrine subfamily *Lampropeltinae.* This subfamily contains but a single species, *A. elegans,* which is divided into several North American subspecies, all called glossy snakes, which are an oviparous group closely related to the pine, gopher, and bullsnakes. Like them, *A. elegans* has a relatively narrow head that is still distinct from its slender neck, but unlike *Pituophis, Arizona* is characterized by the smooth, shiny dorsal scales from which its common name is drawn. These scales occur in as few as 25 or as many as 35 rows, there are two prefrontal scutes, and the anal plate is undivided. In lifestyle, *Arizona elegans* is an efficient burrower that emerges onto the surface only after dark to seek its prey of sleeping lizards and, sometimes, small rodents—both of which it may overcome by constriction. Although entirely nonvenomous, like both the pitvipers and the rear-fanged colubrids, glossy snakes have semielliptical daylight pupils—which in darkness enlarge to a circular shape.

69 TEXAS GLOSSY SNAKE
Arizona elegans arenicola

Nonvenomous   See **Kansas Glossy Snake.**

Abundance   Endemic to Texas, *A. e. arenicola* is uncommon in the northeastern part of its range—an extended peninsula of sandy-soiled terrain that stretches from the state's central cross-timbers into its eastern pine forest—yet this race of glossy snake is one of the more abundant serpents encountered on warm spring and early summer nights almost everywhere on the Rio Grande plain south of Falfurrias and Hebbronville.

Size   Adults are most often 20 to 30 inches long, and rarely exceed 3 feet. *Arizona elegans arenicola* is recorded to $54\frac{5}{8}$ inches in length, however.

Habitat   *Arizona* means "dry area" and *arenicola* is "sand-loving"—the primary siliceous habitat of glossy snakes. South of San Antonio this reptile is occasionally found in cropland, but is more abundant in the patches of Tamaulipan thorn woodland that still exist between Duval County and the Mexican border.

In the northeastern part of the Texas glossy's range, sandy-soiled terrain is often used as hay-growing pasture, and here the author has found this race in both Lee and Milam counties. Even farther from its South Texas population center, *A. e. arenicola* has been recorded east of the Trinity River by James Dixon of Texas A&M University, who defined this subspecies in 1960.

Prey   The behavior of recent captives suggests that *Arizona elegans* feeds mainly on lacertilian prey (whiptails, race runners, and spiny lizards are numerous in the Texas glossy's range), most probably scented out after dark while they sleep. Small mammals are perhaps also sometimes taken, although few newly caught individuals accept mice as food.

Reproduction   Egg-laying. Little reproductive data is recorded, but in September and early October up to 2 dozen young, $9\frac{1}{2}$ to 11 inches in length, emerge from buried clutches of $2\frac{3}{4}$-inch-long eggs.

Coloring/scale form   Dorsolateral ground color is off-white, marked, between snout and vent, by 41 to 60 (average 50) large, reddish brown vertebral blotches with very thin dark borders. Unique to glossy snakes, the definitive marking is the pale longitudinal line that runs along the spine just behind the crown. A brown band masks the eyes and crosses the cheeks, and the venter is uniformly white. The smooth dorsal scales, which reflect the nacreous patina suggested by the glossy's name, occur in 29 to 35 (average 32) rows at midbody, and there are 2 prefrontal scales.

Similar snakes   The **Kansas glossy snake (70)** is distinguished from the Texas race by its slightly more numerous (41 to 69, average 55) vertebral blotches and its lower number (29 to 31) of midbody dorsal scale rows.

Behavior   All three Texas glossy snake races are thought to have once been members of an ancient, xeric-adapted fauna that occupied a dry corridor joining the desert Southwest to the Florida peninsula. After this arid-land community was fragmented by the cooler, wetter climate that prevailed along the Gulf Coast during the late Pleistocene, *A. e. arenicola* presumably survived in relict populations confined to pockets of sandy, desertlike soil in eastern and southern Texas. Here, *A. e. arenicola* is almost never seen above ground except well after dark.

70 KANSAS GLOSSY SNAKE
Arizona elegans elegans

Nonvenomous   Large Kansas glossy snakes may bite if molested.

Abundance   Uncommon. Like other *Arizona elegans*, the Kansas glossy's abundance seems to vary radically. In 1948, D. L. Jameson and A. C. Flury's exhaustive West Texas fieldwork failed to turn up a single Kansas glossy snake, yet *A. e. elegans* was more numerous than any other snake collected by Charles McKinney and R. E. Ballinger (1966) in the lower Panhandle. In the shrub desert surrounding the Guadalupe Mountains, an area included in Jameson and Flury's study that deemed *A. elegans* to be a rare snake, Frederick Gehlbach of Baylor University found Kansas glossies to be not uncommon.

Although *A. e. elegans* is unevenly distributed across its approximately 200-mile-wide range, which stretches from Big Bend to northern Kansas, it may be both more fossorial and more common than the sporadic records of its presence would suggest. In wet years it may even be common, for during the summer rainstorms of 1999 these animals turned up throughout the southern Trans-Pecos where almost none had been seen for years.

Size   Slightly larger than other glossy snake races, adult *A. e. elegans* ranges from 20 to 47 inches in length.

Habitat   The Kansas glossy is a western plains and northern Chihuahuan Desert subspecies whose habitat varies markedly. Throughout the drier parts of its range this animal is rarely found, and it is equally uncommon in the intensively cotton- and sorghum-farmed parts of the panhandle. Kansas glossy snakes are seen more often, however, in the sandy-soiled prairie grasslands of north central Texas and the western panhandle, as well as in grassy parts of the Marfa and Marathon basins.

Prey   While recent captives are more willing to feed on mice than are members of the more southerly Texas glossy snake race, the Kansas glossy snake's prey is, nevertheless, probably mostly lizards (kangaroo and pocket mice have been found in the same burrows as *A. e. elegans* and are likely to constitute intermittent prey).

Reproduction   Egg-laying. See **Texas Glossy Snake.**

Coloring/scale form   Like that of all *Arizona elegans*, the Kansas glossy's definitive marking is the pale vertebral line that runs along the neck just posterior to the skull (*elegans* refers to this animal's presumably elegant dorsolateral patterning). A brown band masks its eyes and crosses its cheeks, while its dorsolateral ground color is beige to off-white. This is patterned, between snout and vent, by 41 to 69 (average 55) large brown vertebral blotches with thin dark borders. (A slightly different color morph is reported by Abilene Zoo director Jack Joy, who in Tom Green County found large Kansas glossy snakes with a faintly pinkish ground color and olive-brown dorsal blotches.) Unlike all other large, brown-blotched terrestrial serpents in Texas, glossy snakes have uniformly white bellies, their smooth dorsal scales occur in 29 to 31 midbody rows, and there are 2 prefrontal scales.

Similar snakes Southwest of a line through Del Rio, San Saba, and Gainesville, the Kansas glossy snake is replaced by its subspecies, the **Texas glossy snake (69)**, which has both statistically fewer dorsal blotches (41 to 60, average 50 between snout and vent) and fewer dorsal scale rows, 29 to 35 (average 32). The **bullsnake (67)** has a pale, speckled head, keeled dorsal scales, 4 prefrontal scales, and an enlarged rostral. It lacks the glossy snake's whitish vertebral line along the nape. The **Great Plains rat snake (74)** also lacks the glossy snake's light vertebral line just behind the head, while its venter is pigmented with dark gray and its anal plate is divided.

Behavior Unique to glossy snakes among North American colubrids is the ability to alter the shape of their pupils from round (during darkness, when they are active) to elliptical in sunlight, although pitvipers also vary the configuration of their pupils from vertical slits in bright light to an elliptical shape after dark.

71 PAINTED DESERT GLOSSY SNAKE
Arizona elegans philipi

Nonvenomous See **Kansas Glossy Snake.**

Abundance Uncommon. Perhaps because of the very harsh desert terrain it inhabits, *A. e. philipi* seems to be even more unevenly distributed than other races of glossy snake. Although its abundance varies radically from place to place, it has been found in parts of the Franklin Mountains north of El Paso as well as eastward throughout the sandy lowlands extending as far as Hudspeth County.

Size See **Kansas Glossy Snake.**

Habitat El Paso County and a bit of western Hudspeth County harbor animals found nowhere else east of the hundredth meridian because of this area's long stretch of sand dunes. This Sahara-like milieu harbors a biotic community that includes such sand-adapted animals as the Apache pocket mouse and the most westerly of Texas glossy snakes, *Arizona elegans philipi*. In places other than the West Texas dunes, the Painted Desert glossy snake's favored habitat consists of creosote- and blackbrush-covered sandy or gravelly slopes, sagebrush flats, and dry grassland.

Prey See **Kansas Glossy Snake.**

Reproduction Egg-laying. See **Texas Glossy Snake.**

Coloring/scale form   Like most arid-land reptiles whose dorsolateral camouflage must mirror the pallid, sometimes pinkish hue of its prevailing desert substrate, the Painted Desert glossy snake is paler than its eastern relatives, with golden brown dorsal blotches often compressed over its spine into a waisted, hourglass shape. The white vertebral/nuchal stripe characteristic of glossy snakes is present, but as a seemingly sun-bleached version of its eastern subspecies it lacks the latter's well-defined dark masks although a faint umber line running from its eye to the corner of its jaw suggests this marking. *Arizona elegans philipi* also differs from more eastern glossy races in having a slightly longer tail (about 15 percent of its total length).

Similar snakes   The subspecies **Kansas glossy snake (70)** has statistically fewer dorsal blotches (41 to 69, average 55) and fewer dorsal scale rows (29 to 31, average 30). The **Sonoran gopher snake (68)** has a pale, speckled head, keeled dorsal scales, 4 prefrontal scales, and an enlarged rostral scute; it lacks the glossy snake's whitish vertebral line along the nape.

Behavior   The Painted Desert glossy snake—the subspecies name honors Philip M. Klauber, whose father, Lawrence M. Klauber, defined this race in 1946—is similar in behavior to the state's two more easterly glossy snake subspecies: its activity cycle is one of exclusively nocturnal foraging on the surface and subterranean retreat during dawn, daylight, and dusk. See **Texas Glossy Snake.**

Rat Snakes
Genus *Elaphe*

Texas Rat Snake, *Elaphe obsoleta lindheimerii*
Baird's Rat Snake, *Elaphe bairdi*
Great Plains Rat Snake, *Elaphe guttata emoryi*

The genus *Elaphe* is a member of the colubrine subfamily *Colubrinae*— a group of powerful, oviparous constrictors represented in the eastern United States by five species: *E. obsoleta*, which includes five races of the nominate black rat snake; *E. bairdi*, Baird's rat snake; *E. guttata*, the corn snake/great plains rat snake; and *E. gloydi* and *E. vulpina*, the two fox snake species. Adult *Elaphe* have weakly keeled dorsal scales and generally unkeeled lateral scales; juveniles lack scale keels. The number of dorsolateral scale rows varies by species as well as, to some extent, individually. The black rat snake races have from 25 to 33 rows, Baird's rat snake usually has 27 rows, corn/Great Plains rat snakes have 27 to 29 rows, and the fox snakes have 23 to 27 rows. The anal plate of all American *Elaphe* is divided.

Except for the fox snakes, American *Elaphe* undergo marked ontogenetic, or age-related, changes in color and pattern. At hatching juveniles are strongly blotched or crossbarred and are difficult to differentiate as to subspecies, but with age and growth many lose their contrasting juvenile pattern and become either more indistinctly marked above or, in the case of the yellow rat snake, strongly striped.

Because of their propensity for farms and barnyards, members of the genus *Elaphe* have received the official common name of rat snake, though they are more widely, and erroneously, known by the public as chicken snakes. (A foraging rat snake will eat both baby chicks and eggs but it is the proliferation of their preferred rodent prey among piles of debris or within unused buildings that draws these reptiles to farmyards.)

With the exception of the fox snakes, rat snakes are also agile climbers that can ascend straight up moderately rough-barked tree trunks; with more difficulty they usually can climb even smooth-trunked trees. This ability is crucial to the ecological niche of American *Elaphe*, for arboreal refuge is central both to these animals' avoidance of predators and to the acquisition of their own prey; young rat snakes usually feed on small lizards and tree frogs, while adults consume rodents, juvenile rabbits, and birds. Most of these creatures are killed or immobilized by constriction, though where there is no room to wrap body coils around a victim—in the confines of narrow rodent burrows, for example—small prey is simply grasped in the jaws and swallowed.

72 TEXAS RAT SNAKE
Elaphe obsoleta lindheimerii

Nonvenomous   Texas rat snakes are vigorous in their own defense and if threatened often make several mostly bluffing, openmouthed strikes. Pressed further, *E. o. lindheimerii* may defecate in fear, emit musk from its cloacal glands, and ultimately bite—though the pressure of its jaws is slight and only scratches usually result.

Abundance   Very common. One of the handful of the state's truly abundant large terrestrial serpents, the Texas rat snake is the long, brown-mottled snake that most often appears in suburban neighborhoods throughout the eastern two-thirds of Texas. It is likely to be found high in trees or, in human-populated areas, hidden in barns, henhouses, abandoned buildings, and machinery. After the grayish young hatch in late summer, they often turn up around both rural and suburban houses; like the adults, they may nip when picked up.

Size   Adult Texas rat snakes are slender but long, averaging 42 to 72 inches—dimensions that have earned *E. o. lindheimerii* the nickname "piney woods python." The record length is just over 7 feet.

Habitat   Abundant in both deciduous woods and bordering pastureland, this reptile is named for pioneer naturalist Ferdinand Jacob Lindheimer, who collected the type specimen near his home in New Braunfels, Texas. This westernmost race of *Elaphe obsoleta* also occurs in almost every terrestrial and aquatic-margin environment from upland pine/hardwood forest to coastal prairie marsh.

Prey Both juvenile and adult Texas rat snakes feed almost entirely on warm-blooded prey, especially birds and their nestlings—on which *E. o. lindheimerii* is a major predator. (A flock of blue jays and other passerines screaming at a Texas rat snake coiled high in the branches is a common woodland sight.) Also called "chicken snake" for its attraction to the rodents, eggs and chicks to be found in henhouses, *E. o. lindheimerii* is equally likely to be seen by the residents of wooded subdivisions who set out cage birds on their patios. Larger prey such as small mammals is overpowered by constriction, which hatchling rat snakes employ instinctively, though they learn the mechanics of swallowing prey head first only by trial and error, initially attempting to ingest young mice sideways or from the rear until they discover that does not work.

Reproduction Egg-laying. Hatchling Texas rat snakes are 12 to 14 inches long, with lead-gray crowns striped by a pair of solid chocolate lines that form a forward-facing spearpoint. Another chocolate-colored band masks the eyes and extends rearward only as far as the posterior upper labial scales. Juveniles' backs have a pale gray ground color, boldly patterned with darker-edged, irregularly shaped brown dorsal and lateral blotches which enlarge and, along with their ground color, darken as they mature.

Coloring/scale form Adult Texas rat snakes' large, dark brown rectangular vertebral blotches are separated by smaller, yellowish brown transverse areas about 4 scale rows in width; reddish skin may be evident on the sides of the neck. Older adults are darker in color. The pale venter is blotched with dark squares partially obscured by a grayish overwash, while the underside of the tail tip is usually solid gray. Albinism is rare but existent among *E. o. lindheimerii,* with a whitish 4-foot-long female reported from Williamson County by Tim Cole. Of the 27 midbody rows of dorsal scales, those along the spine are most strongly keeled.

Similar snakes The **Baird's rat snake (73)** is faintly striped above and lacks dorsal blotches; juveniles are grayer than young Texas rat snakes, with dark transverse vertebral bars. The similar-looking juvenile **Great Plains rat snake (74)** has a black-edged brown V on its pale crown. Another dark-edged brown band crosses its snout, masks its eyes, and extends posteriorly onto its neck, while a pale subcaudal midventral stripe is centered between dark distal borders. The **prairie kingsnake (76)** has smooth scales and an undivided anal plate.

Behavior The Texas rat snake's wiry musculature and sharp-edged belly scales make it an agile climber, but it also patrols creekbanks from the water and has been captured swimming across the middle of large lakes.

73 BAIRD'S RAT SNAKE
Elaphe bairdi

Nonvenomous Although some Baird's rat snakes are entirely nonaggressive even when first picked up in the field, other individuals may hiss and nip if cornered.

Abundance Very uncommon. Native only to Texas and 3 or 4 small, disjunct ranges in northern Mexico, *Elaphe bairdi* seems to be spottily dispersed in even the best habitat. Although its primary range is the Trans-Pecos, it is also found on the western Edwards Plateau: back roads in the vicinity of Leakey, Vanderpool, and Barksdale are the site of a number of nocturnal sightings, especially after summer rainfall.

Size Adults are usually between 24 and 40 inches long; one enormous specimen measured 62 in.

Habitat *Elaphe bairdi* inhabits three very different primary environments: (1) both montane forest and lower elevation canyons throughout the southern Trans-Pecos, (2) the very different oak/juniper forested riparian corridors of the central hill country, and (3) the barren Cretaceous limestone bluffs and canyons of the Pecos River drainage, where Baird's rat snakes are rare. Although much of this range includes arid terrain, most of it unsuitable habitat, for *Elaphe bairdi* occurs primarily in comparatively mesic canyon biomes (one small male taken just before shedding was unable to rid itself of its old skin until it had soaked in a pan of water for several days).

Prey Like other rat snakes, *Elaphe bairdi* is a generalized predator on small vertebrates, constricting prey that includes birds and their eggs, lizards, rodents, and other small mammals. Lizards and nestling rodents are probably the primary food of the young.

Reproduction Egg-laying. Mating during May and early June results in the midsummer deposition of usually fewer than 10, 1¼ by 1-inch-wide smooth-shelled eggs. Like the eggs of other rat snakes, the whole clutch usually adheres to form a single cluster that, after 70 to 85 days, hatches into 11- to 13-inch-long gray, dorsally dark-barred offspring. As they mature, juveniles undergo an ontogenetic color and pattern change, losing their prominent dark brown cross-dorsal bands during their second year in place of the longitudinal brown stripes of the adult.

Coloring/scale form *Elaphe bairdi* is a subtly beautiful snake. Beneath a translucent sheen, the forebody of adults is washed with a golden tint—the result of myriad tiny orangish crescents, one of which rims the forward margin of each dorsal scale. From the eyes to the rear of the skull the crown is dark mahogany, followed by a pair of moderately wide brown dorsolateral stripes. These stripes have a crosshatched appearance because only part of each scale that makes them up is pigmented with brown. A rare, yellowish tan color phase dimly marked with gray stripes occurs west of Big Bend, while an extraordinarily colored individual with rusty-hued cross-dorsal bands was found in the Chisos Mountains by former Big Bend National Park Superintendent Roland H. Wauer. The lips and chin are light gray-brown to pale yellow, colors that continue beneath the forebelly, then darken to pale salmon, scalloped with gray, under the tail. The weakly keeled dorsal scales are arranged in 27 rows at midbody.

Similar snakes   The adult **Texas rat snake (72)** has an entirely dark brown head and neck and rectangular chocolate dorsal blotches along the length of its trunk.

Behavior   Like those of the Baird's sparrow and sandpiper, this animal's name honors Spencer Fullerton Baird. As secretary of the Smithsonian Institution throughout the middle third of the nineteenth century, Baird fueled much of the burst of zoological discovery that accompanied the opening of the West. Often in partnership with Charles Frederick Girard, he first described some 24 southwestern snake species and subspecies.

74 GREAT PLAINS RAT SNAKE
Elaphe guttata emoryi

Nonvenomous   Although a large individual may nip if picked up roughly, most wild Great Plains rat snakes are easily handled.

Abundance   Common in Texas, *Elaphe guttata emoryi* is much less abundant in other parts of its range. It is protected as a threatened species in both Illinois and Colorado.

Size   Most adults are 2½ to 3½ feet long; the record is 60¼ in.

Habitat   A grayer, drier habitat-living race of the eastern corn snake, *E. g. emoryi* occupies terrain that varies from upland prairie to tidewater marsh to bottomland forest. In the western part of its range, an even grayer color morph with smaller dorsal blotches is found in the arid northern Chihuahuan Desert. Here, *Elaphe guttata emoryi* is an especially chthonic animal, for it inhabits inaccessible rock crevices far below the surface. In places where big Great Plains rat snakes are almost never seen, very large individuals are sometimes driven from deep subsurface haunts by flash flooding; Robert Webb (1970) reports 1 active individual found 60 feet underground.

During the warmer months some subterranean caverns provide food— *E. g. emoryi* is a regular predator on Mexican free-tailed bat nursery colonies— while in winter, caves, rock quarries, and abandoned building foundations offer temperate shelter. At this season Great Plains rat snakes have been found brumating alongside both Texas rat snakes and copperheads, while the cellar of one derelict farmhouse in Woods County, Oklahoma, served as a hibernaculum for 6 Great Plains rat snakes and 27 eastern yellow-bellied racers.

Prey   *Elaphe guttata emoryi* eats mostly warm-blooded animals that it kills by constriction. Rodents, as well as birds and their young, are its primary prey. (The author observed one Brewster County, Texas, Great Plains rat snake wedging its way up the furrowed bark of a cottonwood in whose lower branches a pair of vermillion flycatchers were frantically defending their nest.) Frogs and lizards are also sometimes preyed upon, but smaller snakes are not ordinarily taken.

BROWN-BLOTCHED TERRESTRIAL SNAKES

Reproduction   Egg-laying. The first description of reproduction—of a typical clutch of 15—was published by John E. Werler in 1951:

"On June 14 . . . a 44¾-inch-long female from near Brownsville laid 5 smooth, adhesive eggs. Ten more were deposited the following day, averaging 1.8 inches in length, 1.1 inches in width. Slits first appeared in 2 of the eggs on Aug. 7, and these snakes emerged from their shells on August 8. Two additional snakes escaped from their shells on August 9, another on August 10, and the last two on August 12."

The subspecies eastern corn snake, *E. g. guttata*, typically deposits 20 to 30 much smaller eggs, while the westernmost *E .g. emoryi* populations lay only a dozen or so relatively much larger eggs that produce offspring up to 4 times as heavy as those of eastern *E. guttata*. Geographically intermediate populations are similarly intermediate in clutch number, egg size, and average hatchling weight. The record size clutch for *E. g. emoryi* is probably that of a Murchison County female maintained by Gus Renfro of Brownsville, which deposited 25 fertile eggs during the first week in July. After 68 days her emerging hatchlings ranged from 11 to 15½ inches in length. The members of a smaller litter maintained by the author had grown to about 29 inches in length after 14 months; at 9 years of age one of these animals measured 44 inches and weighed just under 3 pounds.

Coloring/scale form   The Great Plains rat snake's most distinctive marking is the diamond-shaped brown arrowhead shape (whose point lies between the eyes) that patterns its crown. Forward of this marking and below it a dark-edged brown mask crosses its snout, masks its eyes, and continues rearward past its supralabial scales. Like its eastern subspecies, the corn snake, the Great Plains rat snake's dorsolateral color and pattern vary according to geographic location. As the substrate—which snakes' dorsal camouflage must match—becomes lighter in color as one moves westward, a majority of *E. g. emoryi* display correspondingly paler dorsolateral hues. For example, most Great Plains rat snakes living in southwest Texas have a paler, grayer ground color than more easterly individuals, and are patterned with smaller, more numerous, and lighter-hued dorsal blotches because in the predominantly whitish, limestone-substrate portions of south and southwest Texas, light-hued *Elaphe guttata* are likely to survive better than their darker-blotched kin.

E. g. emoryi from the northern part of this subspecies' range tend to have larger, darker brown vertebral blotches on a medium brown ground color, while Great Plains rat snakes from East Texas and Louisiana sometimes have dark orange pigment on their necks, suggesting the genetic influence of the Great Plains rat snake's easterly race, the russet and black-backed corn snake. Among all geographic variants, the belly is blotched with brown—more heavily in eastern specimens—while the underside of the tail has a pair of dark distal stripes bordering its pale midventral stripe. The 27 to 29 midbody rows of dorsal scales are weakly keeled along the spine.

Similar snakes. Adult **Texas rat snakes (72)** have unmarked dark brown heads and necks and solid gray undertails; juveniles have a lead-gray crown and a solid chocolate eye mask. The **prairie kingsnake (76)** has smooth dorsal scales and an undivided anal plate. **Glossy snakes (69-71)** have a pale vertebral line along the nape, a white venter, and an undivided anal plate.

Behavior   This abundant but often secretive reptile is named for William Hemsley Emory, the long-whiskered U.S. boundary commissioner who, in authorizing the initial mapping of the Texas–Mexican border, subsequently saw his name attached to a number of the plants (Emory oak) and animals (Emory's rat snake, *E. g. emoryi*) first described by members of his expeditions. Extremely nocturnal, during its March-to-October activity period *E. g. emoryi* emerges from hiding only well after dark, but when rainstorms drive terrestrial snakes to shelter, Great Plains rat snakes are typically among the first serpents to emerge again.

Trans-Pecos Rat Snake
Genus *Bogertophis*

Trans-Pecos Rat Snake, *Bogertophis subocularis*

This is a new genus defined in 1988 by H. G. Dowling and R. M. Price and named for Charles M. Bogert, head of herpetology at the American Museum of Natural History. It belongs to the colubrine subfamily *Colubrinae*.

It is an oviparous, primarily saxicolous desert- and dry savannah-living genus whose most unique characteristic is the row of subocular scales that separates the eye from the upper labial scales (the 31 to 35 rows of dorsolateral scales are weakly keeled and the anal plate is divided). Despite being commonly termed "rat snake," this genus is considered by some researchers to be more closely related to the bull and gopher snakes, *Pituophis*, than to the rat snake genus *Elaphe*, from which *Bogertophis* was only recently separated. (This genus' slim, muscular body is more similar in configuration to that of the rat snakes than to the bull/gopher snakes, however, and is the reason its members were long considered to be *Elaphe*.)

Whatever its genetic affinity with related genera, *Bogertophis* is made up of only 2 species, one of which, the Trans-Pecos rat snake, occurs in the area covered here. This big-eyed, delicate nocturnal serpent has a somewhat flattened head, much broader than its slender neck and, at least toward humans, has an extremely gentle, tolerant disposition. It typically constricts medium- and large-sized prey but often chooses not to constrict smaller animals.

75 TRANS-PECOS RAT SNAKE
Bogertophis subocularis

Nonvenomous Trans-Pecos rat snakes almost never defend themselves against human beings.

Abundance Uncommon. *Bogertophis subocularis* is among the numerous cryptic nocturnal Chihuahuan Desert serpents which, despite being widespread, are seldom seen by humans.

Most *B. subocularis* are encountered on dark, humid nights between May and September on back roads through Val Verde, Terrell, Presidio, Brewster, and Jeff Davis counties. Other *B. subocularis* have been found as far north as the Guadalupe Mountains, but most of this species' range is northern Mexico, and its greatest concentration in the United States is probably along the Rio Grande's Big Bend.

Size Adult *B. subocularis* measuring 30 to 48 inches long are most often seen in the wild—though the author found a 12¾-inch neonate with a fresh umbilical scar in Big Bend National Park late in September, and other juveniles turn up from time to time. Specimens have been recorded to 5½ feet in length.

Habitat This arid land reptile's macrohabitat includes the northern Chihuahuan Desert's barren flats and slopes of ocotillo, lechuguilla, and sotol cactus, as well as Trans-Pecos Texas' less xeric short-grass prairie and oak–juniper woodland at altitudes of more than 6,500 feet in the Davis Mountains. Everywhere in its range the Trans-Pecos rat snake is found on and around rocky outcroppings and stony, heavily fissured road cuts.

Prey Despite the preference for lacertillian prey shown by a majority of newly captured individuals, in its natural setting *B. subocularis* appears to be a generalized feeder on smaller vertebrates, with the exception of other snakes. The author once observed a well-fed Trans-Pecos rat snake coiled on a cave ledge below a layer of flightless young Mexican free-tailed bats, while herpetologist Damon Salceies observed a rare instance of predation by this nocturnal hunter.

A wild adult *B. subocularis* which he had been watching from a distance with a flashlight flushed a crevice spiny lizard from its nighttime hiding place on a roadside rock ledge. Darting from beneath the thin layer of dirt that hid it from view, the lizard, as is typical, ran only a few feet, then paused and soon became drowsy, shutting one eye and then the other. Meanwhile, with the predatory concentration that characterizes all ophidian hunters, the Trans-Pecos rat snake crept gradually nearer its prey. Finally, holding its head and forebody motionless to avoid attracting the crevice spiny's attention, the rat snake drew its posterior body forward, gathering its coils behind its head. Then, belying the docile nature this species shows toward humans, the rat snake abruptly shot forward in a shower of flying dirt to pin the lizard in its open mouth, instantly encircling its prey with loops of its body.

Reproduction   Egg-laying. First accomplished by Jonathan Campbell at the Fort Worth Zoo during the 1960s, captive propagation of this species has since become widespread. Twenty-five pairings among *B. subocularis* maintained by D. Craig McIntyre reveal that only during a brief annual period of fertility will the female accept a mate, for nearly all these copulations took place between June 18 and 30.

Deposited during July, August, and September, the proportionately large eggs range from 3 to 11 per clutch and require a comparatively long incubation of up to 88 days. (Some *B. subocularis* clutches have taken more than 100 days to hatch, but since serpent embryos begin developing as soon as the egg is formed, longer incubation in the nest cavity may mean only that the mother has not retained her eggs for as long as females whose eggs hatch after shorter incubation.)

This species' long incubation and late-season breeding pattern—one road-killed Davis Mountains female was still gravid with unlaid eggs in late August, and the eggs of captives often hatch as late as Thanksgiving—means that the higher elevations of this animal's range have become quite cold by the time its young are ready to emerge from the egg. Therefore, rather than face this hostile time of year abroad, newborns may remain below ground until the following spring, perhaps emerging only rarely during their first year. (Another possibility, suggested by the presence of apparently fresh umbilical scars on neonate *B. subocularis* discovered in late spring, is that with the advent of cold weather this species' embryos may cease development within their eggs so that whole clutches may winter below ground, hatching only in the following year's warming temperatures.)

Delicate little creatures 11½ to 13 inches in length, hatchling *B. subocularis* are paler than the adults but share the same dorsal pattern. Sexual maturity is reached in 2 to 3 years, and fertility can last for at least an additional 13 seasons. (McIntyre's females have produced fertile eggs at more than 16 years of age, and one individual—which now holds the species' longevity record of 26 years—was captured as an adult in 1971 and has since laid more than 60 fertile eggs.)

Coloring/scale form   Against a soft, mustard-brown dorsolateral ground color, a pair of parallel black lines, one on either side of the spine, are joined by 27 to 41 dark crossbars that form a series of H-shaped patterns along the spine. On the tail these crossbars become squarish saddles. Populations living north of I-10 may be paler, those in rocky terrain nearer the Rio Grande more orange or rust in ground color. (Pale yellow *B. subocularis* with no vertebral stripes and only faint dorsal patterning also exist. In 1964 the first of these "blonds" was found in southern Brewster County by Dennie Miller of the Chihuahuan Desert Research Institute; since then other similarly colored individuals appear periodically from the lower Pecos River area to southern Presidio County. Some Trans-Pecos rat snakes from north of El Paso exhibit a light gray ground color, and even albinism has been reported.)

The Trans-Pecos rat snake is unique among North American serpents in possessing 40 pairs of chromosomes instead of the usual 36 or 38, while its scalation is also unusual. A row of small subocular scales (from which the

181

species' Latin name, *subocularis*, is derived) separates the scales of its upper lip from its eye. The venter is a silky off-white on the throat that darkens to olive buff by midbody; some individuals show dim undertail striping. Only the 7 vertebral rows of dorsal scales, which occur in 31 to 35 rows at midbody, are keeled.

Similar snakes Classified with other North American rat snakes in the genus *Elaphe* until 1988, the Trans-Pecos rat snake has now been shown—by H. G. Dowling and R. M. Price—to be genetically distinct enough to warrant taxonomic placement in a new genus, *Bogertophis*. (This genus includes only one other species, the Baja California rat snake, *B. rosalie*.) No other North American serpent shares either the Trans-Pecos rat snake's mustard brown dorsolateral ground color or its distinctive dark, H-shaped vertebral pattern.

Behavior Like many xeric-adapted reptiles, *B. subocularis* responds to the harsh climate of its Chihuahuan Desert range by restricting its movements on the surface to temperate summer nights. During the day, as well as for what may be as much as several months' winter brumation, it remains within this succulent desert's subsurface labyrinth of creviced limestone. Living mostly in this sheltered milieu, the Trans-Pecos rat snake may have never needed to evolve strong fight-or-flight behavior for, illuminated by headlights, *B. subocularis* typically makes no attempt to escape or to defend itself when picked up.

Kingsnakes, Milk, Scarlet, and Long-Nosed Snakes

Genus *Lampropeltis*

The milk snake and kingsnake genus, *Lampropeltis*, is part of the colubrine subfamily *Lampropeltinae*. This subfamily includes both the rat and pine snake genera, *Elaphe* and *Pituophis*, respectively, to which *Lampropeltis* is more or less closely related since captives of all three genera have hybridized and produced viable offspring. All *Lampropeltis* have scales so smooth they appear polished, and indeed *lampros* and *peltas* mean "shiny scaled" in Greek. All *Lampropeltis* have an undivided anal plate and are noted for their ophiophagus inclination—predatory behavior aided by their resistance to the venoms of the various pitvipers that share their habitat. *Lampropeltis* also cannibalize smaller members of their own species.

In the eastern and central United States there are four species of *Lampropeltis*, some called milk snakes and some called kingsnakes, though there is no significant taxonomic difference between the two. Of these four species, only one, the gray-banded kingsnake, *L. alterna*, is not subspeciated. A second species, *L. calligaster*, the prairie kingsnake, contains three subspecies, while the third species, *L. getula*, the common kingsnake, has five subspecies and several localized color morphs. The fourth species, *L. triangulum*, the milk snake, has eight subspecies. (The prairie kingsnake has 21 to 27 dorsolateral scale rows; eastern forms of the common kingsnake have 21 to 25 rows; milk snakes, 19 to 23 rows; and the gray-banded kingsnake, 25 rows.)

Brown-blotched Kingsnakes

Genus *Lampropeltis*

Prairie Kingsnake, *Lampropeltis calligaster calligaster*

76 PRAIRIE KINGSNAKE
Lampropeltis calligaster calligaster

Nonvenomous This mild-tempered reptile may vibrate its tail in fear, but even when picked up in the wild it seldom nips humans.

Abundance Uncommon. Prairie kingsnakes are widely but sparsely distributed across a huge range that covers both the Great Plains and its adjacent eastern woodlands. *Lampropeltis calligaster* is so secretive, however, that in spite of being a quite sizable snake, it is only rarely seen.

Size Adults average 24 to 36 inches in length; the record is 58⅛ in.

Habitat As its common name implies, the prairie kingsnake is predominantly an inhabitant of grassland. This includes not only the dry tall-grass prairie of the upland plains but flood-prone salt-grass savannah and grassy barrier island dunes along the upper Gulf Coast—where piles of driftwood are a good microhabitat.

Prey Like other kingsnakes, *L. c. calligaster* is a powerful constrictor, but one more oriented toward warm-blooded prey than other kingsnakes; food animals include mice, rats, gophers, moles, and birds. Frogs and toads, lizards, and other snakes are also less frequently reported as prey.

Reproduction Egg-laying. No natural nests are recorded, and hatchling *L. c. calligaster* evidently live deeply fossorial lives, for very few wild newborns have been observed. In captivity, clutches of 6 to 17 smooth-shelled eggs are deposited during late June and July, and then hatch into relatively small, 6- to 8-inch-long young (one such captive-born specimen has been maintained at the Oklahoma City Zoo for over 13 years).

Coloring/scale form The prairie kingsnake's yellow- to light olive-brown dorsolateral ground color is usually patterned with 50 to 55 irregular brown vertebral saddles; its sides are marked with jagged brown spots. A short, yellow-brown vertebral stripe extends forward along the nape from its anterior back; the dark borders of this stripe widen, then come together on the forecrown to form a spearpoint-shaped marking; anterior to this spearpoint a dark stripe runs across the prairie king's snout, masks its eyes, and extends posteriorly past the rear of its jaw.

Lampropeltis calligaster calligaster also exhibits ontogenetic color variation, darkening with age and sometimes developing, from its dorsal blotches, four dimly defined dusky lengthwise stripes. Among very old prairie kingsnakes the entire dorsum may have darkened to a solid umber. The yellowish to cloudy gray venter—*calligaster* means "beautiful belly"—is checked with large, rusty brown rectangular blotches. The smooth dorsal scales occur in 25 to 27 midbody rows, and the anal plate is undivided.

Similar snakes The **Great Plains rat snake (74)** has weakly keeled vertebral scales, a pale buff rather than olive-brown ground color, a dark-edged undertail tip and, unlike *Lampropeltis*, a divided anal plate. **Texas** and **Kansas**

glossy snakes (69–70) have a pale longitudinal line along the nape, at least 29 rows of dorsal scales, and an unmarked white belly.

Behavior   Prairie kingsnakes are secretive reptiles that seldom emerge from beneath rocks, clumps of grass, or the depths of small mammal burrows. John MacGregor has found *L. c. calligaster* to be quite diurnal during springtime in Kentucky, but in the more southerly part of its range foraging typically takes place at dusk in spring and fall, but occurs only well after dark during the hottest months.

Pale-speckled Kingsnakes
Genus *Lampropeltis*

Speckled Kingsnake, *Lampropeltis getula holbrooki*
Desert Kingsnake, *Lampropeltis getula splendida*

77 SPECKLED KINGSNAKE
Lampropeltis getula holbrooki

Nonvenomous   If molested, the speckled kingsnake may swell its neck and bite with determination. If treated gently, however, it quickly becomes accustomed to handling, although if one's hands smell of its prey it may try an exploratory nip.

Abundance   Fairly common. *Lampropeltis getula holbrooki,* which is named for the father of American herpetology, John Edwards Holbrook, occupies a mostly wooded eastern and central Texas range. The speckled kingsnake's territorial influence is much broader than this, however, for to the west *L. g. holbrooki* shares a huge zone of intergradation with its subspecies, the desert kingsnake.

Size   Recorded to 74 inches in length, adult speckled kingsnakes are robust, cylindrically bodied reptiles whose muscular necks are as large in diameter as their heads. Most adults are 18 to 36 inches long; hatchlings are 6 to 9 inches in length and about the thickness of a pencil.

Habitat   Despite the extent of its northward distribution, *L. getula* is basically a southern animal that occupies a variety of terrestrial and semiaquatic environments, among them pine and deciduous woodland (where rotting logs and stumps are a favored microhabitat), grassy pastures, estuarine wetlands (including saline tidal flats), and salt grass- and succulent-covered barrier beach dunes where speckled kingsnakes are found sheltering beneath driftwood. During wet spring weather, along the upper Gulf Coast *L. g. holbrooki* occurs with some frequency in brackish and freshwater marshes and inundated riparian bottomland, around abandoned farms, and along the edges of crop fields and drainage ditches.

Prey   Speckled kingsnakes are scent-oriented hunters that prey on a variety of smaller vertebrates. Other snakes, including members of their own species, are especially favored. Although pitvipers are formidable adversaries that may strike and poison them repeatedly, kingsnakes are resistant to the effects of Cortaid venom and are able to overcome these vipers by immobilizing them with constriction. Then the kingsnake's powerful neck and jaw muscles let it work its way forward to engulf the head of the viper. (Sometimes, however, after a pitviper's bite the kingsnake chooses not to consume its prey.) Small mammals, birds, fish, and frogs are also taken; a favorite food is turtle eggs, which are not punctured but swallowed whole.

Reproduction   Egg-laying. See **Desert Kingsnake**.

Coloring/scale form   Each shiny black or dark brown dorsal scale bears a yellowish white spot—creating, among adults, a uniformly pale-speckled back and sides. (Juveniles are also profusely light-freckled, but many of their light-colored spots are clumped together in pale lines that cross the back, leaving dark intervening areas similar to those of the eastern and Florida kingsnakes.) The venter is predominantly yellow, checked, or blotched with black; the glossy dorsal scales—*Lampropeltis* means "shining skin"—are arranged in 21 to 23 midbody rows.

Similar snakes   A western race, the **desert kingsnake (78)**, is distinguished by its predominantly black venter and crown, its 23 to 25 dorsolateral scale rows, and its large dorsal areas of black or dark brown scales.

Behavior   *Lampropeltis getula holbrooki* is almost always encountered on the ground where, as a slow-moving serpent, its principal defense against large predators is to retreat into burrows or beneath sheltering debris. It can also climb, although slowly, in search of bird eggs, and it swims well, as it often does in both flooded bottomland and coastal tidal flat milieus.

78 DESERT KINGSNAKE
Lampropeltis getula splendida

Nonvenomous   Like other kingsnakes, *L. g. splendida* is for the most part a docile animal when approached or even handled in the wild. Yet if threatened, even a small individual may put on a valiant defensive display, drawing its neck into an S-shaped curve, vibrating its tail tip, and striking open-mouthed. Big kingsnakes can bite with conviction, but most of their strikes are bluffs; frightened desert kings are more likely to defecate and discharge odorous musk.

Abundance   Uncommon. This xeric-adapted race of *L. getula* is widespread in northwestern Mexico and western Texas. North of the U.S. border it is most numerous in the thorn brush of the Rio Grande Valley. Desert kingsnakes are also widely distributed throughout extensive montane areas west of the Pecos River, but they are not common there, nor in the intervening low-lying Chihuahuan Desert except in artificially watered areas like the irrigated fields around Balmorrhea, where this subspecies is sometimes abundant. Elsewhere in northwestern Texas, even the largest desert kingsnakes may spend most of their lives as burrowers. After torrential rains in Andrews County had flooded many snakes from their subsurface haunts, Damon Salceies found a gravid female *L. g. splendida* almost 5 feet long.

Size Adults average 22 to 38 inches in length; the record is 60 in.

Habitat *Lampropeltis getula splendida* may occur in almost any vegetated rural habitat in the western half of Texas. Yet—despite its common name— the desert king generally inhabits the more mesic parts of its range and is most often found near water tanks or within riparian corridors. Here, the soil is soft enough for burrowing and the desert king is more likely to find its favored prey of other snakes and buried reptile eggs.

Prey This arid land–living kingsnake feeds on other snakes, lizards, and small mammals, as well as on clutches of reptile eggs detected beneath the surface by smell. In part because of its resistance to pitviper venom, *L. g. splendida* is also able to prey on the young diamond-backed rattlesnakes which, in early autumn, are extremely common within its range. (At this kingsnake's scent even huge western diamondbacks, far too big to fall prey to any *Lampropeltis*, instinctually edge backward, hiding their heads with a body coil and often raising a loop of the body as a shield since the pitviper's normal venom defense is ineffective against *Lampropeltis getula*.)

Reproduction Egg-laying. Courtship and copulation among desert kingsnakes take place between March and June, with combat rivalry between competing males taking part as both lie prone alongside each other. The victor then switches between inserting the right and left hemipenes during repeated copulations. Clutches of 5 to 12 narrowly elliptical, adhesive-surfaced eggs are deposited in late June or July, sometimes buried as deeply as a foot to prevent drying, through their moisture-permeable shells, in the extremely low humidity of this animal's western range. After about 60 days of incubation the 8½- to 10-inch-long hatchlings emerge, each weighing about ⅕ ounce. Brightly yellow-speckled with pale vertebral cross-lines and as shiny as porcelain figurines, hatchlings are marked with a row of big black vertebral squares. As individuals from the eastern part of the range mature, their dark vertebral areas may be fragmented by encroaching yellow flecks; western specimens are more uniformly dusky above.

Coloring/scale form This beautiful kingsnake is notable for its glossy black or very dark brown dorsum, finely speckled with off-white or yellow. Some of these light-hued flecks may join to form narrow, pale yellow crossbands, between which large black or dark brown dorsal rectangles are only faintly pale-speckled. Light yellow scales usually predominate along the lower sides. West of the Pecos River, even more strikingly colored *L. g. splendida* make up a considerable percentage of the population. Posteriorly colored like individuals from the eastern part of the range, this Chihuahuan Desert color phase—called "sock-heads" by enthusiasts—has a jet-black head and neck with only a bit of yellow labial scale edging. The venter of both adult and young is mostly black or dark gray, with white or pale yellow blotches marking the ventral plates of the intergrade specimens found throughout the south central Great Plains. The dorsal scales are arranged in 23 to 25 rows at midbody.

Similar snakes   An eastern subspecies, the **speckled kingsnake (77)**, is distinguished by its largely unmarked, more uniformly yellow- or white-speckled back, sides, and head, by its predominantly yellow, black-blotched venter, and its 21 to 23 midbody rows of dorsal scales. Intergrades with the speckled kingsnake prevail along the eastern portion of the desert king's range, where most individuals exhibit characteristics (such as partially pale cross-patterned dorsums and yellow and black bellies) that combine the attributes of both races.

Behavior   Although these snakes are generally reported to be exclusively terrestrial and fossorial, the author nevertheless captured an adult near the top of a mulberry tree in Brewster County. This 35-inch-long male had just swallowed two fully feathered young kingbirds (whose bodies, feet, and beaks were outlined beneath its distended skin) and was in the process of sizing up two more of the first pair's nestmates.

Red- and Black-banded Milk and Kingsnakes
Genus *Lampropeltis*

Louisiana Milk Snake, *Lampropeltis triangulum amaura*
Mexican Milk Snake, *Lampropeltis triangulum annulata*
New Mexico Milk Snake, *Lampropeltis triangulum celaenops*
Central Plains Milk Snake, *Lampropeltis triangulum gentilis*
Gray-banded Kingsnake, *Lampropeltis alterna*

79 LOUISIANA MILK SNAKE
Lampropeltis triangulum amaura

Nonvenomous   Louisiana milk snakes seldom bite even when first picked up in the wild. Like other members of the kingsnake family, occasional individuals may nip and hang on tenaciously, but most *L. t. amaura* are so small that these nips are inconsequential.

Abundance   Uncommon to rare. Although *Lampropeltis triangulum* is one of the world's most widely distributed ophidian species, the Louisiana milk snake is sparsely distributed throughout the pine forest and more open oak–greenbrier woodland of eastern Texas. Rarely encountered because of their retiring, semi-subterranean lifestyle, all the *L. triangulum* races have long been sought by reptile enthusiasts entranced by their bright colors. As a result, for years every milk snake subspecies was protected in Texas, although now it is thought that collectors' impact on the natural population has been minimal. Despite the major incursions both logging and agricultural/residential land clearing have made into its original longleaf pine forest home, *L. t. amaura* is no longer classified as a threatened animal.

Size   Recorded to 31 inches in length, most adult Louisiana milk snakes are much smaller, averaging only 16 to 24 inches and attaining a girth no thicker than a forefinger.

Habitat   The Louisiana milk snake is by no means principally an inhabitant of the state for which it is named. Along Texas' Gulf shoreline *L. t. amaura* inhabits both sandy beach dunes and barrier islands, where it is found beneath driftwood, planks, and littoral debris marking the spring tide line. Inland, Louisiana milk snakes live in pine and hardwood forests, where both fallen and upright dead trees standing in riparian bottomland seem to be a preferred microhabitat. In this environment Louisiana milk snakes are cryptic, fossorial inhabitants of thickly layered forest-floor detritus. When late winter rainfall makes this vegetative milieu too saturated for subsurface life, Louisiana milk snakes may wedge their slim bodies into the narrow crevices beneath loosened shingles of pine bark or, for cold weather brumation, tunnel their way deep into these decaying trees' soft interiors.

Prey   Much of the diet of *L. t. amaura* consists of the small serpents that, along with its secondary prey of skinks and spiny lizards, share its forest-floor microhabitat of leaf litter and humus.

Reproduction   Egg-laying. See **Central Plains Milk Snake.**

Coloring/scale form   The typical Louisiana milk snake is characterized by a partially black snout—often so mottled with white that the animal seems to have been nosing into flour—while the posterior portion of its head is entirely black, followed by a pale collar. Broad red dorsolateral bands, ranging in number from 13 to 21 (average, 16), are spaced along its trunk, pinched in at the belly line by their narrower black borders. Between these black rings are light-hued dorsolateral bands (considerably less broad than the Louisiana milk's red body bands), whose color varies from light yellow among more southerly ranging individuals subject to gene flow from the deep yellow-banded Mexican milk snake, to white among *L. t. amaura* living in the pine/oak woodland at the northeastern edge of the range. Many individuals living in this northeastern part of the range are so heavily clouded with dark gray that the typical bright milk snake pigmentation is only dimly visible; it is from this color variant that the race's name, *amaura*, Greek for "dark," is drawn. Among each of the Louisiana milk snake's many color morphs, the belly is off-white or light gray along a central strip. Red and black pigment encroaches onto the outer portion of the ventral scales, however, while the dorsolateral scales are arranged in 21 rows at midbody.

As this great variation in color suggests, southwestern milk snakes are difficult to define with precision because their ranges overlap so intricately. Not only are there broad zones of intergradation where the territories of adjacently ranging subspecies meet, but Bern Tryon, formerly of the Houston Zoo, has pointed out that throughout the ranges of the Louisiana, Mexican, and New Mexico milk snakes, individuals typical of neighboring races can be found. For example, D. Craig McIntyre recently found a perfectly typical Louisiana milk snake in LaSalle County, deep within the range of the Mexican milk snake. This is a characteristic pattern among what are known as ring species: groups of related organisms that sometimes interbreed across intersecting species lines while at other times overlapping in range without evident genetic exchange.

Similar snakes   Milk snakes' red and pale yellow or white dorsolateral hues never touch as they do on the **Texas coral snake (91)**. Unlike *L. triangulum*, the coral snake has black body bands as broad as its red ones, while it also has a divided anal plate. The darker red and golden yellow dorsolateral bands of the subspecies **Mexican milk snake (80)** seldom narrow at the belly line and are often suffused with black along the spine; this race has a black-blotched midventral area. Another subspecies, the **central plains milk snake (82)**, has even more profuse white flecks on its head and snout and a higher number—20 to 32 (average, 26)—of narrower, more orangish dorsolateral rings. The **Texas long-nosed snake (86)** is marked with roughly rectangular red and black vertebral saddles above black-speckled yellowish lower sides. It has 23 rows of dorsal scales, its unmarked venter is off-white, its elongate snout is tan, and under its tail lies a single row of subcaudal scales unlike the double row characteristic of other nonvenomous snakes.

Behavior   Like other milk snakes, *L. t. amaura* seems to suffer less inhibition of movement from low temperatures than most other southern snakes. In chilly conditions that render neighboring serpents so slow moving that photographing them is easy, Louisiana milk snakes are still able to mount a fast-wriggling flight when discovered, a trait that may enable *L. triangulum* to forage later into the fall and begin breeding earlier in the spring than competing species.

Cool weather tolerance also adapts these animals to forage effectively during the hours of darkness, to which their coloring is also suited, for milk snakes' contrasting dorsal hues appear to function at least in part as nocturnal camouflage. Although in daylight these bright colors instantly draw the attention of human eyes, at night—the only time Louisiana milk snakes are abroad—red looks gray to even color-visioned snake predators such as owls. (Mammalian carnivores that feed on small terrestrial serpents are largely color-blind.) Moreover, by approximating dark shadows, the milk snake's black crossbands break up the visual continuity of its serpentine shape, while its intervening pale dorsolateral rings further fragment its profile against the light-dappled patchwork of the nighttime forest floor. These contrasting body bands are probably also effective in deterring carnivores, for both the mimicked coral snakes and milk snakes have a significantly lower average incidence of predator-caused injuries than do similarly sized, nonbanded serpents living in the same habitat. This imitation of a dangerous look-alike is further substantiated by the fact that the greater the distance between the home range of a milk snake population and that of the nearest resident group of coral snakes, the less similarity there is in their markings.

80 MEXICAN MILK SNAKE
Lampropeltis triangulum annulata

Nonvenomous   Mexican milk snakes grow large enough to bite effectively in self-defense, but do so only if seized roughly.

Abundance   Uncommon. Found north of Mexico only in southern and south central Texas, *L. t. annulata* is widespread throughout both the remaining brush country of the Rio Grande floodplain and the irrigated farmland that has replaced much of the area's native vegetation. According to most references' range maps, the Mexican milk snake also occupies much of the Edwards Plateau, but this seems to be largely a historical phenomenon, for milk snakes are virtually never found in this part of the state today.

Size   The largest North American milk snakes, adult *L. t. annulata* average 20 to 32 inches in length, while the record is a truly huge 54 in.

Habitat   Mexican milk snakes are most often observed in the Tamaulipan thorn woodland of the lower coastal plain. (Named for Mexico's most northeastern state, this tangle of catclaw acacia, paloverde, tamarisk, cenizo, and ocotillo formerly stretched almost halfway from the Rio Grande to San Antonio. In species diversity, it was among the richest biotic communities in the United States, but its dense vegetation grew on fertile, level land, and the agricultural boom of the 1950s leveled most of its thorn brush, eliminating the tropical birds, mammals, and reptiles that ranged only as far north as this jungle of spiny legumes and succulents.) Another very different habitat, also characteristic of the Mexican milk snake, is the coastal barrier islands, where these animals are found under driftwood deposited by high tide.

Prey   Like most *Lampropeltis*, milk snakes are powerful constrictors of other serpents, from rattlesnakes to smaller members of their own species. Other prey includes lizards and small mammals, both of which are usually immediately accepted as food by recent captives.

Reproduction   Egg-laying. See **Central Plains Milk Snake.**

Coloring/scale form   Fourteen to 20 (average, 18) broad, dark red dorsolateral bands, often peppered along the spine with black, cover the upper trunk. The lower edges of these reddish bands (*annulata* is "ringed" in Latin) extend onto the otherwise pale gray belly scales, where they are cut off by blotchy strips of black pigment that occupy the midventral area. Narrower black body bands border each side of these red bands, separated by wide intervening yellow bands. A few light anterior labial spots sometimes mark the otherwise black head, and the smooth, glossy dorsolateral scales are small and arranged in 21 rows at midbody.

Similar snakes Milk snakes' red and yellow (or white) body bands touch only its black bands, never each other; in contrast, the **Texas coral snake (91)** has adjacent red and yellow bands. Unlike the milk snakes, its body bands entirely encircle its trunk, its black bands are about as broad as its red bands, and its anal plate is divided. Where their ranges intersect, the **Louisiana** and **Mexican milk snake (79–80)** races show intermingled characteristics. To the west, *L. t. annulata* merges with the **New Mexico milk snake (81)**, which is distinguished by its greater average number of red dorsolateral bands (22), black dorsolateral rings much thinner than its broad white (rather than yellow) pale body bands, and its distinctly light-hued midventral area. The **Texas long-nosed snake (86)** has rectangular red and black vertebral saddles, predominantly yellowish to cream-colored lower sides speckled with dark scales, a long brown or pinkish snout, and 23 rows of dorsolateral scales. Its belly is off-white, and a single row of scales lies beneath its tail.

Behavior As vividly tricolored reptiles, milk snakes are anything but milky in appearance, their name apparently having stemmed from early attempts to explain their presence in dairy barns. These smallish kingsnakes were probably drawn there in search of nestling mice, but it seemed likely to early farmers that these snakes could have subsisted in their barns only by twining up the legs of dairy cows to suck milk from their udders. Seen mostly on rural roads long after dark, *L. t. annulata* is typically spotted moving quickly across the pavement; it is virtually never found basking in the roadway warmth that lures so many other serpents.

81 NEW MEXICO MILK SNAKE
Lampropeltis triangulum celaenops

Nonvenomous See **Louisiana Milk Snake.**

Abundance Rare. Although its range encompasses both the Trans-Pecos and, above the caprock formation, the western quarter of the Texas panhandle, the New Mexico milk snake is almost never seen. A majority of the few recorded *L. t. celaenops* were encountered at night crossing Trans-Pecos ranch roads during May and June.

Size Most adults are between 14 and 22 inches in length; the largest of 7 Texas individuals measured 25¼ in.

Habitat In West Texas' intermittently montane terrain, one habitat in which the author has seen two individuals is the evergreen/hardwood woodland of the Guadalupe Mountains. A similar environment in which New Mexico milk snakes have also been found is the riparian corridors that penetrate the

Davis Mountains. To the north, in a grassland milieu another New Mexico milk snake was recently found near Highway 176 in Andrews County, while an entirely different habitat—one seemingly inhospitable to a species whose other races live in well-vegetated habitats—is the waterless northern Chihuahuan Desert. In this severely arid biome, *Lampropeltis triangulum celaenops* has been found on rocky plateaus and bluffs north of Sanderson, as well as in the even harsher desert of Big Bend's Black Gap Wildlife Management Area.

Prey   Like other kingsnakes, the New Mexico milk snake feeds primarily on smaller snakes, lizards located by scent in the crevices where they retreat for the night, and burrow-dwelling rodents.

Reproduction   Egg-laying. See **Central Plains Milk Snake.**

Coloring/scale form   The 17 to 25 (average, 22) broad carmine dorsolateral bands are bordered by narrower black bands separated by equally narrow off-white bands; within the latter, scattered brown flecks may impart a grizzled appearance. The New Mexico milk snake's black body bands are often slightly wider over its posterior spine, its midventer is largely without black pigment, and its black snout is flecked with white. Arranged in 21 rows at midbody, the smooth dorsal scales have an enamel-like surface to which the genus' Latin name, *Lampropeltis*, or "shining skin shield," refers.

Similar snakes   In the eastern part of its range the New Mexico milk snake shares the territory of the **Texas coral snake (91)**, whose red and sulfur-yellow body bands touch (milk snakes' red dorsolateral bands are bordered only by black bands). Because their ranges overlap so broadly, Texas' four milk snake races can be difficult to distinguish, but the **central plains milk snake (82)** has narrower, more numerous (average, 26), orangish dorsolateral bands; along its ventral midline, splotchy black pigment separates the lower edges of these bands. The **Mexican milk snake (80)** also has a black-pigmented midventer, deep yellow body bands and fewer, wider red bands (average, 18). The **Texas long-nosed snake (86)** has rectangular red and black vertebral saddles, 23 rows of dorsal scales, and an off-white venter whose undertail scales occur in a single row.

Behavior   In addition to winter dormancy, milk snakes living in the western United States typically undergo a similar subsurface retirement, or aestivation, to escape the summer heat and aridity. Even during spring and fall these animals spend most of the daylight hours deep in subterranean crevices, however (the individual pictured here was found at dawn on a rocky Big Bend trail), where the humidity is higher and the temperature more constant than on the surface. *Lampropeltis triangulum celaenops* is seldom abroad except on still nights of high humidity, when the preponderance of males suggests that most individuals have not emerged in search of prey, but are instead seeking the pheromone scent trails of reproductively receptive females.

RED- AND BLACK-BANDED SNAKES

82 CENTRAL PLAINS MILK SNAKE
Lampropeltis triangulum gentilis

Nonvenomous   See **Louisiana Milk Snake.**

Abundance   Generally very uncommon. Sparsely distributed across the central Great Plains, *L. t. gentilis* can nevertheless be locally common during early summer in some places. Yet, because this primarily fossorial snake is seldom found at the surface—and then almost always beneath the cover of flat stones or other sheltering debris—it is rarely seen even in these areas.

Size   Most adult central plains milk snakes are 16 to 24 inches long; the record is just over 36 in.

Habitat   Little is recorded of this animal's natural life history in Texas. Near Barnhart, several individuals were found beneath rocks in early spring, discoveries that parallel *L. t. gentilis* records elsewhere in the wide sweep of basin and rangeland this animal inhabits. Nevertheless, its specific habitat preferences are largely unknown. It has been found both on brushy hillsides and in rolling, short- or tall-grass prairie, especially where the soil was slightly moist, broken with large rocks, and loose enough for burrowing. Such a conspicuous, slow-moving reptile would find it dangerous to expose itself on the surface of its largely coverless habitat, but where *L. t. gentilis* lives below ground and what behaviors it employs there remain largely a mystery.

Prey   Nothing is recorded of prey taken in the wild, but the young probably feed mainly on lizards, skinks, and miniature serpents such as blind snakes and *Tantilla*, as well as on earthworms and insects. In captivity, like other milk snakes adult *L. t. gentilis* readily constricts and feeds on other snakes and small rodents.

Reproduction   Egg-laying. The reproduction of captives indicates that after springtime breeding and gestation this race of milk snake deposits clutches of up to 10 1¼- by ⅝-inch-long adhesive-shelled eggs. After 65 to 80 days' incubation these hatch into 7½- to 11-inch-long young whose colors are somewhat brighter than those of their often rather pallid parents.

Coloring/scale form   Among *L. t. gentilis*, both dorsal pattern and color are highly variable. Its black snout and forehead are usually, but not always, mottled with white, while individuals from the northern plains have less vividly colored reddish orange dorsolateral bands than those from North Texas, whose population intergrades with more brightly colored southern subspecies. Yet in both areas the central plains milk snake's reddish dorsolateral bands are more numerous (20 to 40, average 26) than those of most other milk snakes, and are suffused with black scales over the posterior spine. These bands are bordered by narrow black rings that sometimes almost entirely encircle them low on the sides and outer belly. The intervening yellowish gray dorsolateral rings only intermittently cross the darkly pigmented midventer. There are 21 midbody rows of dorsal scales.

Similar snakes   Even the approximate distribution of western milk snake races is difficult to define because individuals typical of adjacently ranging subspecies can be found throughout the territory of their neighbors. For example, the central plains race intergrades with the **Louisiana milk snake (79)** as far south as Fort Worth, where the latter is distinguished by its fewer (average, 16), wider and brighter red dorsolateral bands, as well as by its partially pale midventral area. The **New Mexico milk snake (81)** also has fewer, wider, and brighter red body bands (average, 22) and a lighter-hued midbelly. The **Texas long-nosed snake (86)** has rectangular red and black dorsal saddles, black-speckled yellowish lower sides, and an unmarked off-white venter distinguished by its single row of subcaudal scale.

Behavior   Perhaps because so much of its habitat consists of open grassland, like other milk snakes *L. t. gentilis* is an extremely fossorial creature that seldom risks emerging from cover. During cool weather, rather than basking to elevate its temperature, it may seek warmth by coiling against the underside of sun-heated flat rocks. In this sort of environment, during the spring of 1998 the first albino central plains milk snake ever recorded was found, in Kansas, on a rock-strewn prairie in one of the few places where a seasonally surfacing population of *L. t. gentilis* has been identified.

83 GRAY-BANDED KINGSNAKE
Lampropeltis alterna

Nonvenomous   When first picked up in the field, a large gray-banded kingsnake may give a single frightened nip, but unless severely mistreated it will not bite a second time.

Abundance   Widespread but uncommon. The range of *L. alterna* is now known to include 15 Texas counties, adjacent Eddy County in New Mexico, and much of the northern Mexican state of Coahuila—although because gray-banded kingsnakes are almost entirely fossorial for most of the year and were consequently thought to be extremely rare, despite their broad range and widespread population, for decades this species was protected by the state of Texas. *Lampropeltis alterna* is no longer classified as threatened, however, since over 90 percent of its U.S. habitat occurs either on private ranchland or within state and national parks. Nevertheless, to some extent *L. alterna* remains a controversial species. Influential magazine articles have maintained that it is disappearing, but the prevailing scientific view is that neither the 50 to 100 gray-banded kingsnakes taken from the Trans-Pecos every year by collectors nor those run over by traffic are ecologically significant, mainly because those losses are unlikely to increase since the great majority of *L. alterna* are inaccessible to snake hunters except where a few road cuts and canyon bluffs border public roads.

   Although this snake was for many years a little-studied animal, the gray-banded kingsnake's existence has been known for over a century; the type specimen was collected in the Davis Mountains by E. Meyenberg in 1901. This dark-hued specimen was formally described by A. E. Brown, who named it *Ophibolus alternus* for its alternating broad and narrow dorsolateral bands. For the next 47 years this species, renamed *Lampropeltis alterna* after it was found to be a true kingsnake, was known only from the Chisos, Davis, and Sierra Vieja mountains, from a single locality near Bakersfield in Pecos County, and from the Mexican state of Coahuila. Then, in 1948 a pale, broadly orange-banded kingsnake unlike any previously reported from the Trans-Pecos was discovered 9 miles west of Dryden. This animal was thought to be a new, orange-banded type of kingsnake, which was formally described by A. G. Flury and named *Lampropeltis blairi* after University of Texas herpetologist W. F. Blair. Flury's classification was in error, however, for some 20 years later Ernest Tanzer found both orange and dark gray-banded young kingsnakes emerging from a single clutch of eggs laid by a wild-caught Juno Road female. This established that both wide-orange-banded *L. blairi* and narrow-banded *L. alterna* were really a single species, so that now *Lampropeltis alterna* is the proper term for all of Texas' gray-banded kingsnakes. Herpetoculturists now breed thousands of these beautiful snakes every year in captivity, but wild-caught individuals still carry some cachet, and the chance of capturing one attracts enthusiasts from all over the world to Trans-Pecos Texas during the gray-band's activity and breeding season in May and June.

Size   Adult *L. alterna* average 28 to 34 inches in length. Those from the Chisos and Davis mountains average slightly smaller, with a bit narrower heads and more forward-pointing eyes. The record is a 58-inch-long male "Blair's phase" found 17 miles west of Rocksprings in Edwards County.

Habitat   To avoid the harsh surface conditions of the Northern Chihuahuan Desert, the gray-banded kingsnake spends the majority of its life in a more sheltered environment beneath the surface. The limestone substrate that makes up the subterranean world in this region is penetrable by a large snake like *L. alterna* only where crevices caused by weathering and geologic uplifting permit subsurface movement, however, and graybands are therefore restricted to broken, rocky habitat. In terrain ranging from stony low-lying flats adjacent to bluffs or arroyos to montane rock faces as high as 6,500 feet, canyons, craggy ridges, talus slopes, and boulder piles are this animal's preferred microenvironment. The limestone faces of road cuts offer the same conditions, and until recently gray-banded kingsnakes were assumed to be exclusively saxicolous since almost all sightings came from such rocky environs. Yet during the summer of 1999 the author found an adult male gray-band in a yucca/grassland milieu several miles from the nearest rocky bluff.

Prey   Moving slowly through the maze of interconnecting crevices that underlie the Trans-Pecos' broken limestone topography, *L. alterna* feeds on the lizards that, at dusk, descend into its chthonic warren in search of shelter. On the surface, where it sometimes hunts, *L. alterna* uses its prominent ventral scales to grip rough-surfaced stone, inching its way across rock faces while searching every crevice for the earless, side-blotched, and spiny lizards that sleep there. In this stony habitat Salmon and Hollister observed an adult male gray-band trying to pull a crevice spiny lizard from a crack in a roadside rock cut where the lizard had wedged itself for the night, while the author found a desert side-blotched lizard in the stomach of a road-killed *L. alterna*. In captivity, most wild-caught adults feed readily on mice, and while gray-bands are clumsy at conventional constriction they may immobilize such small prey by pressing it against the side of their enclosure. Lizard and snake eggs are also reportedly eaten by *L. alterna* (the young are exclusively lizard eaters), while Ed Acuna and Dan Vermilya found a big female gray-band near Big Bend National Park filled with eggs that turned out to be those of scaled quail. Canyon tree frogs and other small amphibians are also taken on occasion, although ophiophagy—eating other snakes, which is common among most kingsnakes—appears to be rare.

Reproduction   Egg-laying. No reproductive behavior has been recorded for gray-bands in the wild, but extensive captive breeding of *Lampropeltis alterna*—successful propagation was first described by James Murphy of the Dallas Zoo—has led to the thorough documentation of its courtship and breeding. Clutches of 3 to 13 eggs, 1¼ to 1⅝ inches in length, are deposited from late May to July. Following a 60- to 80-day incubation the young pip through their leathery eggshells but remain coiled within the eggs for another couple of days, peeking out from time to time while adsorbing the last of their yolk sacs. Well-fed *L. alterna* reach reproductive maturity in their second or third year (wild females may become gravid at as small as 24 inches), and in captivity can live more than 20 years.

Coloring/scale form   The species name *alterna*, drawn from Latin, refers to the arrangement of the gray-banded kingsnake's dorsolateral bands. These bands are so widely spaced along its body that they were assumed to be only the alternate markings between a second set of invisible, yet genotypically present, intervening bands. The great variety made possible by such unique color and patterning has made this animal an obsession to many herpetoculturists, among whom it is said that "no two *alterna* are exactly alike." That may not be entirely true, but gray-banded kingsnake populations are highly polytypic, and both wild and captive-bred individuals seem to present an almost infinite variety of color and patterning.

Ground color varies from black to light gray, though two principal color phases prevail (the original terms *alterna* and *blairi* are still used to distinguish these color types, despite the fact that many specimens are intermediate between them). Individuals from the lower Pecos and Devil's river drainages are most often pale gray, with orange dorsal saddles delineated by narrow, sometimes thinly white-bordered black edges. Among the more northerly and westerly specimens known as *alterna* morphs, heavier pigmentation is likely, and thin black bands, sometimes narrowly split with red, are separated by still thinner intermediate, or "alternating," dark bands or vertical rows of small black spots. These differences are loosely tied to the hue of the background rocks on which these populations live. In the southern part of the range where the paler "Blair's" form more often occurs, these snakes inhabit a chalky desert substrate of limestone or naviculite; at higher elevations to the north and west, more moisture allows lichens to encrust the dark, volcanic rhyolite, and here more heavily pigmented *alterna* prevail. Because both sorts of young emerge from the egg clutches produced in both regions, natural selection undoubtedly determines which color phase is best camouflaged against the local background rock and is thus most likely to survive. The gray-banded kingsnake's ventral coloring varies almost as much as that of its dorsum, ranging from off-white to, in the Davis Mountains, almost entirely black. There are 25 midbody rows of dorsal scales.

Similar snakes   The light-hued color phase of the **mottled rock rattlesnake (104)** is somewhat similar in pigmentation to some pale-phase *L. alterna*. The heads of both species are triangular, but rattlesnakes have both a rattle and a dark, distinctly depressed heat-sensing pit midway between the nostril and the slit-pupiled viperid eye (like other subterranean or nocturnal serpents, gray-banded kingsnakes have bulging eyes with prominent round pupils).

Behavior   The gray-banded kingsnake's movement on the surface is sporadic, fluctuating according to both season and weather. Most of its infrequent forays occur on warm spring and early summer nights with low or falling barometric pressure, especially when rainfall has recently occurred and the humidity is higher than normal. During times of extreme drought, even these desert-adapted animals are stressed by lack of water, and in the very dry summer of 2000 one was photographed, after having ascended a set of stone steps, drinking water from a puddle on the porch of a house in Terlingua Ranch near Big Bend. Surprisingly, the sometimes gaudy colors of *Lampropeltis alterna* are difficult to see at night except in the beam of a spotlight. Red looks gray after dark, and the variegated dorsolateral patterning of *L. alterna* masks its serpentine shape against shadowy rock faces.

Scarlet Snakes
Genus *Cemophora*

Florida Scarlet Snake, *Cemophora coccinea coccinea*
Northern Scarlet Snake, *Cemophora coccinea copei*
Texas Scarlet Snake, *Cemophora coccinea lineri*

Cemophora is part of the colubrine subfamily *Lampropeltinae*, establishing its member species as close relatives—as one would expect from their glossy scalation, subterranean lifestyle, and bright dorsolateral colors—of both the milk snake/kingsnake group and the southwestern long-nosed snakes. Like the latter group, *cemophora* have a hard, pointed rostral scale, presumably to help them unearth their buried food. This characteristic is the source of this animal's species name: Greek for *phoros* ("having") and *cemo* ("snout").

Unlike both king- and long-nosed snakes, however, scarlet snakes are specialist feeders on reptile eggs that only when driven from their burrows by heavy rains, or on warm, humid evenings emerge from their burrows to move about on the surface. This oviparous, monotypic genus consists of a single species, *C. coccinea*, a beautiful burrower of the southeastern and western Gulf coastal plains whose back and sides are marked with bands or saddles of red, black, and white or yellow; the yellow and red bands are separated by bands of black. This species' head is narrow and not overly distinct from its neck, its pointed snout is red, its belly is an unmarked off-white, its smooth dorsolateral scales are arranged in 19 rows, and its anal plate is undivided.

84 NORTHERN SCARLET SNAKE
Cemophora coccinea copei

Nonvenomous It is almost impossible to induce the northern scarlet snake to bite.

Abundance **Threatened. Protected by the state of Texas.**
Yet *Cemophora coccinea copei* is fairly common, for during May and June northern scarlet snakes are sometimes abundant on East Texas back roads. Within the state's eastern forests it may even be locally abundant in pine flatwoods, wet prairies, bottomland forest, and both coastal and inland sandhill habitats, for in most of these environments drift fence surveys regularly catch *C. c. copei* on late spring and early summer nights.

Size Adult scarlet snakes are 16 to just over 32 inches in length; the slim, very rarely seen hatchlings are 4½ to 6 inches long.

Habitat A primarily fossorial inhabitant of sandy-soiled pine, hardwood, and mixed forest environments, *C. c. copei* also evidently frequently forages abroad, for it is sometimes found in open terrain some distance from woodland. Here, it occurs most often along the borders of swamps and stream banks and in agricultural fields. Jim Ashcraft reports that in the wetter southern part of its range, in riparian forest near Beaumont during minor flooding, northern scarlet snakes are sometimes found on the sandy, white pine-covered ridges that rise above intervening boggy ground harboring baygall and magnolia.

Prey Reptile eggs are this animal's preferred food—in search of which *C. c. copei* apparently forages widely on the surface. (To puncture the leathery shells of eggs too large to swallow whole it has developed enlarged upper posterior teeth.) Northern scarlet snakes may also take small lizards, snakes, and nestling rodents. See **Texas Scarlet Snake.**

Reproduction Egg-laying. Breeding occurs from March to June, with oviposition occurring between May and August. The 3 to 8 eggs, 1 to 1¼ inches in length, hatch from July to October into 5½- to 6-inch-long young.

Coloring/scale form Adult *C. c. copei* have a grayish or yellowish white ground color, with up to 32 broad red dorsal saddles prominently bordered with black. Their lower sides are flecked with brown and their elongate snouts are orange-red, as is the crown, which is sometimes capped by a circular marking edged with black. The anterior-most black vertebral band usually touches the parietals, there are usually 6 supralabial scales, and the unmarked venter is white.

Yet this appearance is only one manifestation of the scarlet snake's lifelong ontogenetic change in appearance. This reptile's pattern and coloring alter so much during the course of its life that hatchlings, adults, and very old individuals look like different species. Hatchlings are off-white, with pink dorsal saddles that extend only a short way down their sides, where they are surrounded by black lateral flecks. As northern scarlet snakes grow older these flecks coalesce to form the dark lower borders of steadily reddening dorsal blotches, which eventually develop a broad, solid black edging. Among very old *C. c. copei*, the red vertebral color dulls, their once-carmine saddles fade to mahogany, and their formerly white intervening spaces become tarnished with tan or gray.

Similar snakes The **Louisiana milk snake (79)** usually has a white-flecked black nose, dorsolateral bands that extend onto its red, white, and black ventral scales, and 21 rows of dorsal scales. **Texas coral snakes (91)** have red and yellow dorsolateral bands that border one another and extend unbroken across their bellies; the coral snake's stubby, rounded snout is jet black, its anal plate divided.

Behavior One of the most deeply subterranean of serpents, the northern scarlet snake (whose subspecies name, *copei*, honors Edward Drinker Cope, professor of geology, minerology, zoology, and comparative anatomy at the University of Pennsylvania) seldom appears in the open except on late spring and early summer nights. Yet, in search of buried reptile eggs, from time to time it forages furtively abroad. Its only defense is to dig its way out of sight as rapidly as possible, although in the loose, sandy soil it favors the northern scarlet snake can disappear with surprising rapidity. It does so by pressing its tapered snout into the ground at a shallow angle and wagging its head from side to side, rooting up a pair of little earthen berms that quickly collapse inward over its foreparts. Thus partially concealed, *C. c. copei* discontinues its sideways cephalic motions and forces its head almost straight down into the ground. There, it may continue to move forward like a big earthworm. At other times it seeks out subterranean crevices or the tunnels of small mammals to go deeper, for during building excavation northern scarlet snakes have been uncovered as much as 6 feet beneath the surface.

85 TEXAS SCARLET SNAKE

Cemophora coccinea lineri

Nonvenomous See **Northern Scarlet Snake.**

Abundance **Threatened. Protected by the state of Texas.** Endemic to this state and widely separated in range from any other member of its species, the Texas scarlet snake is a rare animal. Only a handful of individuals have been recorded, including the type specimen discovered in Kenedy County by Ernie Liner. This most southwesterly living scarlet snake's scarcity has given it such mystique that a myth has sprung up among reptile enthusiasts that *C. c. lineri* is descended from a handful of Florida scarlet snakes (*C. c. coccinea*) accidentally transported to South Texas in a load of oil field drilling pipe.

Size   This race of scarlet snake grows to a length of at least 26 inches.

Habitat   Almost the only habitat in which *C. c. lineri* has been observed is a narrow band of sand-floored baygall thicket adjacent to the Laguna Madre and a three-county extension of this coastal vegetative zone that extends inland into the Tamaulipan thorn woodland of the Rio Grande plain.

Prey   Although evidently a sometime constrictor of lizards and small snakes, *C. c. lineri* seems to feed largely on reptile eggs, which it punctures with the slightly enlarged teeth located in the rear of its upper jaw. One newly captured individual brought to the Houston Zoo drank nearly a quarter of the contents of a hen's egg from a shallow dish, then over the next 8 days consumed 9 Texas spiny lizard eggs. For months afterward, however, it refused both eggs and small snake and lizard prey; another captive *C. c. lineri* lived nearly a year in captivity feeding solely on fresh hen's egg yolks while refusing both living and dead lacertilians and small serpents. (Jim Ashcraft, who has elicited feeding responses among northern scarlet snakes by providing them with deep soil in which to burrow, suggests that exposure in an open cage may have inhibited the feeding of both these individuals.)

Reproduction   Egg-laying. See **Northern Scarlet Snake.**

Coloring/scale form   Basic color, pattern, and scutellation are similar to those of the northern scarlet snake, *Cemophora coccinea copei*—from which this subspecies was formally distinguished in 1966 by Kenneth Williams, Bryce Brown, and Larry David Wilson. Both the northern and Texas races have an off-white dorsolateral ground coloring, although at all stages of maturity the Texas race's hue is brighter and less grayish. Seventeen to 24 heavily black-bordered carmine to mahogany-red vertebral saddles mark its dorsum, while the Texas scarlet snake's anterior-most black vertebral band usually touches its parietals. There is an elongate orange-red snout, but the crown and cheeks are wrapped in a glossy jet-black cap, marked only with a tiny white postcranial bar. There are 6 supralabial scales and the venter is uniformly white.

Similar snakes   Scarlet snakes typically exhibit ontogenetic variation, their pale, pinkish young growing first redder and then darker and more brownish with age, but among Texas scarlet snakes a black cap replaces the red crown typical of other scarlet snake races and the black border below its vertebral saddles does not join across their lower edges. The **Texas coral snake (91)** has a rounded black snout, adjacent red and bright yellow dorsolateral bands that cross its venter, and a divided anal plate. The **Mexican milk snake (80)** also has a black, sometimes white-speckled nose, a red, white, and black venter, and 21 midbody rows of dorsal scales. The **Texas long-nosed snake (86)** usually has rectangular black dorsolateral saddles, black-speckled yellowish lower sides, 23 rows of dorsal scales, and a single row of undertail scales (unlike the double row typical of every other harmless snake).

Behavior Few observations of Texas scarlet snakes have been made in the wild, but the activity cycle of *C. c. lineri* is probably similar to that of its two subspecies. Captives remain buried in the loose sand of their cage bottoms during the day, emerging only at night, when their bright colors, by visually breaking their serpentine outline, may function primarily as nocturnal camouflage.

Long-nosed Snakes
Genus *Rhinocheilus*

Texas Long-nosed Snake, *Rhinocheilus lecontei tessellatus*

The genus *Rhinocheilus,* whose name is taken from the Greek (*rhinos* for "nose" and *cheilo* for "lip") in reference to its extended rostral scale, is part of the colubrine subfamily *Lampropeltinae.* Within this large subfamily, related genera include those of the similarly brightly hued scarlet, milk, and kingsnakes. *Rhinocheilus* are oviparous, characterized by slender heads, a long, pointed snout, smooth dorsolateral scales arranged in 23 rows, and an undivided anal plate. These beautiful, busily patterned, tricolored snakes, of which only one subspecies is native to central North America, are associated with arid and semiarid grasslands, where they are secretive, capable burrowers. By day, long-nosed snakes may be found hidden amid sheltering rocks, in crevices and rodent burrows, or under debris, but by evening they often prowl widely on the surface, especially during or following rains. Like their milk snake relatives, long-nosed snakes seem to be more tolerant of cool weather than most serpents, foraging late into the crisp hours after midnight; even in the high altitudes of the Davis Mountains, the author has found *R. l. tessellatus*, abroad on decidedly chilly roadway pavement.

If threatened, the long-nosed snake may hide its head beneath a body coil, or even autohemorrhage, spontaneously bleeding a drop or two from its cloaca. Nasal hemorrhaging has also been noted, but the biomechanics of this presumably defensive maneuver remain unknown. An occasional individual may rear into an elevated S posture and bluff-strike if provoked, but its mouth always remains firmly shut—at least if it is an adult, since juveniles, for some reason, are apt to nip if picked up. *Rhinocheilus lecontei* is an efficient constrictor but consumes smaller food animals without first suffocating them. Lizards seem to be this species' preferred food, but individuals from southern parts of the range also accept small rodent prey immediately after capture; young ground-nesting birds are reportedly eaten as well.

86 TEXAS LONG-NOSED SNAKE
Rhinocheilus lecontei tessellatus

Nonvenomous   Adult *R. l. tessellatus* almost never bite, even if picked up suddenly, but an occasional individual defecates and writhes in agitation, sometimes discharging blood, musk, and feces from its vent.

Abundance   Uncommon. Sparsely distributed in both central Texas and the state's Stockton Plateau, the Texas long-nosed snake is more often found in Trans-Pecos and New Mexico grassland, and it may be fairly numerous. *Rhinocheilus lecontei tessellatus* is probably most abundant, however, in the Tamaulipan thorn brush savannah of the Rio Grande plain.

Size   Most adults are 16 to 30 inches long; the record is 41 in.

Habitat   A burrower—and rooter for hidden prey—in the dry, gravelly soils of prairie and thorn brush grassland, the Texas long-nosed snake is sometimes found near the moisture of stock tanks and intermittently flowing streams, almost always long after dark. It also occurs in the northern Chihuahuan Desert, however, for the author has found this animal in some of the Trans-Pecos' harshest desert biomes, including the arid, rocky slopes of the Black Gap Wildlife Management Area, often in weather too cool for most other snake species to be abroad.

Prey   Despite its enlarged rostral, the Texas long-nosed snake is not primarily fossorial; instead, it uses its sharply pointed snout to root lizards from beneath the layer of soil in which desert-living lacertilians shelter for the night. In 1966 Charles McKinney and R. E. Ballinger found only lizard remains in 14 *R. l. tessellatus* taken in the panhandle. (Much too swift to be captured by the slow-moving, long-nosed snake during the day, open plains- or rock-living lizards are vulnerable to scent-hunting snakes at night when they sleep wedged into crevices or buried beneath a layer of sand.) Abilene Zoo director Jack Joy reports observing a Texas long-nosed snake using its pointed snout to root out sleeping racerunner lizards. Rodents are also taken by the South Texas population—perhaps preferentially, for a number of captives from LaSalle and McMullen counties refused reptilian food but immediately recognized small mammals as prey. Although no more than ½ inch in diameter, these *R. l. tessellatus* had no difficulty in constricting adult mice with a loop of their muscular trunks. Yet the long-nosed snake's small mouth limits its prey to animals smaller than those eaten by similarly sized serpents like young rat and bullsnakes.

Reproduction   Egg-laying. Four to 9 eggs are deposited in an underground nest. After 2 to 2½ months, the 6½- to 9½-inch-long young emerge, pallidly marked with pink dorsal saddles and dark-speckled whitish sides.

Coloring/scale form   Its elongated rostral scale is the source of both this creature's common and scientific names: *rhino* is Greek for "nose" and *cheil* means "lip." (*Lecontei* honors John Eatton Leconte, an army engineer who, after organizing the defense of Savannah during the War of 1812, devoted himself to herpetology.) In reference to the long-nosed snake's multihued, mosaic-like dorsolateral patterning, *tessellatus* is Latin for "tiled."

Although the coloring of all *R. l. tessellatus* tends to darken and intensify with age, separate populations vary in both hue and marking. Specimens from South Texas have equally sized vertebral blocks of red and black, lightly black-speckled yellow sides, and white bellies. In the northern Trans-Pecos, Texas long-nosed snakes may either resemble those from the southern part of the range or have larger red dorsal rectangles separated by sometimes hourglass-shaped wide black dorsolateral bands. Among this population there is less yellow, and the pale venter may be dark-splotched. In all areas the snout is reddish, there are 23 midbody rows of smooth dorsal scales, and, as in no other nonvenomous serpent in North America, the scales beneath the long-nosed snake's tail usually occur in a single row like that of the pitvipers.

Similar snakes   Each of the four races of **milk snake (79-82)** that occur within the range of the Texas long-nosed snake has a stubby black snout, narrow black dorsolateral crossbands, a vividly colored venter marked with black, pale gray, and red, and 21 rows of dorsolateral scales. A double row of scales is found under the tail.

Behavior   In 1967, McCoy and Gehlbach established that some *R. l. tessellatus* employ defensive behavior in which bloody fluid mixed with anal gland musk is discharged through the cloaca. If more severely stressed, such an autohemorrhagic individual may hang limply, presumably imitating a moribund carcass. Alternatively, with its head buried in its coils for safety, the Texas long-nosed snake sometimes elevates its curled tail tip, waving it about in a threatening pose thought to evoke the similarly banded, about-to-strike head of the coral snake.

MILDLY VENOMOUS REAR-FANGED SNAKES

Night Snakes
Genus *Hypsiglena*

Texas Night Snake, *Hypsiglena torquata jani*

The genus *Hypsiglena* is classified within the colubrine subfamily *Xenodontinae*, a category containing a host of rear-fanged (or "differently toothed") snakes, a number of which also have mildly toxic saliva. Like dangerously venomed serpents such as the pitvipers, the Texas night snake also has the vertical pupils to which, in Greek, *Hypsiglena* refers. Yet, like most *Xenodontinae*, tiny *H. t. jani* is harmless to humans, lacking both toxic venom and an aggressive temperament. Along with the Texas subspecies, more westerly living night snakes are divided into several races that can be difficult to differentiate. All share small size and a variable but pale, earth-toned ground color patterned with a big, elongate chocolate-brown blotch on each side of the neck. The dorsolateral scales are smooth and arranged in from 19 to 21 rows, and there is a divided anal plate. Among *H. torquata* the saliva is toxic only to tiny prey species, however, and these quiet, cryptic animals emerge, as their common name indicates, from hiding only as daylight wanes, after which they are active far into the hours of darkness. Primarily terrestrial, Texas night snakes may be locally common in areas where small lizards are abundant and numerous flat rocks provide surface cover.

87 TEXAS NIGHT SNAKE
Hypsiglena torquata jani

Mildly venomous Although its weakly toxic saliva has a partially paralytic effect on its amphibian and diminutive reptile prey, the Texas night snake does not bite larger creatures. In self-defense it does, however, threaten to do so by raising its slightly triangular head and making abrupt little bluff-strikes.

Abundance Variable, sometimes locally common. This widespread though seldom seen reptile inhabits a variety of dry, terrestrial environments within a large range that includes a narrow strip immediately adjacent to the southern

Gulf Coast and all of Texas west of the Edwards Plateau. A small, disjunct population of Texas night snakes lives in northeastern Texas. *Hypsiglena torquata jani* is sometimes fairly abundant in the hill country's oak/juniper savannah, in the Tamaulipan thorn brush of the Rio Grande plain, and in the Trans-Pecos, where its pale color morph can be one of the most common snakes. It is also found in considerable numbers in the grasslands of the Texas Panhandle.

Size   Most adults are 10 to 14 inches in length, but *H. t. jani* is recorded to 20 in.

Habitat   Its favored microhabitat is sandy or gravelly terrain broken by rocky bluffs or overlaid with flat stones and fallen branches. In South Texas this race is often found in the neighborhood of stock tanks and irrigation ditches. In the Trans-Pecos, as well as in the Texas Panhandle, it occurs in both short-grass prairie and around rocky outcroppings—in the Davis Mountains, Texas State Parks biologist Linda Hedges has found *H. t. jani* at more than 6,000 feet in elevation.

Prey   Mostly lizards, although smaller snakes and tiny frogs have been reported. Worms and insects may also be taken by adults, and neonates probably feed largely on invertebrates.

Reproduction   Egg-laying. In northern Tom Green County, former Abilene Zoo Director Jack Joy observed a copulating pair of Texas night snakes on May 10. Other records are of clutches of 4 to 6 proportionately large eggs—up to 1⅛ inches in length and ½ inch in diameter, found between early April and late June beneath stones, decaying vegetation, and other debris. John E. Werler (1951) reported an incubation period of 54 days, after which the 5.7-inch to 6-inch young emerged; 13 days after hatching these neonates ate newly hatched rusty lizards but refused the small anole lizards that were offered from time to time, indicating an innate preference for the ground-living lacertilian prey these youngsters would be likely to encounter in their natural environment.

Other litters of young have behaved differently, however. A gravid female found in a road cut 9 miles north of Sanderson by reptile breeder Jim Costabile deposited two similarly sized, torpedo-shaped eggs on June 1. These hatched on July 31 into 5½-inch-long young which showed no interest when presented with the scent of locally common toads, a chirping frog, and a tiger salamander. Interest, but no feeding behavior, was elicited by the scent of whiptail, earless, spiny, and canyon lizards, as well as by that of a Texas banded gecko, and ground as well as five-lined skinks. Only the odor of invertebrates—beetle larvae and pin-headed crickets—produced an immediate feeding response.

Coloring scale/form   Dorsolateral ground color is beige, marked with 50 or more irregular brown vertebral blotches and numerous small dark lateral spots. (Along the Rio Grande from east of Big Bend to the Quitman Mountains in southern Hudspeth County, much lighter-hued night snakes prevail. Probable intergrades with the more westerly spotted night snake subspecies, *H. t. ochrorhyncha*, these animals are smaller and slimmer than their more easterly ranging relatives and have only little, pale brown dorsolateral spots separated by larger areas of off-white ground color.) Night snakes' most distinctive characteristic, however, is their large coppery eyes, slit by a vertical hairline pupil reminiscent of the eyes of vipers. The big, chocolate-brown blotch that marks the nape and each side of night snakes' necks is also definitive, and is the source of this species' Latin name, which means "neckringed." The venter is white with a faint silvery sheen. Except for slightly ridged vertebral scales above the anal region of adult males, the 21 midbody rows of dorsal scales are smooth and the anal plate is divided.

Similar snakes   Their tiny upturned snouts distinguish **western** and **Mexican hook-nosed snakes (64–65)**, which have only 17 rows of dorsal scales, round-pupiled dark eyes, and no large, dark brown nuchal blotches.

Behavior   Active between April and late October, *H. t. jani* has an elliptical pupil whose vertical aperture protects the eye's light-sensitive optic rods in daylight, yet allows for more radical expansion after dark than a circular pupil. (North of the Rio Grande, this configuration is shared only with the pitvipers and other rear-fanged colubrids.) Befitting this adaptation, captives invariably spend the daylight hours hidden beneath the sand in their cages, coming to the surface to prowl only well after dark. Ordinarily entirely terrestrial, the Texas night snake also climbs into low vegetation: north of Sanderson, Connie McIntyre found an adult *H. t. jani* 4 feet off the ground in thorny shrubbery.

Black-striped Snakes
Genus *Coniophanes*

Black-striped Snake, *Coniophanes imperialis imperialis*

The rear-fanged genus *Coniophanes* is contained in the colubrine subfamily *Xenodontinae*; its members often have toxic saliva that allows them to overcome the lizards, small snakes, amphibians, and nestling rodents on which they prey. Among black-striped snakes, those toxins have caused severe local inflammation in humans, while internal bleeding has been associated with bites by the related Mexican genus, *Conophis*. Black-striped snakes' heads are moderately distinct from the neck, their scales are smooth and arranged in 19 rows, and the anal plate is divided. *Coniophanes imperialis* is the only species in this predominantly subtropical genus found north of the Mexican border, and even in its sole U.S. habitat in Texas' lower Rio Grande Valley, it is a secretive serpent only occasionally seen abroad, always after dark; it is more often found hidden beneath moisture-retaining surface litter.

88 BLACK-STRIPED SNAKE

Coniophanes imperialis imperialis

Mildly venomous   The longitudinally grooved rear teeth for which *C. imperialis* is noted allow it to intro-duce salivary toxins into its small vertebrate prey. Yet its small size and calm temperament mean that it is unlikely to bite a human being—in whom its saliva has produced severe local inflammations but no lasting effects.

Bryce C. Brown (1939), who as a young man allowed a black-striped snake to bite him on the hand as an experiment, reported that the sharp initial pain was similar to a bee sting but lasted much longer. Within an hour the dis-comfort had reached his elbow and his slightly swollen hand had grown tem-porarily numb, a condition that remained for several days, though Brown eventually recovered and went on to pursue a successful career in herpetol-ogy at Baylor University.

Abundance   **Threatened. Protected by the state of Texas.** *Coniophanes impe-rialis imperialis* is a predominantly Mexican reptile known in the United States only from Cameron, Hidalgo, and Willacy counties where, before World War II, it was quite numerous. Today, because elimination of the Rio Grande Valley's native thorn woodland by agricultural and residential clearing has devastated much of the area's wildlife, black-striped snakes are seldom encountered.

Size   Adult *C. i. imperialis* are 12 to 18 inches in length; the record is 20 in.

Habitat   The Tamaulipan thorn thicket—particularly its riparian arroyos and seasonally filled watercourses and resacas—was the black-striped snake's original home. This tangle of catclaw acacia, paloverde, tamarisk, cenizo, and ocotillo, named for Mexico's most northeastern state, formerly covered the lower Gulf coastal plain with one of the richest biotic communi-ties in the United States, harboring tropical fauna like *C. i. imperialis* which ranged no farther north than the Rio Grande Valley.

In what is left of this thorn brush, the semifossorial black-striped snake's microhabitat on the surface consists of natural or man-made debris (on the outskirts of Harlingen, black-striped snakes are edificial, turning up around buildings beneath long-discarded trash and construction material). See **North-ern Cat-eyed Snake.**

Prey   This reptile's prey is mostly small frogs and toads, lizards, and smaller snakes.

Reproduction   Egg-laying. In Chiapas, Mexico, clutches have been found to number up to 10 eggs that in the area's tropical heat and humidity can report-edly require as few as 40 days to hatch into 6½-inch-long young.

Coloring scale/form   This slender colubrid is notable for both its small head, hardly distinct from its neck, and for the three dark dorsolateral stripes—a single prominent black vertebral line and a wider dark longitudinal stripe low on each side—that run the length of its medium brown body. In contrast, the black-striped snake's venter shades from orange to pink, with a bright red undertail.

Similar snakes   None. No other serpent within its range is likely to be mistaken for the black-striped snake.

Behavior   This secretive, semitropical serpent typically forages from late evening to early morning, avoiding daytime activity by burrowing into sandy soil or hiding under cacti, fallen palm fronds, or logs. Like other snakes with brightly hued undertails, *C. i. imperialis* typically everts this part of its belly when harassed.

With its foreparts lowered, it may then wave its elevated tail tip back and forth in a gesture presumed to approximate the threatening head of a venomous reptile such as the coral snake. Unlikely as this seems, the technique may work, for Frederick R. Gehlbach (1981) found fewer old, healed injuries among species like the coral, long-nosed, and black-striped snakes that raise and wave their colorful undertails, than among species that did not employ this defensive technique.

Cat-eyed Snakes
Genus *Leptodeira*

Northern Cat-eyed Snake, *Leptodeira septentrionalis septentrionalis*

The subtropical genus *Leptodeira*—"thin-necked" in Greek—is classified within the colubrine subfamily *Xenodontinae*. It is oviparous, and its members have smooth scales arranged in 21 to 23 dorsolateral rows and a divided anal plate. South of the Rio Grande, several other species and subspecies of *L. septentrionalis* are common, but only the nominate race is restricted, in the United States, to the lower Rio Grande Valley and the adjacent Gulf Coast. Here, the northern cat-eyed snake's tropical affinities are evident, however, for it resembles other wiry, arboreal Central and South American serpents in that its large, coppery-gold eyes have the vertically elliptical pupils characteristic of many rear-fanged, weakly venomed tropical colubrids, while its broad head, extremely slim neck, and slender body also echo the configuration of many rear-fanged Central and South American species such as the vine snakes. Although *L. septentrionalis* is sometimes found in aquatic or bankside rushes and sedges, like vine snakes it is principally arboreal. A predominantly nocturnal hunter, it becomes more active when rainy periods bring out small frogs and result in aggregations of their eggs and tadpoles. By day, *L. s. septentrionalis* usually secrets itself in surface debris, stump holes, beneath fallen logs, or in the leaf crowns of bromeliads or climbing vines. Its venom quickly immobilizes frogs and lizards, but what effect these toxins might have on humans remains unknown.

MILDLY VENOMOUS REAR-FANGED SNAKES

89 NORTHERN CAT-EYED SNAKE

Leptodeira septentrionalis septentrionalis

Mildly venomous   The longitudinal grooves scoring this slender colubrid's paired, slightly enlarged rear teeth enable *L. s. septentrionalis* to channel its mildly toxic saliva into small prey, which is quickly immobilized by the serum's narcotic effect.

Abundance   **Threatened. Protected by the state of Texas.** This tropical serpent is northern (*septentrion* in Latin) only in relation to its Mexican and Central American relatives. It inhabits the United States nowhere but at the southern tip of the Rio Grande Valley and along the lower Gulf Coast, where, because little of its native thorn brush and riparian woodland habitat remains, it has become quite rare.

Size   Adults average 14 to 32 inches in length (females are slightly longer), with bodies no thicker than a forefinger among even the largest individuals.

Habitat   Principally a Latin American species, fairly common in good habitat, in the United States the northern cat-eyed snake's habitat includes the jungle of coastal thorn brush known as Tamaulipan woodland. The remnants of this ecological community can be found along the Gulf Coast from Tampico north to Texas' Kleberg County, where at one time this mass of catclaw acacia, paloverde, tamarisk, cenizo, and ocotillo harbored an entire tropical ecosystem that rivaled East Texas' "Big Thicket" in species diversity. But during the 1950s an agricultural boom leveled most of this native subtropical vegetation, and a majority of the Mexican birds, mammals, and reptiles, including *L. s. septentrionalis*, that historically ranged only this far north now remain as relictual, diminishing populations isolated in a handful of the Rio Grande floodplain's widely separated preserves. In what remains of this subtropical thicket, the northern cat-eyed snake's favored microhabitat is dense vegetation bordering ponds and watercourses. Sometimes sheltering in the bowls of bromeliads during daylight, the cat-eyed snake's arboreal agility affords it an effective means of flight from danger.

Prey   Predominantly pond and tree frogs, and their eggs. In much of its Latin American range, *L. s. septentrionalis* preys heavily on the red-eyed tree frog, whose eggs and tadpoles it finds by creeping carefully through dense foliage after dark, guided by scent. Adult frogs are seized and then envenomed using the cat-eyed snake's long rear teeth. Though such prey is usually quickly overcome, it is typically chewed for several minutes before being swallowed. Captive *L. s. septentrionalis* have also fed on smaller snakes, minnows, and mice.

Reproduction   Egg-laying. Incubation periods of several clutches deposited by Mexican females varied from 79 to 90 days; except for their somewhat bolder dorsal patterning, the 9-inch-long young resemble adults.

Coloring scale/form   The northern cat-eyed snake's slender dorsum is alternately crossbarred with rectangular khaki and dark brown blocks; its light-hued crown bears a distinctive darker oval with a rearward pointing apex. Its bulging golden eyes, however, are this animal's signature. Shared with other rear-fanged, mildly venomed colubrids, as well as with the pitvipers, the irises of *L. s. septentrionalis*—which are the source of its perfectly descriptive common name—are slashed with sharply defined, catlike vertical pupils. The pale underchin and throat shade to light orange at midbody and salmon beneath the tail, while the outer ends of many of the belly scales, which have a slightly darkened posterior border, are peppered with brown. The 21 to 23 midbody rows of dorsal scales are predominantly smooth, although some are pocked by tiny apical pits.

Similar snakes None. No other serpent within its range is likely to be mistaken for the northern cat-eyed snake.

Behavior As might be inferred from its big, cat-like eyes, *L. s. septentrionalis* is an exclusively nocturnal serpent. Like the lyre snake, a similarly rear-fanged desert-dwelling colubrid, the northern cat-eyed snake has pursued an evolutionary strategy very different from that of the thick-bodied, sedentary pitvipers (whose toxins are predigestive agents that, in the bodies of large, hard-to-swallow prey, partially break down the victim's carcass in order to ease its passage down the throat and accelerate digestion). Instead, cat-eyed snakes have developed toxins only as potent as they need to subdue their mostly anuran prey, while maintaining a slender, agile body that allows them to both hide and forage effectively within thick vegetation.

Lyre Snakes
Genus *Trimorphodon*

Texas Lyre Snake, *Trimorphodon biscutatus vilkinsonii*

The rear-fanged genus *Trimorphodon*—a term that means "three types of teeth"—is characterized by dentition unique among North American snakes. Posterior to a set of conventional, inward-curved teeth located in the front of the mouth, a second set of barely visible small teeth is present. These are followed, far to the rear of the jaw, by the pair of enlarged, grooved fangs with which members of this genus envenomate small prey. As a result, *Trimorphodon* has been placed in the colubrine subfamily *Xenodontinae*, or "differently toothed."

Lyre snakes—whose common name is derived from the dark, ostensibly lyre-shaped marking on their crowns—live in habitats ranging from sea level to over 7,000 feet in elevation throughout the southwestern United States and Central America, but only one subspecies occurs in Texas, in a range restricted to the western Trans-Pecos not far from the Rio Grande. Here, Texas lyre snakes have been found in open Chihuahuan desert, rocky hills and mountains, and wooded canyons, with a preferred microhabitat of exposed rock faces and huge piles of boulders where they typically shelter in weather-generated crevices.

Emerging from these hiding places early in the evening, *Trimorphodon biscutatus vilkinsonii* typically remains active far into the night, for its eyes are exceptionally adapted to dim-light foraging. Lyre snakes are the only southwestern U.S. snake with both a vertically elliptical pupil and a lorilabial scale between its loreal and its paired labial scales. This pair of labial scales is what the name *biscutatus* references—the Greek *bi*, or "two," and *scutatus*, or "scale." Dorsolaterally, the Texas lyre snake has from 21 to 27 rows of smooth scales and an anal plate that may be either divided or undivided. The lyre snake's slim neck and broad head, which allows room for its enlarged salivary glands, as well as its elliptical pupils suggest its status as a rear-fanged serpent. Yet, despite its copious, mildly toxic saliva and its considerable body size, *Trimorphodon biscutatus* rarely bites and even if handled (carefully) it poses no threat to humans.

90 TEXAS LYRE SNAKE
Trimorphodon biscutatus vilkinsonii

Mildly venomous   Vertically slit hairline pupils mark *T. b. vilkinsonii* as a mildly venomous serpent whose posterior upper jaw carries a pair of slightly enlarged, grooved teeth. Related to the New World rat snakes, *Elaphe*, rather than to the pitvipers, the genus *Trimorphon* developed rear fangs, a broad, viperlike head, and vertically slit pupils. Lyre snakes pose little danger to humans, however, for unlike the vipers they cannot inject venom. Instead, after a bite *Trimorphodon biscutatus* engages its rear fangs, down whose lengthwise furrows its toxic saliva is squeezed by contractions of its jaw. Though the Texas lyre snake is typically reluctant to bite humans, if roughly restrained it tends to thrash about wildly, and large individuals are big enough to bite with conviction, perhaps depositing painful saliva into a wound.

Abundance   Threatened. Protected by the state of Texas. First described by E. D. Cope in 1886, from a specimen collected in Mexico's Sierra Madre Occidental by Edward Wilkinson, at the time of L. M. Klauber's review of the genus in 1940, *T. b. vilkinsonii* was known from only three other specimens. Yet Texas lyre snakes seem to be broadly if spottily distributed across the northern Chihuahuan Desert, for these secretive animals turn up every summer in widely separated locales across Trans-Pecos Texas. Often these sites are hidden nooks in the granite bluffs along the River Road west of Big Bend National Park in Presidio County. Although years pass in which no one sees a single *T. b. vilkinsonii* in this area, at other times these reptiles seem to be almost abundant. Marty and John Walmsley—who chanced to venture out during a period when lyre snakes were active—found 5 individuals during the 3-day Easter weekend, then another 2 on the same May night, all of them between Tornillo Creek and Ivey's Spring west of Lajitas, except a single individual found in a never-before-reported habitat high in the Chisos Mountains near the national park's Basin Campground. This animal—a male like all the others and therefore almost certainly abroad primarily in search of female pheromone scent—was abroad in rainy, 60°F weather.

The decision by the Texas Department of Parks and Wildlife to make illegal the possession and captive reproduction of this race has proven to be less important than to regulate automobile traffic through its critical habitat. Before the human population of the El Paso area exploded, Texas lyre snakes were encountered regularly on the Trans-Mountain Road, which bisects the Franklin Mountains, where this subspecies is now either extinct or exceedingly rare.

Size According to Augustus Rentfro, who has studied all three races of lyre snakes, this medium-sized colubrid's average adult length is about 30 inches, with most individuals falling into the 24-to-36-inch range. The record is 41 in.

Habitat This slim, saxicolous reptile is most often found in jumbles of fallen boulders or along fissured bluffs. Like most chthonic, arid land–living serpents, it leaves its creviced daytime retreats only well after dark. Earl Turner has observed *T. b. vilkinsonii* in a variety of habitats, including barren desert flats, in Presidio County's Pinto Canyon, and at the mouth of Santa Elena Canyon on the Rio Grande, where he discovered a small female on a ledge overhanging the river.

Prey The Texas lyre snake probably feeds on any smaller vertebrate, but Dave Barker found only lizard remains in the feces of several newly caught *T. b. vilkinsonii*. While spiny lizards and skinks are accepted as food by captive lyre snakes, Rentfro reports that these serpents greatly prefer racerunners as prey. The way in which Texas lyre snakes capture this lacertilian prey became evident when Dallas herpetologists Dave Blody and James Murphy observed one large individual methodically search a stony arroyo wall for the several species of lizards that had squeezed into its crevices for the night. Warm-blooded prey is also taken and may even be preferred; Shaw and Campbell (1974) propose that for many lyre snakes the primary prey is bats. After reading this, Rentfro, searching for a way to fatten his prospective breeding stock but fearing "acquiring some dreadful disease" from bats, turned to the hyperabundant food source of nestling English sparrows—which his lyre snakes "enthusiastically accepted." Most other recent captives feed readily on mice.

Reproduction Egg-laying. This enthusiastic feeding allowed Rentfro's females to quickly gain weight, and in late June frequent copulation was observed. The females rapidly vibrated their tails when courted by their mates but no biting or dominance wrestling was seen. In late July one 28-inch-long female deposited 7 adhesive-shelled oval eggs, averaging 1⅛ inches in length and ⅝ inch in diameter. After a 77-day incubation period these hatched into 8-inch-long young dramatically different in appearance from their dull brown parents. These hatchlings were a soft silver-gray with 25 sharply defined, white-edged black bands between snout and vent. There was no lyre-shaped marking on their crowns, for only two irregular black spots could be seen on their otherwise unmarked heads. After shedding, the young fed on small spiny and racerunner lizards.

The only hatchling *T. b. vilkinsonii* ever discovered in the wild was found by Damon Salceies during October in Brewster County, Texas, on Pepper's Hill between Lajitas and Terlingua. Mired in roadside tar, this thin, 7-inch-long neonate—whose photograph is included here—had a recent umbilical scar indicating it had hatched only a few weeks previously. Wild-born Texas lyre snakes may remain mostly below ground for their first several foraging seasons, since it may be unnecessary for juveniles—or females—to venture beyond the shelter of their residential rock piles to capture much of their lacertilian prey.

Coloring scale/form   The adult Texas lyre snake's ground color is a flat, medium brown, with 17 to 24 very widely spaced, triangularly shaped dark brown dorsolateral saddles (so widely spaced that Hobart M. Smith has suggested that some unique genetic suppression obscures what would be expected to be intervening dark-hued markings between them). Broadest over the spine and outlined by an irregular yellowish border, each of these brown triangular saddles has a paler, cinnamon-hued center. Lower on the sides, each of these saddles tapers to a point no more than a single scale in width at the belly line, although across the tail the saddles become narrow brown bands.

The Texas lyre snake's wiry neck supports a wide, oval-shaped head notable for the big, pale, slit-pupiled eyes associated with a venom system. Among more westerly subspecies, the somewhat lyre-shaped dark brown cephalic marking (the source of this reptile's common name) is evident. Yet the crown of most Texas individuals shows little more than a trio of chocolate smudges. The anterior venter is yellowish or pinkish brown, becoming buff on its posterior third. A small facial scale called a lorilabial is located between the loreal and upper labial scales, the dorsal scales are smooth, usually arranged in 23 rows at midbody, and the anal plate is usually divided but may sometimes be undivided.

Similar snakes   None. No other serpent in the Trans-Pecos shares the Texas lyre snake's slim trunk, broad head, and widely spaced, triangularly shaped vertebral saddles.

Behavior   Exceptional climbers, *Trimorphodon* have strongly developed musculature that encases their wiry trunks and enables them to traverse and even ascend vertical rock faces with powerful waves of concertina-motion ribwalking. Exclusively nocturnal in the wild, Texas lyre snakes may have less innate aversion to bright light than other night-hunting reptiles because, according to Barker, captives are willing to emerge in the evening to explore even a well-lit room, using the distinctive gait—head held high off the ground—typical of *Trimorphodon*. Wild Texas lyre snakes usually restrict their rare appearances in the open to early and midsummer, primarily during periods of elevated humidity following rainfall. Yet Blody and Murphy observed *T. b. vilkinsonii* moving about on a rainy night in March, while L. M. Klauber, speaking of western subspecies, noted that *T. biscutatus* seemed to be very tolerant of low temperatures, foraging abroad on nights too cold for other nocturnal species.

CORAL SNAKES
Family *Elapidae*

The family *Elapidae* is composed of predominantly neurotoxically venomed tropic or subtropics-living snakes, including the cobras, mambas, kraits, and their allies, while the large group of New World elapids that is made up of many coral snake species is also predominantly tropical, with even North American *Micrurus* favoring a warm climate and an at least locally mesic microenvironment. All elapids have enlarged, frontally grooved (*proteroglyphous* in Greek) anterior fangs. In most species, including the American coral snakes, these grooves are folded over to make an enclosed tube, at whose lower, forward end is the discharge/injection orifice. At its upper end, each fang—no more than a millimeter or two long in most coral snakes—is connected to a small venom gland located at the rear of the jaw. The jaw muscles compress both this gland and the cells that secrete the coral snake's complex and potent yet minuscule quantity of neurologically destructive venom. (This is why corals typically seize their prey and then hold on, chewing, until it has been immobilized.)

Elapids are of exclusively Old World distribution except for 3 genera of North and South American coral snakes; *micrurus* is the only member of the family *Elapidae* in eastern and central North America.

Coral Snakes
Genus *Micrurus*

Texas Coral Snake, *Micrurus fulvius tener*

In the eastern United States, the genus *Micrurus* has but a single species, *M. fulvius*, sometimes called the Harlequin coral snake, which is divided into two races, the eastern coral snake, *M. f. fulvius*, and its western subspecies, the Texas coral snake, *M. f. tener*. Both races are ringed with red, yellow, and black, with only the two warning colors of a traffic signal—red and yellow—touching. (In this country, all nonvenomous red-, yellow-, and black-banded snakes have their red and yellow bands separated by a black band, though this does not hold true in Latin America.)

Coral snakes are also shaped differently from other red-, yellow-, and black-banded North American snakes. The head is flattened, with a rounded black snout, and there are both 15 rows of smooth dorsolateral scales and a divided anal plate.

Moreover, they behave differently, for the harlequin coral snake can be a dangerous reptile, in part because its temperament is so unpredictable: *M. fulvius* may suddenly and reflexively bite sideways in response to even a gentle touch. Alternatively, the body may be flattened, brightening its colors by exposing patches of skin between the scales and hiding the head beneath the trunk while waving a coiled tail tip aloft as a predator decoy.

Because coral snakes have short, immovable fangs and a comparatively small head, a myth has arisen that they can nip only the tip of a finger or toe, and then must chew deliberately to administer venom.

Actually, while *M. fulvius* is not able to make the long, lunging strikes of large pitvipers or to inject pressurized venom deeply into muscle tissue, it does not need to, because coral snakes are perfectly capable of pinching out a tiny fold of skin between their exceptionally wide-gaping jaws to bite an arm, leg, or foot. A single quick bite, moreover, one that just penetrates the skin, is all this animal needs to mortally envenomate its reptilian prey, and the same is to some extent also true of a human adversary.

Another erroneous belief is that one can safely lift a coral snake by its tail, but *M. fulvius* is able to rapidly change ends by adroitly climbing its own dangling body. (Like other snakes, *M. fulvius* tend to do this only if they are dangled; if their foreparts are allowed to touch the earth they generally forget about climbing their own bodies and resume merely trying to crawl away.)

Coral snakes have very small, beady eyes and are apparently unable to see well. Yet because of the inclination of *M. fulvius* to whip its foreparts from side to side, biting anything against which it bumps its head, an angry coral snake can be an aggressive creature. Its first response is often the decoy maneuver of raising its tail like an about-to-strike head and then suddenly snapping outward with its previously hidden jaws.

Harlequin coral snakes inhabit open woodlands, hammocks, and fields, as well as suburban backyards. They hide under fallen tree trunks, beneath discarded litter, in mats of vegetation or the recumbent stems of lawn grasses. Yet *M. fulvius* is seldom seen, in spite of being common throughout most of its range, because it has such a secretive nature.

91 TEXAS CORAL SNAKE
Micrurus fulvius tener

Venomous   Since its venom is made up primarily of neurotoxically destructive peptides, *Micrurus fulvius* (along with the Mojave rattlesnake) is the most virulently toxined snake in North America. The lethal dose for a human adult is estimated to be as little as 5 to 10 milligrams of venom, which is approximately the same potency as the venom of most cobras. Immediate pain usually accompanies a coral snakebite, but since nervous system impairment may not manifest symptoms for several hours, antivenin should be ready before the onset of neurological problems.

Yet few people are harmed by coral snakes. If unmolested, *M. fulvius* is so

nonaggressive toward people that virtually everyone bitten has first touched or handled the animal. Moreover, many coral snake bites result in no enveno-mation at all (partly because at only about an ⅛ inch in length the coral's rigidly fixed little fangs are too short to penetrate shoe leather or thick cloth-ing), and only about 1 percent of North American venom poisonings involve coral snakes.

Nevertheless, *Micrurus fulvius* is adept at biting a large adversary. Its mouth can gape open to form a surprisingly wide biting surface, and its strong jaws can easily press those small fangs through the skin anywhere on the human body. In addition, as hollow hypodermic needles, coral snake fangs are designed to both puncture skin and rapidly inject venom. (Janis Roze, the world's leading authority on coral snakes, has observed that during a bite *Micrurus* also typically releases a small additional amount of venom from glands located in its lower jaw.) The common myth is that *M. fulvius* must chew deliberately to infuse its venom, and though coral snakes certainly bite and chew, agitated individuals do so with sufficient vigor to instantly deposit their toxins onto a pinning stick or inject them into a thick leather handling glove much less penetrable than human skin. In confined areas, *Micrurus fulvius* can also move very quickly, suddenly twisting its head to snap side-ways. See **Venom Potency Table.**

Abundance   Common. Throughout the eastern third of Texas, *M. f. tener* inhabits mostly wooded environments, either pine forest—where it is uncommon—or more open oak hickory woodland, including both cross tim-ber hillsides and riparian bottomland. To the west, these riparian corridors allow the Texas coral snake to range across the oak–juniper savannah of the Edwards Plateau, and to penetrate the arid eastern reaches of the northern Chihuahuan Desert. Here, if even a bit of terrestrial leaf litter, fallen grass, or other vegetative detritus offers shelter for its small ophidian prey, *M. f. tener* is sometimes found in virtually waterless canyon milieus. The Texas coral snake is also entirely at home in residential areas where stone walls and land-scaped shrubbery provide both cover and a habitat for the ground, ring-necked, brown, and earth snakes on which it feeds (as a largely diurnal forager, *M. f. tener* is far more likely to be seen in suburban areas than its nocturnal look-alikes, the milk snakes, which are rare to nonexistent in cities). The author has often been called to suburban backyards and even porches to remove Texas coral snakes—sometimes quite early in the spring since this is a comparatively cool weather–adapted snake.

Size   Texas coral snakes are larger than commonly thought: 74 adult females averaged 26½ inches in snout–vent length, 93 males just over 24 inches. The record is a 47¾-inch-long specimen from Brazoria County.

Habitat   Active throughout the year during warm weather, *Micrurus fulvius tener* occupies a variety of terrestrial milieus, most often at least partially wooded. These include the eastern pine forest, Central Texas' oak–juniper brakes, and the thorn brush woodland of the Rio Grande plain. Either rock crevice cover or thick plant litter is important, both as a hiding place and as habitat for the semisubterranean serpents on which coral snakes prey.

Prey   Coral snakes feed largely on other snakes, but lizards—especially slen-der, snakelike lizards such as skinks—are reportedly also taken, although captive coral snakes of both eastern and Texas races are typically reluctant to feed at all, no matter what prey is offered. In the wild, ophidian prey (which can be proportionately very large: sometimes longer than the coral snake which devours it) is located by active scent-tracking. On a Central Texas riverbank the author discovered a 26-inch-long female *M. fulvius* in the process of envenoming a young Texas rat snake. The rat snake was first immobilized and then, very gradually, swallowed. That evening, as coral snakes often do when captured, this animal disgorged the rat snake—which turned out to be nearly an inch longer than the coral itself. Northeast of Austin, a Texas coral snake found by Tim Cole also disgorged a checkered garter snake of nearly its own size.

Slender-bodied lizards (especially snakelike glass lizards and skinks), as well as small amphisbaenians, are also reportedly consumed, though much less frequently than ophidian prey. Cannibalism among *M. fulvius* has also been observed, which means that males much smaller than their prospective mates approach them only at the risk of being eaten. The food of hatchling coral snakes in the wild is unknown, but a captive brood raised by the author fed sporadically on small earth and brown snakes, and 3 of the 6 reached adulthood.

Reproduction Egg-laying. "No other North American snake has been reported to breed from late summer to late spring, then lay its eggs in midsummer," wrote herpetologist Hugh Quinn in 1979. Seldom bred—or even successfully maintained—by herpetoculturists, *M. f. tener's* 3 to 8 white, sausage-shaped eggs—1⅛ inch in length by ⅜ inch in diameter—are laid during June and July. These hatch 2 months later into 6½- to 7½-inch-long young, which in two Central Texas clutches in the author's experience were very slender: no more than ⅜ inch in maximum body diameter.

Identical to the adults in color and marking, in the wild coral snake neonates evidently lead almost entirely fossorial lives, perhaps for years since they have so rarely been seen abroad; hatchlings cared for by the author virtually never emerged from a deep layer of cage-bottom litter, even to feed.

Coloring/scale form *Micrurus fulvius tener* is the only black-, red-, and yellow-banded serpent in Texas whose red and yellow bands touch. "Red against yellow, kill a fellow" seldom turns out to be the case, but it is a good phrase to use in quickly identifying a coral snake. The Texas coral snake's trunk is completely encircled with 14 to 20 equally broad red and black bands separated by much narrower yellow rings. Both its head and tail are banded only with black and yellow; the nape and posterior crown are marked with a wide yellow band. Partially albino coral snakes have also been found, with white bands replacing normal individuals' black pigmentation. (This very rare color morph has ordinary red and yellow bands, however.) Whatever its color, the Texas coral snake's bright dorsolateral bands continue unbroken across its belly, while its undertail has a double row of scales like that of most nonvenomous snakes. There are 15 midbody rows of smooth dorsal scales and its anal plate is divided.

Similar snakes   Among both **milk snakes** (79–82) and **scarlet snakes** (84–85) the red and pale yellow or white crossbands do not touch—black dorsolateral rings separate them: "Red against black, venom lack." Unlike coral snakes, whose tails are entirely black and yellow, milk and scarlet snakes' red crossbands occur all the way to their tail tips. The **Texas long-nosed snake** (86) may have a few red and creamy yellow scales that touch, but only in the speckled edging of its dorsal saddles. Its venter is mostly white, its protruding, pointed snout light brown or orange.

Behavior   Like many North American serpents, coral snakes tend to be diurnal in spring and fall, becoming nocturnal during the heat of the summer. Yet, judged against the behavioral norms of other North American serpents, coral snakes are more like their elapid relatives the cobras—which also exhibit a wide range of behavioral flexibility. Coral snakes simply do surprising things. When Connie McIntyre was called to rescue a Texas coral snake from a suburban backyard, the animal seemed lethargic until it was touched. Then it began *Micrurus fulvius'* typical thrashing and sideways snapping, then made a dash for shelter. As it squeezed under a rock, McIntyre took hold of its about-to-disappear tail and pulled it out—only to find that in the second or two its foreparts had been out of sight the coral snake had discovered and seized a rough earth snake, *Virginia valeria striatula*, which it held wriggling in its jaws. In these situations, *M. fulvius* typically hangs on tenaciously (a quality described in its subspecies name, *tener*) until its venom has paralyzed its prey, then works its jaws forward across the shingled scales of the victim toward its head.

To what degree coral snakes' bold patterning functions as a warning has long been an area of controversy. Experiments with clay snakes painted to resemble corals and laid out in Central American forests indicate that far fewer attacks from predatory birds occurred on brightly banded than on plain-hued models. Yet, to realize their full defensive potential, the coral's bright body bands may need to be combined with its distinctive threat behavior. For example, opossums confronted with both artificial replicas and dead coral snakes were not frightened. Only when live *Micrurus fulvius* actively raised and slowly wagged their yellow- and black-banded tail tips (presumably in a threatening imitation of their similarly patterned heads) did the opossums exhibit concern. See **Louisiana Milk Snake.**

CORAL SNAKES

PITVIPERS
Family *Viperidae*

This group of dangerously venomous, lengthily front-fanged snakes contains two subfamilies, *Viperinae* (true vipers) and *Crotalinae*, or pitvipers. The latter subfamily consists, in the eastern and central part of North America north of Mexico, of the genera *Agkistrodon*, or copperheads and cottonmouths, and *Sistrurus* and *Crotalus,* or rattlesnakes. (Pitvipers' common name is derived from the well-defined heat-sensing pits, one of which deeply indents on each side of the snout between eye and nostril.) These heat-sensitive facial organs let pitvipers pick out warm-blooded prey against a kaleidoscope of less-warm background temperatures. In addition, the sensitivity and positioning of these pits allows the pitviper to strike almost unerringly even in complete darkness. The strike is particularly effective because a pair of long, hollow fangs, each attached to a rotatable maxillary bone within a distal socket, is located at each front corner of the upper jaw. When the pitviper lunges toward its prey each maxilla is rotated anteriorly to direct its fang almost straight forward to jab its victim; when the snake closes its jaws the maxilla rotates posteriorly to fold its fang against the roof of the mouth.

Each of these fangs (if either breaks off it is quickly replaced by the anteriormost in a row of proto-fangs lined up just behind it) intersects a hollow, tubular duct against which its upper opening is sealed by sphincterlike muscles. Each of these paired ducts leads, in turn, to a venom gland, or lumen, set in the outer rear third of the skull. (In conjunction with the contracting musculature that surrounds it, these big lumens broaden the rear of the pitviper's head into the distinctive, triangular viperid shape.) *Crotalinae* also share a vertically elliptical pupil with the mildly venomous North American colubrids, but unlike most nonvenomous snakes, pitvipers have a single row of subcaudal scales.

Pitvipers' control of both their fangs and their venom glands is highly evolved, allowing these animals to choose both the depth of its fangs' penetration and the amount of venom expended during a strike. Because of this element of choice on the snake's part, many purely defensive bites are "dry," meaning no venom is injected, since the snake is trying to merely deter rather than kill its attacker.

Actually, even where prey is involved, pitviper venom is only partially a killing device. The primary function of pitvipers' toxic mixture of cell-destroying proteases is to predigest food animals. *Viperidae* are thus able to ingest larger, more calorically valuable prey animals, which may supply more than a quarter of the pitviper's annual caloric needs in a single meal. This is made possible in part because pitvipers' cell-destroying venom has rendered the often lumpy carcasses of their prey into softened masses of partially digested tissue. Like everything else about pitvipers, the action of their venom is far from random inside envenomed prey. Cell-dissolving enzymes disintegrate the dying animal's skin and muscle and, after the victim is swallowed, open its viscera and finally expose its skeleton to further digestive disintegration. (The simpler, less elaborately evolved venom of elapids is much more lethal.)

Copperheads and Cottonmouths
Genus *Agkistrodon*

Southern Copperhead, *Agkistrodon contortrix contortrix*
Broad-banded Copperhead, *Agkistrodon contortrix laticinctus*
Trans-Pecos Copperhead, *Agkistrodon contortrix pictigaster*
Western Cottonmouth, *Agkistrodon piscivorus leucostoma*

The viperine subfamily *Crotalinae* contains all North American members of the genus *Agkistrodon*, commonly known as copperheads (highland moccasins) and cottonmouths (water moccasins). Both sets of common names are descriptive, for dry land–living copperheads have unmistakable coppery- to russet-colored crowns, while a glimpse of the pinkish white interior of the largely aquatic cottonmouth's oral cavity gaping in defensive threat makes clear the reason for its name. Likewise, these creatures' scientific designation, *Agkistrodon*, is drawn from the Greek *ankistron*, or "fishhook," and *odon*, or "tooth," which describes these pitvipers' curved, fishhook-like fangs. *Agkistrodon* feed on a variety of both endothermic and ectothermic prey—from grasshoppers and cicadas to amphibians, ground-dwelling birds, and mammals up to the size of muskrats. Both copperheads and cottonmouths give birth to live young, often only every second year among northern copperheads, and perhaps also among cottonmouths from the more northerly parts of the range. Both species' neonates have a pale yellowish or greenish tail tip that they subconsciously use as a wriggling, worm-like decoy to lure small prey within striking range (excited adult copperheads and cottonmouths exhibit the same instinctive tail whirring, and despite lacking a rattle can produce an audible buzzing sound as their tail tips vibrate against dry vegetation).

92 SOUTHERN COPPERHEAD
Agkistrodon contortrix contortrix

Venomous   While poisoning by any race of *A. contortrix* could be fatal to a very small child, records of the Antivenin Institute of America show that throughout the United States, regardless of the kind (or lack) of treatment, over a 10-year period not a single death resulted from 308 copperhead bites. This is largely because *A. contortrix* has short (³⁄₈ inch maximum length) fangs, and because its toxins are only about half as destructive to tissue as those of an equal quantity of most rattlesnakes' venom. Even animals as small as cats, which are often bitten due to copperheads' prevalence in wooded suburban neighborhoods, usually survive *A. contortrix* envenomation, 221 although they typically experience substantial tissue loss and sloughing of the skin. See **Venom Potency Table.**

Abundance   Very common. In much of the eastern third of Texas, southern and broad-banded copperheads are the most numerous venomous snake.

Size   The largest of the copperhead subspecies, individual *A. c. contortrix* from the southeastern United States have reached a record size of 52 inches. Most individuals are much smaller, however, with a majority of adults measuring 24 to 30 in.

Habitat   Southern copperheads are almost always found in tree-shaded areas where fallen leaves, logs, and branches afford these terrestrial ambush foragers an intricately patterned background against which their dark-edged dorsolateral crossbands provide beautifully cryptic coloration. Heavy vegetative ground cover also shelters the southern copperhead's small, forest-floor-living prey which, if it is numerous, can support as many as 6 or 7 adult copperheads on a single acre. In one North Texas study plot, a majority of intergrade southern/broad-banded copperheads marked and subsequently recovered were found within 100 yards of where they had been released a year earlier.

Prey   Copperheads take whatever small prey is most seasonally available. Year in and year out, however, deer mice and white-footed mice are probably the principal food source of *A. c. contortrix*—followed by anurans (in spring, large numbers of puddle-spawning frogs are taken). Large insects such as cicadas can also be a major, if only periodically available food source as they emerge en masse from underground. When excited by nearby prey, young copperheads slowly twitch their yellowish or grayish green tail tips in a subconscious, tantalizing imitation of a wriggling caterpillar—a maneuver that may lure small frogs and lizards within striking range.

Reproduction   Live-bearing. See **Broad-banded Copperhead.**

Coloring/scale form   This eastern subspecies' most distinctive characteristic is its beige, sometimes almost pinkish ground color, which is marked with 13 to 20 pale-centered, dark-bordered, reddish brown dorsolateral bands. Often the right and left sides of these bands do not line up along the spine, where they are cinched, or contorted, into an hourglass configuration—a shape that gave rise to the Latin name *contortrix*. The tan, wedge-shaped crown bears a pair of dark posterior spots, while the prominent supraocular plates of all *Agkistrodon* are part of a sharply angled intersection between the crown and the flat, undercut cheeks. Posterior to its slit-pupiled, coppery-colored eyes, the southern copperhead's cheeks (supralabial scales) are marked with a pale, reward pointing V whose upper border is defined by a dark line leading from the eye to the rear of its jaw; just below and behind its nostril is the pitviper's dark, heat-sensing pit. The southern copperhead's whitish venter is only slightly mottled along its midline; distally, it is marked with large brown ovals. The 23 to 25 midbody rows of dorsal scales are weakly keeled, there is a single row of ventral scales beneath the tail tip, and the anal plate is undivided.

Similar snakes   Where the ranges of the southern and **broad-banded copperhead** (93) races meet along a broad strip stretching from the Gulf Coast to central Oklahoma, individuals intermediate in pattern between these sub-species prevail. The western broad-banded race can be distinguished, how-ever, by its more darkly mottled venter, the absence of dark borders on its reddish tan dorsolateral bands, and the almost equal width of these bands at the belly line and along the spine. The nonvenomous serpent most commonly mistaken for the southern copperhead is the **eastern hog-nosed snake (60)**, especially in its coppery color phases. Sometimes similarly patterned, these short, heavy-bodied snakes inhabit the same tree-shaded suburban neighbor-hoods as the southern copperhead, and like it often show little fear of humans. But the hog-nose's raised forehead, round-pupiled dark brown eyes, compar-atively thick neck, and prominently upturned snout are distinctive, as is its divided anal plate and the double row of scales beneath its tail. As a juvenile, the **western cottonmouth (95)** resembles the young southern copperhead, but it is a dusky gray-brown serpent, with dark dorsolateral bands. Unlike neonate copperheads, newborn *A. p. leucostoma* also have a wide, dark band across their cheeks and are seldom found away from water in the copperhead's dry woodland habitat.

Behavior   Most often abroad at dawn or dusk between March and Octo-ber, copperheads are low-energy-budget predators. Because they may eat no more often than once every 3 weeks, even during the months in which they are most active, *Agkistrodon contortrix* often lives virtually alongside small mammal populations. During late spring and summer both snakes and rodents may be simultaneous residents of the sheltered microhabitats beneath logs and human debris such as sheets of plywood or metal siding. The author has found nests of baby mice within a few feet of a coiled, quiescent copper-head whose presence had failed to excite the parent mouse into moving her brood. Although normally entirely terrestrial, after floods southern copper-heads have been seen on sloping boughs above high water, and in Lee County the author once discovered an intergrade *A. c. contortrix* coiled inside a dead stump protruding from several inches of standing water.

93 BROAD-BANDED COPPERHEAD
Agkistrodon contortrix laticinctus

Venomous   Although all pitvipers will bite if sufficiently provoked, copperheads of all races are singularly docile, and when found around suburban houses can be gently picked up with a stick, placed in a trash can or other large container, and easily moved to safety. See **Southern Copperhead.**

Abundance   Very common. *Agkistrodon contortrix laticinctus* is confined to the central third of Texas. Along the eastern side of its range, in a wide north–south band it intergrades with its subspecies the southern copperhead while, to the west, from Del Rio north along the Pecos River the broad-banded copperhead intergrades with its westerly Trans-Pecos race. Although this animal's range includes a great deal of open country, in such terrain *A. c. laticintus* is mostly confined to riparian corridors that approximate its preferred microenvironment of mesic woodlands with plentiful ground cover. Since this description also fits many tree-shaded urban neighborhoods, throughout the eastern part of its range the broad-banded copperhead is sometimes abundant in city suburbs. Readily adapting to the presence of humans, *A. c. laticinctus* (as long as it is not molested by people, cats, or dogs) does well in creek bottoms and vacant woodlots located in the midst of housing developments.

Size   The record length for this race is just over 37 inches.

Habitat   Almost everywhere in its range the broad-banded copperhead occurs in either riparian or upland woods on a carpet of fallen oak leaves or pine needles—against which its russet dorsal patterning makes it almost invisible. This reptile is also locally abundant in the live oak/cedar brake bottomland of the Edwards Plateau.

Prey   Primarily small rodents, nestling ground birds, spiny lizards, frogs, and large insects. Newly metamorphosed cicadas, which periodically emerge in swarms numbering thousands per acre, at times account for a large percentage of this reptile's prey, but deer and white-footed mice are the staple diet of most copperheads. Like other copperheads, *A. c. laticinctus* is also successful at surviving within a small area—thus avoiding the increased exposure to predation that extensive foraging entails. This success is a result of 2 sets of extraordinary predatory adaptations. First, pitvipers have excellent night vision, heat-sensing facial pits, sophisticated venom, and delicately manipulable fangs that require only a short, rapid thrust to kill a majority of the small prey animals that come within striking range. Second, as mostly ambush hunters, they use comparatively little energy, and the slow metabolism this lifestyle permits allows copperheads to thrive on as little as one kill every few weeks.

Reproduction   Live-bearing. Courtship begins with the male advancing to touch the female with his snout and, if she does not move away, rubbing her back with his chin. If she is receptive she will remain stationary, often flattening her body, waving or vibrating her tail and, as a preliminary to mating, eliminating waste from her cloaca. Copulation is initiated only when she opens her cloaca to receive the male's hemipene, after which the pair can remain linked for several hours. Although prior breeding by the female tends to deter subsequent mating attempts by other males, spring copulation by a female carrying sperm from a previous autumn pairing can probably produce a litter sired by 2 males. Born during the latter part of July and all of August, broad-banded copperhead litters number 4 to 8, with most neonates—which have paler pigmentation than their parents—measuring 7½ to 10 inches in length.

Coloring/scale form   *Agkistrodon contortrix laticinctus* is defined by its light brown ground color and its 11 to 17 reddish tan dorsolateral bands—almost equally wide at the belly line and along the spine, for which it is named *laticinctus* for "broad-banded." To accommodate this pitviper's large venom glands, the rear of its skull broadens to more than 3 times the width of its narrow neck; ahead of its eyes and slightly below the level of its nostrils lie its dark, heat-sensing pits. The pale venter is generally mottled with reddish brown. Arranged in 23 (occasionally 25) rows at midbody, the dorsal scales are weakly keeled, and under the tail the belly plates are arranged in a single row behind the vent; the anal plate is undivided.

Similar snakes The **southern copperhead (92)** is typically a light, sometimes almost pinkish tan subspecies noted for the hourglass-shaped, chocolate-bordered dorsolateral bands that narrow to solid brown bars across its spine; its buff-colored venter is only laterally splotched with large brown ovals. **The Trans-Pecos copperhead (94)** is distinguished by its chestnut to near-black venter, interrupted by pale lateral intrusions. Its dorsolateral crossbands often bear a pale central aura around a mahogany-hued spot just above the belly line, as well as by a whitish bordering wash, while the area between these bands may also be almost white. On average, there are more undertail scales (52 to 59 compared to the broad-banded's 40 to 54). Seen from above, **hognosed snakes (60–63)** have a proportionately thicker neck than any pitviper, beady little eyes with round pupils, a bulbous forehead, and a markedly upturned snout. They also lack the copperhead's grayish tail tip, and have a divided anal plate and a single row of undertail scales. Newborn copperheads are distinguished from young **cottonmouths (95)** by the pale, rearward-facing V that marks the copperheads' cheeks; neonate cottonmouths have blackish cheeks and, unlike the copperhead, seek shelter in water.

Behavior Copperheads and cottonmouths are the only North American members of the genus *Agkistrodon*, which apparently originated in Asia during early Miocene times, then spread to the New World over the Bering land bridge. Here, these ancestral pitvipers gradually gave rise to the more highly evolved rattlesnakes. Like those of most temperate-zone reptiles, copperheads' activity patterns vary considerably throughout the year. After early spring emergence from winter denning, *A. c. laticinctus* seeks an optimal temperature of 78 to 84°F by basking during the sunniest hours and hiding beneath woodland debris at other times. As midday temperatures climb with the advent of summer, copperheads grow largely crepuscular, foraging mostly at dawn and twilight except on overcast days or when soil and vegetation are damp; in the hottest weather of midsummer they are abroad mainly at night. Because the copperhead is among the least agile of snakes—its only capacity for rapid motion is in the darting jab of its strike—its predatory forays characteristically involve little more than deliberate travel from one ambush site to another, although sedentary prey such as nestling birds and rodents are sought by scent. If threatened, *Agkistrodon contortrix* may both emit musk from a pair of anal glands and vibrate its tail in agitation.

MOCCASINS

94 TRANS-PECOS COPPERHEAD

Agkistrodon contortrix pictigaster

Venomous   See **Southern Copperhead.**

Abundance   Uncommon. Confined to Trans-Pecos Texas, *A. c. pictigaster* is essentially a xeric-adapted race of an eastern woodland species living at the western limit of its biological capacity. How this came to be is illustrative of the slow but unending alteration that occurs to all habitats, and of the struggle plants and animals face in trying to continue living in ever-changing environments. Because the northern Chihuahuan Desert is of more recent origin than much of its resident wildlife, a number of species—including *A. c. pictigaster*—persist in relict populations confined to the vicinity of the scattered permanent springs and streams remaining from the wetter climate of the late Pleistocene. Yet many sightings of *A. c. pictigaster* occur not around desert springs but in dry canyon-laced terrain in Terrell, Val Verde, and Crockett counties.

Size   Most adults are 18 to 26 inches in length; the record is 32⅞ in.

Habitat   Although most U.S. copperheads are associated with wooded, mesic bottomland, this westernmost race is found throughout the Trans-Pecos—where springs and seasonally moist canyons are its favored habitat. Nevertheless, biologist Kelly Bryant reports frequently seeing this race in the arid terrain of Big Bend Ranch State Park but has yet to see a Trans-Pecos copperhead in several years' fieldwork in the far more mesic Davis Mountains uplands—though records exist of this subspecies' presence there at over 6,000-foot elevations.

Prey   Both West Texas' canyonlands and shrub desert are well populated with the small rodent species that copperheads feed on everywhere in their range—as well as a host of abundant, and possibly preyed-on, lizard species. See **Broad-banded Copperhead.**

Reproduction   Live-bearing. See **Broad-banded Copperhead.**

Coloring/scale form   Some individuals of this strikingly colored subspecies are distinguished by an off-white or even silvery ground color unlike that of any other copperhead. The back and sides of *A. c. pictigaster* are patterned with 13 to 19 broad, cinnamon-bay to seal-brown dorsolateral bands, each of which usually bears a pale aura just above the belly line, centered with a mahogany spot. (Juveniles tend to be somewhat lighter hued, with more contrasting colors, while large adults have usually darkened into a medium brown ground color.) The heavily mottled belly, typically mahogany to black but interrupted with pale lateral intrusions, is unique to this subspecies and is the source of the Trans-Pecos copperhead's scientific name: *picti* means "painted" and *gaster* is "stomach." The tail is gray-brown above, with thin grayish or greenish crossbands, while a single row of subcaudal plates lines its posterior tip. The 21 to 25 midbody rows of dorsal scales are weakly keeled, and the anal plate is undivided.

Similar snakes   The **broad-banded copperhead** (93) is somewhat less reddish above, generally has more uniformly colored, lighter brown body bands, a much less heavily mottled belly, and a lower average number of subcaudal scales (37 to 54 vs. 52 to 59 among *A. c. pictigaster*). In the field such distinctions are largely meaningless, however, because southern, broad-banded, and Trans-Pecos copperhead subspecies only gradually diverge into their pure forms across an east–west sequence of gradual clinal variation.

Behavior   Because this race of copperhead is part of a basically mesic-adapted species, its ability to thrive in a region now much drier than at any time in recent history is due partly to the widespread ophidian capacity for enduring extended periods of hostile conditions—heat, drought, or cold—as long as some portion of the year allows active foraging. Yet few other moist-climate snakes are found in the harsh Chihuahuan biome, so energy conservation may be the Trans-Pecos copperhead's edge. The minimal caloric expenditure that lets ambush-hunting pitvipers like *A. c. pictigaster* thrive on a single kill per month even during its primary activity period in this region's brief, late-summer rainy season is undoubtedly a major factor in its survival here.

95 WESTERN COTTONMOUTH
Agkistrodon piscivorus leucostoma

MOCCASINS

Venomous   Despite the cottonmouth's formidable reputation, very few people are bitten by this reptile (only about 7 percent of Texas' snakebites involve cottonmouths), and even fewer are seriously injured; throughout the United States, the mortality rate is less than 1 person per year. Envenomation by *Agkistrodon piscivorus* may result in substantial tissue death, however, because these big aquatic vipers have up to ⅝-inch-long fangs and huge venom storage lumens which, from the largest individuals, can yield hundreds of milligrams, dry weight, of venom. While its toxins are less potent than those of most large *Crotalus*-genus rattlesnakes—Sherman Minton estimates the lethal dose for a healthy human adult as about 150 milligrams—the hemorrhagic effects of cottonmouth venom are pronounced. See **Venom Potency Table.**

Abundance   Locally very common. Although the majority of presumed cottonmouth sightings are actually those of *Natricine* water snakes, western cottonmouths are extremely numerous in some places, especially on the Gulf coastal plain. Near Sinton, as well as on rice field levees near Egypt, Tex., at times the author has seen a basking cottonmouth every few hundred yards. Such dense populations can even make themselves known, in still air, by scent, as is sometimes the case around forest-enclosed ponds in East Texas where the musky smell of *Agkistrodon piscivorus* can sometimes be detected.

Size   The record *A. p. leucostoma*, taken on the Neches River by George O. Miller, was a fraction of an inch over 5 feet in length. Most western cottonmouths are much smaller, however. Of 306 recorded individuals, only a few males—which grow larger than females—were longer than 3 feet, and the great majority measured between 20 and 30 in.

Habitat   Although western cottonmouths are generally found within ½ mile of permanent water, they are not limited to aquatic environments. They favor leutic microhabitats primarily because of the more plentiful prey and better cover available there. But they do quite well in entirely dry milieus. Dry forest, grassland, and even cornfields (where they hunt for rats) are also occupied. During spring, flooded prairie with a large population of breeding frogs is a prime foraging site. Salt marshes and the low-lying saline barrier islands bordering the Gulf Coast also harbor large numbers of western cottonmouths, yet the density of *A. p. leucostoma* populations tends to vary widely, with large areas of apparently prime wetland being almost entirely devoid of these reptiles.

Prey   The western cottonmouth is likely to feed on any vertebrate small enough to swallow. Frogs are probably this pitviper's most frequent prey, but *A. p. leucostoma* (its Greek-derived subspecies name means "white-mouthed") is an indiscriminate feeder whose diet alters with the availability of different food species. Water birds, smaller snakes—including copperheads and other cottonmouths—are also reported, as are a variety of fish species, although game fish are generally too fast for cottonmouths to capture. Like other aquatic serpents, *A. piscivorus* also feeds on carrion and is consequently drawn to wounded and dying fish dangling from fishermen's stringers.

Reproduction   Live-bearing. Reproduction follows the usual viperid pattern of slow growth, delayed maturation, and low reproductive frequency. But the enhanced foraging opportunities afforded by their rich aquatic habitat often give female cottonmouths a better chance than terrestrial vipers of acquiring the increased body fat necessary for successful pregnancy. (Unlike the many terrestrial viperids that may require two years' hunting to acquire enough fatty tissue to nourish their large, well-developed young, some female *A. piscivorus* breed every year.)

During early spring courtship, adult male cottonmouths typically follow a female's pheromone scent trail, sometimes even across lily pads. If they encounter another male engaged in the same pursuit, dominance behavior is likely to ensue, with each combatant attempting to force down the other's foreparts. Pairing initially involves tongue flicking of the female's back by the male, followed by rubbing his chin along her spine, after which copulation may last several hours.

Because gestation among snakes is not as uniformly timed as that of birds and mammals, fertilization may be delayed for weeks while sperm remain viable in the cloaca. Up to several months after copulation, therefore, the 8- to 11-inch-long young are born, usually during August, September, and early October. They are so stoutly proportioned that gravid females bear only 3 to 12 offspring per litter (while similarly sized water snakes typically deposit dozens of their much more slender young). Newborn western cottonmouths are both more brownish and more clearly patterned than adults, with dark dorsal bars and lateral blotches. Their tails have gray-green tips which, in a predatory technique shared with their relatives the copperheads, are instinctively flicked back and forth in the excitement of seeing prey, thus unconsciously imitating the movements of a worm or caterpillar, which can lure small frogs and toads within striking range.

Coloring/scale form Adult western cottonmouths are dark gray-brown, with broad, dimly defined lateral banding. (Some individuals' dull dorsal coloring results from a film of water-deposited sediment and algae: clean water–living cottonmouths show more distinct patterning.) Very old cottonmouths, however, may be entirely dark gray or black. In daylight, the pupils of the large, grayish eyes are vertical black slits easily discernible from a safe distance; at night in the beam of a flashlight they are oval or elliptical during the few moments it takes them to close against the glare. Definitive but less evident is the dark orifice of the heat-sensing pit located between the eye and nostril, and the pronounced taper from the thick posterior trunk to the cottonmouth's attenuated little tail. Especially among females the tail seems out of proportion to the heavily proportioned trunk, while the posterior trunk of males contains its hemipene and is somewhat larger. The keeled dorsal scales occur in 25 rows at midbody, and the subcaudal scutes display a unique pattern by which, even from their shed skins, *Agkistrodon* can be identified: behind the undivided anal plate a single row of belly-wide scale plates occupies the undertail tip.

Similar snakes The dark, heavy bodies and aquatic habitat of **large water snakes (30–38)** often cause them to be mistaken for the western cottonmouth. All water snakes lack the cottonmouth's heat-sensing pit between eye and nostril, however, and have clearly visible *round* pupils. *Agkistrodon piscivorus* also behaves differently from water snakes, which neither gape in threat nor vibrate their tails in agitation. Also unlike water snakes, the cottonmouth swims in a leisurely way, its whole body floating buoyantly, with the head held high. Water snakes swim by squirming rapidly along, their bodies drooping below the surface when they stop. Juvenile **copperheads (92–94)** are lighter brown and have dark-edged beige cheeks unlike the cottonmouth's dark labial scales.

Behavior The most widespread story about the cottonmouth concerns the water-skier purportedly killed by a flurry of bites after tumbling into a "nest" of these reptiles. For years various retellings of this fictitious event have circulated in boating circles, and an even more absurd fantasy about a cowboy killed by western cottonmouths while crossing the Nueces River on horseback appeared in the television special *Lonesome Dove*. All such episodes are untrue: no water-skier or river-fording horseman has ever suffered multiple *A. piscivorus* envenomation. These scary myths originate in people's observations of the large number of harmless water snakes that, during late summer, become concentrated in drying creeks and stock tanks, where they are mistaken for nests of cottonmouths. Cottonmouths do not "nest," however, and though groups do sometimes aggregate in such aquatic refugia, none ever attack en masse; in the water cottonmouths quickly dive and flee even when approached stealthily. On land, where *A. piscivorus* is too heavy-bodied to flee effectively, some individuals hold their ground and gape open-mouthed, although the cottonmouth's notorious widespread jaws actually signal a comparatively passive defense gesture, for such snakes often fail to strike even when prodded with a boot.

RATTLESNAKES
Genera *Sistrurus* and *Crotalus*

All rattlesnakes (as well as copperheads and cottonmouths) are contained in the viperine subfamily *Crotalinae*, which includes both the pigmy and massasauga rattlesnake genus *Sistrurus* and the generally larger and more widespread genus *Crotalus*.

Pigmy Rattlesnakes and Massasaugas
Genus *Sistrurus*

Western Pigmy Rattlesnake, *Sistrurus miliarius streckeri*
Western Massasauga, *Sistrurus catenatus tergeminus*
Desert Massasauga, *Sistrurus catenatus edwardsii*

Two of the three species of *Sistrurus* (a name drawn from the Latin *sistrum* for "rattle" and the Greek *oura* for "tail") occur in the United States, where both *S. miliarius* and *S. catenatus* are divided into three subspecies. These are generally small, excitable rattlesnakes with slender tails and rattles so attenuated that their whirring warning can be difficult for a human to hear. Although in Florida the dusky pigmy rattlesnake can at times be present in immense numbers, the other two races of pigmy rattlesnake, and all three races of massasauga, are now uncommon even in suitable habitat.

Sistrurus are quite different from members of the genus *Crotalus*. The latter have much smaller crown scales, while *Sistrurus* are characterized by a set of 9 large cephalic scale plates that resemble those of both nonvenomous snakes and the copperheads and cottonmouths from which rattlesnakes are thought to be descended. (Both pigmy and massasauga *Sistrurus*-genus rattlesnakes are believed to belong to an ancient group of pitvipers. All rattlesnakes, however, including the more highly developed *Crotalus,* are believed to have a single common ancestor, in whom the rattle evolved only once. Although venom potency among *Sistrurus* is quite high, as small pitvipers their venom gland capacity is not large and their fangs are relatively short.)

The dorsolateral scales of pigmy and massasauga rattlesnakes are keeled, both the anal plate and subcaudal scales are undivided, and, as on all pitvipers, the pupil is vertically elliptical. The head is distinctly wider than the neck, but not nearly as broad, proportionately, as that of rattlesnakes belonging to the genus *Crotalus*.

96 WESTERN PIGMY RATTLESNAKE

Sistrurus miliarius streckeri

Venomous   See **Dusky Pigmy Rattlesnake.**

Abundance   Generally uncommon. The western pigmy rattlesnake is seldom encountered even by those working in the midst
of its East Texas its range since it is an extremely cryptic animal which
spends the day hidden beneath ground cover. In biologically generous riverbottom and palmetto flatland habitats it can be numerous, however.

Size   Adults usually measure 14 to 20 inches in length; the record is 25⅛
inches.

Habitat   Favored habitat includes loblolly/longleaf pine forest, riverbottom
hardwoods, wet sawgrass prairie, and palmetto lowlands. *Sistrurus miliarius
streckeri* also occurs in the riparian corridor of sycamore, pecan, black willow,
and mustang grape that traces the Trinity and Red river systems northwestward,
allowing this fundamentally eastern bottomland forest animal to penetrate an
extensive dry, upland area. Along the upper Gulf Coast, *S. m. streckeri* was formerly found in most places where there was both heavy vegetation and abundant surface water. Such sites recently included low-lying woodland in the
Alvin/Liverpool/Angleton section of Brazoria County and the swampy portion of Matagorda County between Cedar Lane and the coast. Extensive
urbanization and agricultural development have eliminated a majority of this
animal's Texas habitat, however.

Prey   Small reptiles, amphibians, and insects constitute most of the diet of
adult *S. miliarius*. For the first several months of their lives the young have
yellowish tail tips (just anterior to their rattles) that involuntarily twitch with
excitement when prey is nearby, thus functioning as wriggling worm- or cater-
pillar-like decoys to attract frogs and lizards.

Reproduction   Live-bearing. Primarily autumn breeders—males have been
observed in rivalry combat at this season—*S. miliarius* typically gives birth in
late summer after winter-long sperm storage by the female. A captive pair
maintained at the Fort Worth Zoo bred repeatedly throughout September,
with the female giving birth some 8½ months later to 3, ⅒-ounce, 5⅓-inch-
long young with pale yellow tail tips. In the wild, Kenny Wray of the University of Texas, Arlington, found a gravid female *S. m. streckeri* near
Clarksville which gave birth to very tiny young between 3 and 5 inches in
length. These neonates would likely have had to seek minuscule invertebrate
prey since in captivity they were incapable of taking food items larger than
the cricket frog legs on which they were fed.

Coloring/scale form   *Sistrurus miliarius streckeri* was coined in 1883 by
S. Garman from the Greek for "rattle" and "tail," while the subspecies name
honors herpetologist John K. Strecker, for whom the Mexican hook-nosed
snake, a chorus frog, and Baylor University's Strecker Museum are also
named. *Sistrurus miliarius streckeri* also has unusual coloring for a rattlesnake.

Its gray dorsum is widely spotted with black and marked with a russet tan vertebral stripe, while its lower sides bear a double row of dark spots that may overlap onto the whitish, faintly stippled venter. This little rattlesnake's head is proportionately narrower than that of larger rattlers, and boldly black-striped on both its crown and cheeks, where its large, slit-pupiled eyes are obscured by a dark mask. The strongly keeled dorsal scales are arranged in 23 to 25 rows at midbody, the crown is capped with 9 large scale plates, the anal plate is undivided and the rattle is so small it may go entirely unnoticed, giving rise to the myth of the "rattleless ground rattler."

Similar snakes The **western massasauga (97)** has larger, more closely spaced brown dorsolateral blotches, lacks a distinct vertebral stripe, and has 25 rows of dorsal scales at midbody. It has a prominent, proportionately wider and longer rattle, and as a grassland animal is not found in the pigmy rattlesnake's woodland/wetland habitat.

Behavior Entirely terrestrial, *S. m. streckeri* may rattle its tail from beneath ground cover, although its rattle is so minuscule that the sound is difficult to hear. If exposed in its hiding place, this little pitviper does not raise its forebody into the defensive posture that enables *Crotalus* genus rattlesnakes to strike up to half their body length. Instead, a threatened *S. m. streckeri* may flatten its trunk and if touched, snap without coiling—though its strike never extends more than a few inches.

97 WESTERN MASSASAUGA
Sistrurus catenatus tergeminus

Venomous Few envenomations by *Sistrurus catenatus tergeminus* take place in the wild (the great majority of snake venom poisonings occur while handling captives) because western massasaugas are retiring animals that avoid human-inhabited areas. In addition, this snake's nocturnal habits—out of 60 recorded field observations, not a single instance of daytime activity was noted—further reduce its chance of encounters with humans. Massasauga envenomation itself is likely to be less serious than that of larger, *Crotalus* genus rattlesnakes because this reptile's fangs are usually no more than ⅜ inch in length, while its venom capacity is also comparatively low. Only 15 to 45 milligrams (dry weight) can be obtained even by artificial milking, which produces more venom that a snake could expel on its own. Therefore, a mortal bite to a healthy human adult (for whom a probable lethal dose would be 30 to 40 milligrams) is very unlikely. Despite some serious envenomations, most massasauga bites resemble those suffered by Rick Pratt, former director of Houston's Armand Bayou Nature Center, and Jack Joy of the Abilene Zoo, both of which caused no permanent damage.

Abundance Uncommon. Throughout the broad north–south swath of Great Plains grassland stretching from the Texas Gulf Coast north through the panhandle the western massasauga has probably always occurred in somewhat localized populations. In those areas, they were formerly numerous, however. According to John E. Werler (1978):

"This reptile was very abundant in some parts of the state more than 50 years ago. In the early 1900s one Armstrong County farmer . . . killed 50 or 60 during one wheat season."

Even as late as the early 1970s it was not unusual to find concentrations of western massasaugas: both the author and Jonathan Campbell of the University of Texas at Arlington remember seeing as many as 40 of these animals in a night's road cruising on the prairie west of Fort Worth. Yet this localization of its populations has made *S. c. tergeminus* vulnerable to human expansion: intensive crop cultivation has depleted Texas grassland populations, while residential development and the destruction of their wintering dens have all but eliminated the western massasaugas living between Fort Worth and Weatherford, as well as those living along the now heavily human-populated Gulf Coast.

Size   Most adult *S. c. tergeminus* are about 2 feet in length; the record is 34¾ inches.

Habitat   The western massasauga is primarily a prairie animal, and in what little of that original Great Plains ecosystem still grows big bluestem and Indian grass, *S. c. tergeminus* continues to exist, spending the daylight hours hidden either below ground or in clumps of prickly pear or bunchgrass, the latter habitat being noteworthy because within such clumps the daytime humidity is significantly higher than in surrounding areas.

Prey   *Sistrurus catenatus tergeminus* is an opportunistic predator on a variety of small vertebrates: 18 stomachs contained 9 pocket and harvest mice, 3 whiptail and rusty lizards, 2 ground snakes, 1 lined snake, 2 leopard frogs, and a shrew.

Reproduction   Live-bearing. Breeding occurs both spring and fall, with a courtship that begins, as Joseph Collins (1974) writes, when:

"The male crawls along beside the female with quick, jerking movements of his body. His tail bends beneath her until their cloacal openings meet and copulation occurs. Sperm from the autumn pairings remains viable in the female's cloaca throughout the winter, fertilizing her developing eggs only in spring. Pregnancy lasts 15 to 16 weeks, with litters of 5 to 13 young, 7 to 9 inches long, being born during July and August."

Coloring/scale form   *Sistrurus* are thought to be similar to the first rattlesnakes to branch from their moccasin-like *Agkistrodon* ancestors, for they retain the 9 large forecrown scale plates of the copperheads and cottonmouths. The western massasauga's 38 or more big brown vertebral splotches are closely spaced along its gray-brown dorsum; below its narrow, almost oval brown-striped crown a white-edged chocolate mask hides its pale, vertically pupiled eyes and stretches back across its cheeks. Its venter is mottled with gray. Arranged in 25 rows at midbody, the dorsal scales are keeled; the anal plate is undivided.

Similar snakes   The **desert massasauga (98)** is a slightly smaller, paler, arid-land race formally distinguished—though these distinctions do not hold true

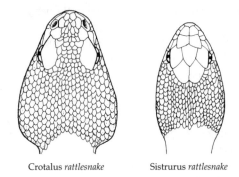

Crotalus *rattlesnake*   Sistrurus *rattlesnake*

for many individuals of intermediate parentage living in areas where the ranges of these two races overlap—by its fewer (35 to 37) dorsal blotches on a creamy ground color, its uniformly white venter, and its 23 midbody rows of dorsolateral scales. The **western pigmy rattlesnake (96)** is distinguished by its gray dorsolateral ground color, its widely spaced blackish dorsal bars or blotches, and its russet tan vertebral stripe. It has but 21 rows of dorsal scales and a diminutive rattle. All other rattlesnakes living within the western massasauga's range have crowns covered with small scales.

Behavior   In cool weather this nocturnal reptile sometimes thermoregulates by seeking the heat-retaining asphalt of little-traveled roads. Unlike more active serpents intercepted as they cross pavement on hunting or breeding forays, *S. c. tergeminus* typically coils quietly at the edge of the asphalt, soaking up its warmth. Later in the night as the roadways cool, every massasauga will once more withdraw into the grass. Yet western massasaugas are also very sensitive to elevated temperatures. Dmi'el (1972) reports diminished activity above 93°F, and few massasaugas are seen on the roads after hot weather begins. By July, even in areas where it was abundant in late spring *S. c. tergeminus* seems to be almost nonexistent, although the first cool, damp autumn weather always draws a few individuals back to the sun-warmed pavement before they enter winter dormancy.

98 DESERT MASSASAUGA
Sistrurus catenatus edwardsii

Venomous   No record exists of human envenomation by this retiring southwestern massasauga race, but the potency of its toxins is almost certainly the same as those of its subspecies, *Sistrurus catenatus tergeminus.*

Abundance   Very uncommon. Although distributed over a large range, the desert massasauga is unevenly dispersed and is extremely difficult to find even during its late spring activity period.

Size   *Sistrurus catenatus edwardsii*'s subspecies name honors Dr. L. A. Edwards, who—for Charles Girard's and Spencer Baird's subsequent scientific description—collected the type specimen of this subspecies in northern Mexico. Adults average less than 18 inches in length, while the record specimen measured only 20½ in.

Habitat   This misleadingly named serpent is not a true desert dweller and only occasionally occurs in Texas' arid northern Chihuahuan biotic province. Here, individuals have been found north of the Christmas Mountains and on arid flats near Hen Egg peak, but far more often, in both the Trans-Pecos and the panhandle, *S. c. edwardsii* inhabits short-grass prairie. That of the Marfa Basin in southwest Presidio County is one such milieu, while in South Texas, desert massasaugas have a very fragmented distribution, with one localized population occurring in mesquite/prickly pear savannah near Norias in Kenedy County, with another group living in the grass-covered dunes along the inland side of the Laguna Madre.

Prey   *Sistrurus catenatus edwardsii* captured in the thorn brush of the lower Gulf coastal plain typically choose laboratory mice as prey over small reptiles or amphibians, but two adults taken in the Presidio County grasslands would feed only on whiptail lizards.

Reproduction   Live-bearing. A pair of long-term captives maintained by Tim Cole bred during the second week in April; three 8-inch-long young were born 95 days later to the very plump, 18-inch-long female. After their first shed at 9 or 10 days of age, these newborns immediately began to feed on nestling mice. See **Western Massasauga**.

Coloring/scale form   This little pitviper is a xeric conditions–adapted race of the western massasauga, which it resembles except for its paler dorsal coloring, its fewer (35 to 37) dorsal blotches on a creamy ground color, its uniformly whitish venter, and its 23 midbody rows of dorsal scales. See **Western Massasauga**.

Similar snakes   The desert massasauga is the only rattlesnake within its range whose head is capped with the 9 large scale plates typical of its *Sistrurus* genus. The **western diamond-backed rattlesnake (100)** has a mottled grayish back patterned with white-edged vertebral diamonds, a distinctly black-and-white-ringed tail, and 25 to 27 dorsal scale rows at midbody. The **prairie rattlesnake (102)** is browner in ground color and also has 25 to 27 rows of dorsal scales at midbody, as well as numerous small cephalic scales between the large supraocular scales that flank its broad, triangular crown. Exhibiting eerily similar dorsolateral coloring, size, and body shape is the **Mexican hog-nosed snake (63)**; at night, in the beam of a flashlight it takes a close look, checking for the viper's rattle, to be sure whether a desert massasauga or Mexican hog-nose is at hand. (This is an interesting case of parallel evolution—in configuration, coloring, and habitat selection—among unrelated snakes, for the Mexican hog-nose shares both of the desert massasauga's geographically separated ranges, favoring the same, sandy-subsoiled short-grass prairie on the western plains and mesquite savannah in southern Texas.)

Behavior   Almost entirely nocturnal, *S. c. edwardsii* is almost never seen except shortly after dark during its late spring/early summer activity period, when individuals appear coiled along the edges of roads.

Rattlesnakes
Genus *Crotalus*

Canebrake Rattlesnake, *Crotalus horridus atricaudatus*
Western Diamond-backed Rattlesnake, *Crotalus atrox*
Northern Black-tailed Rattlesnake, *Crotalus molossus molossus*
Prairie Rattlesnake, *Crotalus viridis viridis*
Mojave Rattlesnake, *Crotalus scutulatus scutulatus*
Mottled Rock Rattlesnake, *Crotalus lepidus lepidus*
Banded Rock Rattlesnake, *Crotalus lepidus klauberi*

This evolutionarily advanced genus is exclusively of New World derivation and distribution, with numerous species occurring from southwestern Canada and central New Hampshire south to Argentina. In the United States, this genus is best represented west of the Mississippi River. East of the Mississippi, only two *Crotalus* species occur, the timber and the eastern diamond-backed rattlesnakes.

The rattlesnakes of this genus have large, well-developed rattles—a characteristic for which, from the Greek *krotalon*, or "rattle," the genus is named. The rattle is a connected string of enlarged, interlocking hollow scales which, like a long fingernail, breaks off periodically. What primarily distinguishes *Crotalus* genus rattlesnakes from those in the genus *Sistrurus*, however, are the many small scales covering the center of their broad crowns. (Both *Sistrurus* and the *Agkistrodon* pitvipers and nonvenomous North American snakes have 9 large scale plates covering the tops of their heads.)

Crotalus genus rattlesnakes have a pair of long fangs, each attached to a rotatable maxillary bone. As these fragile, tubular teeth break off during hunting—or are simply shed (rattlesnake fangs generally function for less than 2 months during the activity season)—they are replaced by the forwardmost fang in the row of developing protofangs waiting just behind. In order to accommodate such radically enlarged dentition, when the rattler's mouth is closed, its fangs lie folded against the roof of its mouth. When the snake's mouth is opened wide, the fangs can be voluntarily erected, and in striking they are directed almost straight forward. Penetration of their target's skin, followed by venom injection, occurs in a fraction of a second, with the amount of venom expended regulated by the snake. The venom itself is a complex combination of enzymes and proteins that varies both among species and within populations of a single species.

Like a majority of pitvipers, *Crotalus* genus rattlesnakes are wait-and-ambush hunters. Using chemosensory testing, they position themselves along active small mammal trails and then, when a rodent scampers past, suddenly strike and release it. The animal is often able to dash away but, after allowing its venom time to immobilize its stricken prey, the rattler typically sets off to trail it by scent—a process in which experiments have shown that rattlesnakes are able to differentiate between the trails of nonenvenomated and envenomated animals of the same species.

99 CANEBRAKE RATTLESNAKE*
Crotalus horridus atricaudatus

Venomous   Like other *Crotalus* genus rattlesnakes, this large and potentially dangerous serpent is of variable disposition. If startled while moving, some canebrake rattlers freeze motionless but remain stretched out and silent, while other individuals coil and begin rattling while a potential threat is still some distance away. Others attempt a headlong dash for safety, rattling furiously, while still other individuals may strike suddenly, with or without rattling.

The venom is geographically variable, being predominantly hemolytic throughout much of the range, but reportedly more highly neurotoxic among members of both the Gulf and Atlantic coastal plain populations, for laboratory studies as well as field evidence suggest that the venom of some *C. h. atricaudatus* from South Carolina and Florida westward to Texas may contain a larger percentage of neurotoxically active peptide components than the venom of the subspecies timber rattlesnake of the northern and central United States. Immediate systemic collapse has occurred after canebrake envenomation in the Southeast, and the same sort of immediate shock and near-lethal systemic failure has also occurred in East Texas. See **Venom Potency Table.**

Abundance   Threatened. In Texas, canebrake rattlesnakes are creatures of the eastern pine and hardwood forest that in places reaches westward as far as Lee and Burleson counties, where the author has found many individuals, as well as south along the Gulf Coast as far as Matagorda County. Overall, the canebrake may be withstanding the pressures caused by human expansion more successfully than its rapidly declining northern subspecies, the timber rattlesnake; where prime habitat remains, *C. h. atricaudatus* persists in both farming communities and wooded parks and preserves.

Size   This southern race of the timber rattlesnake is adult at 44 to 54 inches in length. Historically, adult female canebrakes averaged about 48 inches in length, males somewhat larger. Populations not impacted by human-caused mortality are now very rare, however, and since both the largest individuals and adult males—which tend to wander farthest and spend the most time

---

*In 1973, George Pisani et al. compared the characteristics that had traditionally separated the timber from the canebrake rattlesnake and found the two were subspecifically different. Nevertheless, a number of researchers continued to feel that subspeciation was unwarranted. Therefore, in 1986 Brown and Ernst repeated the 1973 study. Adding average adult size and average pattern differences using specimens from the eastern United States, where the two forms are most distinctly differentiated, Brown and Ernst concluded that taxonomic separation was indeed proper.

exposed to human predation—are now reduced in most wild populations, there seems to have been a recent demographic shift among canebrake rattlesnakes toward a younger and more female-weighted population. Nevertheless, where humans are scarce even contemporary *C. h. atricaudatus* regularly attain 60 inches in length, with the largest individuals slightly exceeding 72 in.

Habitat   Throughout the southeastern states, *C. h. atricaudatus* is found most often in low-lying deciduous forest, where it seems to especially favor the dense thickets of moist riparian corridors. (Here, during the latter part of the eighteenth century it came to be known as the canebrake rattlesnake for its prevalence in the impenetrable cane thickets, or brakes, which at that time matted every damp clearing in the Southeast.) In extensive natural areas, radio telemetry–equipped *C. h. atricaudatus* have maintained home ranges that varied from the 10 or fewer acres utilized by gravid females to as many as several hundred acres covered by wide-roaming adult males. Like those of other large snakes, however, timber rattler territories are now defined largely by the presence of man, for sooner or later the more wide-ranging individuals typically (and usually fatally) stray into suburban yards and parking lots.

Prey   Prey is almost entirely warm-blooded and primarily mammalian. Juvenile *C. h. atricaudatus* take mostly white-footed mice—even newly born canebrakes are large enough to eat adult mice—as well as, occasionally, amphibians and lizards. A 28-inch-long female found beneath the author's Lee County house was discovered in the act of eating a leopard frog. Afterward, she would not take even small mice for weeks, but after growing very thin eventually began to accept rodents and quickly regained normal body weight. In contrast, the stomachs of 30 large individuals collected in Louisiana contained 10 rabbits, 8 mice, 6 rats, and 1 fox squirrel. No reptiles or amphibians were found to have been eaten, although spiny lizards are readily taken by young canebrakes in captivity, and cannibalism of its own kind has also been observed. A different and exclusive prey orientation was exhibited by a 3-foot-long *C. h. atricaudatus* captured by D. Craig McIntyre. After this individual had refused small mammal prey for weeks, McIntyre was about to release it for fear it would starve when he accidentally discovered its sole food requirement was birds—a diet on which it then thrived for years. (Research suggests that pitvipers can acquire this sort of exclusive prey preference by successfully killing a particular food animal early in life.)

Reproduction   Although, because of its longer seasonal activity period the canebrake rattlesnake may attain sexual maturity earlier in life than the late-maturing northern timber race, fecundity is still low because most females produce young only once every two to four years. Parturition occurs in mid- to late summer, with litters varying from 3 to 19 (between 6 and 10 is the usual number of offspring). Neonates, which average 13½ inches in length, are similar in pattern to adults, but are paler, with a light gray ground color.

Coloring/scale form   The entirely black tail (in Latin, *atri-caudatus* means "black-tailed"), cinnamon-hued vertebral stripe, and 21 to 29 dark dorsolateral bands—usually in the form of forward-pointing chevrons—are definitive. The russet vertebral stripe is most colorful nearest the head and fades toward the tail, where dark pigment prevails.

In the Southeast, the canebrake's ground color varies from yellowish gray through pale brown to buff; rarely, a dull pink or lavender individual is photographed. Farther west, in Texas this snake tends to be duller, with a medium brown to olive ground color and light-hued borders outlining its dark bands. Sometimes, however, the posterior third of the trunk is so thoroughly suffused with black pigment that any pattern is difficult to discern. The crown is much paler than the dorsum, and on the sides of the head the big, slit-pupiled eyes are partially obscured by the pitvipers' characteristic dark mask. The dull yellowish venter may be smudged along its edges with patches of darker pigment, and usually reflects the dorsal ground color, also darkening toward the tail.

Both ontogenetic variation and sexual dimorphism—the latter rare among snakes—occur in *C. h. atricaudatus*. As this pitviper ages, its body darkens, obscuring the contrast between its creamy youthful ground color, black dorsolateral chevrons, and rusty vertebral stripe. Males are grayer than females, so the oldest and largest males—one of which is pictured here—are far less colorful than young females. Among southern *C. horridus*, more individuals have 25 midbody rows of keeled dorsal scales than among northern and western populations, where 23 rows are most common. Like that of other rattlesnakes, the anal plate is undivided.

Similar snakes   The **prairie rattlesnake (102)** and the **western diamond-backed rattlesnake (100)** both have light-hued lines on the sides of their heads and light-and-dark banded tails. **Pigmy rattlesnakes (96)** and **Massasaugas (97–98)** have 9 large scale plates crowning their heads.

Behavior   This is a more secretive and less flamboyant rattlesnake than the eastern diamond-backed rattler, which shares much of its habitat, a characteristic that allows *C. h. atricaudatus* to persist in areas of human habitation. This success is partly due to the quieter temperament of this nocturnal forager, but it also reflects how well *C. h. atricaudatus* blends into forest floor debris. A few fallen leaves, a stick or two, and a patch of dark soil can render a coiled 4-foot-long canebrake virtually invisible, especially when there is sufficient litter for it to slide beneath, leaving only the eyes and nostrils exposed. Before spring foliage has cut visibility in the woodland understory an occasional individual is also sometimes to be found basking in a patch of sunlight at the base of a tree or next to a fallen log.

100 WESTERN DIAMOND-BACKED RATTLESNAKE
Crotalus atrox

Venomous   Nearly all of the most serious cases of snakebite treated in Texas hospitals are inflicted by *Crotalus atrox*, the western diamond-back. Heaviest serpent in the Southwest and statistically the most likely to inflict serious harm (*atrox* is Latin for "frightful" and indeed, many western diamond-backs are quick to coil, rattle, and strike if approached too closely). This large reptile's venom contains roughly 17 percent neurologically active peptide components, 30 percent tissue-digestive proteases, and 53 percent blood-metabolizing toxic enzymes. Injection of this complex, ever-changing venom mix is characterized by immediate severe pain, along with swelling, weakness, sweating and chills, faintness or dizziness, elevation or depression of pulse, nausea, vomiting, and/or swelling of the regional lymph nodes.

The western diamond-back is a dangerous reptile partly because, like many other venomous snakes, its temperament is unpredictable. This wide range in behavior is based on temperature (cool snakes are more docile), recent hunting success or failure (hungry snakes are more irritable), and the degree to which the animal has been disturbed. It is also a function of this reptile's individual temperament, and some *Crotalus atrox* are innately more aggressive than others.

Yet few people die from western diamond-backed rattlesnake bites. Widely available care at hospital facilities accustomed to combating hypovolemic shock has cut the fatality rate to less than 10 percent, even among heavily envenomated patients, those who succumb are mostly children, whose body fluid volume is too small to accommodate the plasma leakage brought about by the venom toxins' perforation of their capillaries. In cases of heavy envenomation, peripheral morbidity, including the loss of digits and even limbs, is still fairly high, however, especially when aggravated by ill-advised first-aid procedures. See **Venom Potency Table**.

Abundance   Very common. *Crotalus atrox* is the most numerous and widespread venomous snake in the western 75 percent of Texas. Because of its bold temperament and frequently diurnal foraging pattern, in this area it is also the most likely pitviper to be noticed, both in remote areas and around farm buildings that shelter rats and mice.

Size   Adults average 3 to 4 feet in length, yet because newborns are so numerous in early autumn, at this time of year a majority of *C. atrox* are less

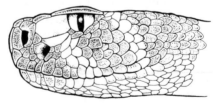

Western diamond-backed rattler

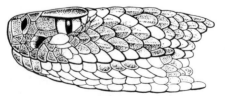

Prairie and Mojave rattlers

than 20 inches long. Huge western diamond-backs also occur. These are always males, since among pitvipers this is the larger gender, and among diamond-backs the largest males weigh up to 20 percent more than the biggest females. Several recorded western diamond-backs have measured from 7 to just under 7½ feet in length, but when these dimensions are obtained from carcasses instead of live animals the numbers are distorted since the bodies of such large snakes have usually been stretched grotesquely, from their own weight, by being hung up. This can add more than 20 percent to a big serpent's length, making its true size difficult to determine.

Extremely large *Crotalus atrox* like these are not extremely old snakes, but true genetic giants. Many western diamond-backs have spent long lives in confinement—the record is nearly 26 years—without reaching remarkable size, and most giant *Crotalus atrox* come from areas known for harboring exceptionally large individuals. The gene pool of Starr, Hidalgo, and Willacy counties in Texas regularly produces western diamond-backs over 5 feet in length (in this area, Greg Lasley observed a copulating pair, both of which were more than five feet long). Other large western diamondbacks have been reported from the equally rich agricultural region along the Texas–New Mexico border near Carlsbad.

Habitat   *Crotalus atrox* can be found in nearly every terrestrial habitat within its range. These snakes are especially abundant on the Gulf Coast barrier islands, in the South Texas Tamaulipan thorn woodland, and in the northern part of Big Bend National Park. Compared to other rattlesnakes that share more specific habitat niches within its range, *Crotalus atrox* is a generalist—an animal whose microhabitat overlaps to the east, the habitat of the mesic bottomland-living canebrake and pigmy rattlesnakes; to the northwest, the grassland inhabited by prairie and massasauga rattlesnakes; and to the west, the mountainous/saxicolous environs of the rock and black-tailed rattlesnakes. Western diamond-backs also share the creosote desert and mesquite tarbush zone typical of the arid-adapted Mojave rattlesnake. (In this harsh terrain, during years of severe draught *C. atrox* seems to be at the edge of its adaptive capacity; the author has found diamond-backs so thirsty that when doused with water, instead of fleeing or coiling as they ordinarily would, they instead turned their heads upward to drink.)

Prey   *Crotalus atrox* feeds mostly on mammals. Newborns swallow full-grown mice without hesitation while, among the largest adults, squirrels, prairie dogs, cottontails, and even young jackrabbits are possible prey. Ground-living birds are also taken, but very small rodents are ignored, perhaps because the effort required to capture them is not warranted by their minimal food value.

Reproduction   Live-bearing. Photographs of large *Crotalus atrox* engaged in dominance combat—agonistic encounters usually provoked when two similarly sized adult males meet along a receptive female's pheromone scent trail—are common postcard fodder. Copulation is prolonged, sometimes occurring without interruption for more than 24 hours. Litters average 9 to 14, with most newborns measuring between 9 and 13½ inches in length. Shortly after their birth in late August, September, and early October, small western diamond-backs are often encountered by humans because they are both abundant and unwary as they disperse across unfamiliar terrain.

Coloring/scale form   Dorsolateral coloring is dark-speckled gray-brown, vertebrally patterned with the big, light- and dark-edged "diamonds" for which the species is named. On the posterior dorsum these markings become obscure, but its widely varying overall coloring is less helpful in quickly identifying *Crotalus atrox* than is its boldly black-and-white banded "coon tail." (Dorsal ground color varies partly because this species' population is so large; the author has seen one nearly all-black wild diamond-back, as well as several almost patternless specimens, two of them taken from old barns in central Texas. This region is also home to albino/leucistic *C. atrox*—including a pale but dark-eyed hypomelanistic individual that has fathered a line of pale color morphs that are now bred in captivity by Tim Cole of Austin.)

A chocolate gray band, its anterior and posterior edges lined with white, diagonally masks each cheek, partially camouflaging the big, pale, slit-pupiled eye. The light-hued lower border of this band intersects the upper lip midway along its length, while the white posterior edge of the dark cheek stripe runs from behind the eye directly to the rear corner of the mouth. The venter is unmarked yellowish white, the heavily keeled dorsal scales are arranged in 25 to 27 rows at midbody, and only 2 internasal scales intersect the rostral. Like that of all pitvipers, the anal plate is undivided.

Similar snakes   The **prairie rattlesnake (102)** has more rounded brown vertebral blotches, which on its posterior trunk elongate into narrow crossbands. More than 2 internasal scales intersect its rostral, while the white posterior border of its dark subocular cheek band curves backward above the corner of its mouth. The **Mojave rattlesnake (103)**, found only in the central and southwestern Trans-Pecos region, has 2 or 3 big, rough-edged scales between the supraocular plates of its anterior crown—the diamond-back has several much smaller scales. See **Mojave rattlesnake (103)** for illustration. The Mojave rattler's white tail bands are also sometimes noticeably wider than its black caudal rings, its more cleanly defined vertebral diamonds elongate on the posterior third of its back into crossbands like those of the prairie rattler, and its white postocular line curves backward above the posterior corner of its mouth. The **canebrake rattlesnake (99)**, with which the western diamondback shares a crosstimbers range, has an entirely dark tail, a russet vertebral stripe, and black, chevron-shaped cross-dorsal bands. **Rock rattlesnakes (104–105)** lack diamond-shaped vertebral markings and have only 23 midbody rows of dorsal scales. The crowns of both southwestern **massasaugas (97–98)** are dark-striped and capped with 9 large scale plates.

Behavior   Most western diamond-backed rattlesnakes follow seasonally structured activity patterns. By late May or June, this reptile's predatory forays have split into early morning and evening periods, while the high daily temperatures of July and August limit its foraging to the coolest part of the day, long after dark. In winter, most *C. atrox* seek shelter in communal dens, although sometimes for relatively brief periods; on the Rio Grande plain and coastal islands many individuals are fully active during midwinter warm spells.

Even in the cooler parts of its range some *C. atrox* venture abroad at midday during winter, although they remain close to their dens from late November through March.

In spring, this concentrated population enhances males' chances of mating with emerging females before they disperse—when *C. atrox* may move as far as 3 miles to its summer feeding range—but it renders the emerging snakes vulnerable to predation by humans. In their attempts to flush wintering *Crotalus atrox* from brumation dens, participants in the Southwest's annual rattlesnake hunt also kill hundreds of other subsurface-living animals. Banned by most states for the ecologically absurd practice of pumping gasoline fumes into rock crevices and earthen burrows, these roundups remain popular springtime carnivals in Texas. Large roundups such as those promoted by the town of Sweetwater, as well as the many roundups held at smaller venues, unfortunately continue to operate without what should be the prompt intervention of the Texas Department of Parks and Wildlife (more progressive policies enacted in both Louisiana and Florida prohibit using gasoline to collect wildlife, while in Georgia all wild snakes are protected).

101 NORTHERN BLACK-TAILED RATTLESNAKE
Crotalus molossus molossus

Venomous So few bites are recorded that the specific pathology of black-tail venom is little known. At roughly 79 percent the lethality of western diamond-backed rattlesnake venom, black-tail toxins are quite potent and are thought to have a primarily anticoagulant action. Yet a recent envenomation—a bite on the finger of a healthy adult man by a 3-foot-long black-tail—brought about minimal hemaetic necrosis but set off severe systemic shock within 15 minutes.

Abundance Uncommon. Found only occasionally on the western Edwards Plateau, black-tailed rattlesnakes are more numerous in the deserts, mountains, and canyons of the Trans-Pecos. Here, especially during rainy periods following long droughts, *C. m. molossus* can be temporarily abundant. The enhanced scent-carrying capacity of humid air can send individuals in search of prey as well as mates (in the case of pheromone-seeking males), and at the mouths of the rhyolite-walled canyons south of Alpine, human residents may relocate one or more black-tails from their yards every day following heavy rains.

Size Although adult *C. m. molossus* are generally less than 32 inches in length, the largest black-tail on record is the 52-inch-long male captured and measured by the author on the edge of a rocky Davis Mountains arroyo in September 1995.

Habitat *Crotalus molossus molossus* is most common in broken terrain: canyons, vegetated gullies, and wooded mountainsides. On the western

243

Edwards Plateau, black-tails live in brushy limestone canyons; west of the Pecos River they are found in desert terrain broken by rocky bluffs and canyons. In the pine–oak forests of the far western mountains, black-tailed rattlesnakes go up as far as the land itself; the author has found individuals at over 7,000 feet on the south rim of the Chisos Mountains.

Prey   Adult *C. m. molossus* feed mostly on small mammal prey. Wood rats are abundant in the westernmost parts of black-tails' range and probably constitute this species' major prey there, for black-tails are often found waiting in ambush near the rats' runways and burrow entrances. Unlike most other large crotalids, however, newly captured black-tails from the southeastern Trans-Pecos apparently feed mostly on lizards and are sometimes reluctant to accept domestic mice as food.

Reproduction   Live-bearing. Two females from Brewster County found while gravid deposited litters of 7 and 8 young (all of which measured between 8 and 10¼ inches in length) in late July.

Coloring/scale form   Calling to mind the jagged, light–dark harlequin patterning of Navajo blankets, the dark band running along the black-tailed rattlesnake's spine is inlaid with patches of pale scales. In Texas, this reptile's ground color ranges from brownish to silver-gray, with sometimes very boldly contrasting patches of off-white vertebral scales. (Black-tails from the Chiricahua and Huachuca Mountains in southern Arizona often have beautiful lemon-hued dorsal patches and nearly golden lower sides.) The dark-hued posterior crown is speckled and spotted, the forecrown covered by a wide black band that obscures both the heat-sensing viperid pit and the slit-pupiled eyes before tapering rearward to a point just above the posterior corner of the jaw. As its common name indicates, this animal's tail is a uniformly sooty black. A majority of Texas' black-tails have 27 midbody rows of keeled dorsal scales, but individuals vary between 25 and 29 rows. The pale venter may have a yellowish cast, clouded and mottled in places with gray, and the anal plate is undivided.

Similar snakes   No other rattlesnake in the Southwest has a black forecrown and tail and creamy vertebral scales enclosed by dark pigment.

Behavior   Almost always found in either rocky or xeric environs, *Crotalus molossus molossus* seldom emerges from shelter until evening, and may forage in comparatively cool weather. Despite temperatures near 60°F, three individuals from Kerr County were abroad as late as December 12; other black-tails have been found in the Trans-Pecos as early as mid-February. Like other pitvipers that orient on the body heat of their predominantly endothermic prey, black-tails are unbelievably sensitive to faint vibrations of warmth. The heat-sensing pits between eye and nostril let one individual in the author's experience accurately track the movements of a lighted cigarette from more than a foot away, even through the glass wall of its cage front.

244

102 PRAIRIE RATTLESNAKE
Crotalus viridis viridis

Venomous   Findlay E. Russell's work with the toxins
of *Crotalus viridis* (1980) indicates that prairie rattler toxins have only about half the tissue-necrotizing effect, and
less than a third of the blood-destroying potency of western
diamond-backed rattlesnake venom. Yet, due to its large complement of neurotoxically active peptide components the prairie rattlesnake's overall venom potency is slightly greater per unit of measure than
that of the western diamond-back. Most prairie rattlesnakes are much smaller
than adult diamond-backs, however, and besides having shorter fangs, their
average venom capacity is only 35 to 110 milligrams (dry weight)—the largest
diamond-backs produce 175 to 600 milligrams—and as a result the prairie
rattler's potential threat to humans is considerably less than that of the western diamond-back. See **Venom Potency Table**.

Abundance   Along gully and canyon drop-offs, or in places where agriculture has not plowed under native grassland, *C. v. viridis* may inhabit any part
of Texas' western grasslands. South of the panhandle, *C. v. viridis* is uncommon on the Stockton Plateau and in most of the Trans-Pecos, with populations inhabiting the pastureland of the Marfa Basin, as well as the more xeric
grasslands of the northern Marathon Basin. As the most northerly ranging
pitviper (*C. v. viridis* lives throughout the long sweep of open country that
stretches from Texas to southeastern Alberta and Saskatchewan), its reproductive replacement rate is low, with litters being deposited only every third or
fourth year, a pattern that enormously potentiates any additional pressure
placed on its numbers from either human predation or habitat destruction.

Size   Although this slender pitviper reaches a maximum of 4½ feet in length,
the majority of adults are between 2 and 3 feet.

Habitat   The prairie rattlesnake, like the massasauga, is a grassland animal.
But because this prairie environment offers little cover, *C. viridis* spends more
time in small mammal burrows than any other western pitviper. On these
windswept grasslands the deep tunnels of gophers, ground squirrels, and
prairie dogs are usually the only available shelter—shelter which, at times, *C.
v. viridis* shares with not only their resident rodents but with burrowing owls,
toads, and a host of invertebrates.

Prey   An ambush specialist like a majority of pitvipers, *Crotalus viridis* is
adept at making the most of the few hiding places its rangeland habitat provides, coiling inconspicuously beside any outline-masking bush or rock shadow.
Yet it is a more active forager than strictly sit-and-wait predators like the rock
rattlesnakes, having been described by *Crotalid* authority Harry Greene as
a "mobile ambusher." This means that *C. viridis* maximizes its chances of
encountering prey by seeking out and patrolling sites such as gopher colonies
and prairie dog towns, where food animals are most concentrated. Other prey

reportedly includes baby rabbits, ground-nesting birds, and among the young, lizards.

Reproduction   Live-bearing. The prairie rattlesnake's interrupted reproductive schedule is an example of the adaptations typical of pitvipers living in high latitude environments. Because the northerly foraging season is too brief to build up in a single year the reserves of body fat necessary to nourish developing offspring, females typically give birth as infrequently as every third or fourth year, a pattern that may prevail even among members of the species living farther south. Because female prairie rattlesnakes are only periodically receptive, it is imperative for as many as possible of them to be found by males during their sporadic fertile periods, so communal denning (where all the sexually receptive females available in any particular year find themselves surrounded by a host of males as they emerge from winter brumation) is an important part of this animal's reproductive strategy. It is also important for gravid females to follow an energy-conserving regimen of nocturnal sheltering beneath the earth and midday basking on sun-warmed stones in order to devote all their hard-won reserves of body fat to the final development of their young. Gravid female *Crotalus viridis* move about very little and feed rarely if at all during their final weeks of gestation. Birth of the 8½- to 11-inch-long offspring occurs from late August to October in Texas.

Coloring/scale form   Thirty-five to 55 oval brown blotches and crossbands line the center of the prairie rattlesnake's tan dorsum. (This animal's Latin species and subspecies names seem to be a misnomer, for *viridis* means "green," though prairie rattlers from the northern Great Plains are occasionally reported with a faintly greenish ground color.) Frequently waisted over the anterior spine, these blotches elongate into crossbands on the posterior third of the trunk. *Crotalus viridis* is also unique in having more than 2 internasal scales touching its rostral scale, while along its cheeks a pair of thin white seams—the higher of which curves backward above the corner of the mouth—border a dark ocular band. Arranged in 25 to 27 rows at midbody, the dorsal scales are keeled, the unmarked venter is yellowish white, and the anal plate is undivided.

Similar snakes   The **western diamond-backed rattlesnake (100)** has bold black and white bands around its tail (the prairie rattler's tail is ringed with brown), diamond-shaped, dimly white-edged anterior vertebral blotches, 2 internasal scales intersecting its rostral, and a white upper-cheek stripe that runs straight to the posterior corner of its mouth. The **Mojave rattlesnake (103)** may have wider white caudal bands than the diamond-back, separated by black rings and more sharply defined white-edged vertebral diamonds. Two internasal scales touch its rostral, and a distinctive double or triple row of large, rough-edged scales lines the center of its crown (here, the prairie rattler has 4 or more rows of much smaller, smoother scales). The **rock rattlesnakes (104, 105)**, which do not inhabit prairie grasslands, lack the prairie rattlesnake's brown vertebral ovals and white cheek lines. These little reptiles have 23 rows of dorsal scales, and only 2 internasal scales touch the rostral.

Behavior   Prairie rattlers are most likely to forage abroad between 80 and 90°F. In the northern portion of their range this makes for a short annual activity period, yet this snake's adaptation to life below ground (including months-long winter denning), combined with its ability to exploit the rich bird and small mammal life of the Great Plains, enables it to range farther into Canada than any other serpent except the bullsnake, hog-nose, and garter snakes. Where *C. viridis* is able to bask after dusk on sun-warmed roadways, however, it, like other rattlers, can respond with startling suddenness to intrusion, employing the radiated warmth of its substrate to strike abruptly even from an extended, noncoiled posture.

103 MOJAVE RATTLESNAKE
Crotalus scutulatus scutulatus

Venomous *Crotalus scutulatus* is probably the most dangerous serpent living north of Mexico. This is due to its combination of an unusually aggressive, quick-striking defensive behavior and its extremely potent venom. This great potency is characteristic both of *C. scutulatus* native to California's Mojave Desert and to most individuals living in Arizona, whose mutual venom type is referred to as Mojave A. This venom's lethal dosage for a human adult is reportedly no more than 10 to 15 milligrams (dry weight), a toxicity that approaches that of the cobras, while a large individual can be milked of up to 90 milligrams of it. (Although pitvipers can typically deliver only about a third of this milked volume, in the case of Mojave Type A venom that is still more than double a lethal human dose.) West Texas–living *C. s. scutulatus* reportedly carry the less virulent toxins of Mojave Type B venom. See **Venom Potency Table**.

Abundance In Texas, *C. s. scutulatus* occurs primarily in Brewster, Presidio, Jeff Davis, Terrell, and Pecos counties. The author has found both adult and young Mojaves to be not uncommon here, in arid, low-lying desert near the Christmas Mountains and to the north of Marathon, as well as in montane environments such as the high meadows of the Davis Mountains and the slopes of Elephant Butte; in both milieus, after late summer rainfall *C. s. scutulatus* can outnumber the region's ubiquitous western diamond-backed rattlesnakes.

Size Mojave rattlesnakes are relatively slender, with a majority of adults measuring less than 32 inches. The record is just over 54 inches.

Habitat Much of the range of *C. s. scutulatus* is windswept Mexican tableland at 2,000- to 6,800-foot elevations. Nevertheless according to Frederick Gehlbach (1981), along the Trans-Pecos Mexican-U.S. border:
"The Mojave rattlesnake prefers the shortest grass and fewest shrubs at lowest elevations. . . . Overlap between the diamondback and Mojave in the mesquite-tarbush zone is [perhaps a result of] an invasion by the Mojave over the last hundred years. . . . The most logical scenario evokes the all-too-familiar theme of desertification: as grassland is degraded into desert shrubland, the [dry-adapted] Mojave rattler moves in."
    In Texas, this desert biome includes creosote bush flats along the Rio Grande west of Big Bend, while *Crotalus scutulatus scutulatus* is also present,

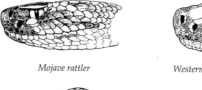

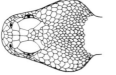
Mojave rattler

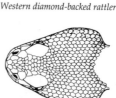
Western diamond-backed rattler

but less common, in the grassland around Marfa. Thomas Van Devender and C. H. Lowe (1977) believe that the Mojave is uncommon in these areas because it faces strong competitive interaction with the prairie rattlesnake, *C. v. viridis*. Mojave rattlesnakes do not enter into more than the southwestern fringes of the Great Plains communities occupied by the prairie rattlesnake, although in the absence of *C. viridis*, the Mojave inhabits both plains grassland and oak woodland communities in northern Mexico.

Prey   Little is reported, but the Mojave rattlesnake's prey probably consists primarily of rodents. Such small prey does not require the extreme potency of venom typical of some Mojave populations, so this snake's great venom toxicity may have evolved primarily as a defense against predation.

Reproduction   Live-bearing. One brood of *C. s. scutulatus* conceived after copulation on October 2 at the Fort Worth Zoo was born 9 months later on July 23.

Coloring/scale form   The distinctive scalation that caps its crown distinguishes the Mojave rattler from the several other rattlesnake species it resembles. Between its supraocular plates—the big flat scales that cap its eyes—the midsection of the Mojave's crown is shingled with a double or triple row of enlarged, rough-edged scales. (It is from these unique scales, or scutes, that the Mojave receives both its Latin species and subspecies name *scutulatus*.)

   Crotalus scutulatus scutulatus is also unusual in that individuals living in different parts of its range differ not only in overall color—a common trait among snakes—but in pattern as well. In some areas, such as the Rio Grande's Black Gap region, the anterior part of the resident Mojaves' backs closely resembles that of the western diamond-back, and there is even speculation of hybridization with *Crotalus atrox*. These Mojaves' posterior backs, however, are patterned with brown dorsolateral crossbands that resemble the posterior dorsal markings of the prairie rattlesnake. In contrast, *C. s. scutulatus* from the Christmas Mountains of southern Brewster County are known for their almost silvery ground color and distinctly defined white-edged dorsal markings quite different from those of the typical diamond-back. (Unlike the vertebral diamonds of more easterly Mojave populations, these vertebral markings share the ovoid form of prairie rattlers' anterior dorsal blotches.)

A third variation is seen among Mojave rattlesnakes living on the dark rhyolitic substrate of Texas' Brewster and Fort Davis counties. These animals characteristically display the diamond-shaped vertebral forebody patterning of their more easterly relatives, combined with much darker coloring. Their crowns are solid charcoal to chocolate (almost as dark as that of a black-tailed rattlesnake), while both their dorsal blotches and lateral stippling are a similar rich brown, with little of the pale edging that outlines the vertebral blotches in other populations. Finally, some grassland-living Mojaves show dusty greenish dorsolateral tones.

Among all these groups, narrow black and—usually—distinctly wider white bands encircle the tail, the pale venter may be darkly smudged along its edges, and the lower half of the basal rattle segment usually has a bold yellowish hue. The diagonal white line bordering the rear of the Mojave rattlesnake's brown ocular mask passes (like that of the prairie rattler) well above the posterior corner of its mouth. Arranged in 25 rows at midbody, the dorsal scales are keeled, more than 2 of its internasal scales touch its rostral, and the anal plate is undivided.

Similar snakes　The very similar-looking **western diamond-backed rattlesnake** (100) is distinguished by the 4 or more rows of very small scales that cover its forecrown and by its more mottled, less cleanly defined vertebral diamonds. These fade posteriorly but do not elongate into brown crossbands on the rear of its trunk as do those of the Mojave. The western diamond-back also has nearly equally wide black and white tail bands, its upper postocular white line directly intersects the posterior corner of its mouth, and the basal rattle segment is horncolored, although in the eastern part of the Mojave's range every one of these differences becomes blurred. The **prairie rattlesnake** (102) is unique in that more than 2 of its internasal scales touch its rostral scale. The center of its forecrown, unlike the Mojave's, is evenly covered with 4 or more rows of smooth little scales, and along its spine its foreparts are patterned with rounded brown blotches, usually white-edged vertebral blotches or diamonds. **Rock rattlesnakes** (104–105) have heavy dorsolateral speckling and irregular dark crossbands, and lack the Mojave rattler's characteristic row of enlarged midcrown scales.

Behavior　In Texas, adult Mojave rattlesnakes are typically small but very hot-tempered. When only mildly threatened, individuals may lower their heads, raise their tails, and slowly flick their rattles from side to side like a metronome—a particularly menacing gesture in light of their extremely toxic venom. Pressed further, *C. s. scutulatus* is, as cowhands put it, "a bitin' fool." Throughout its range the author has seen angry but unassaulted Mojaves strike out, over and over in quick succession, hitting nothing but thin air, but creating a sufficiently formidable prospect to deter almost any natural assailant.

104 MOTTLED ROCK RATTLESNAKE

Crotalus lepidus lepidus

Venomous   Because deep penetration is not necessary to kill its diminutive prey, *Crotalus lepidus* has very small fangs. According to L. M. Klauber (1956), these seldom measure more than ¼ inch across their curve. Rock rattlesnakes' venom, however, contains a high percentage of potent neurotoxic peptide components. Except for reptile fanciers and zoo personnel, there is little danger of being bitten by one of these little pitvipers, though, because rock rattlesnakes' inaccessible mountain and desert habitat, as well as their inclination to withdraw into crevices at the first vibration of human footsteps, make a hostile accidental encounter highly unlikely.

Abundance   Uncommon. In areas of suitable habitat, mottled rock rattlesnakes are thinly distributed over much of the westernmost quarter of Texas, but even in their favored Trans-Pecos canyons these animals are not abundant.

Size   The smallest of West Texas' rattlesnakes, *C. l. lepidus* averages under 24 inches in length; the record length is 32½ inches.

Habitat   Mottled rock rattlesnakes occupy a range of environments, but two quite different primary habitats prevail. In the northwestern part of its range this almost exclusively rock-dwelling animal inhabits igneous canyon ledges and bluffs and evergreen mountain woodland at altitudes above 4,500 feet. To the southeast, in a less exclusively saxicolous milieu, a population of much paler-hued *C. l. lepidus* lives on the barren sandy mesas and within the shallow Cretaceous limestone canyons of Terrell, Crockett, and Val Verde counties. In both areas this species is a surprisingly skillful climber, successfully negotiating near-vertical rock faces.

Prey   *Crotalus lepidus lepidus* seems to feed primarily on lacertilian prey: there are reports of desert side-blotched, rusty, and spiny lizards taken in the wild. Smaller snakes, mice, and occasional amphibians are also probably eaten, as are large *Scolependra* centipedes. One average-sized adult *C. l. lepidus* attacked these 9- or 10-inch-long chilopods just as it would a large rodent or lizard: striking 2 or 3 times in rapid succession, then withdrawing into a defensive coil to wait for its venom to take effect. After the centipede—whose sizable fangs and toxic venom enable it to kill and feed on snakes nearly its own size—succumbed, it was swallowed headfirst like any other prey. Like other small, desert-living crotalids, banded rock rattlers may consume less than their own body weight in prey each year, which may mean that only 3 or 4 mice or lizards are taken during each activity season.

Reproduction   Live-bearing. Its small litters and probable alternate-year reproductive cycle mean that *Crotalus lepidus* has the same low fecundity—and therefore heightened vulnerability to human predation or disturbance—as northern pitvipers contending with short activity seasons. The 2 to 4 young

250

are born in late summer or early autumn, 9 to 11 months after mating. The earliest account of parturition came from John Werler (1951):

"A 20.15-inch-long female [taken on] the Blackstone Ranch in Terrell County . . . gave birth to three young on July 21. The newborns averaged 8½ inches in length and differed from their pale, indistinctly banded parent in being more vividly colored, with dark gray crossbands. Food taken includes young rusty lizards . . . and newborn mice. Another pair, from the Chinati Mountains in far southwestern Texas, bred early in October but, like other high-altitude, desert-living crotalids, did not produce young until the following September."

See **Banded Rock Rattlesnake.**

Coloring/scale form *Crotalus lepidus lepidus* is folklore's celebrated "pink" and "little blue" rattlesnake. While not ever really blue (although sometimes quite pink), by matching the prevailing pigmentation of its background substrate the mottled rock rattlesnake's variable dorsal hues offer camouflage from both its lizard quarry and its color similarly-visioned avian predators. Mottled rock rattlesnakes from the Davis Mountains, where brownish maroon granite is prevalent, have numerous dark primary blotches on a variegated, muddily russet—less often, pinkish buff—ground color. In contrast, *C. l. lepidus* living along the Rio Grande, as well as those from the Stockton and western Edwards Plateaus, live on pale limestone and have ground colors of chalk to faintly bluish gray. Their dark cross-dorsal bars occur mostly on the posterior body, where there is also considerable dark speckling that approximates the mottled coloring of the lichen-encrusted rocks on which they spend most of their time.

Among all rock rattlesnakes, the wedge-shaped head is much wider than the wiry neck and is crowned with small scales. The slit-pupiled eyes are often masked by a dark stripe, there is a dark, heat-sensing pit posterior to the nostril, and 2 internasal scales touch the rostral. The 23 midbody rows of dorsal scales are keeled, and the anal plate is undivided.

Similar snakes Against a predominantly pale, unspeckled ground color, the **banded rock rattlesnake (105)** has distinctly defined, jagged-edged blackish crossbands throughout its length. Adult *C. l. klauberi* also usually lack a dark postocular stripe, and the rear of their crowns is likely to be marked with a pair of large brown spots absent in the mottled race. The **desert massasauga (98)** is a grassland serpent distinguished by its 9 large cephalic scale plates and the pair of brown stripes that band its crown.

Behavior Texas' rock rattlesnakes may be the only serpents easier to hear than to see. As one walks across montane talus slopes it is not unusual to notice one of these little reptiles buzzing its rattle from a rocky niche beneath the shingles. Yet *Crotalus lepidus* may also have a characteristic curiosity, for in order to watch—and rattle at—an intruder, individuals will withdraw into crevices less deeply than they might for their own protection.

During spring and fall, as well as on overcast days, rock rattlesnakes engage in extensive diurnal foraging, especially after thunderstorms, when individuals emerge onto the still-moist rocks. In summer *Crotalus lepidus* is more often abroad at night, avoiding the midday heat by coiling against tree trunks or, in the low desert of Val Verde and Terrell counties, under rock overhangs or low bushes. Although seemingly inactive at these times, these little pitvipers are fully alert and poised to strike any lizard that darts through their patch of shade.

105 BANDED ROCK RATTLESNAKE
Crotalus lepidus klauberi

Venomous   See **Mottled Rock Rattlesnake.**

Abundance   Uncommon. *Crotalus lepidus klauberi* is almost unknown as a pure race in Texas, for only the genetic influence of this predominantly Mexican subspecies may be present in the state's most western county.

Size   See **Mottled Rock Rattlesnake.**

Habitat   The banded rock rattlesnake is named for Lawrence M. Klauber, chairman of the board of the San Diego Gas and Electric Co. and the author of the two-volume *Rattlesnakes: Their Habits, Life Histories, and Influence on Mankind.* For the most part, this small, usually inconspicuous reptile inhabits saxicolous montane terrain from 3,500 to over 7,000 feet in elevation. In Texas, its range is primarily the Franklin Mountains north of El Paso, where the male pictured here was found.

Prey   See **Mottled Rock Rattlesnake.**

Reproduction   Live-bearing. Among the *C. l. klauberi* observed in Chihuahua, Mexico, during September, Barry Armstrong and James Murphy (1979) note that courtship began as "the male directed rapid head bobs onto the dorsum of the female. Tongue-flicking occurred at the same speed." Unlike most autumn-breeding serpents, which simply retain viable spermatozoa throughout the winter to permit springtime fertilization, female *Crotalus lepidus* evidently become gravid immediately after fall copulation and experience a true 9- to 10-month gestation, protracted by winter dormancy. First propagated in captivity in 1975 by Dave Barker of the Dallas Zoo, breeding pairs of banded rock rattlesnakes were initially only seasonally cooled to elicit the dormancy of their normal winter brumation. Then, San Antonio Zoo reptile supervisor Jozsef Laszlo and curator Alan Kardon found that in addition to the mild chill of a simulated winter, *C. l. klauberi* fared better if kept year-round at temperatures—76 to 80°F during the day, 67 or 68°F at night—considerably cooler than those preferred by lowland serpents.

The problem was that at these lowered temperatures the reproductively delicate females tended to either reabsorb their developing fetuses or give birth to malformed offspring. Finally, it was discovered that in addition to maintaining banded rock rattlers in a comparatively cool overall environment throughout the year, a "winter" of up to 14 weeks at even lower temperature should follow a pair's autumn copulation—but only if the newly gravid female had unrestricted access to an electrically heated "hot rock" on which to bask.

This artificially warmed ceramic surface mimicked the radiated heat of the sun-warmed rocks and ledges of banded rock rattlesnakes' high-desert habitat, which pregnant females seek out during warm winter days, and providing it resulted in consistently produced litters of healthy, 7½- to 8-inch-long neonates with bright yellow tail tips, most of which weighed just over ¼ ounce at birth.

Coloring/scale form   In Texas, *C. l. klauberi* with silvery dorsums patterned solely by sawtooth-edged black crossbands have been found just north of El Paso. Some males from Arizona have a beautiful pale green ground color (the "green rattler" of southwestern folklore is *C. l. klauberi*) while female banded rock rattlers from the same area are grayish or even faintly lavender—a type of sexual dimorphism known primarily among Old World snake species such as the European adders and African boomslangs; such dimorphism is not as evident among the few Texas-living *C. l. klauberi* as it is in more westerly populations. Among both groups, however, the white wash bordering the vertebral edges of the black dorsolateral bands recalls the typically lighter-hued perimeters of the lichen patches that cover the rocks and boulders among which this little rattlesnake lives.

Similar snakes   See **Mottled Rock Rattlesnake (104)**.

Behavior   See **Mottled Rock Rattlesnake.**

RATTLESNAKES

GLOSSARY

Adhesive-shelled eggs Eggs with a sticky surface that causes them to adhere in a cluster when laid (the shells soon dry out, but the eggs remain stuck together).

Aestivation The hot weather-induced dormancy of many reptiles and amphibians.

Allopatric Having a separate or discrete range.

Amelanistic Color phase almost entirely lacking black pigment.

Amphiuma Large, eel-like aquatic salamander with small legs and no external gills.

Anal plate Scale covering the cloacal vent.

Anaphylaxis Antigen-antibody reaction caused by sensitivity to a foreign protein such as antivenin; capable in extreme cases of producing severe shock, respiratory impairment, coma, and death.

Anchor coil The lowermost loop of the body of a coiled snake; this serves the animal as a foundation from which to strike.

Anerythristic Color phase almost entirely lacking red pigment.

Annelid Segmented worm or leech; most commonly the earthworm.

Anterior Toward the head.

Antibody A globulin produced in reaction to the introduction of a foreign protein.

Antiserum The fluid portion of the blood of an animal previously infused with a reactive foreign protein.

Antivenin Crystallized serum produced from the antibodies of animals infused with venom; able to partly neutralize venom's effects on the victim's tissue by blocking the toxic enzymes' access to their target cells.

Antivenin Index A compendium of antivenins available in the United States (including those for non-indigenous snakes) from the Arizona Poison Center at the University of Arizona Medical School in Tucson. Antivenin for indigenous North American pitviper and coral snake venoms is produced by Wyeth Laboratories in Philadelphia.

Anuran   Frog or toad.

Aposematic   Warning signal: sound, posture, coloration, etc.

Arachnid   Eight-legged invertebrate—spiders, scorpions, mites, and ticks.

Arthropod   Segmented invertebrate with jointed legs—insects, arachnids, and crustaceans.

Azygous scale   A single scale, that is, not one of a bilateral pair.

Belly line   The horizontal line of intersection between the venter, or belly, and the lower sides of the body.

Brumation   The winter dormancy of reptiles and amphibians.

Caudal   Pertaining to the tail.

Cephalic   Pertaining to the head or crown.

Chemoreception   The perception of chemical signals such as scent particles by the smell/taste mechanism of olfactory and veromonasal glands.   See **Jacobson's organ.**

Chin shields   The central scales on the underside of the lower jaw.

Chthonic   Below or within the earth.

Cloaca   Lower chamber of the digestive, urinary, and reproductive systems of birds, reptiles, and amphibians, which opens to the outside through the anus, or vent.

Colubrid   A member of the largest worldwide family of snakes, *Colubridae;* most North American species are harmless.

Compartment syndrome   The pressure of extreme edema, which after severe envenomation may rarely cut off blood flow to a limb, causing the death of its tissue. Some authorities believe this to be a cause of local necrosis that warrants surgical alleviation by fasciotomy; most maintain that necrosis is due almost exclusively to the enzymatic, digestive action of the venom itself.

Congeneric   Within the same genus; species belonging to the same genus are congeneric.

Conspecific   Within the same species; subspecies, or races, of a single species are conspecific.

Corticosteroid   Steroid often used to treat venom poisoning; it originates in the adrenal cortex and its effects include the enhancement of protein replacement, the reduction of inflammation, and the suppression of the body's immune responses.

Crepuscular   Active at dusk or dawn.

Crossband   Among snakes, a pigmented strip running from side to side across the back.

Crotalid   A pitviper; a member of the family *Viperidae,* subfamily *Crotalinae;* in the United States: rattlesnakes, cottonmouths, and copperheads.

Cryotherapy   Treatment of an injury with cold. Dangerous when a snakebitten extremity is radically chilled, since this can cause tissue death. (A cold pack on the wound may slightly reduce pain; another on the forehead may help to offset the nausea that often accompanies pitviper poisoning.)

Cryptic   Serving to conceal or camouflage.

Debridement   The surgical removal of (venom-saturated) tissue.

Depauperate   Diminished in species diversity.

Dichromatism   The presence of two or more color phases within a species or subspecies.

Diel   Daily or daytime.

Disjunct   Geographically separate.

Distally   Toward the periphery, or sides, of the body.

Diurnal   Active during the day.

DOR   Initials of Dead On Road, an abbreviation for vehicle-slain wildlife, originally coined by rattlesnake authority L. M. Klauber. It is now in general use for all kinds of animals and offers a rough but useful indicator of the presence of fauna in an area.

Dorsal   Pertaining to the back.

Dorsolateral   Pertaining to the back and sides, usually the entirety of the back and sides.

Dorsum   The back and upper sides.

Duvernoy's gland   A gland that produces some of the venom of rear-fanged colubrid snakes; named for the French anatomist D. M. Duvernoy, who first described it.

Ecdysis   The shedding of a reptile's outer skin. See **Exuviation.**

Ecotone   Transition zone between differing biological communities, such as the border between forest and meadow.

Ectotherm   Animal whose temperature is almost entirely determined by its environment.

Edema   Swelling of tissue due to the release of fluids (primarily from the vascular and lymphatic systems) into the interstitial tissue spaces.

Elapid   A rigidly front-fanged, venomous serpent of the family *Elapidae,* such as the coral snake. Elapids are characterized by a large proportion of neurotoxically active peptide venom fractions.

257

Endemic   Found only in a particular area.

Endotherm   Internally heat-regulating animal.

Envenomation   Infusion of venom.

Enzyme   Organic agent capable of producing the metabolic breakdown of tissue into its component proteins.

Exuviation   A shed; the sloughing of the entire outer covering, or *stratum corneum,* of a snake's body. This process first occurs soon after birth, then occurs every few weeks to months (more often if the snake has been injured; less often as the snake grows older) throughout the animal's annual foraging period. This process can occupy from ten minutes to several hours. Rattlesnakes add a new basal rattle segment with each exuviation; the terminal segments are periodically broken off.

Fasciotomy   Surgical incision into the fascial band enclosing a muscular compartment. This is usually done in an attempt to prevent tissue destruction from excessive hydraulic pressure caused by the fluid released by the venom's perforation of the capillary walls and pumped into the tissues by the heart. Fasciotomy is of questionable value except as an emergency measure to save a limb in immediate danger of general necrosis due to vascular constriction.

Form   Subspecies or race.

Fossorial   Adapted to burrowing; subterranean.

Frontal scale(s)   Scale(s) located on the crown, or top of the head between the eyes.

Genotype   Genetic makeup of an individual.

Gravid   Pregnant.

Hemotoxic   Destructive to blood, blood cells, or the vascular system.

Hemipene   The bi-lobed, therefore Y-shaped, penis of serpents and lizards.

Herpetoculture   The husbandry and breeding of reptiles in captivity.

Hibernation   Dormancy during winter.

Holotype   The specimen from which the description of a species or subspecies is derived.

Hydric   Well watered.

Hydrophytic   Plant life adapted to living in standing fresh water.

Hypovolemic shock   Shock due to a loss of fluid from the circulatory system. In snakebite, this occurs when the arteriole and venule walls are perforated by venom enzymes.

Infralabial scales   The scales that line the lower jaw.

Indigenous   Native to an area; not introduced.

Infrared perception   Apprehension of the infrared band of the light spectrum.

Intergradation   The gradual genetic alteration of one subspecies into another across a geographical continuum.

Intergrade   Intermediate individual or population which often exhibits some combination of the characteristics of two or more species or subspecies.

Internasal scales   Scales just posterior to the rostral scale on top of the snout, anterior to the prefrontals.

Jacobson's organ   Double-sided sensory organ located in the roof of the mouth of serpents and some lizards into which the tips of their forked tongues are pressed. When a snake flicks it tongue, molecules that adhere to its sticky surface are carried into the mouth when the tongue returns to its sheath, then placed in ducts in the roof of the mouth. These ducts lead to veromonasal epithelia containing the chemosensory neurons which have evolved highly specific, inherited selective recognition of the chemical signature of appropriate prey species.

Keel   Small longitudinal ridge creasing the centerline of a dorsal scale.

Labial scales   Large scales lining the outer edges of the upper and lower jaws (**supralabial scales** line the upper jaw; **infralabial scales** line the lower jaw).

Lacertilian   Pertaining to lizards.

Lateral   Pertaining to the sides.

Lecithotrophy   Yolk-nourished embryos.

Leucistiphosis   The nourishment of embryos by means of an egg yolk.

Leutic   Still, nonflowing water.

Linear constriction   Pressing a prey animal against a stationary object—such as the side of a burrow or rock crevice—to immobilize it.

Ligature   Binding a limb with a circulation-impairing band such as a tourniquet.

Littoral   Pertaining to the margins of bodies of water; shoreline.

Live-bearing   Reproduction by means of fully-formed young born in membranous sheaths, which are immediately discarded.

Loreal scale   Scale between the preocular and nasal scales.

Lumen   Venom-generating and storing gland.

Lysis   The breakdown or metabolism of cells or tissue by a peptide or enzyme.

Matrotrophy   Nourishment of embryos by nutrient exchange from the mother's blood.

Maxillary bones   Paired bones at the front of the upper jaw that in anterior-fanged venomous snakes carry the fangs. Among pitvipers the maxillary bones are able to rotate outward separately, swinging each fang tip forward independent of the other.

Mesic   Moderately watered; moist.

Midventral   The center of the belly.

Milieu   Environment or habitat.

Morph   Short for morphological; of variant appearance. For example, a color phase.

Morphological   Pertaining to an animal's appearance (as opposed to its genetic makeup).

Natricine   Large water snakes of the genus *Nerodia*.

Nasal scales   Scales through which the nostrils open.

Necrosis   Death of bone or soft tissue.

Neonate   A newborn, offspring.

Neurotoxic   Destructive primarily by impairing neuromuscular function. Among the most dangerous effects of ophidian neurotoxins is the blockage of acetylcholine receptor sites in the upper spinal ganglia.

Noetenic   Retention of the juvenile form or coloring into adulthood.

Non-indigenous   Not native to an area: therefore, introduced.

Nuchal   Pertaining to the neck.

Ocular   Pertaining to the eye.

Ocular scale   Scale covering the eye.

Ontogenetic   A change in morphology due to aging.

Ophidian   Pertaining to snakes.

Ophiophagous   Feeding on snakes.

Oviparous   Egg-bearing or laying: producing young by means of eggs that hatch outside the body.

Oviposition   Egg-laying.

Ovoviviparous   Live-bearing. Producing young by means of membranous eggs, whose membrane-encased embryos remain within the mother's body until hatching, at which time they are deposited as fully developed offspring.

Paraphyletic   Genus or species-level groups of organisms which, due to significantly differing habits, morphology or physiology, have emerged from their ancestral families and, rather than replacing them, now exist alongside their progenitors in slightly different niches.

Parietal scales   Pair of large scales located on the rear of the crown.

Parotid gland   Organ that secretes saliva in mammals and most of the venom in pitvipers and elapids.

Parthenogenesis   Reproduction by the development of an unfertilized egg.

Parturition   The process of giving birth.

Phenotype   Physical characteristics of an organism.

Pheromone   Primarily hormone-derived chemical substance released by an animal that influences the behavior of others of the same species.   Ophidian pheromones include both general scents used for locating the retreats, hiding places, or microhabitat of other individuals of the same species and male-attracting scents excreted by breeding-condition females.

Placentophosis   Nourishment of embryos by nutrient exchange from the mother's blood.

Plate   Large scales covering the crown, or top of the head, as well as the venter, or belly.

Polyvalent antivenin   An antivenin produced from a combination of antibodies and therefore useful against the venom of a genus or related group of venomous snakes. Wyeth's polyvalent antivenin is a single crystallized serum developed to treat the bites of all North American pitvipers: rattlesnakes, copperheads, and cottonmouths.

Posterior   Toward the tail.

Postocular scales   Scales bordering the posterior edge of the eye.

Preocular scales   Scales bordering the anterior edge of the eye.

Primary band   A snake's more distinct and complete dorsolateral crossbands (as opposed to the irregular, broken markings which may occur between them).

Proteinase   Proteolytic, or tissue-dissolving, enzyme.

Proteolysis   Destruction of tissue due to the inability of venom-weakened cell walls to withstand their internal fluid pressures.

Race   Subspecies.

Range   The area thought to be the entire geographic distribution of an organism.

Relict population Contemporary remnant group of a species formerly found over a broader range.

Riparian The banks or bottomland along streams or rivers.

Rostral scale Scale covering the tip of the snout, frequently enlarged among burrowing species.

Ruderal Agricultural.

Saxicolous Inhabiting or growing among rocks.

Scute Scale plate.

Scutellation Scalation; the arrangement of scales.

Serosanguinous Swollen with blood.

Sexual dimorphism A morphological difference (in coloring, pattern, size, configuration, or other trait) according to gender.

Siren Large aquatic salamander shaped like an eel but possessing forelegs and external gills.

Spermatogenesis Generation of spermatozoa.

Squamata The order of classification comprising snakes and lizards.

Subcaudal scales The scales lining the undersurface of the tail posterior to the cloacal opening.

Subocular scales Small scales separating the lower edge of the eye from the supralabial scales.

Subspecies A group or cluster of local populations that, to a significant degree, differs taxonomically from adjacent groups or clusters.

Supralabial scales The scales that line the upper jaw.

Supraocular scales The scales on the sides of the crown above the eyes.

Sympatric Overlapping or corresponding ranges; occurring in the same area.

Syntopic Overlapping or corresponding microhabitats; occurring in the same pond or beneath the same log.

Temporal scales Scales along the side of the head behind the postocular scale(s) and between the parietal scales and the supralabial scales.

Terminal segment Among *Sistrurus* and *Crotalus,* the last, or posteriormost rattle segment. Because rattles break off periodically, there are rarely more than 8 or 10 segments in a series no matter how old the snake. See **Exuviation.**

Thermoregulation Control of body temperature—usually by an ectotherm—by moving toward or away from warmer or cooler areas.

Variant   Individual or population difference—most often in color or pattern—not judged to be of sufficient genetic magnitude to warrant recognition as a subspecies or race.

Venom fractions   The approximately three dozen discrete toxic proteins—principally peptides and enzymes—that make up reptile venoms. Most of these fractions can be isolated from the venom mix by electrophoresis and dialysis.

Vent   The posterior opening of the cloaca.

Venter   The belly.

Ventral   Pertaining to the belly.

Ventral scales   The transversely elongate scale plates, or scutes, that line the underbody of most snakes.

Ventrolateral   On the outer edge of the venter and the lower sides of the body.

Vertebral   Along the spine.

Vitellogenesis   Generation of ova.

Viviparous   Live-bearing. Among snakes this means retaining the developing young (in their membranous egg sacs) within the body cavity of the mother until their birth/hatching, which occur simultaneously.

Vomeronasal organ   The primary chemical sense that snakes use to orient themselves in their environment and to detect prey is vomerolfaction, which is the perception of scent particle carried into the mouth by the tongue, then placed in the vomeronasal, or Jacobson's organ, located in the roof of the mouth. See **Jacobson's organ.**

Xeric   Arid.